THE COMPANION GUIDE TO

Madrid
and Central Spain

D0783368

THE COMPANION GUIDE TO

Madrid and Central Spain

ALASTAIR BOYD

COMPANION GUIDES

First published 1974
Second edition, revised and updated, 1986
Third edition 1988

Reissued 1996
Companion Guides, Woodbridge

ISBN   1 900639 07 6

Companion Guides is an imprint of Boydell & Brewer Ltd
PO Box 9, Woodbridge, Suffolk IP12 3DF, UK
and of Boydell & Brewer Inc.
PO Box 41026, Rochester, NY 14604-4126, USA

Printed and bound in Great Britain by
Hartnolls Limited, Bodmin, Cornwall

Maps and Plans

Contents

✤

Illustrations

ILLUSTRATIONS

Panorama, Segovia
The Cathedral tower, Segovia (J. J. Farquharson)
The Alcázar, Segovia (J. J. Farquharson)
The town square, Piedrahita
El Barco de Avila
The high vault of the Cathedral, Plasencia

Hospital de Santa Cruz, Toledo   350 and 351
Casas Colgadas, Cuenca (after face-lift)
The Cathedral, Cuenca
Casas Colgadas (before face-lift)
Village street in the Vera (Avila)
Farmhouse near Cuenca
Sierra de las Mamblas (Burgos) (J. J. Farquharson)
Hamlet near Soria
Pastrana
Priego
Co-Cathedral of Soria, Cloister capitals
San Baudelio de Berlanga (Soria)
Towers
  1. Romanesque, Santa Maria del Azogue, Benavente
  2. Plateresque. Morón de Almazán
  3. Baroque. The Clerecía, Salamanca
  4. Baroque. The Cathedral, El Burgo de Osma

All photographs are by author or by courtesy of
the Spanish Tourist Office, unless otherwise stated.

Introduction

❧

The first word of the title of this guide is MADRID and the capital itself occupies about one-sixth of the text. But I must make it clear at the outset that I do not recommend Madrid as a touring centre except for its own province, the royal palaces of El Escorial and Aranjuez and the university town of Alcalá de Henares. I treat it first because many people will fly there and will probably want to see the pictures in the Prado, even if they are proceeding elsewhere. Having done so, I leave Madrid and commence the circuit that gives body to the words AND CENTRAL SPAIN at Burgos. Obviously the capital is accessible from anywhere on the circuit and vice versa, yet it need not form part of the itinerary of anyone with a car who knows it already and wants to avoid it.

The Central Spain of the book consists of about one-quarter of the country. The suggested route deals in some detail with twelve of the fifty modern provinces and enters the territory of three more. It includes thirteen cathedral cities (nine of which are provincial capitals) and two capitals without cathedrals. The route does not – cannot in the space – respect the boundaries of the mediaeval kingdoms; it takes in the larger parts of Old and New Castile and the more southerly regions of the old kingdom of León. With the exception, due to a twisted ankle of two excursions in the province of Cuenca, I have mentioned no place that I have not personally visited.

If the route were followed in its entirety it would take several months and few readers, if any, will have time or inclination for this. However, it is easily broken down into sections. The first major city for motorists entering Spain by Irún, Bilbao or Santander will be Burgos. Chapters two to six cover Burgos, Palencia, Valladolid, Zamora and Salamanca, from where one can break off for Portugal or take the western approach to Andalusia. Then come Segovia, Avila and Toledo, which can themselves absorb an entire holiday. From Toledo there are many choices. My route runs cross-country, south of Madrid, to Cuenca and then north through Guadalajara and Soria (including the delightful and little-known cathedral towns of Sigüenza and El Burgo de Osma). But this could equally be joined as a variant of the usual route north by someone heading home from Andalusia.

One of my main objects is to encourage people to use the provincial towns as centres for regional touring. The capital of a province is usually but not *always* the best centre. For instance, Covarrubias is a very good centre for the easterly regions of the province of Burgos; Medina de Rioseco is a better centre for the Palencia/Valladolid area than either of the bigger cities and Brihuega is much preferable to near-by Guadalajara. Some hotels I have used are mentioned in the text and these are summarised and expanded in an appendix. There is also an appendix on eating and drinking. For deeper coverage of these aspects of travel a Michelin guide is useful. I also advise the reader to go to the tourist office, which exists in all provincial capitals and some other towns of historical and artistic interest (for addresses see pp.435-437). These bodies distribute – free – provincial and town folders and hotel lists. If one's preferred hotel or hotels are full, the tourist office will help find alternative accommodation. For intelligent touring a map of the whole country is not detailed enough and the Firestone series covering Spain in nine sheets, scale 1:500,000 can be recommended. There is also a road atlas called Mapa Oficial de Carreteras published by the Ministry of Public Works (Ministerio de Obras Públicas) and available from Madrid bookshops. The tourist office folders contain useful town plans.

Now to the content of this book. The reader without previous knowledge of Spain may find the amount of text devoted to religious art and architecture a little forbidding and be surprised by the lack of 'country houses' in our sense. It is therefore important to understand the nature of a country that has been too harsh to encourage people to live in it for pleasure – most of the Castilian plateau or *meseta* is about 2,000 feet above sea level and is subject to extremes of temperature. Most people have heard the phrase 'Castles in Spain' and indeed there are still thousands (literally) of these, some very dramatically sited and making a great impact on the skyline. But most of them are ruinous. This leaves the Church as the trustee of the best buildings and the finest artefacts in the land.

How did this come about? The overwhelming factor is the Moorish invasion of AD 711, which by 725 had overrun the whole land apart from a few isolated pockets and driven a wedge far up into France. It took Christian Spain nearly 800 years to re-establish complete control over the whole land mass. The life-force of the various kingdoms – Asturias, León, Castile, Navarre, Aragón etc. – was spent in this endeavour. When an area was reconquered, it had to be re-populated and when this had been done the achievement was invariably symbolised by the building of a church or churches. And a wall would surround the new settlement. And the nobility would build their houses within the wall, forts within a fort. Also they took over Moorish castles or built new ones to consolidate their feudal status vis-à-vis the Crown. And then the municipalities took steps to protect themselves against their feudal protectors. Eventually the Crown knocked down the castles in order to bring its over-mighty subjects to heel and then proceeded to erode and finally nullify municipal rights as well. But none of this gave rise to any but the most severely utilitarian type of building. It was the Church that provided the glamour of the cathedrals, with their daring architecture and rich fittings, and of the great monastic foundations where a mitred abbot or abbess would enjoy the privileges of a feudal lord, while encouraging arts and skills unknown in the secular sphere.

Let us turn to the people. In a book of this length and type giving a lot of detailed information it has been possible to include very few personal anecdotes. So a few general remarks seem called for. Some knowledge of Spanish – or even a phrase book – will make the traveller's journey more enjoyable. Receptionists and hall porters in good hotels (four stars and up) and Paradors will probably have some basic English. Lady employees of the Patrimonio Nacional (controlling certain monuments, mainly royal palaces) speak good English. Madrid as a whole makes pretty good shift with foreigners. Otherwise, one is thrown back on Spanish, pidgin Spanish, sign-language or *simpatía* and laughter. George Borrow remarked that Spaniards hated foreigners to speak their language well and refused to listen to them when they did, and to this day pidgin Spanish will not only achieve communication but go down very well. I am as nearly bilingual as most Englishmen and have often heard it said with *disapproval*: he speaks *almost* like a Spaniard. So no one should get a hang-up on perfect Castilian or nothing.

Once communication is established on one level or another, the traveller will find the average Spaniard really prepared to be involved with him. He will seldom be brushed off by someone too busy or too bored to help. Any enquiry about meals, hotels, railways, roads, buses, petrol – services of any kind – will become public property in a restaurant or bar and be bandied about until a consensus of opinion emerges. This can be confusing but it is nearly always fun. And it is not all based on idle curiosity about the newcomer. There is a substratum of brotherly co-operation to even the greatest inquisitiveness. No one who breaks down or has a puncture need feel abandoned. Someone will not only come by but stop and do something. I think most people will find the level of *concern* for a stranger higher here than in England, France or Italy. In many places, particularly in the country, this concern will not be accompanied by financial interest. Mechanics will often do small jobs on cars – fixing an indicator, cleaning a plug – for nothing. But this disinterest decreases the nearer one is to a large tourist centre. It is almost impossible to recommend a rigid scale of tipping but some ideas are given in the appendix on hotels.

Finally, someone may ask: Why go to Central Spain at all when there is so much coastline and you have said yourself that the interior never encouraged the Spaniards themselves to live in it for pleasure? Well, *chacun à son goût* of course. For anyone interested in art or architecture the great cathedrals and great painters are quite a sufficient draw, in fact a 'must'. And even those with only marginal interest in these things, who feel like me that the various *costas* are becoming intolerably crowded and ugly, may like to investigate new pastures. The cluttered coastline has the strong but limited appeal of sun and sea. The Centre has sun, air, great buildings, great light and great space – above all space. By European standards Spain is a large country, the horizons are usually distant and the landscape is often superb – even where it is monotonous the space, light and air persist. And if the radial arteries to and from Madrid are avoided, there is still remarkably little traffic on the roads. Certainly, the climate can be tough but the Spring and Autumn are usually delightful. Food and drink are more truly regional and cheaper. And in the Centre one finds Spaniards. But a good wine, they say, needs no bush. I now pray the reader to join me in Madrid or Burgos or Toledo or wherever he pleases and judge for himself.

CHAPTER ONE

Madrid

᪣

Among European capitals Madrid has always had to concede seniority and antiquity to Rome, Paris and London. There have been Palaeolithic finds and there is some evidence of Roman and Visigothic settlements but the capital of Spain only emerges into history with any clarity during the Muslim occupation. It is said that the fifth independent Emir of Córdoba raised a watch-tower on the platform now occupied by the royal palace. If so, this must have been between 852 and 886, the limits of his reign. Majerit, as it was then called, was successfully raided and sacked by Ramiro II of León in 932 but it did not pass permanently into Christian hands until its capture by Alfonso VI with the help of the people of Segovia in 1083 or – some say – 1085, the year of the capture of Toledo.

After its reconquest from the Moors Madrid did not immediately acquire much importance. It was not until 1202 that Alfonso VIII granted it a *fuero* or charter of rights. It was first host to the peripatetic *cortes* or parliament in 1309. Alfonso XI repeated these gatherings in 1329 and 1335. It is impossible to say where they were held. There was no permanent building here or anywhere else in the country specifically designed for the purpose. The choirs and porches of churches were among the places used, serving in just the same way for the assemblies of local elders. Early municipal councils were called *consejos* and those who formed part of them *consejales*. The latter term has been preserved for town councillors, though the civic building where they meet is called the *ayuntamiento* after the *ayuntados* or co-opted members who were required to attend the deliberations.

In 1346 Madrid acquired a grammar school. Peter the Cruel improved the *Alcázar* or fortress that had grown up on the same site as the Moorish one. The people of Madrid supported Peter in his unsuccessful contest with his half-brother

13

Henry of Trastamara. After the change of dynasty John I gave the lordship of Madrid to León V, dispossessed King of Armenia; this curious act of grace and favour lasted until John's death in 1390. In order to improve its relations with the Trastamaras Madrid emptied the municipal purse on lavish celebrations of the marriage of Henry III to Catherine of Lancaster, granddaughter of Edward III of England. John II held a parliament in Madrid in 1421 and his favourite Alvaro de Luna kept up a residence in the town. In 1434 came the great flood (hard to imagine on the banks of the meagre Manzanares) and in 1438 the great plague. On the death of Henry IV, called the Impotent, in 1474 – he was the first king to die in Madrid – the local nobility turned out for the little Princess Joan, of dubious paternity, whose claim was supported by Portugal. The subsequent war of succession was won by Ferdinand and Isabel and again Madrid had been on the wrong side. Understandably the *Reyes Católicos* (this was the title later conferred on the royal couple by the Pope) showed Madrid no special favour and Isabel established her first court at Valladolid.

In 1509 Ferdinand, now a widower, held a parliament in the church of San Jerónimo to proclaim himself regent in the names of his daughter, Joan the Mad, herself recently widowed by Philip the Fair, and of her son, Ferdinand's grandson Charles. On Ferdinand's death in 1516 Charles wrote to the Madrid town council announcing that he would exercise the kingship jointly with his mother. The arrival of Charles I of Spain in search of funds to make himself Charles V of the Holy Roman Empire and accompanied by foreign place-seekers was not popular. Nobody liked the pretentiousness of 'Your Majesty' instead of the traditional 'Your Highness' or the conversion of simple monarchy into empire. Along with most of the other Castilian towns Madrid joined the Revolt of the Commoners (see pp. 154–155), which failed, and was once again out of favour.

The red-letter year in Madrid's history is usually taken as 1561, when Philip II abandoned Toledo and set up his administration in the *Imperial y Coronada Villa* (Charles V had eventually conferred this sonorous title on Madrid, even though he preferred both Toledo and Valladolid as seats of government). Among the reasons for Philip's move were the over-mighty attitude of the Toledan clergy, which did not please him at all, and his desire to be nearer the great work he was to carry out at El Escorial. There was no official declaration of the new administrative centre as capital and it is interesting to note that Madrid is still a *villa* (the term, similar to French *ville*, was used throughout Castile in the Middle Ages to describe a small fortified town, usually the seat of a feudal lord) and has never graduated to the rank of city. The modern capital of over three and a half million inhabitants is rather proud of this idiosyncracy.

At the time of the reconquest from the Moors it is thought Madrid might have held some 12,000 inhabitants. After this there was a very slow expansion – in the time of Charles V there were only 2,500 houses and approximately 15,000 inhabitants – until the arrival of the court in 1561. During the reigns of Philip II, Philip III and Philip IV there was a fairly rapid growth, including the present Plaza Mayor, which was a fairground outside the mediaeval wall and the Buen Retiro Palace and Park, all of which Philip IV enclosed within a *cerca*, a mud pallisade of no defensive value which acted as a fiscal limit and, it was fondly hoped, as a sanitary cordon in times of plague. There was virtually no further extension of the area of the capital between the death of Philip IV in 1665 and the accession of Isabel II in 1833, when some development took place along the present Calle de la Princesa. Between 1860 and 1914 the area immediately to the north of the centre was built, mainly in a style we should call Edwardian. By the end of this period the town had little over half a million inhabitants and must have been at its most agreeable. Wide boulevards had been built on the French model outside the old core; what was lacking in antiquity had been made good in terms of space, air, light and charm. It was quite an achievement, considering the fundamentally unpromising terrain on which Madrid is built. The population increased only a little between the First World War and the end of the Civil War in 1939. Then everything changed very rapidly. The decision taken by the winners of the Civil War to turn Madrid into an industrial as well as administrative capital was admittedly delayed by the Second World War but when the explosion came it was shattering. It shattered the war-scarred relics of Edwardian charm; it increased the population seven-fold in a quarter of a century; it fogged a limpid sky and clear skyline and made nonsense of the old adage that a *madrileño* prayed to go to Heaven and then for a little window to look down from Heaven on his beloved Madrid. On some days he would be hard put to see it even with celestial light.

And yet, something remains. Despite these unattractive developments Madrid still manages to retain a certain crispness and sparkle, particularly on a bright Spring or Autumn day when the wind is not concentrating the smog over the capital. Then the good air from the Spanish steppes fills the lungs and brightens the eye; then the many bars serving delicious *tapas* (see pp. 441-2) beckon to an apéritif and whet the appetite before a leisurely lunch in one of the excellent restaurants that abound at all prices. And the sense of well-being receives a boost from the manifest conviction of the inhabitants themselves that this is the good life with its noise and fumes and competitive driving and thronged department stores and huge government buildings and high-rise flats and lurid smoky outline. 'For me,' I was told by an enthusiastic government official, 'Madrid is the quintessence of Spain.' One may quarrel on aesthetic or environmental grounds with what they have created but there can be no doubt whatever that they are enjoying it and this is infectious.

THE PRADO

It is received wisdom that there is nothing to see in Madrid but the Prado. This is far from true, for there are other excellent museums and some highly evocative corners remain in the old quarter. Madrid is a town that grows on you. However, the **Museo Nacional del Prado** is so much the most important single attraction possessed by the capital that it demands to be described before anything else. Situated in the Paseo del Prado, the building was undertaken for Charles III by the Neo-Classical architect Juan de Villanueva. It was designed to house a natural history museum and an academy of sciences. In 1818 it was redesignated as a museum of painting and sculpture and in this capacity it opened to the public in 1819. In 1872 the Prado acquired the pictures and sculptures from the Museo de la Trinidad, which had been formed in 1837 with works of art from the suppressed convents of Avila, Segovia, Toledo and Madrid. In 1865 the collections ceased to be the private property of the Crown and in 1869 passed into the hands of the Patrimonio Nacional.

During the Civil War the contents were sent out of the country by the Republican Government. The museum was reopened in 1940. The collection is not only one of Spanish painting but includes many foreign works commissioned or bought by the Spanish rulers. These and other legacies have ensured an important display of both Flemish and Italian works. The Dutch and English schools have only token representation but the French, reflecting Bourbon taste, is more ample.

There are two main floors which I shall call the ground floor and the principal floor. There are three entrances: the Puerta de Goya facing the ballroom entrance of the Ritz; the Puerta de Velazquez, facing the Paseo del Prado; and the Puerta de Murillo facing the Botanical Gardens. I shall refer to the 'Ritz', 'Paseo' and 'Botanical' entrances. For several years now the museum has been in the throes of renovation, including the installation of an air-conditioning plant. Some rooms are still closed to the public on this account. The old numeration of the long galleries and other rooms by Roman numerals and letters is, at the time of writing, still in place but I do not use it in this edition, as it is due to be superseded by a new system. The plans of the two main floors on pp. 16-17 simply show the regions of the museum in which the national schools and the painters of greatest renown will be found when the process of renovation is complete. Rather than attempting to indicate the exact location of works my aim has been to distinguish the most important trends in Spanish painting and in the purchases of the monarchs. To this end I have divided my remarks into seven sections, in which the artists are treated as nearly as possible in chronological order so as to relate their works to Spanish history.

It is intended by the museum authorities that the revised layout should not diverge greatly from the original. Thus, the two essential tributaries of the Spanish mainstream, the Flemings and the Italians, retain their rooms on the right and left respectively of the principal floor, entering from the 'Ritz' end of the building. The Spanish sixteenth and seventeenth centuries will occupy, as before, the long gallery running almost the whole length of the building on this level. Velázquez maintains his pivotal position at the centre of the museum. But the new plan includes some undoubted improvements. Goya – this is the biggest change contemplated – will occupy both main levels of the block at the 'Botanical' end of the

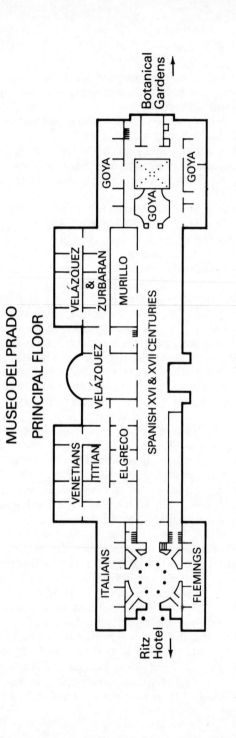

MUSEO DEL PRADO
PRINCIPAL FLOOR

Botanical Gardens

GOYA
GOYA
GOYA

VELÁZQUEZ & ZURBARAN
MURILLO

VELÁZQUEZ

SPANISH XVI & XVII CENTURIES

VENETIANS
TITIAN
ELGRECO

ITALIANS
FLEMINGS

Ritz Hotel

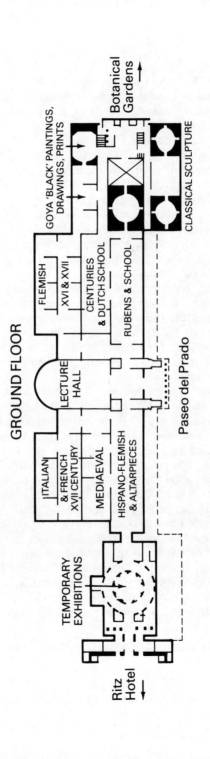

GROUND FLOOR

Ritz Hotel →

TEMPORARY EXHIBITIONS

ITALIAN & FRENCH XVII CENTURY

MEDIAEVAL

HISPANO-FLEMISH & ALTARPIECES

LECTURE HALL

Paseo del Prado

FLEMISH XVI & XVII

CENTURIES & DUTCH SCHOOL

RUBENS & SCHOOL

GOYA 'BLACK' PAINTINGS, DRAWINGS, PRINTS

CLASSICAL SCULPTURE

Botanical Gardens →

building. Pending this move his tapestry cartoons and some of his portraits continue, along with his 'black paintings' on the ground floor near the 'Ritz' end; after the move the space vacated by him will be devoted to the Italian and French seventeenth and eighteenth centuries. One of the greatest improvements, in my view, has already taken place: this is the consolidation of the Flemish sixteenth and seventeenth centuries, including Van Dyck and Anthony More, on the ground floor in a dozen or so rooms off the long gallery devoted to Rubens and his school. The core room at this level immediately facing the 'Paseo' entrance (and corresponding to the great Velázquez room on the principal floor above) has become a lecture hall, in which talks are given two or three times a week.

If any confusion results, as well it may, either from the transitional arrangements or from some change in the eventual plan, the most useful publication to acquire is the slim format *Guide to the Prado* by Consuelo Luca de Tena and Manuela Mena, which has a double index, both by catalogue number and by artist, which considerably facilitates the location of any work actually on view. Readers should note that figures italicised in brackets in the text of the present book indicate catalogue numbers. The opening hours are from 10.00 to 17.00 hours in winter and 10.00 to 18.00 hours in summer from Tuesdays to Saturdays inclusive and from 10.00 to 14.00 hours on Sundays throughout the year. There is rather a claustrophobic cafeteria in the basement. Though Spaniards have finally been granted free museum entry like the British, foreigners still have to pay. However, the charge is not prohibitive and the ticket is valid also for the Nineteenth Century Collection and for Picasso's *Guernica,* both housed in the nearby Casón del Buen Retiro. The Prado is closed on Mondays throughout the year and this is the case with most other museums and collections in the capital, so the prudent traveller will remember that in Madrid the rule is 'Never on Mondays' and devote this day to one or other of the excursions described in the next chapter.

Romanesque and Mozarabic frescoes – Hispano-Flemish retablos and panels – the Flemings – Rogier Van der Weyden – Gerard David – Hieronymus Bosch – the elder Breughel – the German School.

Starting our visit chronologically, we should first seek out the Spanish 'primitives', which occupy the long gallery on the ground floor at the 'Ritz' end of the building. The very earliest paintings are awaiting a new home off this gallery. They are expected to be on view again from 1985. The main items are the Romanesque wall paintings of the twelfth century from Maderuelo (Segovia), which depend mainly on folds, wings and linear anatomy for their effect, and the remarkable frescoes from San Baudelio de Berlanga (Soria). Most of the murals of this remote Mozarabic church were transferred onto panels and sold to private collectors. This has since been described as 'one of the most intolerable operations of Elginism', though the British in this case were not to blame. Now six of them have been returned to 'temporary indefinite deposit' by the Metropolitan Museum of Art, New York. Said to date from the first half of the twelfth century, they depict beasts and scenes of the chase and are completely secular in theme in marked contrast to those of Maderuelo. They rely on mass rather than line and have been attributed to a Muslim artist. The great humped boar or bear (it is hard to tell which) is memorable.

Romanesque and Mozarabic painting was confined to a few churches in León and Old Castile and Northern Catalonia. The development of a Spanish school of painting on panels was slow to come. Native energies were absorbed by the seemingly endless Reconquest of the Peninsula from the Moors, who had landed in 711 and were not dispossessed of their last kingdom, Granada, till 1492. In troubled times art tended to be portable. Kings carried their favourite images at the saddlebow. Creative ingenuity found its outlet in tiny ivory diptyches, jewellery, church plate, clasps, bindings, caskets, processional crosses and the like – all things that could move easily with their owners. When the Christian sway became more firmly established and there was a demand for larger works on flat surfaces, Spain turned to Flanders. The long gallery is dominated by *retablos* or reredoses containing panels in the Hispano-Flemish style, mounted in gilt Gothic frames. (I am going to italicise and translate Spanish words only on their first appearance in the text; in case of later doubt they can be found in the glossary on pp. 423-30. The first painters – inferior in status to masons, goldsmiths or woodcarvers – sought to preserve the rich relief of gold and silver ware, brasses, ivories, enamels etc by the use of stamped gold backgrounds. In the Catalan and Aragonese masters in particular there is a strong tradition of raised and gilded gesso called *estofado* to pick out hems, borders, staffs, crooks, crowns and haloes. The Martyrdom of Saint Vincent (*2670* and *2671*) uses this technique for the saint's halo and the wooden staffs and tunic buttons as late as 1450, while it is also pronounced in the two panels (*2668* and *2669*) devoted to the passage of the corpse of Saint James the Great (Santiago) to Compostela.

Far greater sophistication is evident in the works of the fifteenth and sixteenth century Flemish masters, shown in five rooms off the principal floor rotunda at the 'Ritz' end of the building; the legend 'Escuela Flamenca' points the way. There is no work in the Prado certainly attributable to the Van Eycks, who are generally credited with the invention of oil painting, yet two panels by the Master of Flemalle showing Saint John the Baptist with a monk (*1513*) and Saint Barbara reading with her back to a fire (*1514*) recall the precision and spaciousness of the Arnolfini couple in the National Gallery. These works easily outstrip those of any indigenous Spanish artist of the time. Rogier Van der Weyden (d. 1464) is well represented by the triptych (*1888, 1889* and *1891*) with grisailles on the outer faces of the doors (*1890* and *1892*); also by the exquisite Pietá (*2540*) and the great Descent from the Cross (*2825*), painted in 1435. Having failed to buy this, Philip II commissioned Michel Coxcie to make a copy of it and this – a work of staggering faithfulness – now hangs in the Escorial. The original, now before us, came to Spain eventually in the bequest of Queen Mary of Hungary, sister of Charles V. Against a traditional gold background the figures have the connecting rhythm of a stone frieze. From left to right and top to bottom the interplay of hands and feet leads inexorably to the skull on the ground. Christ seems quite weightless with the spirit fled. This is one of the greatest paintings of the Gothic world.

The next generation gives us the gem-like Virgins of Gerard David (1450-1523), represented here by the delightful version with coral beads (*1537*) and the Rest on the Flight into Egypt (*2643*), in which the blue-green landscape plays a more important role than ever before. David is closely followed by Adrian Isembrandt (d. 1551). Quentin Metsys contributes the striking Christ presented to the People (*2801*). In the work of J. Gossaert also called Mabuse (1478-1533/6) and Bernard Van Orley (1492-1542) we find pronounced Mannerist tendencies – see the former's Virgin of Louvain (*1536*) in which the overwhelming exedra is designed to show off a sophisticated knowledge of contemporary decorative motifs. We are moving fast towards unbridled Mannerism – a style ostentatiously familiar with the fashionable tricks of the Italian Renaissance. Gossaert, however, also shows recessive Gothic tendencies in his Van Eyckian Christ between the Virgin and Saint John (*1510*).

One of the specialities of the Prado is the collection of fifteenth- and sixteenth-century Flemish paintings of a humorous or grotesque character formed by Philip II. The next room contains the Haywain (*2052*) by J. Van Aeken, commonly known as Hieronymus Bosch and in Spain as el Bosco (c. 1450-1516). Those who are able to scramble onto the bandwagon of life do so; others attempting to ascend with ladders are crushed under the wheels. The Pope, the Emperor, a king and a duke follow behind discussing the whole matter objectively while Christ opens His arms somewhat helplessly in the sky. J. Patinir (1480-1524) uses props borrowed from Bosch in his Charon crossing the Styx (*1616*). The room contains no fewer than three Rests on the Flight into Egypt, in which the importance of landscape and country activities continues to increase. In Gerard David's time the Virgin and Child had still filled the foreground. Patinir maintains the pose used by David and borrows the basket but adds a great deal of the rural husbandry (*1611*); in his son's version (*1612*) the central group has almost disappeared. Bosch's great Garden of Delights (*2823*), which defies description, has as its theme the transitory nature of sensual pleasure; it was bought by Philip II in 1593 during his declining years in the Escorial. Pieter Breughel (1525-1569) made trips to Italy but allowed himself to be little influenced by the new fashions; his painting career extended over a mere ten years and he is deliberately archaic. Though he is less inventive of fantastic forms, the figures in his Triumph of Death (*1393*) are rather more solid than Bosch's brittle shells for souls. Devotees of backgammon will notice a board and some counters along with a scattering of cards bottom right. The skeletons win the day, pushing all humanity into a vast coffin, something like a tank-landing craft.

The German School is represented by Lucas Cranach the Elder, Hans Baldung Grien and Dürer, whose fancy self-portrait (*2179*) was lost by England to Spain in the sale of Charles I's collection by Cromwell, as were a number of other splendid pictures now in the Prado. The then Spanish ambassador was a perceptive buyer and the Commonwealth did remarkably bad business in this sale. Dürer's Adam (*2177*) and Eve (*2178*) were presented to Philip IV by Queen Christina of Sweden (along with an equestrian portrait of herself). Charles III would have consigned them to the flames for indecency, had it not been for his court painter, Mengs, who locked them away in the Real Academia de San Fernando, where they remained for nearly a century.

Hispano-Flemish School (cont.) – Renaissance Influence – Antonio Moro – Sanchez Coello – the Spanish Seventeenth Century – Ribera

It took Hispano-Flemish and Spanish painters more than a century to drop iconographic formulae that had been devised for different and more prestigious materials than oil paint and find their liberty, along with a new kind of bondage, in the discoveries of the Renaissance. In the long gallery on the ground floor the School gradually emancipates itself from its dependence on gold leaf but not without reluctance. The Master of the Eleven Thousand Virgins strives for the illlusion of gold thread in an altar-cloth (*1294*). The Master of La Sisla achieves a greater naturalism but sticks to stamped gold leaf for royal and celestial headwear and church plate. Pedro Berruguete (1450-1503), painter to Ferdinand and Isabel, is to be found in a room opening off the main gallery. His vivid scenes also rely on the stamped gold technique for canopies and curtains. The Auto de Fe (*618*) is perhaps his best-known work. The anonymous Virgin of the Catholic Sovereigns (*1260*) shows Ferdinand and Isabel with two of their children and Torquemada all kneeling, flanked by saints. Hereabouts too are works by Fernando Gallego (active 1466-1507), whom we shall meet again in Salamanca, and the talented Juan de Flandes (d. 1519). See particularly his

Resurrection of Lazarus (*2935*), Ascension of the Lord (*2937*) and Coming of the Holy Spirit (*2938*). Also worthy of note are the robust Passion scenes by Rodrigo de Osuna and the big Saint Michael of Zafra (*1326*) of c. 1480. These works are all still predominantly Gothic in feeling.

With Vicente Masip, Juan de Juanes and Juan de Correa the halo becomes a mere circlet and the artists rely more on cunning compositions. Both Masip and his son-in-law Juanes show strong Renaissance influence in their achitectural passages, while in Correa's Nativity (*690*) a Renaissance arch frames a pastoral landscape. Correa's gold rims and borders are drawn very fine in his Death of the Virgin (*671*), a beautiful painting combining the best of the Gothic and Renaissance worlds. The italianate Juan de Borgoña (1470-1555) retains gold haloes in his fine Magdalen and Dominican Saints (*3110*). Louis de Morales, *el divino Morales* as he is called, whose glossy finishes are rather repellent, finally abandons the gold standard altogether. Pedro Machuca and Yáñez de la Almedina have seen Raphael. Machuca's Deposition from the Cross (*3017*) is a Mannerist work mixing the new know-how with the old Spanish taste for the macabre. Yáñez's graceful Saint Catherine (*2902*), inspired by Leonardo da Vinci and Andrea del Sarto, firmly marks the ousting of the Flemish influence by the Italian in religious painting.

This tendency was less marked in the case of portraiture, in which Spain was to excel. A key figure here was Anton Van Dashorst, alias Sir Anthony More in England and Antonio Moro in Spain. He was born in Utrecht in 1519 and died in Antwerp in 1576. Summoned to Spain in 1550, he can be said to have exercised the most important influence on Spanish portraiture after Titian. At this juncture it is therefore worth seeking him out among the Flemings in the rooms off the long gallery devoted to Rubens and his School. To reach him one must cross the vestibule immediately inside the 'Paseo' entrance on the ground floor. Moro's rich stuffs and jewels point the way to Sánchez Coello, while el Greco cannot have been unaffected by the locating of faces, hands and ruffs like islands in an almost uncharted sea of black. The marvellously painted suede gloves anticipate Velázquez. Among some splendid portraits one may single out Mary Tudor (*2108*), who married the future Philip II of Spain in 1554 as his second wife, only to die in 1558. It is a work of Victorian realism, showing the Queen at 38, eleven years older than her husband with a red rose in her hand and a compressed mouth. In almost the same pose is the painter's wife Metgen, who accompanied him on his trip to England to paint the royal likeness. Moro is especially good with women.

It is now time to embark on the main Spanish gallery which runs almost the whole length of the building on the principal floor. Starting at the 'Ritz' end, we find Sánchez Coello (c. 1530-1588), who succeeded Moro as court painter, and Pantoja de la Cruz (1549-1608), who is better with clothes than their wearers. There is a perspicacious portrait by Coello of the sallow Philip II (*1036*), in which Moro's influence is abundantly apparent. The same artist's renderings of Philip's daughter Isabel Clara Eugenia alone (*1137*) and with her sister (*1034*) and of the resentful, over-regimented young prince Don Carlos (*1136*) are all exceptionally good pictures of children under the stress of their position. Then come large laudatory historical paintings by A. de Pereda (1603-1678), Jusepe Leonardo (1616-1656) and Fray J. B. Maino (1568-1649), whose Adoration of the Kings (*886*) is a very skilful piece of composition and colouring. Fray Juan Rizzi's two military portraits (*887* and *1127*) show signs of lessons learned from Velázquez.

Our attention is next arrested by José de Ribera (1591-1652), who spent most of his working life in Naples, where he became known from his small stature as el Españolito. Perhaps as a result of his size he painted on a grand scale. He is a specialist in ageing skin, wrinkled saints and tactile effects in general – see Jacob receiving Isaac's blessing (*1118*) – achieved with the vigorous strokes of a dragged brush. But his pleasure in these effects does not lead to feeble design. The Martyrdom of Saint Bartholomew (*1101*) is a most arresting composition, as is the Trinity (*1069*) with Christ sliding from the knees of God the Father onto a shroud held up by putti. As a model for the penitent Magdalen (*1103* and *1105*) he drew on his memory of his beautiful daughter, who was seduced at the age of seventeen and later abandoned by the bastard Don John of Austria, son of Philip IV and la Calderona (not to be confused with Don John of Lepanto fame, son of Charles V). Saint John the Baptist (*1108*) wears the pagan smile that entered Spanish painting via Leonardo and Raphael. Ribera is no mean painter, though his excessive contrasts of light and shade for their own sake become something of a cliché. As we proceed down the long gallery, an opening on the left beckons to the unmistakable Grecos. Anyone in a hurry can take the prodigious Cretan at this point but a more logical approach is via the Italians.

The Italians – Fra Angelico – Botticelli – Raphael – Andrea del Sarto – Bellini – Giorgione – Veronese – Tintoretto – Titian – el Greco

The 'Escuela Italiana' is reached from the principal floor rotunda on the opposite side to the Flemings. We are immediately confronted by the glowing Annunciation (15) with the expulsion from Eden included on the left by Fra Angelico (1387-1445). Here we are back in an enchanted realm of golden haloes and golden wings and a golden shaft of sun, down which the dove of the Holy Spirit slips effortlessly to the seated Mary in her loggia with its blue star-spangled vault. Nearby are three of four pictures painted by Botticelli (1445-1510) illustrating the story of Nastagio degli Onesti, a tale from the Decameron; brilliant colours are used and the trunks of the umbrella pines serve to separate different scenes in the same panel. The Death of the Virgin (248) by Andrea Mantegna (1431-1506) is a marvellous little work; the silver-grey landscape with water in the background is so modern it could almost belong to the French nineteenth century. This was another of Charles I's possessions. Thus we come to Raphael (1483-1520). The Portrait of a Cardinal (299) with its 'slight, malignant smile' seems to portray a cool, calculating and ambitious politician. The Virgin with a rose on a table (302) and the Holy Family (301) are among the several paintings in which the young Jesus and St. John are endowed with the little pagan smile that has haunted Spanish painting ever since.

Of the galaxy of Italian painters born between the late 1470s and the early 1490s the majority died young. The Florentine Andrea del Sarto (1486-1531) has caught the Raphael smile in his Saint John the Baptist (579), though in his portrait of his wife Lucrecia (332) his colour-range – greys, greens, browns, russets – depart emphatically from the near-enamel hues of most painters up to and including Raphael. In the next room we come to Giorgione (1478-1531), the

shortest-lived of all, who gives us a crucial example of
the move away from tempera and oil on board to oils on
canvas. With the former technique successive glazes are built
up from a white or pale ground and the light appears to be
thrown outwards; with the latter the artist often works from
a dark ground adding the highlights and the picture seems to
absorb additional light from outside itself. In the Virgin and
Child with Saint Anthony and Saint Roch (228) Giorgione's
brushwork is so relaxed and his tonality so far removed from
the gem-like colours of his predecessors and even of some of
his contemporaries that this might be called the first truly
modern painting in the museum. The point is well made by
comparison with the crude colouring of its neighbour (20) by
Vicenzo di Biaggio (1470-1531) and even with the Virgin and
Child and two Saints (50) by Giorgione's master, Bellini.

We are now on the threshold of the great Venetians. Paolo
Cagliari, better known as Veronese (1528-1588) beckons with
another masterpiece from Charles I's collection, namely Jesus
disputing with the Doctors (491). One feels that this great
decorative artist could never have achieved his mastery of
space, had it not been for Giorgione. Though much scaled
down, the same spaciousness is present in the small Finding
of Moses (502), in which Pharoah's daughter and her
attendants are dressed in the rich stuffs so dear to the artist
and the figures follow an elegant curve against a background
of Renaissance buildings and a bland sky. We come next to
Jacopo Robusti, known as Tintoretto (c. 1518-1594). His
glamorous mauve and pearly-grey lady revealing her bosom
(382) should not obscure the more sober merits of such
portraits as that of a Senator (371). In the same room is one
of the grandest paintings of the age, El Lavatorio (2824);
Christ is shown washing the feet of his disciples and the artist
positively bathes his figures in space and light. This too was
snapped up by Spain in Charles I's posthumous sale. Other
Tintoretto's were bought by Velázquez for Philip IV, notably
the Medianite Virgins (393) and the Episode in a battle
between Turks and Christians (399). A room is devoted to
the Bassanos, a painting family highly considered at the time,
who played an important part in the introduction of still life
and animal themes into Spain; Jacopo's Animals boarding the
Ark (22) was bought by Titian for Charles V.

Thus we come to the most successful Venetian of them all,

Tiziano Vecellio (1487/90-1576), one whom the Gods loved and who died old. He was also loved by Charles V, whom Titian painted first at Bologna in the winter of 1532/33. The resulting portrait with a dog (*158*) – given by Philip IV to our poor Charles I and later bought back for £150 – is a splendid work in which muted green and dull gold predominate. Titian's masterpiece in this vein is the great equestrian painting of the Emperor at the Battle of Mühlberg (*410*), in which boldness of design, consistency of tone and a threatening sky combine to produce a mood of majesty, menace and *movement* that makes Velázquez's and Goya's equestrian portraits seem mere studio exercises with the horse as a necessary prop. This is a magnificent achievement on a technical level, though it is somewhat distasteful to think of so able an artist using the best of his gifts to glorify the ruthless suppressor of native Spanish democracy. The same room contains most of the great Spanish Titians, among them the opulent Danae and the Shower of Gold (*421*), the Bacchanal (*418*), the Salome (*428*), the grief-racked Saint Margaret (*445*), the Offering to the Goddess of Love (*419*) and two version of the Entombment (*440* and *441*). All, it seems, was grist to this mighty mill. Finally, there is the self-portrait (*407*) of the Grand Old Man, painter of powerful kings and great nudes and lover of gorgeous mistresses, in his black robe and skull-cap, still painting strongly in his eighties. Titian had an even greater effect on Spanish portraiture than the Flemish Antón Van Dashorst but he was also capable of such sycophantic hack works as the large Allegory of the Victory of Lepanto (*431*) and Spain to the Rescue of Religion (*430*).

From Titian one can pass directly – and this I think is the proper approach – to Domenico Theotocopouli, el Greco (1541-1614). The Prado is not el Greco's temple to the extent that it is Velázquez's or Goya's. The early Trinity (*824*) painted soon after the artist arrived in Spain, is a work according to the Venetian book of rules. The artist has accepted Titian's view of the role of art and is all set to carve himself a position as court painter. After the shock of Philip II's rejection of him, he chose Toledo as his capital and the Church as his client. Probably this was the making of him, for Philip would have been an intolerably exacting and opinionated master. One is immediately struck by the stunning Adoration of the Shepherds (*2988*) whose focal point is the minute babe from whom all the effulgence flows. The first impression is purely one of phosphorescent light with purples, greens, a jab of orange. Then one sees that the almost absurdly elongated figures are sucked towards the centre by the fascination of the event. The Whitsun (*828*) is a warm, vivid work of his later years with zig-zag highlights on the robes. The Baptism of Christ (*821*), the Crucifixion (*823*) and the Resurrection (*825*) all manage to unite the earthly and heavenly spheres in a diffused subaqueous greenish-yellow light. El Greco's fantastic Mannerist tricks, in particular the elongation, have been adduced as evidence of astigmatism or of extreme spirituality but there is no proof of a defect in vision and ecstasy was fashionable at the time. I think both views miss the essential point of an artist who is really much more remarkable for his colour: he drew and composed with colour rather than simply filling in pre-planned shapes with it. The excitement of his works – and they are undeniably exciting – derives from this rather than from any special elevation of his sentiments. A selection of his portraits of grave gentlemen of the middle rank, in which he was able to explore their heads without bombast, prefigure Velázquez. The small Annunciation (*827*) takes us back to Italy.

Zurbarán and Velázquez

The best introduction to the work of Francisco de Zurbarán (1598-1664) is the series of episodes in the Life of Hercules (*1241-1250*), painted for the Retiro Palace in 1634. The commission was probably obtained for him by his fellow Sevillian, Velázquez. The warm flesh-tones and dark backgrounds show the influence of Ribera but the most important characteristic of the series is its deep involvement with the body as form, the body almost as still life. In his *Inmaculada* (*2992*) the painter sets aside the rule laid down by the Inquisition and clothes his Virgin in blue and purple instead of the obligatory blue and white but he complies with the much more often transgressed requirement that her feet should rest on a crescent moon with the horns turned *downwards*. (A surprisingly literal respect for science forbade even the Virgin to stand within the horns, that is in the solid but eclipsed part of the moon's surface.) Saint Casilda (*1239*) is one of the many female saints painted by Zurbarán in fashionable clothes of the period. The Crucifixion (*2594*) is observed by

Saint Luke (Zurbarán himself), palette in hand. The little *Bodegón* (*2803*) is a masterpiece of still life. Saint Peter the Apostle appears upside down, as he was crucified, to Saint Peter Nolasco (*1236*). This painting gives a taste of Zurbarán's expertise with white robes, which has earned him the sobriquet *pintor de los frailes,* painter of monks. But he is much more than that and it is not hard to see why recent opinion has preferred his firm constructions to Murillo's more vaporous effects. Yet his work, though striking, is still slightly claustrophobic; there is no air round his figures; they are substantial but they do not breathe – that comes with Velázquez.

If the proper place to make up one's mind about el Greco is Toledo (and about Zurbarán Seville), the Prado is equally the place for the great encounter with Diego de Silva Velázquez (1599-1660). Founder and giant of the Madrid School, Velázquez was born in Seville a year after Zurbarán and in the same year as Van Dyck. He studied briefly under the rumbustious Herrera el Viejo and then under the pedantic Pacheco, whose daughter he was to marry. After one abortive attempt he persuaded Philip IV to sit for his portrait and was at once admitted into the royal service as *pintor de cámara.* It was to be a marriage even more complete than Charles V and Titian's with the important difference that the absolutist principle was by now so firmly established in Spain that it was not even shaken by Philip's disastrous reign and required none of the propaganda that had accompanied the foundation of the dynasty. Thus Velázquez was able to look more objectively on his sitters and there is a kind of Olympian detachment in his enormously skilful handling of them.

Off the long gallery on the principal floor, exactly at the centre of the museum, there opens a large room which is Velázquez's monument containing many of his most celebrated works. The Drunkards (*1170*) is a bacchanal painted in 1629 to pay for his first Italian trip – undertaken on the advice of Rubens – which lasted till 1631. Whilst on it he bought various works for the King and on his return painted the big equestrian portraits and the Surrender of Breda. The former, for all their marvellous passages of colour, are not among his most successful works. The portrait of Baltasar Carlos (*1180*) shows the young prince astride his favourite pony – stuffed it looks and stuffed it was, for it died before the painting was

completed. The prince himself died at seventeen. Philip IV
(*1178*) is mounted on another rocking-horse with repainted
back legs – in fact it is not even a rocker because the one
thing that is certain about Velázquez's horses is that they will
never move, they are props fixed for all time. One feels that
the artist didn't really believe in this sort of mock heroics.
The best is perhaps that of the Count-Duke of Olivares
(*1181*) with rump half turned towards the viewer and alarums
and excursions in the background; the presumption of
Olivares in taking the wind out of his King's sails is said to
have given Philip great offence and contributed to the
favourite's fall from grace and exile to the town of Toro.
By contrast, the Surrender of Breda, generally known as *Las
Lanzas* (*1172*) is in a different class. The disdain for Baroque
convention in the placing of the lances is quite remarkable.
But, above all, the painting is a clear statement of Velázquez's
firm belief in the civilised values that required courtesy from
the victorious general and good grace from his defeated
opponent who is delivering the key of the town. The
demeanour of all the figures, who are mostly dismounted, is
a statement of faith in certain rules of behaviour, without
which life would become intolerable.

Also in this room are the beautiful royal portraits in
hunting dress with dog and gun (*1184, 1186, 1189*), in which
black, grey, pearl, buff and suède predominate. In Mariana of
Austria, second wife of Philip IV, at nineteen (*1191*), the
artist paints a superb picture from which he cannot eliminate
the new Queen's ill-favoured and worse-natured countenance.
But his portrait of the daughter of the marriage, Margarita
(*1192*) enables him to seize the chance he could not in all
conscience take with the mother and he gives us an enchanting pink and silver portrait of the little princess. Still in the
main room, the buffoon Pablo of Valladolid (*1198*), black on
buff-grey, is a marvellous statement of corporeality in space.
This and the circumspect fool called Don John of Austria
(*1200*) belong to a series of clowns, which also includes the
bombastic Barbarroja (*1199*). It is worth remarking that while
Velázquez painted a number of portraits of these court enter-
tainers he has left us hardly any record of the leading literary
lights of the Spanish Golden Age such as Quevedo, Lope de
Vega, Tirso de Molina, Góngora, Calderón, Gracián – in fact
he painted no member of this constellation for certain other

than Góngora. We draw the obvious conclusion that the King much preferred the company of triflers to the sharp tongues and minds of the literary world. It also becomes apparent that Velázquez's circle was very small, virtually confined to the court, outside which he does not seem to have felt at all happy. In addition to his painterly duties he also became in due course *aposentador de palacios,* a job that put him in charge of the decoration of royal dwellings and lodgings, and it was while on a visit to the royal tapestry factory in this capacity that he must have conceived the idea of *Las Hilanderas (1173),* painted about 1650 after his second trip to Italy. This great painting is the immediate forerunner of *Las Meninas* in its several sources of light and creation of atmospheric depth.

Velázquez's religious paintings have never captured the imagination of the Spanish public. In the Crucifixion (*1167*) of 1632 Christ is already dead and the head falls forward, robbing the viewer of the requisite agony of expression. The early Adoration of the Shepherds, painted when he was eighteen or nineteen, shows the young painter's determination to demonstrate his mastery of solid three-dimensional objects, for which purpose he coolly borrows the Holy Family and the Son of God – the work might almost have been painted by Zurbarán. Near by are the dwarf buffoons, all painted sitting down out of delicate respect for their deformities. Don Sebastian de Morra (*1202*) and El Primo (*1201*) take themselves very seriously and their seriousness is reciprocated by the artist, quite unironically and with due respect.

Velázquez's most famous work is probably *Las Meninas* (*1174*), painted in 1656. Originally called *La Familia de Felipe IV,* it emphasises his role as *pintor de cámara,* whose essential function was to record the life and growth of the royal family. The main group consists of the little Princess Margarita with her attendants (these are *las Meninas*), including the deformed Maria Bárbola and the page Nicolasito Pertusato who has perkily placed his foot on the dozing dog. Lightly painted behind these are a lady of the household and a court official. The painter is standing back from his canvas to appraise his work. The figure in the doorway is another court official, who is drawing back the curtain to admit more light. The foreground figures facing us are not simply characters in a photograph 'watching the dickie-bird'; they

are looking at the King and Queen whom Velázquez is painting and the royal couple, reflected in a mirror on the rear
wall of the picture, can be imagined just about where we are
standing. By means of this involvement of two figures right
outside it the picture achieves a quite extraordinary effect of
space and depth.

Though he travelled in Italy and painted Pope Innocent X
in 1649, Velázquez was neither so prolific nor such a man of
the world as Rubens. He was made a knight of the Order of
Santiago against considerable opposition by its aristocratic
members. Ortega y Gasset attempted to sustain that he was
at least as interested in his honours and duties as a courtier
as in his painting and adduces the paucity of his production as
if this proved a reluctance to paint. But it must be remembered
that some of his works were burned in the Alcázar fire of
1734 and in any case a limited output may be construed
another way – as a sign of extreme fastidiousness. Although
Velázquez's work lacks the ebullience of Rubens, it certainly
contains less hack or run-of-the-mill stuff than any other
great painter's. The only contemporary who approached him
and whom he respected was Zurbarán, whose painting life
was spent mainly in the service of chapter houses and
monastries. Velázquez eschewed these commissions; he simply
didn't want them. In a sense he was the first fully secular
Spanish painter. He released the figure from its symbolic and
propagandist function. He profited from the plastic lessons of
Zurbarán and breathed a life into them that his contemporary
never achieved. Philip IV may not have encouraged
intellectuals at his court but he deserves lasting credit for
providing his *pintor de cámara* with the working conditions
he needed with few strings attached.

*The Spanish Seventeenth Century (cont.) – Murillo – Carreño
– Claudio Coello – Alonso Cano – The Italian Seventeenth
Century – Luca Giordano (Lucas Jordán)*

Further work by Velázquez and by his son-in-law Mazo is
hung in the long gallery. The next major figure we come to is
Murillo, who is shown in a large room of his own on the left.
Bartolomé Esteban Murillo (1618-1682) belongs as much to
Seville as el Greco to Toledo and Velázquez to Madrid. Much
of his better work is in the municipal museum of the southern

city. Here, however, is the *Inmaculada de Soult* (*2809*), so called as it was carried off in 1813 by the French marshal, whom Richard Ford aptly named the Plundermaster General, and only returned in 1941. Murillo always stuck to the Inquisition ruling that the Virgin must be shown in a white dress and blue robe and aged about fifteen but he invariably broke the scientific stipulation that the horns of the crescent moon should be turned downwards in the better interest of his compositions. (El Greco had given nothing for this convention either but Zurbarán and even Rubens had respected it.) Present in the Prado also are the three much-copied child paintings – the young Saint John the Baptist (*963*), the Children with a Shell (*964*) and the Good Shepherd (*962*), in all of which figure a fleecy lamb or lambs. Mention should also be made of the enchanting (earlier) *Sagrada Familia del Pajarito* (*960*), in which the child Jesus teases a small white dog with the little bird in his hand. Despite the appeal to sentiment Murillo's drawing is never feeble. His child models, though prettified, are carefully observed studies from the picaresque Calle de la Feria in Seville. He has suffered a devaluation in this century due less to any intrinsic weakness of his own than to a change of taste in favour of Zurbarán's devotion to significant form. But there is room in the world for both. Murillo's Landscape (*3008*) takes the romanticisation of nature a stage further than it had previously reached.

The main gallery continues to illustrate the course of Spanish painting during the latter part of Murillo's life and after his death until about 1700. After Velázquez's death and his royal patron's, Juan Carreño became *pintor del rey*. His portrait of the Duke of Pastrana (*550*) shows that he has studied both Velázquez and Van Dyck. To him it fell to paint the unfortunate young Charles II, the Bewitched (*642*) and his mother, the same Mariana who had curdled even Velázquez's brush. Now queen-mother and regent, she came into her own as high priestess of the decline in Spain. Claudio Coello (1642-1693) succeeded Carreño. His religious works are able, facile and Italianate. Pedro Núñez de Villavicencio (1644-1700) has a lively genre scene (*1235*) showing the influence of Murillo. The Miracle of the Well (*2806*) is a good painting by the turbulent Alonso Cano (1601-1667) – this really is a genre scene too. Architect of the west front of Granada Cathedral, Cano had studied with Velázquez under Pacheco and is the only painter of the immediately post-Velázquez period, apart from Murillo, to retain any magic in his brush. He was also a considerable sculptor. The Spanish Seventeenth Century also gave rise to a number of lesser but very respectable practitioners who are represented in the Prado. The most noteworthy are: el Greco's disciple Luis Tristán; the Valencian Francisco de Ribalta who modelled himself on Caravaggio; Juan Antonio de Frias y Escalante, an elegant portraitist of the Madrid School; Francisco Collantes and Ignacio Iriarte, leaders of the new fashion for landscape; the prolific Sevillian Valdés Leal; the Benedictine Father Rizzi, an exponent of sober Spanish Baroque; José Antolínez, rather more colourful and dynamic than his master Rizzi; and Carreño's very competent disciple Mateo Cerezo.

The Italian School of the late Sixteenth and Seventeenth Centuries is destined to come to rest, along with the French, in the ground floor rooms off the Hispano-Flemish section of the long gallery. This collection includes the Crespis, Palma Giovanni, Andrea Vaccaro, Gentileschi, Mario Preti, Massimo Stanzione, il Guercino, Guido Reni and Ancello Falcon. There is no fire left in the belly of any of these painters and the successful resistance put up by the Madrid School – and by Zurbarán in Seville – to the Baroque movement is remarkable when one thinks of the earlier wave of Italian influence. It means that Spain largely avoided this empty rhetorical or vapid mythological type of painting. Even so, the Spanish School as a whole was in decline and foreign luminaries, themselves of no vast merit, were gathering in the wings. Coello's last years were embittered by the rising popularity at court of Luca Giordano, known in Spain as Lucas Jordán. The early works of this immensely prolific painter reveal an almost Flemish devotion to detail but he soon soars into the Baroque stratosphere and becomes expert at covering large surfaces with allegories and battle scenes. He can be quite human in small works such as the Journey of Jacob into Canaan (*157*).

The Flemish late Sixteenth and Seventeenth Centuries – Jan Breughel – David Teniers – Rubens – Jacob Jordaens – Van Dyck – Followers of Rubens – Rembrandt and the Dutch School

Despite the rise of Italian popularity with the Renaissance the Spanish taste for the Flemings was by no means at an end. The long gallery on the ground floor nearest the 'Botanical' end of the building is attractively arranged with mythological scenes by Rubens and followers, alternating with classical statuary from the collection of Queen Christina of Sweden (bought by Philip V on her death) in the recesses; eight of a series of the nine muses are present.

One of the great improvements to the museum has been the bringing together in a dozen or so rooms adjacent to this gallery of the main works in the Prado's extensive collection of late Sixteenth and Seventeenth Century Flemish paintings. One must hope they will not be subjected to any diaspora in the future. Perhaps the most immediately striking work in this area is Ruben's gorgeously rich Adoration of the Kings (*1638*), in which the Child paddles its fingers in the proffered gold and the torsos of the slaves swell majestically under the weight of the treasure chests. This just comes off but Saint George and the Dragon (*1644*) with its flurry of mane and gaping of jaws and smiting of evil comes dangerously near absurdity and the shiny Duke of Lerma (*3137*) is not as appealing to modern taste as it was to that prince of favourites who commissioned it during the artist's first mission to Spain on behalf of the Duke of Mantua. Of the Rubens portraits Maria de Medici (*1685*) wins the prize for its solidity and humanity. Here also are the rollicking Garden of Love (*1690*), the Judgement of Paris (*1669*), Andromeda freed by Perseus (*1663*) and the sumptuous Three Graces (*1670*), snapped up by the King on Rubens' death. Atalanta and Meleager (*1662*) provides the occasion for a stunning landscape, so rich and humid you can practically smell the leaf-mould. The small Judgement of Paris (*1731*) is an early Mannerist work. The enchanting Villagers' Dance (*1691*) has a fine rhythm and humour in the vein of the Breughels but is made mysterious by the classical bacchanalian figures joining hands with the rustic dancers. All these attractions and delights should not cause one to overlook the series of small oils on panels ordered by Isabel Clara Eugenia in 1628;

they are the designs for the set of tapestries celebrating the Eucharist and other Church mysteries which hang in the Convento de Descalzas Reales.

Antony Van Dyck (1599-1641) and Jacob Jordaens (1593-1678) are also well represented. Van Dyck's most admired work here is the oval painting of Sir Endymion Porter (secretary to the Duke of Buckingham) with the artist himself (*1489*) painted about 1635. It has been claimed that only Velázquez could have equalled it but a nasty doubt, as always, creeps in as to Van Dyck's limp conventional hands. Among his religious paintings the pathos of *La Piedad* (*1642*) comes across with great effect; there can be no doubt of Van Dyck's hypersensitivity. By comparison, Jacob Jordaens gives an impression of honest craftsmanship; his pictures all seem built of good painterly masonry. His *Piedad* (*6392*) is fine but more relaxed and resigned than Van Dyck's. In the Painter's Family (*1594*) he has almost escaped from his master Rubens and reverts to a homelier tradition, celebrating family life in a way that seems wholesome but not excessively solemn. The small oil sketch of three versions of a street musician's head is a fresh, free work of surprising modernity. The Flemish collection continues with an impressive display of still-lifes. Some are large and opulent like the joint Rubens and Snyders (*1851*), the Adriaen Van Utrecht (*1852*) and the Frans Snyders (*1757*), whose figures may be by Rubens. Here also are animal studies and sanguinary scenes of the chase by Paul de Vos, Jan Fyt and again by Snyders. Of the smaller works the Osias Beet (*1606*) is exquisite.

One of the nicest painting conceits of the time was the *guirnalda* in which formalised garlands of flowers (painted by one hand, often Flemish) formed the surround of a small religious scene (painted by another hand, often Italian). Jan Breughel (1568-1625), known as 'Velvet' Breughel, is a leading exponent. He was son to Pieter Breughel, the Elder, whose brief and momentous incursion into painting we have already noticed (see p. 21). He became painter to the Archduke Albert of Austria, husband of Philip II's favourite daughter Isabel Clara Eugenia; he enjoyed a close friendship with Rubens, who acted as guardian of his children, and his daughter married David Teniers. He is famous for his lush treatment of the five senses either singly or in various combinations. In Sight and Smell (*1403*) the figures, flowers and bibelots on the table are undoubtedly by him but the rest of the painting is by a number of hands. His large scenes of courtly parties in the countryside are endowed with those marvellous blue-green backgrounds which also appear as backdrops to Rubens' portraits of the Archduke Albert (*1683*) and Isabel Clara Eugenia (*1684*). My personal preference, however, is for his more bucolic works, notably the Country Dance (*1439*) and the Wedding Feast (*1442*). Other favourites of mine are Country Life (*1440*) and the splendid Market and Washing Day in Flanders (*1443*), both of which previously bore Breughel's name but are now attributed by expert opinion to Joost de Momper (1564-1635). By comparison with the Breughels David Teniers (1610-1690) turns out a much more theatrical type of genre scene. His figures lack the self-absorption of his father-in-law's; one feels they are dancing and capering not for themselves but for the spectator. However, his Country Feast (*1786*) is a jolly, jigging piece one can't carp at. His Temptations of Saint Anthony continue the grotesque vein of Pieter Breughel the Elder and Bosch. Many of his popular scenes were to be chosen by Mengs as fitting subjects for the tapestries that now hang in the Escorial and other royal palaces. It is worthy of remark that his picture of the Archduke Leopold William's private gallery (*1813*) is an accurate inventory of paintings and other works of art in his patron's collection, every one of which has been identified; even the table has been located.

No self-respecting national collection is without its Rembrandt and this evidently was the view of Charles III who acquired the Artemis (*2132*) in 1769. Done in 1634, the year of the artist's marriage to Saskia, it is a dazzling display of technical mastery. We do not for one moment believe in the Queen of Pergamum about to drink from the poisoned chalice but we are completely captured by the painter and his model. The self-portrait (*2808*) is said to be a copy of the similar painting in London. If so, it is a very good one, sharing with Goya's self-portrait in 1814 the air of naked disillusion towards the end of a harsh and testing life. This may be a coincidence but Goya would almost certainly have been familiar with the Artemis. Indeed one of his favourite sayings was: 'Velázquez, Rembrandt and Nature'.

The French School – Italians of the Eighteenth Century – the Tieopolos – the Bayeus – Mengs – Goya

In 1700 the Habsburg dynasty came to an end with the death of the unfortunate Charles II. The War of the Spanish Succession, it is true, dragged on till 1713 but by this time Philip V, grandson of Louis XIV of France, was firmly established on the Spanish throne and the way was open for the flood of French taste that swamped the court, if not the country. It is therefore almost impossible to speak of any truly Spanish painting in the first two-thirds of the eighteenth century. In default of native painters we must turn to the French who stepped into their shoes. Both the French and the Italians of this period (and of the previous century) should be sought on the ground floor via the Hispano-Flemish gallery. J. Ranc (1674-1735) became Philip V's court painter. By him are the two enamel-like costume pieces of Ferdinand VI and Charles III as boys. The silver-clad pallid-faced Luis I of Spain as Prince of the Asturias by M. A. Houasse (1680-1730) foreshadows the young man's death in 1724 after only 7 months on the throne, which his father Philip then resumed until his death in 1746. Ranc's successor Van Loo (1707-1771) paints an extra-large, extra-dull set-piece of Philip V and his Family (*2283*). Poussin (1594-1665) is well represented and Claude Lorrain (1600-1682) less so. They were both an essential part of the Bourbon baggage: their works were and are an expression of that kind of refinement which – in French eyes at any rate – has passed Spain by. The large equestrian portrait of Queen Christina of Sweden (*1503*) by Sebastian Bourdon (1616-1671), sent by that fantastic lady to Philip IV after her conversion to Catholicism is of some interest; she is no Garbo with her strong nose and mannish dress but the painting is well done and much to be preferred to the stiff rendering of Philip V (*2326*) by Ranc. With Philip's second marriage to Isabel Farnese the influence of the French School declined. The new Queen added to the collection of earlier Flemish paintings and favoured Italian artists with current commissions. Official court portraiture became the province of J. Amiconi (1675-1752). The new royal palace – the Palacio de Oriente (see pp. 62-6) – was decorated by Conrado Giaquinto (1700-1765) and G. B. Tiepolo (1692-1769), who was assisted by his son G. D. Tiepolo

(1727-1804). The Aragonese Francisco Bayeu (1754-1795) followed the Tiepolos in his oil sketches for the decoration of cupolas and pendentives. Native realism was driven into a tight corner, defended by Luis de Melendez (1716-1780) with his scrupulous treatment of victuals, reminiscent in some passages of Zurbarán. Antonio Carnicero (1748-1814), author of a popular series of bullfight prints, was also a dull glossy portrait painter. The Spanish genius seemed quite unable to shake off the foreign yoke, itself feeble enough. One feels at this point that it has become extinguished, never to revive.

A revival, however, was not far off and it was to be of a prodigious nature. In 1761 Charles III appointed the Bohemian A. R. Mengs (1728-1779) as *pintor de cámara.* Mengs was a theoretician who believed that perfect art could be achieved by combining Greek design with the expression of Raphael, the chiaroscuro of Correggio and the palette of Titian. In practice, he continued in the mythological vein of the Italians to which he lent a Neo-Classical tinge, while his royal portraits are in the high gloss French style. When the royal tapestry factory established by Philip V became operational in 1775 Mengs commissioned wall hangings from genre pictures by David Teniers but he also commissioned new designs from the Bayeu brothers, Francisco and Ramón. It was Francisco, the senior of the two, later to be director of the Spanish Royal Academy of San Fernando, who introduced to Mengs a young fellow Aragonese, Francisco de Goya y Lucientes (1746-1828). Goya had married the Bayeus' sister Josefa in 1771 and Mengs obtained for him too a share of the work in painting designs for tapestries. Goya's 'cartoons', as they are called, found favour with Charles III and once again the Spanish genius stirred to life under the kindling breath of royal patronage, though this time it was to range far and wide beyond the confines of the court, touching on and reviving themes taboo in art since mediaeval times.

It is the intention of the museum authorities to bring together all Goya's work on the two main floors at the 'Botanical' end of the building. The most important portraits were previously in the principal floor rotunda where they are destined to return. If the move has not yet taken place, Goya will be found still on the ground floor at the 'Ritz' end. The largest canvas of all is the Family of Charles IV (*726*). Goya's first patron, Charles III, had died in 1788, leaving his amiable,

slow-witted son an outstanding court painter and his painter
a family hardly distinguished for good looks. But they were
no uglier than the Habsburgs and their consorts who had
confronted Velázquez and Carreño. Also, Goya managed to
treat the King's good-natured, undistinguished face with real
affection, while there are enchanting passages throughout the
whole picture, especially the young couple on the right, the
future Ferdinand VII and the girl he was to marry. Goya
does not attempt to endow the Queen's purse-lipped (she was
toothless) and self-satisfied (she wore the trousers) face with
charm or dignity, both of which it conspicuously lacked, but
he does justice to her well-rounded arms of which she was
inordinately proud. The oil sketches (731, 733, 729 and 732)
are preliminary studies for the family group. The portrait of
the Duke of Alba (2449) with a musical score of Haydn's and
that of a lady artist (2448) are handled with 'Regency'
elegance and a cool palette. In the grey-coated, granite-faced
rendering of Francisco Bayeu (721) absolutely no consideration of prudence, deference or family ties seems to come
between the artist and his sitter, whose stern image lingers a
long time on the retina. Then there is the famous pair of
canvases known as the *Maja Desnuda* (742) and the *Maja
Vestida* (741), whose whereabouts can never be certainly
stated. Sometimes they are in the rotunda and sometimes in
Japan or elsewhere; one must take them where one finds
them if at all. They have been transformed by the breath of
scandal about the painter's relations with the Duchess of
Alba into objects as much of tittle-tattle as of art; the nude
figure, for all its charm, is made of thinner stuff than the
Venuses of Titian or Velázquez. With religious themes Goya
never seems quite at home, though he was obliged to paint
them from time to time and his brother was a priest. The
Crucifixion (745) is an academic work painted as the artist's
offering on his election to the Spanish Royal Academy. The
Holy Family (746) is a rather unpleasant Raphaelesque work
painted under the tutelage of Mengs.

The 'cartoons' for tapestries are quite another matter. In
1870 forty-three of them – carried out between 1777 and 1791
– were discovered rolled up in the basement. In contemporary
eyes they had done their duty but we recognise them as
paintings in their own right, whose importance is much
greater than that of the wall-hangings to which they gave

rise. The earlier pieces such as *La Maja y Los Embozados* (*771*) and *La Feria de Madrid* (*779*) and *Merienda a Orillas del Manzanares* (*786*) have sharp outlines and emphatic colouring in deference to the weavers' requirements. By the time of the last work in the series, however, the enchanting *Gallina Ciega* (*804*), which depicts a sort of game of blind man's buff, it is evident that Goya had achieved complete freedom in his treatment of his subjects and forced the weavers to follow him in his subtle colour-range of blues, grey and browns. These works gave the artist the escape he needed from court portraiture into plebeian life but they do not suffer from the knowing folksiness of Teniers. The vigour of the *pueblo* combines with a magic sense of colour and design to produce art as good as any inspired for nearly a century by religious or mythological subjects.

The so-called black paintings belong to Goya's old age; they were removed from the walls of his *quinta* or country house and transferred onto canvas in 1873. These are the products of his deafness and disillusion but unlike *Los Caprichos*, which are mainly social satires and political lampoons, they are total expressions of disgust with few points of reference to the times. Some shapes and forms from earlier works persist, like the great bulbous rock in the Witches' Sabbath (*756*), which has appeared before in etchings, and the two soldiers bottom right in the same painting, blood brothers of those we shall shortly see in the great Third of May. In the especially horrifying *Duelo a Garrotazos* (*758*) two men attempt to club one another to death, both up to the knees in what I had always thought of as a marsh, though another explanation is that they have deliberately dug themselves in so that neither can flee and one or both must die. The absurd Saturn devouring his son (*763*) is much less terrifying than the curious dog buried in sand (*767*), which conveys the panic of smothering in isolation. It is clear that something broke in these private pictures, something not intended for us. It is no mere coincidence that there had been violent episodes in Goya's earlier life. The French occupation of Spain under Joseph Bonaparte, to which the painter had grudgingly submitted, must have imposed its own strains. At the same time, it is equally clear that his psyche was very tough. He did not go under. In very advanced age he returned to a relatively normal world. His fine portrait of J. B. Muguiro

(*2998*), done when he was 81, could almost be by Manet. The Milkmaid of Bordeaux (*2899*) – few realise she is riding on a donkey – is perhaps his last work.

With Wellington's defeat of Jourdain at Vitoria in 1813 the War in the Peninsula was virtually over and in 1814 the Bourbon Ferdinand VII returned to Spain. The fame of Goya's brush saved him from any serious consequences of his reluctant collaboration. He painted the King on a number of occasions as he had his father and grandfather before him. To this period belong the equestrian portrait of General Palafox (*725*), hero of Zaragoza, and the self-portrait (*723*), which I have already compared with the Rembrandt. But the two most outstanding examples of his work immediately after the Bourbon restoration are undoubtedly the canvases entitled Episode of the Second of May (*748*) and Scenes of the Third of May (*749*). Both were painted six years after the uprising in 1808 of the Madrid populace against the troops of Joseph Bonaparte. But there is a great difference between them. The scene of the struggle between the people and the Mamelukes in the Puerta del Sol is a fine work with none of the frigidity and artificiality of most 'historical' paintings but it lacks the immediacy of its fellow. Various explanations have been advanced for this. One is that Goya saw the firing squad at work from his window and was able to record the stance of the executioners; when the shooting was over he went out with his terrified servant to inspect the corpses in their pools of blood; he was thus able to reconstruct a specific historical fact – make a documentary if you like – before the blood had cooled. Severe doubt is cast on this interpretation by Hugh Thomas in his monograph *Goya: The Third of May 1808* on the grounds that the probable site of the executions was a considerable distance from Goya's house in the Calle Valverde and invisible from it. Furthermore, a number of Goya's etchings from the *Caprichos* and from *Los Desastres de la Guerra,* which antedate the painting, have similar compositions deriving from Goya's general experience of the horrors of the Peninsular War and even, it is suggested, from the work of other artists. Be that as it may, the Third of May obviously continued to boil in Goya's blood and when an official commission came round to commemorate the event, it released all the elements of his experience, however acquired, and possibly an element of guilt deriving from his collaboration. The faceless firing squad represents all the mindless killers, 'shooting on orders', of all time. Its members have their packs on their backs and will simply move on the next job when this one is over. The victims have faces, souls and are reduced to abject fear, though the wearer of the white shirt immediately in the sights of the rifles is somehow able, just for a few seconds, to rise above his companions' and his own despair. The two sides of the picture, the killers and the killed, are drawn together by the outsize lantern casting an even yellow light from the ground and lighting the white shirt of the momentary hero with his Christ-like gesture and the suggestion of the stigmata in his right hand. Over and above its documentary and human interest, this painting sums up Goya's achievement. By comparison with it his portraits are necessarily circumscribed by some polite considerations, as are his cartoons for tapestry, while the black paintings suffer from an overdose of private imagery. Here, unleashed feeling goes hand in hand with technical mastery. The lessons of Velázquez are applied to a world that knew nothing of and cared less for the Baroque gallantries of war. This work – a far cry from the gracious good manners of the Surrender of Breda – could only have been painted by a Spaniard, sensing in his own soul the fury and anger and bewilderment and agony of a people deserted by its rulers. There is nothing like it till Picasso's *Guernica*.

The exhibition of a selection of Goya's prints and drawings, changed every three months, will shortly be resumed on the ground floor near the black paintings. It was from his study of Rembrandt that he learned the possibilities of etching as an art form. His notes of a journey through hell have been widely distributed by the various editions of *Los Desastres de la Guerra*, etched between 1808 and 1813. Here the members of the firing squad in the Third of May make an earlier appearance in the print called 'With reason or without it'. In 'One cannot look' only the bayonets of the aimed rifles jab into the picture space; it is left to our imagination what is behind them. This series alternates with *Los Caprichos, Los Disparates, La Tauromaçuía* and other engravings. Almost at the end of his long life he became a pioneer of the lithograph, the technique of which he learned while living in Bordeaux. After Goya, Spanish painting hastily drew in its horns once more, leaving us the glutinous dignitaries of

Vicente López and the bland bourgeois families of Esteve. Where the people are touched on, it is with the patronising rose-tinted brush of the *Costumbristas,* brightly recording regional dress and colourful fiestas; the course of this development is traced in the Museo del Siglo XIX in the Casón del Buen Retiro.

Miscellaneous

Before proceeding to the Spanish Nineteenth Century mention must be made of the Museum's very small collection of English paintings, to be found on the third floor at the 'Ritz' end. All are portraits except for two pleasant Spanish views by David Roberts. Gainsborough's Dr. Isaac Henriquez Siqueira (*2979*) is more sensitive and no less firm and solid than Reynolds' Mr. James Bourdieu (*2986*). Hoppner and Raeburn are slighter and flashier. Lawrence is dull in his official portraits and slick in his more intimate ones.

The Prado possesses 500 pieces of classical and other sculpture. The former star turn, the Dama de Elche, has gone very properly to the Archaeological Museum. Philip V and Isabel Farnese were responsible for the bulk of the classical collection. I have referred already to the series of the Muses who grace the long Rubens gallery on the ground floor. Most of the other pieces will be found in the basement, which also houses the *Tesoro del Delfín* or Dauphin's Treasure, left to Philip by his father who died before he could ascend the throne of France. This consists mainly of Renaissance tableware of rock-crystal, agate, jade, jasper and similar materials, much of it elaborately decorated with enamelled figures and incrustations of jewels.

THE BUEN RETIRO

The Prado Museum is the main attraction of a zone I shall call the Buen Retiro, whose limits are the Paseo del Prado between the Plaza de la Cibeles and the Atocha Station on the west, the railway tracks on the south, the Avenida de Menéndez Pelayo on the east and to the north the Calle de Alcalá. This all formed part of an estate given by the Count-Duke of Olivares to Philip IV. Much of it still consists of gardens and park. The most important remnant of the

Retiro Palace is the **Casón del Buen Retiro,** a free-standing reception hall built at the end of the seventeenth century. It is to be found five minutes walk directly uphill from the Prado Museum, leaving the royal church of San Jerónimo on the right. In recent years it has been the home of the Prado's nineteenth century collection. The large central chamber with its Luca Giordano ceiling depicting the Origin and Triumph of the Order of the Golden Fleece used to house a number of huge history paintings, which have now been banished to make way for *Guernica,* to which I shall come shortly.

The entrance to the upstaged **Museo del Siglo XIX** is at the lower end of the building nearest the Prado (the Prado ticket is still valid). Downstairs, Vicente López (1772-1850) is best out of court – see his portrait of Goya in old age and of his own father. Here also is Madrazo's vulgar Death of Viriathus (for some account of whose life see index p. ???). Upstairs the rooms devoted to the *Costumbristas* are the most interesting. They belonged to a time in which Spanish writers and artists were beginning to look at their country and countrymen with an eye to the regional peculiarities and customs that had fascinated English writers like Borrow and Ford and Scottish artist, David Roberts. Valeriano Dominguez Bécquer, brother of the poet Gustavo Adolfo Bécquer, acquits himself creditably in this vein. *Aficionados* of the bullfight will enjoy the glossy scene before a *Corrida* by Manuel Castellano, in which each *torero* is surrounded by his gentlemen admirers.

The remaining rooms contain history paintings by Rosales, slick pretty pictures by Palmaroli, some facile works by Fortuny, discreet nudes and winsome children by Pinazo and swift portraits by Sorolla. Finally we come to timid Spanish impressionism, whose main exponent seems to be the pale atmospheric Aureliano de Berruguete. This is not a distinguished collection but it is of period interest and introduces some minor artists we shall meet again in the more intimate surroundings of the Museo Romántico. We shall also see Sorolla again in his own museum.

Skirting the building, we now come to its main portico on Calle de Alfonso XII, facing the Retiro Park. This is the entrance to *Guernica* by Pablo Ruiz Picasso (1881-1973). It was first exhibited in the pavilion of the Spanish Republic at the 1937 Paris 'Exposition Internationale des Arts et Techniques', one year after the outbreak of the Spanish Civil War.

The return of this famous work of art from the Museum of Modern Art, New York, in October 1981 was an event of great importance to Spaniards, symbolising as it did the readmission of Spain by the Western democracies into their club. The work was inspired by the bombing and near obliteration on April 26th, 1937 of the old Basque capital of Guernica by the German Condor Legion on loan to General Franco. Usually you have to queue to get in but not for long. You are conducted towards the object of your pilgrimage along a side gallery with preliminary drawings which show clearly the very rapid and intense design process the work went through in the couple of months immediately after the event. The mother and dead child are much strengthened by the progressive disengagement of the child's head from a central womb-like position until it lolls sickeningly free from the mother's bulk. The drawings of the screaming horse and the warrior's fingers knotted like iron bananas round the hilt of the broken sword are essential preliminaries to the great mural itself, which is so well displayed in its bullet-proof vitrine that it is easy to see, however many people are gathered under the Baroque splendours of the vast Luca Giordano ceiling – of which most seem totally unaware. I think perhaps the first impression of the average person will be of a much cooler work than might have been expected. It is a very large cool tonal painting, restricted to greys, black, white, charcoal and rinsed-out blue. Yet it is utterly compelling. It conveys its message better than any blood bath. Compared with the earlier drawings the horse's head has risen from low centre almost up to the sunflower light bulb. The warrior has been dismembered: severed head, severed arm. The bull has been squeezed towards the left and upwards; he is much more effective right over the outraged mother. Roughly an hour is required for the whole experience. On the way out through the other side gallery look at some of the rejected coloured drawings. Strong colour has been rejected as inappropriate even by an artist who broke out of his austere cubist duette with Braque by reaching for the paint pot. Look also at the strip cartoons, Goya-inspired engravings called *Sueño y Mentira de Franco*. And then depart. Don't attempt anything else unless you go back to the Third of May. And then you will see the difference. Goya has almost but not quite escaped the bondage of the anecdotal 'history' painting. Picasso has soared free and given the world a protest painting that is truly universal.

It is only a few steps from the Casón del Buen Retiro to the Army Museum, the **Museo del Ejército,** which occupies the sole remaining wing of the main Retiro Palace built between 1636 and 1639. Be careful to go uncovered for you are on hallowed ground and whoever does not doff his hat or beret in the presence of so many flags and regimental colours will be severely reprimanded by an affronted corporal. The Navy is much more relaxed about this sort of thing. There are two other museums in the immediate vicinity, both in the Calle de Montalban (see plan on pp. 54-5). This street runs down from the Calle de Alfonso XII, bordering the park, to the Paseo del Prado. Near the top end is the **Museo de Artes Decorativos,** which offers a well-arranged and unfatiguing survey of Spanish furniture, fittings and utensils from the fifteenth to the nineteenth centuries. On the ground floor are ceramics from Talavera and Puente del Arzobispo and a beautiful English alabaster Annunciation of the fifteenth century; also an anthology of Spanish glass from Punic times. Some of the wooden *artesonado* ceilings are attractive, particularly the late fifteenth century Toledan example in room 16, which also contains good lustre ware from Manises. The second floor has regional kitchens from Teruel and Andalusia, while higher up room 46 is fitted out as a Valencian eighteenth-century kitchen, entirely tiled with very charming scenes of a lady and her servants preparing to receive guests. Room 50 with its Pompeian panels is an excellent example of the Neo-Classical taste. Lower down the same street on the same side is the **Museo Naval,** housed in the old Ministry of Marine.

Reaching the Paseo del Prado and turning right, we come very shortly to the **Plaza de la Cibeles,** the hub of the motorised Madrid, whose fountain with the goddess in her chariot, finished in 1792, is another of the beautifications carried out by the good King Charles III. Bearing right round the Central Post Office – an ungainly building of the present century jocularly known as Our Lady of Communications – a short walk up Calle de Alcalá leads to the **Plaza de la Independencia,** in the centre of which is Charles III's **Puerta de Alcalá,** a monumental archway with sculpted groups in soft white stone above the cornice; in these the trappings of war are piled in disused heaps, the discarded plumed helmets frame no warriors' heads and Mars himself has stripped off his armour and turned his back on his admirers. Over the side-openings are reliefs with horns of plenty. This well-meaning structure is robbed of much of its effect by an ill-sited tower-block of flats a little further east along Calle de Alcalá.

The Plaza de la Independencia also contains one of the entrances to the **Parque del Retiro,** which boasts many agree-able features, amongst them the **Rosaleda,** reminiscent of Queen Mary's rose garden in Regent's Park. Near here one comes across some sculpture, including the pensive, reclined figure of Pérez Galdos, 'the Spanish Dickens', by Victorio Macho (1918). In the Spring there is Judas blossom every-where. On the big pond called the **Estanque** rowing boats and canoes can be hired; this turns into a game of aquatic bumper cars on warm, crowded days. Raised on an unusually tall pedestal overlooking the pond is a grand equestrian statue of Alfonso XII, here exalted as the 'Pacifier'; from this vantage point he keeps a stern eye on the recreations of his people. Beyond the water is a broad walk called Avenida de Argentina, which is lined by some of the stone figures rejected on grounds of weight from the balustrade of the royal palace. If we emerge from the park on Calle Alfonso XII, somewhere near the Casón del Buen Retiro and follow it southwards, we come shortly on the right to the railings of the **Jardín Botánico** with examples today of about 2000 herbaceous plants and 1000 trees. (Before the cyclone of 1886 it is said to have possessed some 7000 species.) The garden was founded by Ferdinand VI and carried on by Charles III in his unceas-ing attempt to civilise and improve his new capital – which did not compare at all well with the Naples he had left behind. The single entrace is opposite the Puerta de Murillo of the Prado Museum.

Returning to the Calle de Alfonso XII and continuing in the same direction as before, we come on the right to the Cuesta de Moyano flanking the southern end of the botanical garden. On this slope there are some thirty bookstalls and it is pleasant to browse over these on the way down to rejoin the Paseo del Prado. Or continuing along Alfonso XII under the **Observatorio** with an Ionic rotunda by Villanueva, architect of the Prado, which crowns the south-west hummock of the park, one shortly reaches the Museo Etnológico Nacional (closed), forming a corner with the Paseo de la Infanta Isabel. This describes a great curve and turns into the Paseo de la Reina Cristina, on the right of which are the garden and dome of the **Panteón de Hombres Ilustres,** distinguished less for its architecture than for those gallant protagonists of the Spanish parliamentary system who lie within its walls. Here are Canalejas, assassinated in 1912 when President of the Council and Eduardo Dato who met the same fate in the same job in 1921. Almost facing the iron railings of the pantheon is Calle Fuenterrabia running east. On the right of this is the **Fábrica de Tapices,** successor of the royal tapestry and carpet factory set up by Philip V. It is now in private hands and anyone who can afford a thousand dollars a square metre can order whatever carpet or wall-hanging pleases him. I personally found the products rather disappointing. An unsuccessful attempt had been made to weave some of Goya's black pictures, which were not intended for this medium. Where designs by Goya and other old masters are used, the weavers do not work from the cartoons; instead the outline is wound up on a roller behind the threads and a mere magazine reproduction is used for colour guidance. It seems to me that the factory's best work in this century covers the floors of the Ritz, which opened its doors in 1912. This hotel is held by its devotees to be the best in the world. Those who are not staying there (and those who are) should not neglect the semicircular **Plaza de la Lealtad** onto which it faces. The obelisk in the centre rises over the ashes of the victims of the Third of May, 1908.

THE VILLA (I)

Let us now turn to the Villa or old town, which I propose to treat in two sectors, followed by the northward developments of the nineteenth and twentieth centuries

When Philip II moved the court to Madrid in 1561, he brought with him – I translate from the *Breve Historia de Madrid* by Federico Sainz de Robles – 'all those bureaucratic plagues that always follow in the steps of those who reign or govern: the Privy Seal, the Chanceries, the Secretariats, the Councils, the High Courts and the Lower Courts'. But

Madrid loved these plagues and has loved them ever since. It grew rapidly, attracting in the same author's words 'litigators, eternal students, sophists, retired soldiers, friars founding branches of their order, people looking for official jobs and contracts, bawds with their whores, fairground and market tricksters, purveyors of potions and the occult arts, strumpets who hang about the corners and under the arcades, back-door smugglers here today and gone tomorrow . . . in other words the most select and liveliest elements of the picaresque tradition.' Most of these activities have been cleaned up or tidied away. Only vestiges remain in the Rastro. However, a certain smell, a kind of ghostly essence of this Madrid and the sixteenth century, haven of place-seekers and confidence-tricksters, still remains in the area we are about to explore. And though the picaresque and picturesque may have decreased to shadows of their former selves, the bureaucracy has forged ahead and made great strides, ever faithful to *its* four-hundred-year-old tradition.

Philip III was the first Spanish monarch to be born in the Villa. The year was 1578. When he inherited in 1598, one might have assumed that the status of Madrid would now be beyond dispute and its felicity complete. But this was not to be. Madrid was shortly to pass through six years of intense anxiety. Every student, soldier, friar, bawd, whore, swindler and smuggler must have suffered agonies of speculation over the continuing viability of the place. This was all due to the new King's *válido*, the Duke of Lerma. More than favourites but still a far cry from constitutional prime ministers, the válidos of the later Habsburgs were extremely self-interested managers of the royal circus. Lerma had property and support in Valladolid, which sent a delegation to advocate a move to that city. Madrid fulminated against the fogs and cold airs of so low-lying a place, enclosed by two chest-affecting misty rivers, recently the victim of a pestilence that had decimated the inhabitants and quite inadequately endowed with buildings to house a court. The King vacillated but Lerma was adamant. On January 10th, 1601, the official decree was published. The King left Madrid, followed by the various Councils and Secretariats and Chambers of Commerce; even the important Councils of Castile and of the Indies moved. Valladolid went mad with delight. The future Philip IV was born there. Embassies arrived from Persia and England. Rubens appeared –

he didn't waste his time on places that weren't fashionable. Vicente Espinel, one of the most pungent picaresque novelists, abandoned his benefice in Ronda in order not to miss 'the richest and gayest celebrations that human beings have ever seen' – he loved parties and was eventually reproved for his secular tastes and packed off home. In the meantime, he had hobnobbed with the literary giants Quevedo and Góngora, who didn't want to be conspicuous by their absence either. Rather overwhelmed by all this enthusiasm, the King took to escaping back to Madrid and El Pardo (the palace in which General Franco was later to live, not to be confused with the Prado) and Aranjuez, the oasis on the Tagus. Nor was it long before the arguments in favour of Madrid prevailed. The most persuasive of these was gold, gold for Lerma and gold for his King, whose share was fixed at 250,000 ducats over ten years and a sixth part of all house rents for the same period – that is what it cost to get the King back. On March 4th 1606, Madrid received and forgave the royal prodigal with jubilation.

During the rest of the reign Madrid hummed merrily along. Though little remains of the mediaeval period, enough buildings still stand and enough streets follow their old courses to give a fair idea of the physiognomy of the Villa under the House of Austria. To visit this area we should start at the **Puerta del Sol**, where the gate of this name once stood. Now it is a noisy elliptical meeting point of ten streets. The building on the south side is the old post office completed in 1768, except for the later clock which gives Spain its official time. This is now occupied by the Dirección General de Seguridad, no doubt appropriately as the Puerta del Sol has been a notable sparking off point of Spanish insurrections, amongst them the heroic rising of May 2nd 1808 against the French.

From here **Calle Mayor**, the old main street, runs west. Just to the south of it and accessible by Calle de las Postas or any of the several alleys running in this direction is the **Plaza Mayor** with eight arched entrances. The seventeenth-century bronze statue of Philip III in the centre celebrates his restoration of the court to its proper place; the inscription also tells us that Philip ordered the construction of this plaza, which was finished in 1619. The architect was Juan Gómez de Mora, disciple of Juan de Herrera of the Escorial, from which come the steep-pitched slate roofs, dormer windows and slate-hung spires – then fresh and amazing but now the greatest cliché in Spanish architecture. The plan of the square is simply a neater and more homogeneous version of the typical arcaded Castilian town centre, of which we shall see many rustic examples. The central block on the north side, known as the **Casa de la Panadería** with remnants of stucco decoration on the façade, contained chambers for the use of the royal family when attending public spectacles.

The plaza was witness to many of these over the next two centuries. In 1621, 1648 and 1662 there were public executions of nobles who had fallen from grace. In June 1622 there were celebrations in honour of the simultaneous canonisation of five saints, four of them Spanish including Saint Theresa. In 1623 the plaza welcomed Charles Stuart, Prince of Wales, who came with Buckingham to inspect the King's sister Maria with a view to matrimony. Though a patron of the arts Charles didn't trust the conventional medium of painting to tell the truth about a potential bride. He was right. Maria did not please him and no marriage took place. But Spain had the last word. After his execution many of his finest works of art were bought by the Spanish ambassador at ridiculously low prices and are now among the most prized possessions of the Prado.

During the long reign of Philip IV (1621–1665) things went badly for Spain abroad and not much better at home. Wars were lost in Flanders and Italy. Humiliating peace treaties were signed in Westphalia and at The Hague and in the Pyrenees. Catalonia, Portugal, Sicily, Naples, Biscay and Aragón revolted. But Madrid continued to grow in importance, accumulating ever more rights and privileges. Philip built his new wall, enclosing an area seven times larger than before and certainly at times he must have been tempted to persuade himself that Madrid was the universe and all beyond the wall a snare and a delusion. Charles II, the Bewitched, born in 1661, came to the throne at the age of four. The Queen-Mother, the ill-favoured Mariana of the portraits by Velázquez and Carreño, ruled with even more disastrous favourites than those of the previous reigns. The King was proclaimed of age in 1675. With neither of his wives could he sire an heir. His most positive act was his death in 1700, which gave rise to the War of the Spanish Succession and ushered in the Bourbon dynasty in the person of Philip, Duke of Anjou, second son of the Dauphin and grandson of Louis XIV of France.

From the south-east corner of the Plaza Mayor a brief excursion may be made into the Plaza de la Provincia in which stands the old **Cárcel de Corte**, built as a place of detention for well-heeled prisoners. The architect was an Italian, Crescenzi, and the work was carried out between 1629 and 1634 in sober taste. The building now houses the Ministry of Foreign Affairs. Back in the Plaza and taking any of the exits on the side of the Casa de la Panadería, we rejoin Calle Mayor. Walking west, that is away from the Puerta del Sol, we come first to the little Plaza de San Miguel with the main food market and, just beyond this, to the **Plaza de la Villa** with the **Torre de los Lujanes**, in which Francis I of France was confined after the battle of Pavia. Although very much restored, it is virtually the only building to survive from mediaeval Madrid. Facing it is the **Ayuntamiento** or **Casa de la Villa**. This was begun in 1644 by Gómez de Mora to house the municipality, which had previously had no permanent home. It was extended by Ardemans (first architect of La Granja) and revamped in the eighteenth century by Villanueva (architect of the Prado). The head porter will show the main rooms. The Sala de Goya contains no Goyas but a curious by-product of the Third of May in the shape of a romantic painting of the same subject with women as victims by Palmaroli. The Sala de Actos is like a miniature House of Commons with facing benches and a public gallery. There is a public session of the municipality at the end of every month. The remaining side of the plaza is occupied by the so-called Casa de Cisneros, built about 1537 by a nephew of the famous Cardinal. Now taken over by municipal offices, it is of little interest except for a Plateresque doorway at the rear on Calle Sacramento.

Continuing along Calle Mayor, it is worth making a little stab northwards up the Calle San Nicolás to the plaza and church of **San Nicolás**. Mentioned in the fuero of 1202, this is the oldest remaining place of worship in Madrid. The fourteenth-century brick *Mudéjar* tower has been accurately restored. Recrossing Calle Mayor and taking Calle Sacramento past the rear of the Casa de Cisneros, we come to the Pontifical church of **San Miguel**, seat of the Nunziatura, with a rather

MADRID

The Buen Retiro and the Barrio de Salamanca

Museo Lazaro Galdiano

Museo Taurino

PLAZA MONUMENTAL
DE LAS VENTAS

BARRIO DE SALAMANCA

(1860 – 1884)

PLAZA
DE
ROMA

CALLE DE ALCALÁ

o de
la

to de Valencia
Don Juan

PASEO DE LA CASTELLANA

CALLE DE SERRANO

Biblioteca
Nacional
Mus. Arqueológico
Nacional

CALLE DE

ALCALÁ

CALLE DE O'DONNELL

ESQUERDO

PLAZA
PE
DE
INDENCIA
Puerta de
Alcalá

Correos

MONTALBAN
seol
aval

TONIO MAURA

Museo de Artes
Decorativos

AVENIDA DE MENÉNDEZ PELAYO

ESTANQUE

DOCTOR

Museo del Ejército

zHotel

Museo del
Siglo XIX

PARQUE DEL
R E T I R O

useo del
Prado

ESPALTER

CALLE DE ALFONSO XII

LA
CHOPERA

DEL

ARDIN
OTANICO

PARQUE DEL
RETIRO

A DE MOYANO

PASEO

Museo
Etnológico

Observatorio

Estacion
de Atocha

CALLE INFANTA ISABEL

REINA CHRISTINA

Panteón

Fabrica de
Tapices

successful curved Baroque front and twin belfry towers, which follow the arc of the curve. The best course now is to plunge down one of the alleys going south – Calle del Cordero or Calle Doctor Letamendi will do very well – to Calle de Segovia, which we cross to come to the church of **San Pedro** with a brick tower which seems to belong to the same period as that of San Nicolás. Taking the Costanilla de San Andrés we come to the Plaza de la Paja. On the south side of this is the **Capilla del Obispo**, finished in 1535, with some Plateresque tombs. Continuing uphill we pass under the lee of the brick church of **San Andrés**, incorporating the Capilla de San Isidro with a cupola and lantern. With its giant orders framing the brickwork, its deep corbels under the eaves and bold cornice topped by a balustrade and corner obelisks, this is one of the earliest Baroque buildings in Madrid. But the style never really got off the ground in the seventeenth century, as it was always pinned down and held back by the essential sobriety of the court style of the Habsburgs, which could not shake off the influence of the Escorial. Even after the change of dynasty and despite a few frills and furbelows it remains true that Spanish architecture never fully spread Baroque wings.

Via the Plaza de Carros, where carts used to ply for hire, we come to the Puerta de Moros, site of one of the four gates of the mediaeval town, and from here we take the wide Carrera de San Francisco to the church of **San Francisco el Grande**, in many ways the de jure if not the de facto cathedral, which it far exceeds in size. Joseph Bonaparte wanted to turn it first into a parliament and then into a national pantheon. It was designed by the Franciscan lay-brother Francisco Cabezas and begun in 1776. The royal architect Sabatini took over the work in 1785. The curving front of the friar's plan and the great space under the dome are noble, but the whole must have been much more impressive before the covering of virtually every surface by nineteenth-century painters. The side-chapel devoted to the tutelar saint contains an early work by Goya (1784); this is an academic religious painting done for a competition. The high altar is flanked by choir stalls from the Monasterio del Parral (Segovia). The sacristy has a set of twelve apostles by Ribera hanging above eighteenth-century vestment chests. The chapter-house contains some

Renaissance stalls from the Monasterio de El Paular (see p. 103).

Leaving the façade of San Francisco on our right and taking the Gran Vía of the same name we come to the **Puerta de Toledo**. Breaching Philip IV's wall, this was built in 1827 in honour of Ferdinand VII. It is taller and narrower than Charles III's Puerta de Alcalá, which it resembles in the use of bulky clusters of martial impedimenta in soft white stone on top of the severe Neo-Classical mass. From here Calle de Toledo runs north all the way to the Plaza Mayor. At its junction with Calle Colegiata stands Madrid's undistinguished Baroque cathedral church of **San Isidro**. Finished in 1661 for the Jesuits, it was commandeered by Charles III when he expelled them in 1767 and to it were transferred San Isidro's uncorrupted remains, which had previously lain in San Andrés. It follows the usual Jesuit plan with side chapels opening into one another. The cornice is pronounced, while the capitals are relegated to the role of a decorative motif crowning flat pilasters. The structural drama of pillar, column, capital, arch, vault and buttress is lost. Some changes were made by the Neo-Classical architect Ventura Rodríguez. In 1885 it became the seat of a bishop and provisional cathedral pending the completion of Nuestra Señora de la Almudena, which has been under construction since the beginning of the present century.

From San Isidro it is only a couple of minutes' walk along Calle de los Estudiantes to the Plaza del Cascorro, from which the Ribera de Curtidores, scene of the **Rastro**, runs steeply down to the Ronda de Toledo. We could have tackled it from the bottom but it is better to coast down the slope and take a taxi at the bottom. This famous market comes to life on Sunday mornings. The stalls abound in sunglasses, contemporary gear items, charms and records; a very few trade in junk. Some of the better shops have good things but these are expensive and in short supply, owing to the traditional austerity of Spanish life which has meant that only the grandest families had any furniture to speak of. These days this has led to an imbalance between the demand by the new bourgeoisie for old things to lend tone to modern flats and the supply of such pieces. Anyone hoping for a bargain in antiquities might just as well go to Mallett or Partridge, while those who dislike a crush are better advised to devote

Sunday morning to the book market on the Cuesta de Moyano.

The area enclosed by Philip IV is very roughly bisected by the axis Calle Mayor – Puerta del Sol – Carrera San Jerónimo, running from the royal palace to the Prado. To the south of this line there remain one or two things to be mentioned. Calle Lope de Vega runs from the Paseo del Prado westwards under the northern flank of the Ministerio de Sanidad y Consumo, a brutal red-brick slab of official building, which was the headquarters of General Franco's state-controlled trade union movement. The **Casa de Lope de Vega** is not, however, in the street bearing his name but in the parallel Calle de Cervantes. It is a decent brick house that was occupied by the prolific author of *Fuenteovejuna* and *El Caballero de Olmedo,* to quote only two out of hundreds of titles, between 1610 and his death in 1635. Restored and refurbished, it does not feel very authentic but the general tone is no doubt accurate enough. The Age of Gold lived plain and one sometimes wonders what it would have thought of Bourbon taste. In the same area is Calle (not Paseo) del Prado with the **Ateneo,** a scientific, literary and artistic club founded in 1835. Strangers may join by the month for a modest subscription. The pleasant seedy building has a library distributed in shabby passages, a reading room and cafeteria. The collection of portraits in the long gallery on the ground floor is of no great artistic interest but constitutes a touching national pantheon embracing men of widely different views. Addicts of Spanish nineteenth- and twentieth-century history and literature may like to know that they can find here the likenesses of Echegarray, Pi y Margall, Pérez Galdós, Menéndez Pelayo, General Silvela, Blasco Ibáñez, Canalejas, Pio Baroja, Unamuno, Valle-Inclán, Pardo Bazán, Ramón Gómez de la Serna, Ortega y Gasset, Gregorio Marañón, José Antonio Primo de Rivera, Azorín, Calvo Sotelo, Antonio Machado, Jacinto Benavente and Juan Ramón Jiménez. There they are, a century's worth of worthies, men who took themselves, Life and above all Spain extremely seriously.

THE VILLA (II)

The Palace Hotel facing the Ritz across the Plaza de Cánovas is a good starting point. A little higher up the Plaza de las

Cortes on the opposite side is the **Palacio de las Cortes**. The national parliament was even longer in acquiring a permanent home than the town council. In 1813, on the retreat of the French, the constituent Cortes that had exercised a provisional government from Cádiz was forced to meet in one of the Madrid theatres, and it was not until 1850 that deputies were able to occupy the present building, whose first stone was laid by Isabel II in 1843. The legend over the portico reads **Congreso de los Diputados.** Under General Franco this became a rubber-stamp assembly. Democratic procedures were restored to the hemicycle shortly after his death. Answers to members' questions from the *banco azul,* as the government front bench is called from the colour of its upholstery, are reminiscent of question time in the House of Commons, though the occasion is considerably less noisy. There is also a red light that limits interventions, including those of ministers. Though this practice is in use in many parliaments, it shows no signs of finding favour at Westminster.

Proceeding towards the Puerta del Sol we soon come to Calle Sevilla which runs from the Plaza de Canalejas into Calle de Alcalá almost opposite the **Real Academia de Bellas Artes de San Fernando.** Founded by Philip V in 1744, this began life in the Casa de la Panadería. The museum came into being in 1774 under Charles III, who acquired the actual house. In the first room we are faced with the facility of Sorolla and the Cordoban romanticism of Julio Romero de Torres, whose silky sultry lady appeared on so many thousand-peseta bank-notes of the 1960s. There is a pleasant painting of a woman unmasking by Mengs. Fragonard and Paret of the rippling silks are also here. The room on the left of this has a portrait of Godoy, Queen Maria Luisa's lover, as a pretty page-boy, making a telling contrast with the later picture by Carnicero of the same personage, now the hefty red-faced 'Prince of Peace'.

Beyond the room we first entered is a small chamber containing Jesus and the Samaritan by Alonso Cano and the Tyrant, a courtesan with a deliciously brushed dress by Goya. This ushers us into the heart of the collection. Four monks by Zurbarán bear witness to his vast cosmography of white folds. The Holy Alonso Rodríguez of 1630 is a two-tier work, the earthly and the heavenly spheres firmly divided by a wedge of cloud. El Greco's fusion of the spheres by means of colour is rejected. Baroque lessons have not been learned – or if learned they have not been heeded. Zurbarán's strength lies in *not* heeding. His spirit told him Heaven and Earth were two very different places and should not be whipped up together in the same soufflé. By Goya we have Godoy reading a despatch on the field of battle and Ferdinand VII almost standing in his stirrups on the usual deep-chested tubby mount. The blue background of the Sierra de Guadarrama is reminiscent of Velázquez. The portraits of Villanueva, the architect (*678*), Moratín, the playwright (*671*) and José Luis de Munárriz (*680*) are in his best non-courtly vein. The self-portrait (*669*) is very similar to the Prado's. In the same room are two Inquisition scenes (*673* and *674*), the Madhouse (*672*) and Bulls in a Village (*675*), also the carnival scene called the Burial of the Sardine (*676*). This is one of the best places to meet Goya, represented by several stages of his work in close proximity and removed from the hectoring voices of the Prado guides. The rest of the painting is an anticlimax. A long room contains works by Academicians on election. Beyond this is a room devoted to drawings. Although Perugino, Raphael, Titian, Veronese, Tintoretto, Rubens and Van Dyck are represented, the wall with the Spanish drawings should not be neglected. Among the artists are Carreño, Claudio Coello, Mateo Cerezo, Alonso Cano, Father Rizzi, Francisco de Herrera, Pacheco, Velázquez and the irrepressible Ribera whose splendid little drawing of acrobats steals the show. Here also are Villanueva's designs of 1773 for the face-lift he gave to the original façade of the building by José de Churriguera.

It is only a step from the Academy back to the Puerta del Sol, from which we take Calle Arenal as far as the church of **San Ginés** on the left. Here Quevedo was baptised and Lope de Vega married. The building collapsed in 1642. A much restored version of its replacement, completed in 1645, is what we see now. Almost facing San Ginés, Calle San Martín runs north into the Plaza de Descalzas with the **Convento de Descalzas Reales** or Royal Barefoot Sisters – now occupied by some twenty-five Franciscan nuns. The convent is the first of several national monuments we shall see that are controlled by the Patrimonio Nacional. This body only permits accompanied visits and as the uniformed guides speak English I shall not treat these buildings or their contents in such detail as those in which one can wander at will.

In this case we are right back in the world of the House of Austria. The foundress was Joan, younger daughter of Charles V. The building belonged to Alonso Gutiérrez, the Emperor's treasurer, and the work of adaptation was carried out by Antonio Sillero and Juan Bautista de Toledo, the first architect of the Escorial. The church was built by Diego de Villanueva about 1570. The staircase, which formed part of the original house, is entirely covered with frescoes by Claudio Coello; the family of Philip IV occupies a trompe l'oeil balcony at the top of the stairs. The original sisters were all of royal or aristocratic blood and each founded a chapel on reception into the order. These, often no more than altars in recesses, surround the upper gallery. The **Capilla del Angel de la Guardia** is by Luisa Roldán, 'la Roldana', probably the sculptress of the most popular Sevillian Holy Week float 'la Macarena'. After the **Antecoro** with vestments and the **Coro** containing a swirling Inmaculada by Alonso Cano and a *Dolorosa* by P. de Mena, a specialist in pathetic effects, we are taken to the room hung with eleven tapestries from designs by Rubens (see Prado Museum) celebrating the Institution and Triumph of the Eucharist. Isabel Clara Eugenia, the donor, is represented with the Pope, a cardinal and a saint in number eleven. With their bold designs, predominant blues and greens and pale flesh tones they are visually a great success. Rubens translates well into tapestry and the Escorial will confirm this. But we cannot stay with these hangings long enough to enjoy them. We are implacably beckoned on by the stern cultured young lady guide, whose uniform is a compromise between a nanny's and an air hostess's – with perhaps a touch of the police-woman's.

Back to the gallery and then we whizz through three more chapels. The second of these resembles a doll's house with Pompeian decorations; the third and last contains frescoes by Carreño, Rizzi and Coello and wood carvings by Luisa Roldán. The cell of the Archduchess Margaret of Austria, downstairs, has a very sweet Jesus, sleeping seated, by Alonso Cano, who never fails to surprise. In the **Sala Capitular** or chapter-house there is an interesting selection of religious imagery. In the **Salón de Reyes** hang Isabel Clara Eugenia by Pantoja, and her husband, the Archduke Albert, by Rubens.

The **Relicario** has German, Neapolitan, Philippine, Mexican and many other types of casket for saintly relics. Here the ecstatic inventory of materials employed reaches crescendo. Gold, silver, coral, bronze, ivory, tortoise-shell, mother-of-pearl – these are the entrancing words that the custodians of Spanish art treasures most love to pronounce. At the end of the passage we come finally to the **Sala Flamenca,** containing work that may or may not be by Isembrandt, Gossaert, Juan de Flandes and Titian. One does not have time to form a judgement.

In this area there is another monastic foundation of the Habsburg period. Returning to Calle del Arenal and following it to Plaza Isabel II, we branch right (leaving the Teatro Real on our left) and come shortly to the Plaza de la Encarnación with the **Convento de la Encarnación**, founded in 1611 by Margaret of Austria. The Patrimonio Nacional is in charge here too. The contents of the museum (entrance to the left of the church façade) are less interesting than those of the Descalzas. There are paintings by M. Coxcie, Pacheco, Carreño, Ribera, J. de Pereda, Vicente Carducho, Conrado Giaquinto and Bartolomé Román. The image-maker Gregorio Fernández has two works in polychromed wood, a Flagellation and a recumbent Christ. The sacristy acts as council chamber of the Orden de Hijosdalgo de Madrid – note (*pace* the ballad) that the plural of hidalgo, a gentleman originally forbidden to engage in trade, is *not* hidalgos. The church, which we visit last, was finished in 1616 by Juan Gómez de Mora and restored by Ventura Rodríguez in 1767. It contains an Annunciation by Carducho and some scenes by Francisco Bayeu. The organ is the original one and is played at mass on Sunday mornings.

We have now seen the most important buildings that have survived from the Habsburg dynasty and can turn our full attention to the works of the Bourbons. Let us, therefore, return to the **Teatro Real** begun in 1818 but not completed till 1850, when it was inaugurated with Donizetti's *La Favorita*. The main entrance of this gives on to the Plaza de Oriente, from which we receive the full impact of the eastern face of the **Palacio Nacional**, also called **Palacio de Oriente**. This stands on the site of the Moorish fortress, which was extended and endowed with greater comforts by the Trastamaras, whose tastes ran to luxury in the Moorish style. Charles V tried to confer grandeur through improvements undertaken by Luis de Vargas and Alonso de Covarrubias. Philip II added a new front by Juan Bautista de Toledo. The result of all this patching and cobbling was destroyed by fire on Christmas Eve 1734 – no doubt to the great relief of Philip V, who was thus able to start afresh in consonance with his own tastes.

The first project was drawn up by Felipe Juvara with façades measuring 476 metres each. The only drawback was that the building would have occupied three times the space available. Juvara died and his plan was reduced in extent by Juan Bautista Sachetti. Owing to the lie of the land the new palace, begun in 1738, had to be built up on great basements on the north and particularly on the west sides, almost doubling its height. Seen from the street side, it is a normal palatial building of the period with Doric pilasters framing the piano nobile windows. The salient corner blocks have Corinthian columns in place of the pilasters. The whole is topped off by a firmly stated entablature carrying a balustrade, which incorporates the attic windows as at the country palace of La Granja, whose garden front is by the same architects. The larger-than-life statues of the Spanish monarchs lining the north front gardens and distributed round the Plaza de Oriente belong to the series intended to adorn the balustrade and rejected as dangerous. It's a pity they never got to their skyline, where their extravagant gestures would have been more appropriate.

The entrance is in the south front facing the unfinished new cathedral of Nuestra Señora de la Almudena – a rather unpromising Gothic and Classical hybrid – across the Patio de Armas. Once inside, we are back in the world of national art treasures that has become big business. The Patrimonio Nacional is again in charge. There is a vestibule complete with cafeteria, lavatories and souvenir shop, where we must wait for the next conducted visit. These start every fifteen minutes or so and last nearly two hours, during which time we are shown some 90 rooms. The tours in Spanish are conducted by a footman, those in English by another of the cultured young ladies in uniform. The grand staircase with ceiling by Conrado Giaquinto brings us to the piano nobile and a suite of 19 rooms, in each of which the cicerone declaims a set piece. I will therefore restrict my remarks to what most caught my attention. The **Sala de Gasparini** (called after its decorator) has an astonishing polychrome stucco chinoiserie ceiling with flowers, fruit and birds in high relief, while the **Sala de Porcelana** (1765–1770) is a china chamber in the Neo-Classical style with predominantly white, gold and green porcelain plaques screwed on to a wooden frame; the guide knows the number of the screws. Charles III for whom this was built had already installed one in the Chinese taste at Aranjuez. The furniture throughout is standard palace equipment and very broadly 'Empire'. The bronze and crystal chandeliers made at La Granja show great ingenuity and variety of design – the **Sala Amarilla** has one of the prettiest in the form of a pagoda of glass pendants. The **Comedor de Gala**, made from three of the original rooms with ceilings by Mengs, González Velázquez and Francisco Bayeu, was inaugurated in 1879 to celebrate Alfonso XII's second marriage to Maria Cristina of Habsburg-Lorraine. The chandeliers have become noticeably coarser by this period.

The gallery surrounding the patio is entirely hung with good standard tapestries from among the fourteen kilometres of wall hangings possessed by the Patrimonio. The chapel with a ceiling by Giaquinto contains the bones of Saint Felix. The apartments of Maria Cristina with portraits by Van Loo and Winterhalter include an 'English-style' dining-room with a chandelier representing the horn of plenty. Then come the quarters of Alfonso XIII and his English Queen, Victoria Eugenie. The King's room is in a severe military style with a plain brass bed and his study is furnished with English club furniture and trophies of the chase. His (sparse) library has a collection of paper-weights made from the hoofs of favourite horses and beyond this is the council chamber, a sort of small cabinet room. After these relative intimacies it is with something of a drop in spirits that one regains the 'official' section via the **Cámara Oficial,** in which ambassadors present their credentials. In the **Antecámara Oficial** is a table given by the British parliament to Ferdinand VII for his assistance during an epidemic in Gibraltar. The **Saleta Oficial** is hung with tapestries from genre scenes by Teniers. This brings us to the **Salón del Trono** with a ceiling painted in 1764 by G. B. Tiepolo, *aetat.* 78. The lamps are Venetian. The four lions guarding the throne were saved from the Alcázar fire of 1734.

We have now passed through some 50 rooms, but the

Patrimonio is determined to give us our money's worth and we are next taken through 13 small rooms with paintings, needlework, glass and china. After the Prado none of the pictures need detain us. Not until we are beginning to flag do we reach the best tapestries. The earliest of these are of the fifteenth century – one notes the pale clarity of the heads; the sixth room is the best. The apartments of Charles IV's Queen, Maria Luisa, which follow, are of human rather than artistic interest. Spain, as we saw in the Descalzas, has always been highly conscious of the materials used in works of art – and of the workmanship, the man-hours and -years involved in execution. The weaker the art the more sternly the guide draws our wandering attention to the value of the cut-glass, ivory, ebony, lapis lazuli etc. that went into the objects. We are taken, finally, to the chapel 'treasure' with communion plate and jewels. The Visigothic votive crowns of the seventh century are interesting. The pretty royal crowns seem to have been made for a night at the opera.

On the way to the **Biblioteca** one has a chance to judge the proportions of the central patio, which is 39 metres square. The library of 400,000 volumes is installed in the rooms originally designed for it. Six of these contain a permanent exhibition of books and manuscripts. Among the dependencies that require a separate ticket is the enjoyable **Armeriá Real** on the west side of the Plaza de Armas. The central aisle is flanked from end to end by the accoutrements of mounted knights – between the armour of horse and man the equipment could weigh as much as 115 kilos. There are 44 suits of various kinds made for Charles V alone. At the end of the room is the one worn by the Emperor for Titian's great portrait. On the lower floor are Philip II's encrusted ceremonial suit, the Moorish-style campaigning tent of Francis I of France, captured with its owner at Pavia in 1525 and Alfonso XIII's field writing desk, built into the top of a gun-carriage. At the exit from the Plaza de Armas to Calle de Bailén is the **Farmacia** with retorts, a distilling unit, some pretty china jars from the Buen Retiro factory, glass vessels from La Granja and blue and white containers of Talavera ware.

After the royal palace it is not advisable to attempt anything very exacting the same day. One possibility is the **Museo Cerralbo,** wholly devoted to the tastes of the nobility. This is housed in the mid-Victorian (British chronology) mansion of the late Marquis of Cerralbo on the corner of Calles Ferraz and Ventura Rodriguez the other side of the Plaza de España. The chapel contains an Ecstasy of Saint Francis by el Greco. The picture gallery is dominated by two successful Baroque compositions of Herrera el Mozo (1612–1685), of which Jesus carrying the Cross is the most freely handled and the best designed. Jacob with the Flocks by Ribera is outstanding – really no one can deny *el Españolitto* his determined excellence. Zurbarán has a crisp Inmaculada in which he has correctly treated the moon under the Virgin's feet as a solid but added a pair of upturned horns to the orb, presumably as a concession to popular taste. This is a compromise I have seen nowhere else. There are also works by Luis Tristán, J. Antolínez, Ribalta, Alonso Cano, Magnasco, Mengs, Maella, Bayeu and J. L. David. The grand floor illustrates the florid taste that followed the stolid Isabelline period and drew freely on Renaissance, Baroque, Rococo and Isabelline decoration in the same building and even in the same room. The gallery with Venetian chandeliers leads to a hall of mirrors, whose extravagance defies description.

From the Plaza de España a steep slope runs down to the Estación del Norte. Bearing right past the station and following the Paseo de la Florida for some four or five hundred yards we come on the right to the **Ermita de San Antonio de la Florida** or **Panteón de Goya**. This little church was built between 1792 and 1798 and its decoration was entrusted to Goya. In 1899 the painter's remains were brought from Bordeaux and reburied here in 1919. Disdaining the grandiose effects of Lucás Jordán and G. B. Tiepolo, Goya conceived the simple idea of surrounding the lower part of the central cupola above the cornice with a painted rail on which characters lean or gesticulate in more or less normal perspective. A man sits on the rail with his arse over us, a child straddles it, a white shawl drapes it, two women gossip as they lean upon it. In the central scene Saint Anthony of Padua preaches to a bedraggled assembly and a half-naked man stands up to confess and be saved. Other surfaces are filled with angels upholding or romping on an abundance of white, gold-flecked material but nowhere is it clearly stated who or what is being glorified. There is no representation of Christ, the Virgin or the Faith. The building – deconsecrated in 1927 and now a 'museum' – is not irreligious in feeling but seems to celebrate an undefined

Supreme Being rather than a defined Godhead. Conveniently placed benches make it possible to gaze up at the dome from several positions and young lovers hold hands on these as they contemplate the frescoes. But a certain aura of reverence remains – perhaps more for Goya's genius than for God – and one giggling girl got her face slapped by her escort.

Returning along the Paseo de la Florida to the station roundabout, we shall find a sign to the **Museo de Carruajes**, which is reached through a tunnel on the left of the Paseo de la Virgen del Puerto. This brings us into the gardens laid out under the steep west front of the royal palace by Sabatini but still known by their old name, Campo del Moro. The Carriage Museum is housed in a new building on the site of the old stables. This is one place where the visitor might surely be allowed to wander and ponder at his pleasure under the watchful eye of the Patrimonio. But it is not to be, and the usual breathless round takes place. Among the interesting equipages is a rough canopied litter in which Charles V is said to have been carried on his last journey to Yuste – an honour claimed with more probability by the identical one at Yuste itself. Here too is the coach built in 1832, in which Alfonso XIII was returning with his English bride from their wedding in the church of San Jerónimo in 1906, when a bomb disguised as a bunch of flowers exploded almost under them, killing the coachman and two of the eight horses and causing casualties in the crowd. The royal pair were untouched; they transferred to the following vehicle and the show went on. On the side devoted to more humdrum turnouts there is a *calesa madrileña*, a popular two-wheeler painted in bright bargee colours with a collapsible hood, in which the *majos* and *majas* would spin gaily to the bull-fight. The dash and bounce of these plebeian swells or dandies and their molls was captured with peculiar felicity by Goya's brush.

Back in the Paseo we come shortly on the right to the **Ermita de la Virgen del Puerto** built by Pedro Ribera in 1718. The interior is a Baroque octagon but the façade is more like a miniature Habsburg palace with a few Baroque trimmings and occuli instead of windows on the first floor. The Paseo soon intersects with Calle de Segovia, leading to the **Puente de Segovia**, the first major bridge across the Manzanares, finished in 1584. On the other bank of the river is the **Casa de Campo**, an estate bought by Philip II and now a public park.

From the hummock overlooking the boat-pond one rediscovers Madrid's skyline, badly mutilated but still conserving vestiges of an earlier and more gracious self. Reading from right to left one can pick out the great dome and lantern of San Francisco el Grande, then the smaller dome – also lantern-crowned – of San Andrés, then various other spires leading the eye to the twin towers of the unfinished cathedral. Then come the royal palace, the Hotel Plaza, the skyscraper called the Torre de Madrid and on the far left the Air Ministry, latest and largest child of the Escorial, roofed with slate and built of brick. The sun is red now behind the silhouette of buildings, which becomes quite impressive at this hour. One can find fault with Madrid's brash development but London has little claim to superiority on this score: the view from Parliament Hill is not exactly one to gladden the heart and have we not made a complete mess of London's river? Suddenly it is chilly and, forgetting aesthetic considerations, one wants to feel the warm breath of the town, wants a hot bath, drinks and dinner – all of which Madrid provides extremely well.

Within the confines of the Villa enclosed by Philip IV there are still some places worthy of mention. From the Plaza de España the Avenida de José Antonio – as the Gran Vía is officially called – swoops up on a strip-lit switchback curve of shops and cinemas and cafeterias to a high point before dipping towards the older and wider and more Establishment Calle de Alcalá, lined with banks and ministries and insurance companies. From the top of the switchback Calle Fuencarral runs northwards on a slight bias to the left. Some way up this on the right is the **Hospicio**, begun in 1722 and easily distin-guised by Pedro Ribera's florid Baroque doorway in an otherwise plain façade. This houses the **Museo Municipal,** which deserves a visit for its topographical prints, plans, paintings and above all models of old Madrid. Pedro Texeira's plan of 1656 covers an urban area that has expanded little by the time of the plan of 1768, dedicated to the Count of Aranda. The pride of the collection is the large model, com-pleted in 1830, which shows the Retiro Palace still surrounded by orchards, the bull-ring hard by the Puerta de Alcalá (its successor is much further removed from the centre) and the main lines of access to the Royal Palace by the Calles de Alcalá and Atocha and the Calle Mayor. Even in the early nineteenth century the Villa remains very much as it was in

Velázquez's day. The great gash of the Gran Vía was still 80 years off. A small painting (*1222*) of General Prim entering Madrid in triumph in 1868, looking remarkably like an American Confederate General, is rather touching in the light of his slogan 'No more Bourbons!' which was followed by a Bourbon Restoration in 1874. On the top floor of the museum there is a splendid exhibition gallery, in which I recently found a travelling display of works by William Scott, Victor Pasmore, Patrick Heron, David Hockney, R. B. Kitaj, Boyd and Evans and other standard-bearers of British Art. Madrid has a voracious appetite for contemporary painting and there is a noticeably large number of commercial galleries within the central square mile.

Just south of the Hospicio is Calle San Mateo leading to the **Museo Romántico**. This is in effect a pleasant collection of Spanish 'Victoriana', in which we again meet the Costumbristas, amongst them Cabral-Bejarano – whose juvenile dandy smoking a cigar is amusing – and Valeriano Domínguez Bécquer. The print room illustrates pre-Romantic, Romantic (roughly 1820–1860) and post-Romantic Madrid. Esquivel portrays a group of actors of the time attending a lecture (cf. his poets in the Museo del Siglo XIX)). Vicente López paints a lady miniaturist and Palmaroli paints the poet Bécquer lying dead. When they have no clients, the painters indefatigably paint each other. In the same room as Godoy by Carnicero is an allegory of the Union of England and Spain against France, bloody, beguiling and laurel-crowned. The cabinets are full of toys, dolls, dolls' houses and furniture, fans and other touching things. We end with over-stuffed chairs, pouffes, a lovers' seat, a shawl draped over a piano and some flimsy Hispano-Philippine furniture inlaid with mother-of-pearl. Valeriano Bécquer rings down the curtain with a portrait of a young man taking himself very seriously indeed.

Continuing up Calle San Mateo to the top and turning right along Calle Fernando VI we pass the Art Nouveau building of the Institute of Authors; the same street leads to the Plaza de las Salesas with the ex-convent church of **Santa Bárbara**, built between 1750 and 1758 for Barbara of Braganza, wife of Ferdinand VI. The façade is rather successful with its giant pilasters and white stone relief of the Visitation. The standard Baroque interior contains the tomb of King Ferdinand – an absentee from the Escorial – raised by his brother and successor Charles III to designs by Sabatini. If Charles is generally given credit for polishing up a rustic capital with statues, arches and the like, it is only fair to point out that his elder brother had paved the way, leaving not only many projects but a reasonably healthy exchequer with which to carry them out. He it was who gave the Real Academia de San Fernando its statutes and founded the Botanical Garden. By Spaniards Ferdinand VI (1713–1759) is generally accounted a good king, but he was of a melancholic nature and pined away and died shortly after his wife's death.

We are very near the hub of Cibeles. Calle Conde de Xiquena brings us to the rear of the large red brick War Ministry, once the property of Godoy and confiscated from him on his fall in 1808. Filtering right we come into Calle del Barquillo and some way down this, going towards Calle de Alcalá, is the Plaza del Rey, on the west side of which is the restored **Casa de las Siete Chimeneas** – identifiable still by its seven chimney stacks. This was built about 1557, at which time it stood well outside the then town wall and was surrounded by an orchard. The future Charles I of England was lodged here when he came to inspect Philip IV's sister. A few more steps and we are back on the main artery with the traffic moving fast towards the Gran Vía – which is like nothing so much as the Big Dipper of some never-ending fair. Once I hesitated here in a car and a policeman thrust his flushed, white-helmeted face through the window in a sort of frenzy – an ecstasy almost – of action for its own sake. 'Come on!' he yelled, having seen my Málaga registration plate, 'We are in Madrid . . . we are in Madrid!' Another important rule is to step on the accelerator as soon as the traffic-light goes yellow. If you don't, an indignant taxi-driver will have rammed your boot.

THE NINETEENTH AND TWENTIETH CENTURIES

The main nineteenth century growth of Madrid took place beyond the northern line of Philip IV's wall, whose course is now traced by the Calles de Aguilera, Carranza, Sagasta and Génova. The most important new district was the Barrio de Salamanca (see plan on pp. 54-5), whose rigid grid of wide streets, mansion flats and smart shops was built between 1860 and 1884. This was also the period of construction of the main Spanish railway network and the Marquis of Salamanca, after whom the Barrio is named, played a prominent part in both developments. From our point of view there are only some scattered points of interest in this *quartier,* mainly museums. Let us start from Cibeles. Following the Paseo de Recolletos towards the Plaza de Colón we find on our right the **Palacio de Bibliotecas y Museos,** a complex of vast proportions and French municipal appearance put up between 1866 and 1894. The ground and principal floors to the left of the main portico house the **Biblioteca Nacional,** essentially a working library none of whose manuscripts or incunabula are on display. To the right of the portico at ground level is an art gallery used for contemporary Spanish and foreign exhibitions.

The largest part of the building is occupied by the **Museo Arqueológico Nacional,** whose entrance is at the rear on Calle Serrano. The **Antigüedades Ibéricas y Clásicas,** the Iberian and Classical Antiquities on the ground floor are excellently displayed. Amongst a wealth of material I shall concentrate on exhibits that are indigenous to the Peninsula. The first room contains Paelaeopunic pottery of the eighth to the sixth centuries BC and ninth century BC bronze objects from Huelva, while Ibiza, colonised in 54 BC, provides fascinating clay idols and figurines, in which Egyptian and Attic influences are apparent. From near Alicante come Attic vases and from Lebrija (Sevilla) the mysterious gold 'candelabra' whose real purpose has never been determined. Elche yields interesting Iberian pots from the third century BC to the beginning of the Christian era – though the *Dama de la Galera,* a small alabaster figurine of a Phoenician goddess between two sphinxes, would seem to have been imported. The bronze bulls' heads from Costín (Mallorca), archaically styled, are reminiscent of Crete or Mycenae.

In the next room we come to the famous *Dama de Elche,* no longer isolated in the Prado but properly shown with other products of her civilisation. This arresting bust may represent the Carthaginian goddess of resurrection, Tanit; her hollow core may have housed the ashes of some important person. But she resembles neither a goddess nor a funerary urn. Her narrow face, straight nose, masterful mouth and full chin

would have qualified her as a modern TV presenter. The
head-dress, cap, tassels and necklaces are, of course, the
ritual attributes of some hierarchy but one cannot help think-
ing of her as a portrait and her features remain as firmly
printed on the memory as those of a desirable woman to
whom one might scheme for an introduction. The seated
polychrome stone figure known as the *Dama de Baza* makes
hardly less impact than her neighbour of Elche, with whom
she shares the same full chin. Sculpted in the first half of the
fourth century BC, her face – that of an older woman – might
belong to a very composed Spanish lady of the last century.
It is interesting to note that the colouring of stone carvings
was well-rooted in Spain a millenium and a half before its
adoption on mediaeval tombs. Among the exhibits in this
room one should not overlook the small standing figures
bearing vessels with offerings for the gods from Cerro de los
Santos (Albacete), nor the late romanised Iberian reliefs from
Osuna (Sevilla). *The León de Baena* has a fearsome jaw like
a steel trap. Some of the tiny bronze ex-votos are exquisite.

We pass to the Roman section. Many of the works here are
not indigenous. Some – like the reliefs of the Infancy of
Bacchus – were bought in Italy by the Marquis of Salamanca,
as enthusiastic a collector as entrepreneur. Others were contemporary imports from Rome. But the mosaics are all
Spanish and the bronze tablets with sections of the municipal
laws of various provincial cities are of great local interest.
Bronzes, glass and terra sigillata pottery are also on view –
though the latter seems dull after the imaginative Iberian
products. The Roman influence in the Peninsula did not
diminish with the decline of the Empire. On the contrary,
early Christian or 'Palaeochristian' art owed a huge debt to
Rome, where the first sarcophagi were made – though production ceased after the sacking of the city by Alaric in
410 AD. The *Sarcófago de San Justo de la Vega,* possibly
dating from 315 AD – and if so the earliest piece of Christian
art in the museum – clearly shows its Roman origin in the
toga-clad figure of the 'heroic' Christ. The *Sarcófago de Berja*
of 340 AD is also noteworthy: the left-hand scene, as in San
Justo's, depicts the raising of Lazarus (which was to become
a very popular theme in Romanesque stone-carving), while on
the right Saints Peter and Paul are brought before Nero.
There are more mosaic floors here. The Mosaic of the Muses

and their Teachers on the end wall of the final room belongs to the so-called Art of the Latifundia, produced when the first Barbarian inroads drove sophisticated life from the fortified cities to the large estates of the interior with their civilised villas and dependencies almost forming townships on their own. It was from this refined rural culture that the Emperor Theodosius sprang.

The remaining rooms on this floor are devoted to the Visigothic Kingdom and the Low and High Middle Ages. As throughout the museum, the exhibits are accompanied by models, maps, plans and potted historical summaries, which are earnestly copied by schoolchildren for their exams and 'projects'. The Visigothic section is particularly helpful and informative and is much to be recommended to anyone who has a 'block' about the Spanish Dark Ages. Visigothic carving is usually of the simplest – the two stone fonts are decorated with a helix and with four fishes respectively; stone altar columns are carved with elongated maltese crosses. The golden votive crowns are more elaborate: letters forming the name of the donor dangle from pendents. In the following rooms Arabic and Mozarabic art gain the upper hand over the cruder Visigothic tradition, Arabic ivory caskets and coffers, enamelled or silver-bound, introduce the theme of twinned, entwined birds and beasts which were to become such a feature of Romanesque carving. There is a marvellous ivory cross offered by Ferdinand I of Castile and Sancha his wife to Saint Isidore of León; the minute figures of the frieze are intricately contorted in frozen conflict. A marble Virgin Mother from Sahagún completely encapsulates the Child, a tiny but adult figure with his dexter hand raised in benediction. And there are many other good things, among them Romanesque capitals, Mudéjar carpentry, English painted alabaster reliefs from Nottingham and a kneeling marble figure of Peter the Cruel, whose head is a contemporary portrait, though the torso dates from a century later.

The rooms on the first floor are mainly devoted to furniture, glass, silver, ivories, enamels, ceramics and porcelain of the sixteenth to eighteenth centuries, though some of the ceramics go back to the fourteenth century. We start with the magnificent lustre dishes, large as shields, developed at Málaga and Granada under the Moors, whose skills were transmitted to

Manises and Paterna on the Levant coast, where Morisco craftsmen incorporated Gothic lettering and heraldic beasts in their designs. With the expulsion of the Moriscos in 1609 Aragonese and Catalan production of these wares collapsed but continued at Manises into the eighteenth century. We come next to Talavera ware with hunting scenes on white and blue grounds. Working first for the nobility and monasteries, the factories had turned to more popular utensils by the eighteenth century, giving us such enduring shapes as the bell-bottomed jugs from which *sangría* is still served in tourist restaurants. The eighteenth century also saw the birth of Spanish porcelain manufacture at Alcora from 1727 and then at the royal factory of the Buen Retiro from 1760 with materials and craftsmen brought by Charles III from Naples, where he had founded the Capodimonte factory in 1743. The Retiro products can be divided into two phases. The first, under the direction of Gricci and later of Scheppers, can be identified by the courtly figures deriving from Meissen and Watteau, though one must not forget the more plebeian figures showing Flemish influence, particularly that of Teniers. Both types of figure are an important source of information on contemporary dress. The second period coincides approximately with the reign of Charles IV; it is neo-classical in style with mythological figures and paler colours, reminiscent of Wedgwood and Sèvres. The factory was destroyed by the French invasion of 1808. These rooms are highly recommended for all lovers and collectors of pottery and porcelain. Glass is also well represented by the products of the royal factory of San Ildefonso de la Granja, started in 1736, and by the more popular Castilian glass of the seventeenth and eighteenth centuries. The native Spanish glass makes a welcome contrast with the more pompous French cut-glass table decoration. Those interested in either glass or china should also visit the Museo de Artes Decorativos and the Museo Municipal.

The enormous basement of the Archaeological Museum contains the Prehistoric, Egyptian and Greek Collections. Of particular note is the splendid assemblage of Greek pottery, mainly formed by that enlightened tycoon, the Marquis of Salamanca, which ranges from the 'geometrical' style of the eighth century BC through the great period of Periclean Athens to its decline and the establishment of new centres of production in southern Italy. To this later period belongs Krater *11026* with an amusing scene at the expense of a Falstaffian Zeus. On the way out of the museum anyone who has not visited the Altamira caves (Santander) should take a look at the reproduction of this famous late Palaeolithic painted rock ceiling. Finally, a word of warning. The Prehistoric, Egyptian, Greek, Iberian and Roman sections are open every day but the porcelain and other crafts on the first floor *alternate* with the Visigothic and Mediaeval Collections on the ground floor: you cannot see both on the same day. Happily, the ticket is valid for two days running.

Taking Calle Serrano northwards as far as its junction with Calle Maria de Molina (this is quite a step along a once pleasant street whose trees have been wantonly ripped up) we reach the **Museo Lázaro Galdiano,** housing the legacy to the State of this compulsive collector. The great strength of this museum lies in the 'portable' art I have spoken of in the Prado. On the ground floor, room II has a magnificent collection of Limoges enamels from the twelfth to the sixteenth centuries, also of mediaeval ivories. Room III contains church plate much superior to that of many cathedrals. The *Gran Sagrario de Limoges* of about 1300 is a notable gilt, enamelled and gabled home for the sacrament. Room IV has an interesting collection of jewellery from the Hellenistic and Iberian periods to the Baroque. Rooms V and VI contain small Renaissance bronzes – these idealised figures are meant to be contemplated in the round unlike mediaeval sculpture; they belong to a luxurious almost superfluous art which is absorbed into daily use in such items as door-knockers, inkwells and candlesticks. In room VII we find Celtic and Iberian small bronzes and ex-votos, late Roman and Visigothic clasps and buckles and some interesting mediaeval objects, Arab and Christian, including a Gothic architect's mighty compass.

On the first floor – the old lift of Sr Lázaro's house remains in use – rooms VIII and IX belong to Flemish, German and Spanish primitives. The Aragonese masters in particular rely heavily on raised estofado relief for borders, haloes, crowns etc. Room XII has some English paintings – General Stringer Lawrence by Reynolds is the best; the 'Gainsboroughs' cannot be admitted. In room XVI Carreño's portrait of Mariana of Austria's favourite, Fernando de Valenzuela, shows an

almost good-looking, tight-lipped face over a strict white
collar on a black ground; the courtier's gesture of the hand
on the chest is nervous, even apologetic. Yet this was the
most successful intriguer of the age, *el Duende de Palacio*, the
palace sprite who became prime minister and ended his days
in exile in Mexico. Room XVII contains one of the same
painter's most enjoyable pictures, a portrait of Inés de
Zúñiga, Countess of Monterrey, daughter-in-law of the Count-
Duke of Olivares. This is great fun with the tiny waist, swan
neck surmounted by a pert face, huge skirt, little grey dog and
the pistol attached by a ribbon to the bodice like an innocent
bunch of keys.

The second floor has the best paintings. Room XVIII contains the important triptych by the Master of Avila, who
worked in that city from 1464 to 1476. This has great dynamism; the rigid male gestures are not limp but vibrant; in the
bagpipe scene on the left the folds are almost Vorticist. In
room XIX the Master of Astorga uses cool fresco colours in
his two panels of *c.* 1530 devoted to Santiago. He has accepted
the Renaissance message of figures in space and dropped the
gold standard. Room XX gives us small Flemish works.
Gerard David, Isembrandt, Joos Van Cleve and Bernard
Van Orley are represented. Bosch's Saint Jerome is enjoyable;
for once the subject is not overwhelmed by the fantasy. The
Descent by Quentin Metsys is an unusual close-up of a
familiar scene.

From the end of the Middle Ages we step straight into the
Dutch seventeenth century in room XXI, which contains
Rembrandt's portrait of Saskia done in 1634 – here she is
herself, not Queen of Pergamum. Room XXIII has a small
portrait of Góngora painted by Velázquez in 1622 and below
this the head of a woman claimed as an early work. Zurbarán
contributes one of his blue and purple Inmaculadas of about
1628–1630. The early Adoration by el Greco, of the Venetian
period, is a little essay in fashionable Mannerism. There are
other small studio works and a pastiche Saint Francis with
skull by el Greco's son. Room XXIV contains Spanish
seventeenth-century works. From the dramatic lighting effects
of Ribera, the postures and agonies of Valdés Leal and the
Baroque set-pieces of Cerezo and Antolínez the transition to
the rational clarities and healthy flushed cheeks of English
portraiture is striking. The English room – number XXV – is

at least as good as the Prado's. According to the museum guidebook the portrait of Lady Williams by F. Cotes is 'of ingenuous and aimiable fabrication'. Lawrence's Master Ainslie (1794) is indeed – one must agree – a work of 'superficial refinement'. The American Gilbert Stuart is good with Mrs Merry. Romney's Widow is possibly the best portrait in the room despite the 'profound elegance' of Reynolds's Lady Sondes. Constable's small view of spire and river, catalogued as Salisbury which it cannot be, is delicate and spacious. R. P. Bonington completes the room with a seascape.

It is odd to find Turner with sepia notes of his Italian trip of 1819 in company with two horrible works by Alessandro Magnasco (1681–1747) in room XXVII. One simply cannot admit Magnasco as a 'precursor of Goya' with his technique of very rapid, diffused and ugly highlights – from which Guardi suffers in a lesser degree. Room XXVIII illustrates the Francophile Spanish eighteenth century. Room XXX is mainly Goya's. The Descent from the Cross of c. 1771 is an early work after his return from Rome. The royal confessor, Padre la Canal, is a knowing old man with a slight, wry smile. The best portrait is that of Costillares, the torero, very freely handled. The strange pale Magdalen, belonging to his later years, is held by some to anticipate Renoir.

The third floor is devoted to vestments and stuffs, weapons and a collection of fans – contrary to popular belief these were hardly made in Spain before the end of the eighteenth century, until which time they were mainly imported from France (652,720 of them in 1792 alone). This magpie museum is completed by room XXXVII, containing medals, which are not for the most part the sort you wear. A whole minor art form developed in the Renaissance with heads and busts in low-relief of princes, soldiers and intellectuals. The craze came to Spain with Charles V and Philip II who had their images struck by León Leoni. The custom continued well into the nineteenth century with monarchs, generals and politicians. There are medals here from designs by Pisanello and Dürer, while the heroes treated in lead or bronze or silver range from Luther to Charles V and Cromwell to Voltaire.

Very near Lázaro Galdiano is the **Museo de Sorolla**. One simply descends to the Plaza de Emilio Castelar on the Castellana and crosses into the Paseo del General Martínez

Campos. The painter's house, in which his work is exhibited, is in the second block on the right. Through a garden we enter a never-never land, which brings to mind now Sargent, now Orpen, now Munnings, now McEvoy . . . and even sometimes Lavery. Sorolla lived from 1863 to 1923. Most of his life thus belonged to the pre-First World War period, which did amazingly exist. It is a world of white dresses, billowing sails, sunshades, children skipping and running round a pond, bathers in rippling water, dainty shoes on stepping stones, white shoes that don't pick up a grain of sand on the beach, young ladies stretching and reading on the grass, laughing country wenches at the vine harvest, white sheets, white horses, white floppy hats and the white pillows of the painter's invalid daughter against the white snows of the Guadarrama. There is also smart black for stately mourning. The first room of all contains paintings of figures in regional costume, who provide an appropriately colourful background for this privileged world. In the main studio the white ladies tripping along the seashore must be acknowledged a stunning *tour de force*.

From here it is a very short walk via Calle Miguel Angel, which links Martínez Campos with Eduardo Dato, to the Glorieta de Rubén Darío. Bearing left, we find on the corner with Calle Fortuny the **Instituto de Valencia de Don Juan**. Though it is not open to the public, researchers are admitted and in fact anyone with a cultivated interest in any of its specialities which are: the *Archivo de Altamira* with correspondence between Philip II and his secretaries including Antonio Pérez; the tiles and ceramics including possibly the best collection in the world of Hispano-Moorish lustre ware from Manises and the *Azabaches Compostelanos*, jet figure souvenirs made for sale to pilgrims to Santiago de Compostela dating from the twelfth to the seventeenth centuries. An advance telephone call is advisable to the directress (223 0415, not before midday).

The old Madrid bull-ring was conveniently sited near the Puerta de Alcalá. The present Plaza Monumental de las Ventas lies much farther east along Calle de Alcalá and is best reached by taxi or metro to Ventas. The **Museo Taurino** is installed at the rear of the plaza. Bull-fighting has not generated great art. Its finest moments are preserved in individual memories and the pen renders greater service to the corrida than the brush. The portraits are mostly poor. Costillares (1729–1800), inventor of the *volapie* (the usual way of killing today), appears in several copies or versions of the portrait by Goya in Lázaro Galdiano. There is nothing very good of Pedro Romero (1754–1839), Roque Miranda or Francisco Montes. The Dwarf of Las Ventas, complete with cigar, is the forerunner of the midgets of the *charlotadas* or burlesque fights still popular in the provinces. There is a decent portrait of Juan Belmonte by Vázquez Díaz. There are also a number of bronze heads. And the enthusiast, avid for relics, will find here the bloodied suit worn by Manolete on the day of his death and the head of Perdigón who killed Espartero – another mutual immolation pact. The English lithographs (255) seem to be copied from A. Carnicero in all essentials, apart from the winsome look in the bull's eye and the satirical treatment of the torero in black running gently away with his cape fluttering behind him (last print).

We are left with the area of the University City on the north-west outskirts of the capital. This can be reached either by following Calle de la Princesa from the Plaza de España as far as the Air Ministry or by taking the metro to the Moncloa station. One emerges under the Escorial-inspired Air Ministry very near General Franco's 'Arc de Triomphe', which attaches the Greek letter alpha to the outbreak of the Civil War in 1936 and omega to its ending in 1939. In fact, a whole new alphabet has been written since then. The **Museo de América**, which shares an entrance with the Clínica de la Concepción, on Avenida de los Reyes Católicos is worth a visit for the entertaining exhibition of popular art of America and the Philippines on the ground floor and for two rooms on the first floor. Room X contains a fascinating collection of Inca wooden vessels, pottery and bronze and stone objects – the latter including a carving of an embryo in the womb. Almost every item of Chimu or Mochica ware takes the form of man or beast or fruit. The Nazca culture preferred smooth surfaces to relief but here too the polychrome decoration observes the animal world very closely indeed .One should also seek out the room containing pre-Hispanic goldsmiths' work of the Chimu culture and the 'Treasure of the Quimbayasa' (Colombia) with its skull-cap helmets, embossed drinking flasks, trumpets etc. There are also Inca gold and metal objects. Most of the rest of the museum is devoted to propaganda for the Spanish achievement in South America.

From here continue down the Avenida de la Victoria to the Plaza del Cardinal Cisneros, where a pause for the view of the university sports ground is instructive; the layout is wholly Roman in conception but the main field is occupied by a Rugby pitch. Empires may decline and fall but they leave extraordinarily durable legacies. A little further down is the smoked glass **Musco de Arte Contemporáneo Español.** With its movable screens and panels and disseminated overhead lighting it has all the latest display techniques at its disposal; it therefore invites comparison with the Centre Pompidou. But unlike Pompidou it is, as its name implies, strictly national. Two main streams are evident. The first is the more European in character: the heroes are Picasso, Miró, Gris and Tapiès, all of whom worked either in France or in Barcelona or both. Picasso is less well represented here than in Paris or Barcelona. There is little by Gris, whom some find the most pleasing of the Cubists. Miró's large sketches for a mural in the Senate and *Woman, Bird and Star* (1970) seem to me to transcend his usual impish, spider-like, calligraphic vein. Tapiès emerges as the great poet of surfaces. The second stream is distinctly domestic and will appeal mainly to his-panophiles. It includes Vázquez Díaz's portrait of the owl-eyed Unamuno, some Basque genre scenes by José Gutiérrez Solana, a hymn to the work ethic in the shape of the life-sized *Couple of Artisans,* which looks like bronze but is in fact pressed slate, by Julio López Hernández and several large rather angry abstract paintings done under Franco when this was one of the main ways of letting off steam. But the winner of the domestic stakes is, for my money, Francisco Gutiérrez Cossío (1894-1970). His tonality is reminiscent of Zurbarán and both Two Tables (1954) and Large Table (1962) are very fine paintings.

Still further out, on the left, is the **Palacio de la Moncloa.** Rebuilt after the Civil War (which devastated the whole area of the then budding University City), it was refurnished in the standard neo-classical style common to Spanish royal palaces and used to lodge foreign heads of state on official visits. Nixon slept here. Since General Franco's death it has become the residence and office of the Presidente del Gobierno or

Prime Minister, as its security is easier to guarantee than that of the old office in the Castellana. Anyone who is motor-borne must drive on to the **Puerta de Hierro** (built under Ferdinand VI and now stranded on an island) in order to change direction for the run back into Madrid. From Calle Hilarión Esclava very near the Moncloa metro station buses leave quite frequently for **El Pardo,** where General Franco lived. The journey takes twenty minutes. The first palace on this site was put up in the fifteenth century. Rebuilt in the sixteenth with the addition of the Flemish-style slate spires (said to be the first in Spain, older than those of the Escorial), it was restored in the seventeenth century and enlarged in the eighteenth. It now presents a pleasant buff-coloured exterior in a setting slightly reminiscent of La Granja without the immediacy of the mountains. Neither the palace nor the gardens are open at the time of writing but the inventory of national monuments assures us that the gardens are 'absolutely courtly'. We are, however, allowed to visit the **Casita del Príncipe,** a glorified neo-classical summer house built between 1784 and 1791 by Villanueva for Queen Maria Luisa. This has ceilings by Maella and the Bayeus and contains pastels by Lorenzo Tiepolo. The hall combines stucco figures and Wedgwood-type plaques with speckled mock marble and ormolu trimmings.

I hope no-one will feel, at the end of this chapter, that my treatment of Madrid has been niggardly. The point I wanted to drive home in the introduction was that the capital is not suitable as a sight-seeing centre except for the **Sitios Reales** or royal seats of El Escorial and Aranjuez, the ex-university town of Alcalá de Henares and possibly the monastery of El Paular, which can be included in the last itinerary of the next chapter but is also accessible from Segovia. Anyone who tries to 'do' Segovia, Avila or Toledo on a day trip from Madrid is no friend of mine. By the same token, Madrid itself should not be ticked off in a cursory fashion after ritual homage to the Prado. It is a town that grows on one, particularly in Spring or Autumn. Its late start in the European Capitals Stakes has enabled it to preserve a small town intimacy, particularly around the Plaza Mayor and throughout the area I have described as the Villa. It is, on the whole, very friendly to foreigners. The streets are very clean and public transport, though basic, is efficient. The visual arts are highly esteemed.

There is live theatre at an amazingly low price. Spain has lived through traumas and agonies that most of us have been spared and has emerged in rather good shape. The Spain of the eighties is in a self-confident but not xenophobic mood.

CHAPTER TWO

Excursions from Madrid

❧

OUR first date outside Madrid must be with the Escorial, whose lasting influence on Spanish architecture I have already mentioned. This lies 43 km to the north-west of Madrid, which we leave on NVI for La Coruña, branching left at Las Rozas. Two days are required for a thorough visit; the intervening night is ideally spent at the Escorial itself. The grand Edwardian Victoria Palace Hotel is enjoyable but the more modest Miranda-Suizo is perfectly adequate. The **Real Sitio** or **Real Monasterio de San Lorenzo de El Escorial** owes its existence to a conjunction of circumstances. In his will Charles V bound his son Philip to erect a church incorporating a royal mausoleum. In 1556 he abdicated in Philip's favour. On Saint Lawrence's day 1557 Spanish troops took the French town of Saint Quentin but during the siege the church dedicated to this saint had been destroyed. In recognition of the victory Philip vowed to build him another. Add to this the impression that must have been made on him as a young man by his father's monastic retreat at Yuste and we have the germs of the huge, convent-college-palace, which has been denounced as a cold grim barracks built for a religious maniac and almost equally praised for its dignity and grandeur.

Whichever view is taken, it is appropriate here to say a few words about the extraordinary character of Philip II (1527–1598). Deeply religious, obsessively hard-working, abstemious in eating and drinking, he was at the same time far from averse to women – among his probable mistresses was the celebrated one-eyed Princess of Eboli, widow of his minister Ruy Gómez da Silva – and addicted to paintings of the female nude. He accepted his father's advice to deprive the Spanish nobility of any share in government and ran his unwieldy empire from a private bureau called the *despacho universal* with the aid of his secretaries. His foreign policy which alienated England, France and the Netherlands has been described as 'insane', yet

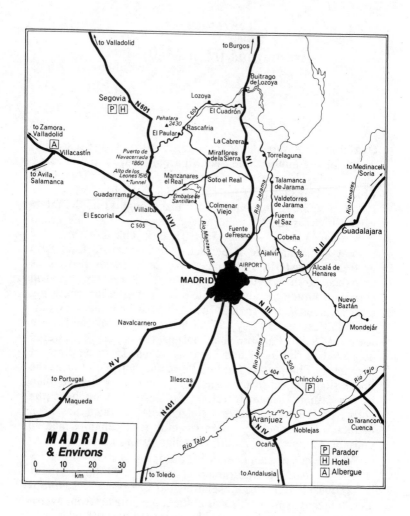

to Valladolid
to Burgos

Buitrago
de Lozoya

Segovia
P H
N 601
Lozoya
C 604
El Cuadrón

Peñalara
2430
Rascafria
El Paular

La Cabrera

to Zamora,
Valladolid
A
Villacastín

Puerto de
Navacerrada
1860
Alto de los
Leones 1516
Tunnel

Miraflores
de la Sierra
Torrelaguna

to Medinaceli
Soria

Manzanares
el Real
Soto el Real

Talamanca
de Jarama

to Avila,
Salamanca

Guadarrama
N VI
Villalba

Embalse de
Santillana

Colmenar
Viejo

Valdetorres
de Jarama

Rio Jarama

Fuente
el Saz

Rio Henares

El Escorial
C 505

Rio Manzanares

Fuente
de Fresno

Cobeña
C 100
N II
Guadalajara

Ajalvir

AIRPORT

MADRID

Alcalá de
Henares

N III

Nuevo
Baztán

Navalcarnero

Mondejár

N V

Rio Jarama

Illescas
C 404
C 300
Chinchón
P

Rio Tajo

to Portugal

Maqueda

N 401

Aranjuez
N IV
Noblejas

to Tarancon
Cuenca

Rio Tajo

Ocaña

MADRID
& Environs

0   10   20   30
km

P Parador
H Hotel
A Albergue

to Toledo
to Andalusia

it was animated perhaps as much by a sense of religious duty as by practical considerations. The Armada fiasco of 1588 began in the spirit of a crusade. Thus, the Escorial may well be seen as the symbol in stone of the Counter-Reformation which Philip conceived it his destiny to lead. The guiding

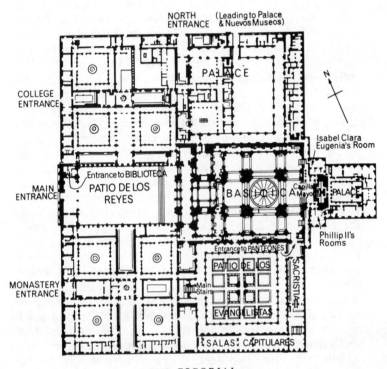

THE ESCORIAL

principles of his long reign – state authority, religious unity and public order – are most aptly expressed in its rigid lay-out and the arrangement of the royal apartments in direct communication with the basilica. In 1598, when he lay dying in the little room from which he could see the high altar, he had little but reverses to look back on abroad but it is unlikely that he blamed himself. It was all in God's hand; success or failure depended on the Almighty; the ruin of his policy did not mean that it had not been right.

Philip's architects served their master well in that they interpreted his ideas with almost uncanny fidelity. In 1559 Juan Bautista de Toledo was summoned from Naples to draw up the plans. He died in 1567 and was succeeded by his assistant Juan de Herrera. The achievement of these two was to put an end to the fussy Spanish Renaissance style known as Plateresque and introduce the plain style generally called *Herreriano* or Herreran, which was to dominate the seventeenth century and persists in some official building to this day. The King intervened at every stage of the work, which was carried out with extraordinary energy by an average labour force of 1000 men. The dome of the basilica was crowned with its cross in 1582 and the last stone was set in place in 1584, though the pantheon was not finished until the reign of Philip IV. Almost all writers remark how magnificently the building holds its own with the surrounding mountains; it is close up that the complaints begin. All the faces are monotonous on first sight, though less so with familiarity. The west is the most varied. Here we make our acquaintance with one of the hall-marks of the Herreran style in the shape of four great ball-topped obelisks placed on the entablature of the portico – which is presided over by J. B. Monegro's statue of Saint Lawrence with a gilded gridiron, the instrument of his martyrdom. There are two other lesser porticos, one for the college and the other for the monastery. The rest of this front is divided into panels by very slightly protruding pilasters, while a horizontal band runs between the second and third of the four storeys. The south front, rising from an outward-sloping basement and entirely unbroken by a single doorway, presents one of the largest, plainest and most forbidding façades in the history of architecture. Its general characteristics are continued on the east side though this is broken by a protruding block containing Philip II's apartments and popularly known as 'the handle' – by the same analogy the rest of the complex represents Saint Lawrence's grid.

We can enter either from the west or north but to get a proper feeling of the scale of the building it is best to start with the **Basílica**, which rises facing the west entrance across the Patio de los Reyes. Its façade is flanked by two towers whose surfaces are variegated by panels and niches. Standing back, one notes the concave buttresses, another Herreran characteristic. On the entablature above the great Doric columns are six kings of Judah, each carved out of a single block of stone by Monegro, though heads and hands are of marble and the sceptres of gilded bronze. We pass into the church through a vestibule under the raised choir. This is covered by Herrera's celebrated flat-centred vault. The King ordered a column to put under this. Herrera complied with a plaster mock-up and had it knocked down under the King's eyes, which led, so they say, to the famous remark, 'Juan de Herrera, Juan de Herrera, with kings one does not play games.' But the architect had got his stresses right and the vault still holds up without support. The interior of the church – based on the original plan for Saint Peter's – is undoubtedly impressive. we note further characteristics of the new style such as semi-circular clerestory windows of three lights above a great thrusting cornice and fluted pilasters running up to a minor cornice underneath. The richness of the retablo pays off in this granite setting. The fifteen gilded bronze figures are by León and Pompeo Leoni; the paintings are by Zuccaro and Tibaldi – the central panel of Saint Lawrence's martyrdom is by the latter. Raised in a recess on the gospel side of the sanctuary is the Leonis' gilt-bronze kneeling group of Charles V with his wife Isabel, their daughter Maria and his two sisters. On the epistle side in an identical position are Philip II with three of his four wives. Mary Tudor is conspicuously missing. The four barrel vaults immediately abutting on the fine plain lantern and the four corner vaulting compartments of the side-aisles are decorated with frescoes by Lucás Jordán. The church has more than forty altars all told; above each of these is a painting or, in one case, a carving – this is a marble Crucifixion by Benvenuto Cellini on the epistle side. The paintings are of no special interest though respectable of their periods; among the artists figure Navarrete, Tibaldi, Lucceto and Carvajal.

To the south of the church is the **Patio de los Evangelistas**, surrounded by the enclosed **Claustro Bajo**, painted by disciples of Tibaldi's. On the west side rises the grand **Escalera Principal** or main staircase, branching into two and overlooked by an arcaded gallery on three sides. This is covered by one of Lucás Jordán's most ambitious ceilings. Standing at the bottom and looking up, one can see poor Charles II on a balcony with his unfruitful bride and his mother Mariana in nun's habit. He is gazing up at his more illustrious ancestors – we must climb some steps to see them – Charles V offering the imperial and the royal crowns to God, while his son Philip offers the whole earth. A little nearer to heaven than either is Saint Lawrence with his gridiron at the foot of the Cross. If we continue round the lower cloister we come, on the south side, to the **Salas Capitulares**, consisting of a very large double chapter-house, designed to accommodate many brethren, with ceilings frescoed in the Pompeian style. The right-hand room contains five large paintings by the deaf Navarrete, appointed pintor de cámara in 1568. He is so mild a Mannerist that his Decapitation of Santiago (which should be a rousing theme for a Spaniard) is almost absurdly limp. The long room to the other side of the entrance contains three works by Ribera, of which the Holy Trinity almost reproduces the theme of Christ in the winding sheet (see Prado no. 1069). At the end of this room is a display of vestments.

Returning to the cloister and circulating to the north-east corner we come to a door marked **Sacristía y Panteones**. Let us take the sacristy first. The main interest consists in the painting by Claudio Coello representing the depositing of a much-prized relic in this same sacristy. Charles II is shown kneeling with the Dukes of Medinaceli and Pastrana and other nobles all gazing at the reliquary containing a host (*la Santa Forma*), which is said to have bled when trampled on by a Dutch soldier in the Netherlands; it was a present to Philip II, an avid relic-collector, from Rudolph II of Germany. Returning to the entrance lobby we now take the steps down to the pantheon of the kings and their (child-bearing) consorts. Over the entrance we are told that the idea was Charles V's, that Philip II chose the place, Philip III began the work and Philip IV finished it in 1654. The architect, who began the work in 1617, was the Italian, Crescenzi who was also to build the Cárcel de Corte in Madrid. The chamber is sited right under the high altar. Finished in rich marbles with gilded bronze trimmings, it is an octagon in shape with four shelves and as many caskets in each face. The kings are all present from Charles V (eventually brought from Yuste) to Alfonso XII with the exception of Philip V, who preferred his own foundation at La Granja and Ferdinand VI whose tomb we have seen in Santa Bárbara, Madrid. On the queens' or

consorts' side is one male, Francisco.de Asís, husband of
Isabel II, who is buried herself on the male or reigning side.
Queens without issue and princes of the blood were consigned
to the **Panteón de Infantes** which was extended in the neo-
Gothic taste by Isabel II, Alfonso XII and Alfonso XIII (who
is still buried in Rome).

We must now retrace our steps across the Patio de los
Reyes and take the stairs which rise from the ticket office to
the **Biblioteca.** This library is a great barrel-vaulted room,
170 feet long, whose ceiling is divided into seven compartments, frescoed by Pellegrino Tibaldi, the best of the Italian
artists imported by Philip II owing to his lack of confidence
in the then state of Spanish painting. Working between 1590
and 1592 in warm colours, he endowed his allegorical figures
with the illusion of volume in space. On the end wall over our
point of entry is Philosophy with Theology on the end wall
facing us. In the vault are personages representing successively
Grammar, Rhetoric, Dialectic, Arithmetic, Music, Geometry
and Astrology. These are the seven liberal arts which together
made up the mediaeval curriculum. Under the golden cornice
each compartment is supplemented with two historical or
legendary scenes relevant to the art in question – these are by
Bartolomé Carducho, also of Italian origin. The room is
lined with its original shelves in two shades of wood designed
by Herrera and contains portraits of Charles V, Philip II and
Philip III by Pantoja, of Charles II by Carreño, of Herrera
himself and of Padre Sigüenza, the second librarian. Down
the centre are display cases containing codices, illustrated
books and manuscripts, including works by Alfonso the
Learned, four autograph works of Saint Theresa of Jesus,
various examples of the Koran, an interesting Arabic natural
history, a fifteenth century bible in Hebrew and the breviaries
of Ferdinand and Isabel, Charles V and Philip II. There is
also a working model supported by four sphinxes of the
Ptolemaic universe with the unmoving world at the centre of
the singing spheres; this was made in Florence to the order of
Charles V.

After the library the best plan is to leave the building and
walk round to the north entrance, leading to **Los Palacios** or
royal apartments and the Nuevos Museos. The former should
be avoided on a week-end or holiday, for they are not large
and become unpleasantly crowded. As in all the royal palaces

the visit is conducted by an official of the Patrimonio, who
tells us what we are seeing, so I shall restrict my comments.
Via four rooms in the neo-Classical style we reach the state
dining-room with tapestries after Bayeu, Wouverman and
Goya. The next ten rooms were furnished by Charles III as a
summer residence. These are all hung with tapestries, many of
them after Teniers, Wouverman (in whose scenes a white horse
always figures), J. del Castillo and Bayeu – here we find *El
Choricero*, who sold pork products to the royal household;
the cartoon for this is in the Prado (room XXXI). In the
fourth and fifth rooms are some delightful tapestries after
Rubens; the finest and the only one woven in the Netherlands
is the scene of Neptune on a conch drawn by two white horses
being cajoled by Calypso from a cloud to calm the storm that
threatens to engulf the ship in the background. In the seventh
room a Pompeian series is contributed by Mengs. From this
suite we emerge into the **Sala de Batallas,** a long gallery once
the guard room, lined with an immense retouched scene of
the Victory of Higueruela over the Moors in the reign of
John II and, between the windows, scenes from the siege of
Saint Quentin. Thus we come to the founder's apartments.
Despite their simplicity they are among the least grim in the
complex, for their windows look out on trees and countryside.
First comes Isabel Clara Eugenia's set of rooms consisting of
parlour, inner sanctum and sleeping alcove, from which a
door leads into a small oratory with a direct view of the high
altar of the Basilica. Next, we pass by a passage behind the
altar and overlooking the Patio de Mascarones on the other
side to the King's rooms, which are distributed exactly like
his daughter's. His parlour looks south-east over a terrace
garden of box hedges with a glowing view towards Madrid.
Through the bedroom (in which he died in 1598) and the
oratory the high altar is again visible. There is little doubt that
Philip copied this scheme from his father's bedroom at Yuste.
Among the pictures is another version of Bosch's Haywain
(cf. Prado room XLIII) and a portrait of the King at 70 by
Pantoja. The remaining rooms follow the outer face of the
'handle'. They are all extremely plain with a dado of blue and
white Talavera tiles. The only concession to luxury is the
splendid series of marquetry doors presented to Philip by the
Emperor Maximilian in 1567. The first room contains engravings and plans, also contemporary paintings of the

palaces of El Pardo, Aranjuez and Valsaín. This leads to the
Throne Room. The purple and gold chair covers are original.
There is a good series of contemporary maps on the walls.
The throne is an armless stool of Charles V's, flanked by
Flemish tapestries representing a kneeling Hercules supporting
a Ptolemaic universe and Atlas supporting a globe with the
signs of the Zodiac. At right angles to this is a room with
mediocre portraits of the kings of the House of Austria.
Duke Emmanuel Philibert of Savoy, effective victor of Saint
Quentin, and Don John of Austria, victor of Lepanto, are
admitted to this company. In the last room with works by the
Bassanos and M. Coxcie is the sedan chair in which Philip
made his last gout-wracked seven-day journey from Madrid
– a shorter version of his father's from Laredo to Yuste for the
same object: death.

We now proceed to the **Nuevos Museos** in the basement.
We begin with Christ crowned with Thorns by Bosch and
works by Memling, Patinir and Marinus Van Reymerswaele.
In a recess are some charming small paintings on parchment
of birds, animals and flowers by Dürer. Via M. Coxcie we
come to Titian and Veronese. By the former the Adoration of
the Kings, the Saint Jerome and the Flight into Egypt are
notable. There is also one of Titian's several Entombments.
Now we enter a long gallery with some outstanding works.
On the end wall to the left of the entrance is a vertical Nativity
by Tintoretto. Following the wall to the right of the door we
find Tintoretto's Magdalen, a lush lady with rich rugs and
drapes and a lap dog; Tintoretto's Jesus in Peter's House;
Tintoretto's Entombment, which almost makes one's loyalty
to Titian tremble; Titian's Last Supper with fine glasses and
napery; Tintoretto's Ecce Homo; Tintoretto's Esther before
Ahasuerus; Veronese's haunting Descent of Jesus into Limbo;
Bassano's Jesus in Emmaeus – and on the end wall Veronese's
vertical Annunciation. The tremendous standard set and so
far maintained dips a little on the remaining long wall with
Guido Reni, Palma Giovanni and Zuccaro. But Titian is also
there with a Saint John the Baptist and Veronese with two
small works, the Eternal Father and a beautiful Descent from
the Cross. Between the Prado and the Escorial Spain owns
the best collection of Venetian paintings in the world outside
Venice.

We return to the Spanish School with Ribera, from whom

we pass to a room with Velázquez's early Joseph's Tunic, akin to Vulcan's Forge in the glowing bodies and rippling muscles of Joseph's brethren. Zurbarán, Valdés Leal, Alonso Cano, Mazo and Carreño are also represented. The **Nuevos Museos** are continued in two large chambers upstairs. One is known as the Sala de el Greco. After the success of his *Expolio* (in which Christ's robe is rent from him) for Toledo Cathedral (1577), el Greco wooed Philip with two small panels, another *Expolio* and the Adoration of the Sacred Name of Jesus, obtaining a commission for a larger version of the latter. This is the painting we see here, popularly known as *El Sueño de Felipe II*, in which the white-faced king, clad in plain black, kneels in company with the richly dressed figures of Saint Paul, the Pope and the Doge. On either side is a treatment of Saint Francis and on the facing wall a Flemish tapestry showing Ferdinand and Isabel extending their sway over the known world. The next room is dominated by el Greco's huge Martyrdom of Saint Maurice and the Theban Legion, commissioned by Philip on the strength of *El Sueño* for the high altar of the basilica. Perhaps more than anything else it is the painter's act of faith in this preposterous scene that makes it memorable. But Philip didn't like it and never commissioned el Greco again. For the decoration of the Escorial he turned to the second rank Italian masters we have seen. Facing the Saint Maurice is Rogier van der Weyden's marvellous Calvary. Against the red back-drop are the grey-robed Magdalen and Saint John, almost like grisailles; Christ's loin cloth is grey; the cross rises from a base of greenish rock. This is in effect a three-tone work with no attempt at illusionistic naturalism. Near by is the copy by M. Coxcie (1499–1592) of the same artist's Descent, which we have seen in the Prado; it is extraordinary that a Renaissance painter should have been able to get under the skin of the Gothic world to this extent. The room is completed by a very large tapestry of scenes during Charles V's capture of Tunis and a small one of the Garden of Delights – but Bosch does not really lend himself to warp and woof.

Before leaving the building it is worth returning to the basement where the **Museo de Arquitectura** gives interesting information on the construction of the Escorial, biographical details of the men most intimately concerned, the cost of the works, the organisation of management and labour etc., combined with an exhibition of some of the machines, ropes and tools used. But the seven opening hours (six in winter) do not allow sufficient time for the monastery and all its contents. A night in the place – the medium-priced Hotel Miranda-Suizo is comfortable and has boiling water – makes a more relaxed visit possible and leaves time for the two casitas. The **Casita de Abajo** in the lower park, built in 1772 by Juan de Villanueva for the future Charles IV, is a forerunner of the same architect's slightly later Casita del Príncipe at El Pardo. Canvases by Lucás Jordán proliferate. At the bottom of the hill is the lower town with a severe parish church built by Fray Antonio de Villacastín, overseer of the Escorial works. Returning to the monastery and taking the road past the west front, which passes under an arch, we come after about 1 km to the **Casita de Arriba**, a pavilion built also by Villanueva for the Infante Gabriel. This was converted for Prince Juan Carlos when a student at Madrid University – hence the modern bathroom. A little before this casita a road to the left winds up to Philip's Seat, a perch among the boulders from which the king would sometimes watch the progress of the work. From here there is a fine view over the undulating oak-scrub, the dome and spires of the monastery, the pine forests on the slopes beyond and, above these, of the highest peaks of the Sierra de Guadarrama.

At 8 km from the Escorial on C600 to Guadarrama is the entrance to the **Valle de los Caidos**. This colossal war-memorial to the fallen on both sides in the last Civil War was built between 1940 and 1959. It consists of monastery, subterranean church in the form of a tunnel driven 262 m into the living rock, and a gigantic cross rising 150 m from its base and equipped with an interior lift and balconies in the arms. The *Guinness Book of Records* is really a more suitable repository of these facts than a guidebook to the delights of old Spain. A visit may be made out of curiosity but aesthetic pleasure is not likely to be derived. The return to Madrid can be made on NVI from Guadarrama.

The **Sitios Reales**, as the royal residences are called, are all situated within fairly easy reach of Madrid. One of their main functions was to satisfy the Spanish monarchs' passion for hunting and shooting, which was particularly marked in Charles III and Charles IV. In his *Episodios Nacionales* Pérez Galdós tells how the latter went shooting from the Escorial the morning after the discovery of his son's involvement in a plot to dethrone him. This was in the late autumn, the season for the boar-hunt in the wooded hills. By contrast, low-lying Aranjuez in the valley of the Tagus, insufferably hot in summer, was pleasant in the spring and if this was a poor season for game there were other distractions such as boating and the theatre. Only 47 km to the south of Madrid on NIV, it is easily visited in a day and the return journey may be varied by a circuit through Ocaña and Chinchón.

ARANJUEZ

Aranjuez grew up near a natural weir in the Tagus which made irrigation easy. In the Middle Ages the place belonged to the military order of Santiago, from which it passed to the Crown in 1522. Charles V built a hunting lodge, which Philip II enlarged. It was Philip too who introduced the English elms, which are such a remarkable feature of the surroundings. The Habsburg buildings were largely destroyed by fires in 1660 and 1665. Philip V undertook a reconstruction in 1727, which was not completed till 1752 under his son Ferdinand VI. Charles III added two wings at right angles to the main front between 1775 and 1778. Driving in from Madrid we cross the Tagus and find immediately on the right the garden called the Parterre to the east of the **Palace**. Taking the first right and flanking the buildings we come to the west front. The grounds and avenues on this side are ill-cared for and shanty bars have grown up among the trees. The impression made by the façade with Charles III's projecting wings is somewhat frigid. Crossing the forecourt to the entrance, we find ourselves back in the hands of our old friend the Patrimonio Nacional. We climb the grand staircase. On the landing where this branches into two is a bust of Louis XIV. Over the well hangs a large La Granja chandelier. Of the 300-odd rooms we are shown 23. Those of us who have been familiarised by the palace at Madrid and Charles III's rooms at the Escorial with the standard decoration of the Bourbon residences will probably feel this is quite enough. The employee, as usual, will point out the salient features of each room. I shall content myself with remarking on the few things by which I was struck. In the queen's study are some rather pretty chairs of Charles IV's time with backs shaped like the high combs used

Goya's *Scenes of the Third of May*, Museo de Prado, Madrid. 'The two sides of the picture, the killers and the killed, are drawn together by the outsize lantern casting an even yellow lighting the white shirt of the momentary hero with his Christ-like gesture and the suggestion of the stigmata in his right hand.'

Goya by Goya.

Manzaranes el Real. 'A bridge takes us over the tip of the Embalse de Santillana and a castle now rises into sight, fulfilling most people's expectations of a "Castle in Spain".'

Plaza Mayor. Alcalá de Henares.

Entering Old Castile. The bridge across the Ebro at Frias.

Left: Seventeenth century stone carving of the Cid at Cardeña.
Right: Tower of the monastery of Las Huelgas, Burgos, 'Church and tower are in the severe transitional Gothic style of the Cistercians.'

Santo Domingo de Silos (Burgos). The doubt of Saint Thomas on the fourth corner pier is 'particularly fine in its flat yet sophisticated handling'.

San Lorenzo, Sahagun (Leon). 'This church of the late twelfth century has a great brick tower composed of receding stages, which are decorated with both round and pointed blind arcades.'

Santiago, Carrion de los Condes (Palencia). Romanesque frieze over the door with Christ in Majesty flanked by the apostolic symbols. Compare the hieratic quality with the shock tactics of the dead Christ below by Gregorio Fernández in the Museo Nacional de Escultura, Valladolid.

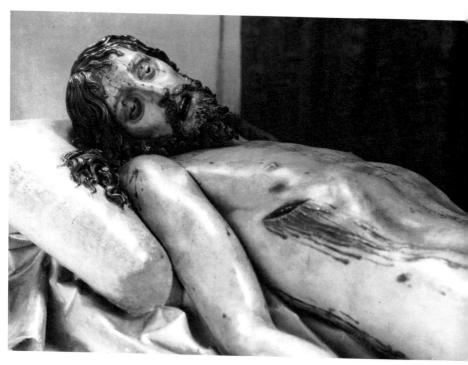

Repentant Magdalen (1664) by Pedro de Mena, Museo Nacional de Escultura,
Vallodolid. He was ' "the most spiritual exponent of the mysticism of the
seventeenth century in Spanish imagery" according to the official catalogue.
This may be so; he took over the eyes and teeth and nails from Gregorio
Fernández but he also had a fine taut streak that raised him above his
material'.

Facade, Colegio de San Gregorio, Valladolid. 'The college . . . was built
between 1488 and 1496. The facade, sometimes described as Gothic-
Plateresque, is in fact one of the last fantastic flourishes of the Isabelline-
Gothic style and has more in common with the work of the wood-carvers of
the great retablos than with that of any silversmith.'

for mantillas. The next room is the **Sala de Porcelana**, predecessor of the china chamber at Madrid and designed by Gricci, the first director of the Buen Retiro factory, in 1763. The intimate family ball-room with padded benches round the walls and portraits of Alfonso XII and Alfonso XIII is distinctly agreeable. The **Sala Arabe**, which was used as a smoking room, is a plaster copy made about 1850 of the Sala de las Dos Hermanas in the Alhambra. The last room has some 200 Chinese paintings on rice-paper of flowers, birds, ways of execution and types of torture etc., which as usual one has not time to digest. On the tour we have passed under a number of Pompeian ceilings and had occasion to note once again the popularity as court painters of Lucás Jordán, Bayeu and Mengs. It is all very much the mixture as before. There is an additional ticket for the **Museo de Historia del Traje**, which displays reproductions of royal and court costumes from the time of Philip II to Charles IV, real clothing from that period onwards, the robes of noble orders, military uniforms and Alfonso XIII's collection of military caps. Benlliure's quaint double bust of Alfonso XIII and Victoria Eugenie employs bronze for the King and alabaster for the Queen. Royal highchairs, hideous cots and curious dressing platforms for highborn babes called *envolvedoras* lead to a collection of eighteenth-, nineteenth- and twentieth-century fans – the most attractive feature of the museum.

On leaving the palace it is worth taking a look at the town. The regular streets of the two-storey houses were laid out in imitation of the Dutch style by Grimaldi, Charles III's ambassador at The Hague. It is a pity the two long sides of the Plaza de la Libertad now carry the heavy traffic of NIV; a bypass is badly needed. The block with the covered walk on the west side contained the house of Godoy, the Queen's favourite, sacked on the night of March 19th, 1808, by the hireling mob set on by supporters of Ferdinand, prince of the Asturias, in whose favour his father Charles IV abdicated the next day. At the south end is the chapel of San Antonio.

If the palace disappoints and the town seems down-at-heel, the grounds and gardens very largely compensate. Immediately inside the entrance to the Parterre garden is a monumental group celebrating the labours of Hercules in the centre of a pond with fountains; the animals he overpowered are sprawled on the imitation rocks round the plinth. The east face of the palace is the only one to conserve remnants of the Habsburg château. By the north corner of this there is a little bridge over a canal called *la ría*, beyond which stretches the **Jardín de la Isla**. This garden, limited by the canal on the south and a great curve in the river on the other sides, is in effect an island. It was laid out by Philip II and the avenues of plane trees have names like Salón de los Reyes Católicos, Calle de la Alhambra etc. It was here that Schiller set his *Don Carlos*. Returning through the Parterre and crossing the main road we enter the Calle de la Reina, a long straight avenue of planes and elms. Between this and the river spreads the extensive **Jardín del Príncipe**. About 1 km along the avenue on the left is the entrance to the **Casa del Labrador** built for Charles IV in 1803. This is the last and largest of the royal 'cottages' of which we have already seen examples at El Pardo and the Escorial. In fact, it is a small palace on two floors. A car ticket can be bought at the gate allowing us to drive right up to the building and to circulate in the park. As soon as we are across the threshold the Patrimonio takes us in hand. There are ceilings by López, Maella and Zacarías González Velázquez. The small sculpture gallery has a frieze and door-cornices in white biscuit-ware, busts of Homer, Socrates and other classical worthies and a musical clock modelled on Trajan's Column. Owing to the pace of the visit the charming paintings of the waterworks at La Granja and views of the Escorial and Aranjuez by F. Brambilla (d. 1842) cannot be properly appreciated. Queen Maria Luisa's dressing-room is a luxurious little box lined with glass, ormolu and wooden panels inlaid with gold and platinum representing the four seasons. After the visit we can walk or drive back through the Jardín del Príncipe, laid out by Charles IV as Prince of the Asturias, to the exit near the town. At the west end, in the crook of a curve in the river, is the **Casa de Marinos**, formerly on the other bank, containing a gondola with a central cabin that belonged to Philip V, the pretty barges with plush-seated and canopied cockpits of Charles IV and Isabel II and the barge and brass and mahogany canoe of Alfonso XII.

Continuing south from Aranjuez on NIV we come after 16 km to **Ocaña**, where Joseph Bonaparte defeated a Spanish army under Areizga on November 19th, 1809. The dour old town's plain brick Plaza Mayor is a country cousin of Madrid's. There is also a bluff brick and flint 'palace' with grilles shaped

like gridirons and a fifteenth-century entrance framed by
an *alfiz* – the Spanish name for a rectangular label or moulding
surrounding a door or window. Leaving the main road and
taking N400 for 6 km we reach Noblejas, from which a road
runs north to **Colmenar de Oreja** with a sixteenth-century
church showing marked Escorial influence in the clerestory
windows. From here it is only 6 km to **Chinchón,** an old villa
near enough Madrid to have been taken up by the madrileños
for week-end and holiday lunches. The compact mass of
housing has a fine Plaza Mayor with wooden galleries over an
arcaded pavement. This is the scene of bullfights held in August
in honour of Saint Roch. Above the plaza rises the parish
church, whose Neo-Classical retablo frames an Assumption by
Goya, pink and pretty but redeemed by the awkward angels
with robust, terrestrial arms and faces. Overlooking the town
on the other side with a sweeping view of the undulating landscape to the north is the squat low castle, which now houses
one of the anis factories for which the place is famous. A
'Chinchón Seco' swallowed in one or at the most two gulps
on a cold morning is an experience everyone should try at least
once. The return to Madrid can be made either by C300,
which joins NIII at Arganda or by C404 rejoining NIV just
south of Valdemoro.

ALCALÁ DE HENARES

It makes a welcome change to turn from court architecture
to the once-famous seat of learning founded by Cardinal-
Archbishop Jiménez de Cisneros at **Alcalá de Henares** 31 km
from Madrid on NII, the road to Zaragoza. Approaching
from the capital, one enters by a plain Neo-Classical arch of
1788, leaving the mediaeval walls on the left. The oldest
stretches of these are Múdejar work of the fourteenth century
and they enclosed one of the main seats of the archbishops of
Toledo. From the arch we quickly reach the Plaza de los
Santos Niños. On the right is the **Iglesia Magistral** of the
fifteenth and sixteenth centuries with a late Gothic west door
and well-composed Herreran stone tower whose balustrade
carries the usual ball-topped obelisks. The rest of the building
has been inappropriately covered with a stucco *esgrafiado*
surface. Inside, we find a Gothic church of fine proportions
by Pedro Gumiel with five bays (rebuilt after destruction in

the Civil War) to the crossing, transepts, sanctuary with a
good grille by Juan Francés and an ambulatory. Under the
high altar is a semi-crypt containing the relics of the child
martyrs, Justo and Pastor. The tomb of Archbishop Carrillo
(who retired in dudgeon to Alcalá on account of his waning
influence over the young Queen Isabel, for which reason he
fought against her at the battle of Toro) used to occupy the
centre of the nave; it was broken up but will be restored and
placed in one of the side chapels. Attached to the church is a
small Escorialesque cloister dominated by the boldly massed
tower. Just to the north of the plaza and accessible either by
Calle San Juan or Calle San Felipe (with the brick seventeenth-
century church of San Felipe Neri on the right) stands the
Palacio Arzobispal, whose most interesting interior features
were destroyed by an explosion in 1939. The main front is of
plain stone with windows surmounted by Renaissance
roundels and an upper loggia of the same period; the window
over the entrance later received a Baroque frame crowned by
a shield. The brick wing at right angles to this was rebuilt in
the 'forties, though the machicolated tower at the south end
is of the fourteenth century. Turning the corner of this, we
come into a small public garden with stone benches and fir
trees. Facing us is the brick façade of the convent church built
by Cardinal Bernardo Sandóval y Rojas in 1618 and dedicated
to his namesake **San Bernardo**. This prelate was an uncle of
Philip III's favourite, the Duke of Lerma, to whose influence
he owed his preferments. He is said to have fulfilled his
function as Inquisitor-General with extraordinary rigour. But
he was also known as a man of taste, a reputation borne out
by the restrained front of his foundation, concealing an
elegant elliptical church with a balconied and latticed interior
window for the Cistercian nuns over each of the six side-
chapels. This work by Sebastián de la Plaza may have served
as model for San Francisco el Grande in Madrid, whose
ground plan is similar.

The area just described is linked to the town centre by the
sensibly arcaded Calle Mayor. Half-way up this on the left is
the **Casa de Cervantes** built in 1955 on the site of the house in
which the author of *Don Quijote* was born. His father held
the post of surgeon and bloodletter in the adjacent hospital,
founded in 1487. A little way up the side street is the Plater-

esque entrance of the Carmelite convent governed by Saint Theresa for some months in 1567. Continuing along the main street we emerge into the large Plaza Mayor, also arcaded on the west side, with a bandstand and a statue of Cervantes. Though none of the buildings is remarkable, this square is conceived on a spacious scale and enjoys the view of a number of decent brick towers with slate spires. At the south end is the ruined church of Santa Maria, destroyed in 1936. Cervantes was baptised here in 1547 – he died in the same year as Shakespeare, 1616.

From the east side the short Calle Pedro Gumiel leads into the Plaza de San Diego with the splendid façade of the **Universidad** on the right. This was founded in 1498 by Alcalá's greatest benefactor, Fray Francisco Jiménez de Cisneros, Archbishop of Toledo. Though of humble origin, Cisneros was in the great line of powerful Toledan prelates. Educated at Alcalá, Salamanca and Rome, he was thrown into prison by Archbishop Carrillo in a dispute over the arch-priest-ship of Uceda. Cardinal Mendoza made him Vicar-general of his own diocese of Sigüenza and proposed him to Isabel as her confessor in 1492. On Mendoza's death in 1495, Cisneros succeeded him in the primacy. His efforts to convert the Moriscos to Christianity were less than happy. When Isabel died in 1504, she left the crown of Castile not to her husband, Ferdinand, but to their daughter, Joan. On the death of Joan's husband, Philip the Fair, in 1506 Cisneros strongly supported Ferdinand's recall and when the King himself died in 1516, Cisneros became regent. But the future Charles I of Spain and V of the Holy Roman Empire, aged 16, administered a severe snub to the old Cardinal by appointing his own tutor Adrian of Louvain in his stead. Cisneros died in 1517 on his way to meet the ruthless young monarch.

In the meantime, the university had become operational in 1508. The first buildings were of brick and so they remained until well after the founder's death. In 1540 the young Rodrigo Gil de Hontañón completed his designs for a grander front in stone. Finished in 1553, this is one of the most successful works of the Spanish Renaissance. The façade is conceived as a whole. The rich central panel is no mere isolated feature, for it completes a square if taken in conjunction with either of its flanks and these in themselves, below the loggia level, also form squares. A short contemplation easily reveals these harmonies. The whole is framed and bound (though in terms of design the package is already strong enough) by the rope motif, representing the girdle of Saint Francis, which had been popular in Gothic façades. This excellent front leads to a courtyard of three superimposed galleries. The balustrade is enlivened by ball-topped obelisks (the only element of High Renaissance decoration to be adopted by Herrera). Swans (the name Cisneros naturally leads to the emblem *cisne*, a swan) abound both as decoration and in support of the Cardinal's shield. This patio is called after Saint Thomas of Villanueva. The next, really a garden surrounded by modest brick buildings, is called the Patio of the Philosophers. But disputes of a very different sort now take place within its walls, for the parts of the University we have seen so far are at present occupied by the School of Public Administration. The third patio can only be glimpsed from here through a locked gate and must be entered through the Hostería del Estudiante, a restaurant whose door is in the Calle de los Colegios at the back.

Returning to the main entrance and turning left, we come to the simple white stone front and belfry of the **Capilla de San Ildefonso**, which contains unexpected riches. Here it is necessary to say something about the Múdejar and Plateresque styles. The former lasted from the twelfth to the end of the sixteenth century and combined Muslim with Christian characteristics. The latter began about 1492 and was played out by the middle of the following century; it derives its name from the work of the *platero* or silversmith, which it resembles in its minuteness and profusion of detail. Though of Renaissance inspiration, it sometimes incorporates both Múdejar and Gothic elements, as is the case in this chapel. The nave is a hall decorated with stucco blind arcades combining Gothic and Plateresque motifs and covered by an artesonado ceiling of Múdejar stamp, whose members are in very low relief so that they almost resemble strapwork. The Franciscan girdle is again in evidence, running the whole way round under the frieze and falling in mock tassels on either side of the sanctuary arch. Beyond this the decoration again combines Gothic and Plateresque elements in an ensemble of distinctly Muslim flavour. The artesonado is richer and the wooden members more strongly defined than in the nave. In the centre is the magnificent but mutilated tomb of Cardinal Cisneros in Carrara marble by Bartolomé Ordóñez. Continuing our circuit of the University building we come to the Calle de los Colegios and enter the **Patio Trilingüe** by the restaurant door. This is named after the famous polyglot bible which Cisneros commissioned in Hebrew, Greek and Latin. It has an arcaded walk only at ground level and gives access to the **Paraninfo** or senate house of 1514–1518, whose proportions are those of a double cube. The lower walls are plain – probably they were intended for tapestries. Above is a stucco Plateresque gallery with six balcony openings on the long side and three at the ends. The wooden ceiling, combining Renaissance coffering with Múdejar workmanship, is painted in blue, red and gold – colours that are repeated in the tribune from which candidates for doctorates expounded their theses. The senate house is still used for some ceremonies by the Universidad Complutense de Madrid. It is sad, though, that this made-to-measure university town does not still fulfil its proper function. Walking east along the Calle de los Colegios towards the modest Baroque chapel of El Cristo de las Doctrinas, we discover that most of the one-time college buildings are now barracks. If other quarters were found for the military, Alcalá could at least be re-occupied by certain faculties. Retracing our steps towards the Hostería, we have a pleasing view of the slate-hatted brick towers of the Colegio de Málaga, founded in 1610 by the first Bishop of Guadix – one of the few colleges still used as a school – and the church of Santa Ursula. Among many other decent buildings the ex-Jesuit church (now parish church of Santa Maria) on the Calle de Libreros running east towards Guadalajara has a façade typical of the early work of the order; the interior distribution includes the intercommunicating side-chapels which were to be adopted also in the church of San Isidro, Madrid. North of the main road Alcalá has a squalid industrial zone and blocks are beginning to rise to the south between the town and the hills. But the nucleus is still unspoilt. A morning may be devoted to sight-seeing followed by lunch at the Hostería del Estudiante. It is advisable to book in advance on a Saturday or Sunday.

There are two places of a certain interest to the south and east of Alcalá, which can easily be visited in an afternoon. Taking C300 towards Arganda for 5 km, we then follow signs to Villalbilla, Valverde de Alcalá and **Nuevo Baztán**, our destination. This is a complete village built by José de Churriguera between 1709 and 1713 for the Navarrese banker and royal treasurer, José de Goyeneche. The surprise of this project is in a sense a negative one, for it displays little of the extravagance usually associated with Churriguera and his family. The two-storey palace with its two slate spires and Escorialesque dormer-windows has a distinct flavour of the previous dynasty and this is not dispelled by a few Baroque mannerisms. The church façade has Herreran obelisks and the parade ground at the back, surrounded by low houses with a first-floor gallery, is almost excessively plain. The village is half deserted and the whole place has a mournful air. From here it is 19 km via Olmeda de las Fuentes to **Mondéjar** with parish church of 1516 and tower of 1560 by Cristóbal and Nicolás de Aldonza. But the main interest lies in the ruined church of **San Antonio**, built between 1487 and 1505 and held to be the first church put up in Spain *a la romana*, that is in the Renaissance style. Despite the affinity of the west door with that of the Medinaceli palace at Cogolludo (Guadalajara) and other Renaissance features such as classical pilasters, the broken ribs at the east end clearly show that a Gothic hall-church vault must have been employed. From Mondéjar we can either return to Alcalá by the same route or turn left at the first cross-roads (5 km) and follow the valley of the Tajuña to join NIII.

Madrid – Colmenar Viejo – Manzanares el Real – (El Escorial) – Miraflores de la Sierra – El Paular – Rascafría – Lozoya – Buitrago de Lozoya – NI to Madrid OR *Torrelaguna – Talamanca de Jarama – Valdetorres – Fuente el Saz – Madrid*

The southern slopes of the Sierra de Guadarrama increasingly provide madrileños with the fresh air they need and no longer get in the capital. This means *urbanizaciones* or developments of a semi-suburban type, which crawl impertinently towards the slumbering flanks of the great massif. The way into this week-end paradise is by C607 to **Colmenar Viejo**, which has an ample church with crocketed spire, a late Gothic north entrance and a respectable Renaissance retablo combining painting with sculpture. From here we take the road for Miraflores, branching left after some 5 km to **Manzanares el**

Real. A bridge takes us over the tip of the Embalse de Santillana and a castle now rises into sight, fulfilling most people's expectations of a 'Castle in Spain'. This was erected by the courtier-poet Iñigo López de Mendoza, Marquis of Santillana, incorporating some older fortifications. His son, the first Duke of Infantado, converted it into a palace, rebuilding the patio with flattened arches on fluted Gothic columns – this is now ruinous. Shortly after, the second Duke charged Juan Guas, the architect of the Infantado palace in Guadalajara, with further improvements. These include the setting of stone spheres like large cannon balls in the upper bodies of the towers and the conversion of the southern *paseo de ronda* into a courtly gallery or loggia which – if not quite as elaborate as that of the' Guadalajara palace – is decorated richly enough with a solid balustrade of diamond-faceted stones under the tracery of the Gothic arcade. Guas was also responsible for the two tiers of pseudo-machicolations, whose design I suspect inspired some of the mouldings in Gaudi's neo-Gothic episcopal palace at Astorga (León). A low outer wall repeats the curves and rectangles of the castle proper. The interior of the parish church is interesting for the wide longitudinal arches resting on grotesquely exaggerated Renaissance capitals. The village does a thriving week-end trade and the bars and restaurants are packed.

Following the river Navacerrada west we rejoin C607 and, crossing this, can return to Madrid via Collado Villalba on NVI – or continuing westwards on C607 to the next intersection and branching left to Collado Mediano and Guadarrama we come easily to the Escorial. If, however, daylight permits, the weather is good and energy high, a much wider circuit may be attempted. Driving east to Soto el Real, we branch left to the summer hill-station of Miraflores de la Sierra, from which a road winds north over the Puerto de la Morcuera (Spanish passes are called *puertos de montaña*, not to be confused with seaports, *puertos de mar*) to Rascafría in the high valley of the river Lozoya. A little to the west of the village is the **Monasterio de El Paular** (also accessible from Segovia). On August 29th, 1390, John I was present at the ceremony of blessing the land on which this monastery was to rise. It belonged to Carthusians until its expropriation by the State in 1836. Untenanted for nearly a century, it was handed by the present régime to the Benedictines in 1954. The Gothic atrium is decorated with coloured shields of the Trastamara dynasty. The great wrought-iron grille is by a doughty ironsmith we shall meet again, Fray Francisco de Salamanca. The church is possibly by Juan Guas assisted by Abdarramán, a Moor of Segovia, but Baroque relining makes the question academic. The glory of the church is the **Retablo** in delicately painted alabaster, one of the finest and most unusual ever made in Spain. The work belongs to the end of the fifteenth century; its grace and delicacy have led to its attribution to Italian craftsmen. Juan Guas has also been advanced as its author but it does not seem likely that this prolific architect of rich designs chiselled the sculpture any more than he carved the detail of his Colegio de San Gregorio in Valladolid. Here the panels, some vertical, others horizontal, depict the traditional scenes including Christ at the Column, the Vía Crucis, the Crucifixion, The Descent, the Death of the Virgin etc. – but special emphasis is given to feminine beauty and the figures stand out clearly with plenty of breathing space. Delightful angels with trumpets surround the Virgin and Child with a bird (this group is a little later). The whole seems to have been executed in that magical interlude between loving late Gothic particularisation (in which it seems the artist can hardly bear to tear himself away from any fold or face or fanciful figure lurking among the leaves) and the Renaissance stereotypes that became the price of clearer design. The free-standing figures on top belong to the Baroque restoration.

To the right and left the retablo is pierced by doorways under trefoil arches, which lead to the startlingly different **Transparente**, designed in 1718 by Francisco de Hurtado, a disciple of the Churrigueras. The term was first used to describe Narciso Tomé's Baroque altarpiece lit by a skylight in Toledo Cathedral but here the purpose is different, for this is a genuine *camarín* or closet behind the altar, in which the Virgin is dressed and her ornaments are kept. The approach is by a large cruciform anteroom with walls painted in imitation of black, porphyry and veined grey marble and hexagonal chapels between the arms. The frescoes are by Palomino and José Donoso; the images by Duque Cornejo, Pedro Alonso de los Ríos and Juan Pascual de Mena. After this extravaganza it is a relief to escape to the pleasant cloister with different vaulting ribs on all four sides. Each Carthusian monk had his own cell round this cloister and would probably be buried under the very ground he trod daily in his lifetime. The central *templete* or pavilion has dials for telling the time by sun or moon. Altogether, this is a very sympathetic and engaging monastery and the retablo should not be missed. If the journey is not possible from Madrid, it can be made from Segovia.

From El Paular C604 leads south-west via Puerto de los Cotos (1830 m) to Puerto de Navacerrada (1860 m), the highest pass of the Guadarrama. N601 then leads down to join NVI to Madrid. Let us, however, assume that there is time to continue the projected circuit. We return to Rascafría and follow the picturesque valley of the Lozoya to the village of this name, from which the road goes on to debouch on NI just beyond El Cuadrón. (Taken in reverse this route provides the only access to El Paular when the passes are cut by snow.) A few kilometres to the north on NI is **Buitrago de Lozoya**, an old fortified town on the river, which swells here into the Embalse de Puentes Viejas. An interesting dog-legged gatehouse and considerable stretches of wall remain. There is also a Mudéjar castle and the church tower is in the Mudéjar tradition. NI may now be followed all the way south to Madrid. But anyone who wishes to meander a little off the main road, though in the same direction, can do worse than turn off left at La Cabrera to **Torrelaguna**, birthplace of Cardinal Cisneros. The crocketed Gothic church tower has a pronounced cornice decorated with the Avila ball-pattern. There is a good standard fourteenth-century interior with a Rococo retablo and two Renaissance pulpits. In the gospel-side apse is a large crucifix said to have been given by Queen Isabel to Cisneros, then her confessor.

Continuing south on C100 for a further 11 km we come to **Talamanca de Jarama** with remnants of Moorish walls and the ruined apse of a Romanesque brick church standing as an isolated feature in the centre of the village. The present parish church also has a Romanesque apse, but of stone. Inside, two pairs of longitudinal arches (cf. Manzanares el Real) of remarkably wide span support a wooden roof. About 1 km to the west of the town is a Roman bridge over the Jarama; the main river has now changed its course and the bridge is hidden in a poplar grove. The road next passes **Valdetorres de Jarama**, where there is a seventeenth-century church of three bays covered by a wooden ceiling; the most interesting features are the unusually flattened presbytery arch and the

Plateresque west door. Thus we come to Fuente el Saz, where there is a choice of routes. Forking right to Fuente el Fresno, we join NI for the final run into Madrid. Or we can continue south on C100 to Cobeña, after which we branch right to Ajalvir and re-enter the capital from the east on NII.

LEAVING THE CAPITAL

As I have explained in the introduction, one of my main objects has been to discourage the selection of Madrid as a base for excursions other than those just described. But this does not mean that some travellers – for example those who arrive by air at Madrid and hire a car – may not want to use the radial network of main roads leading out of the capital in order to join my circuit at some point or other. For their benefit the following routes are briefly outlined.

Madrid – Buitrago de Lozoya – Puerto de Somosierra – Aranda de Duero – Lerma – Burgos

This is NI leading north. For Buitrago see p. 105. Puerto de Somosierra is the 1440 m pass over the Sierra de Guadarrama. This is occasionally closed by snow, and if so, there will be a notice to that effect on the exit from Madrid. For Aranda de Duero see p. 402 and for Lerma p. 136.

Madrid – Puerto de Navacerrada OR Alto de los Leones OR Guadarrama tunnel – Segovia

NVI for La Coruña is followed as far as Villalba, from where N601 branches right to cross the 1860 m Puerto de Navacerrada – the highest of the Guadarrama passes – before descending to Segovia. Continuance on NVI beyond Villalba offers the alternatives of the 1511 m Alto de los Leones or the Guadarrama tunnel (toll), almost obligatory in heavy snows, after which N603 sweeps right from San Rafael and also leads to Segovia. The Navacerrada route, which passes La Granja, is the most attractive of these.

Madrid – Villacastín – Adanero – Olmedo – Valladolid

After San Rafael NVI continues via Villacastín (see p. 272)

to a junction at Adanero, where N403 forks right passing through Olmedo (see p. 187) to Valladolid.

Madrid – Adanero – Arévalo – Medina del Campo – Tordesillas – Toro – Zamora

Same as above as far as Adanero, from where NVI continues via Arévalo (see p. 239) and Medina del Campo (see p. 185) to Tordesillas (see p. 182). From here N122 leads west along the Duero to Toro (see p. 205) and Zamora.

Madrid – Villacastín – Avila – Peñaranda de Bracamonte – Salamanca

From Villacastín on NVI one follows N501 leading west to Avila. The same road then swings north-west to Peñaranda de Bracamonte (see p. 236) and thence to Salamanca.

Madrid – Navalcarnero – Maqueda – Talavera de la Reina – Oropesa – Portugal

This is NV, the main road to Extremadura and Portugal. For Maqueda see p. 293, for Talavera p. 335 and for Oropesa p. 335.

Madrid – Illescas – Toledo

The direct road from the capital to Toledo is N401 via Illescas (see p. 331).

Madrid – Aranjuez – Ocaña – Madridejos – Andalusia

NIV leading south is the main road for Andalusia. For Aranjuez see p. 94, for Ocaña p. 96 and for Madridejos p. 339,

Madrid – Tarancón – Carrascosa del Campo – Cuenca

Leaving Madrid on NIII for Valencia, one continues as far as Tarancón, from where N400 branches left via Carrascosa del Campo (see p. 359) to Cuenca, which is no longer so inaccessible as it used to be.

Madrid – Alcalá de Henares – Guadalajara – Alcolea del Pinar – Medinaceli – Almazán – Soria

NII – the road for Zaragoza and Aragón – leads first to Alcalá de Henares (see p. 97), then to Guadalajara (see p. 368). At Alcolea del Pinar it kicks north and passes under Medinaceli (see p. 380) to à junction with NIII, which leads via Almazán (see p. 383) to Soria.

CHAPTER THREE

Burgos

✼

For the motorist entering Spain by Irún the approach to Burgos sets no problems, for N1 via San Sebastián and Vitoria takes him all the way. The railway follows an almost identical route. Disembarkation at Santander also offers a simple run south on N623. Ferries no longer ply to Bilbao but, in case that service should be restored, it is worth mentioning a short cut by which the tremendous congestion of that port is avoided. Leaving Santurce dock one should contrive to emerge on N634 and once on this follow it for some 6 km in the direction of Santander as far as Somorrostro. From here a local road leads south via Sopuerta to Valmaseda. It is now plain sailing on C631B to the Bercedo cross-roads, where C629 should be selected leading to Villarcayo. The rest of this route, which is simple, is described in greater detail on p. 135.

Whatever the means or route of arrival I shall assume that we meet in **Burgos**. The industrial outskirts are dismaying in their extent and ugliness but most people, I think, will take to the old grey core, which has something of a French air about it. In fact, the houses and shops along the north bank of the Arlanzón always remind me of a northern French quayside, though the river is but a trickle except in heavy rains or melting snows and the house-fronts are separated from it by a fine promenade with espaliered trees called the Paseo del Espolón. This name is derived from the spur-shaped piers of the bridge leading to the main city gateway, the **Arco de Santa María**. The outer face of this arch was added between 1536 and 1553 to an older Gothic gatehouse, which still forms the inner side. Burgos had joined the Revolt of the Commons of Castile in 1520 (see pp. 154–155) and is said to have appeased the wrath of Charles V by erecting this handsome piece of civic architecture in his honour. The Emperor occupies the upper niche of the central panel. On his right is Fernán González, first independent Count of Castile; on his left the luxuriantly bearded and curiously stumpy figure of the Cid. Beneath the

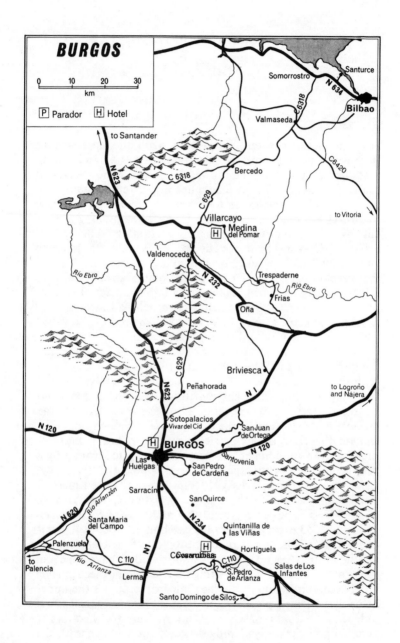

Emperor is Diego Rodríguez Porcelos, the Castilian count to whom the foundation of the city is attributed in 884, flanked in his turn by Nuño Rasura and Laín Calvo, two of the early magistrates known as Merinos. Above the Emperor in a single niche is the guardian angel of the city and above him again are the Virgin and Child. Passing through this gatehouse we come into the cathedral precinct on the south side.

Burgos **Cathedral** is particularly rich in external sculpture and demands a circuit of the outside before we go in. The entrance facing us at the head of a flight of steps is the Puerta de Sarmental, opening into the south transept, but I shall start with the west front. At the lowest stage of this there are three doorways, the centre of which has been given an inappropriate classical pediment, while the pointed tympana of the side doors carry inferior seventeenth-century low-relief scenes. The next stage harbours a rose-window, above which is a gallery with eight statues of the kings of Castile from Ferdinand I, who assumed the title, to Ferdinand III, the Saint, conqueror of Córdoba and Seville and founder of this church. These parts of the front and the lower stages of the towers are in the French Gothic style of the thirteenth century. The upper stages of the towers along with their spires and the balustrade were added between 1442 and 1458 by Hans of Cologne, otherwise Juan de Colonia, who settled in Burgos and was followed in his profession by his son Simón and his grandson Francisco. The balustrade, in the centre of which is a niche with Virgin and Child, carries carved lettering which reads 'Pulchra est et Decora'. The parapet of the right-hand tower spells 'Pax Vobis' in conjunction with a statue of Jesus; the tower on the left has a statue of Saint John the Baptist and the legend 'Ecce Agnus Dei'. Our best course now is to take the ramp, which rises parallel to the west front across the plaza. As we climb, the rich sixteenth-century octagonal lantern slides into view to the left of the towers and now one begins to get the full measure of Burgos. Despite a building span of over 300 years, the church hangs together extraordinarily well; the parts, whatever their date, work together like some imperishable engine invented never to break down. If a connection with the age of iron seems far-fetched, observe the open ribs of the spires, which almost seem to point a finger towards the Eiffel Tower.

At the top of the ramp is the church of San Nicolás. Turning

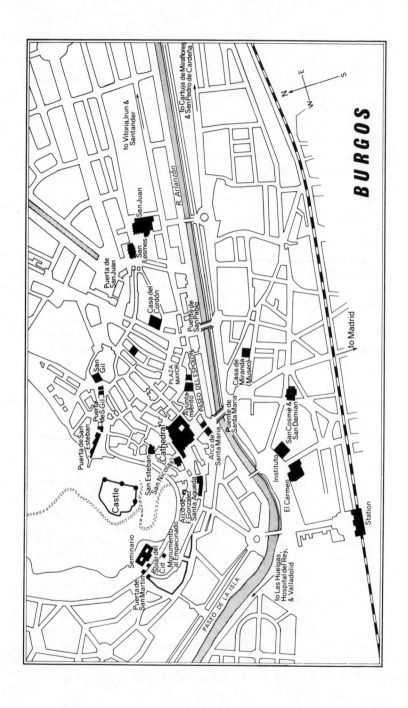

right along the north side of the cathedral we reach the **Puerta de la Coronería** in the north transept face. The tympanum over the door contains Christ with the Virgin and Saint John over a horizontal panel which seems to represent the Church with the saved on the left and the damned (more numerous) on the right, while the lower right-hand scenes of the three archivolts show boiling cauldrons and other salutary horrors. On either side of the doorway (an eighteenth-century modification) are six apostles. The upper part of this façade consists of an open gallery or screen of three main arches, each subdividing into two and then four and sheltering a total of eleven figures. The Puerta de la Coronería is well above the floor level of the transept to which a double staircase descends on the inside. Continuing a few yards, we come to a stone parapet, from which we can survey the chevet with its radial buttresses and the richly decorated extension at the east end called the Capilla del Condestable. This octagon with its tall finials forms the third major element in the interplay of vertical thrusts that is so successful here. A flight of steps leads down to a cobbled yard and we find in front of us a doorway in the eastern face of the north transept at ground level. This is the **Puerta de la Pellejería**, begun by Francisco de Colonia in 1516. Despite the Plateresque framework and the repetitive detail common to the style, the mediaeval formula of figures in the archivolt all moving inwards towards the threatened head-on collision over the doorway is preserved and the bland brutality of the scenes in the upper panels – the decapitation of the Baptist and the martyrdom of Saint John in a pot of boiling oil – come as something of a shock. In the topmost scene of all Bishop Fonseca makes his number with the Virgin. For all the Renaissance mannerisms we have not moved very far from the world of the Puerta de la Coronería, carved over 200 years before. Retreating now as far as the containing wall of the yard allows, we can observe a remarkable ensemble consisting – reading from left to right – of the Capilla del Condestable whose pinnacles, each sheltering four figures under crocketed spires, were completed in 1494 by Simón de Colonia; the chevet, which is the earliest part of the church built between 1222 and 1243; the great lantern built by Juan de Vallejo between 1539 and 1567 to replace Juan de Colonia's structure, which collapsed; the north transept and, finally, the north-west tower. Vallejo's lantern with its two external galleries, corner turrets, Gothic windows, balustrade with silhouetted figures and eight soaring pinnacles, themselves harbouring a further assortment of figures, may sound too much of a good thing, a sort of stone wedding cake. Yet, the masses are firm, the shadows are deep and the details do not distract from the whole.

Continuing round the church and skirting the east wall of the cloister we come to the Calle de la Paloma and turn into a covered walk, which is in fact the lower southern wing of the two-storey cloister. Through grilles opening on to the cloister garden there are fragmentary views of the south side of the church. We emerge from the arcade at the bottom of the steps leading up to the south transept entrance, the **Puerta de Sarmental**, generally considered the finest of them all. To the left of the great doors are Moses and Aaron; to the right Peter and Paul. Immediately over the lintel is a frieze of the twelve apostles sitting and chatting urbanely with books in their hands, as if waiting for a board meeting to begin. The tympanum is enclosed by three archivolts. The inner of these contains kneeling angels, the middle one seated figures including some crowned musicians, while the outermost is devoted to musicians all the way. The whole composition is presided over by Christ dictating his word to the four evangelists accompanied by their symbols; all four write busily though – as we know – with slightly differing results. Two are seated above and one on either side of their master. They work at tall lecterns or desks sloping like draughtsmen's boards. The middle stage of this façade contains a good rose-window with original glass. Above this is an arcaded screen similar to that on the north side, though in this case it shelters thirteen figures, all angels holding candles. These screens have been criticised on the grounds that they rise above the roofs and have no structural role. Yet, the same objection might be voiced against the west front and the gallery of kings and the spires and everything in fact above the high vault, in which case we might as well abandon all interest in or description of Gothic architecture. It seems to me the three main entrances are drawn together by their screens, built round the figure – be it human, angelic or divine – which is an integral part of the building up to and including the highest pinnacle of all.

The cathedral was founded by Ferdinand III and his Bishop, Maurice. On July 20th, 1221, the first stone was laid. Nine years later the first mass was said. The first impression inside is not one of huge size, as at Seville or even Toledo. There are six nave bays to the crossing with a single aisle on either side. Each transept is of three bays. The sanctuary, occupying three bays beyond the crossing, is surrounded by an ambulatory with chapels, the most important being the Capilla del Condestable on the main axis. A completely uniform triforium circles nave, transepts and sanctuary. The clerestory windows do not admit a great deal of light on a grey northern day but the southern rose-window helps the transepts and the lantern looks after the crossing. The horizontal and vertical articulation is interesting. Under the triforium balustrade a continuous moulding runs round the nave and over the engaged columns of the piers, still, so to speak, tying them down. At the next stage, however, the horizontal moulding above the triforium arches is overrun by the ascending columns, which pass on unimpeded to the capitals from which the main vault springs. This vault is not breath-takingly high but the victory of verticality is cleverly assured.

The choir, crossing and sanctuary form virtually a church within a church. To visit them one must apply to the sacristan. The age of Charles V was just as given to lavish emblems as that of Ferdinand and Isabel and the inside of the lantern is no less rich than its outer casing. The four huge piers and the balustrades are garnished with shields. The Plateresque habit of carving the surfaces of the columns themselves with patterns resembling the chasing of silver overspills on to the columns of the arches surrounding the high altar. The interior completion date of 1550 is given. In marked contrast to this sophisticated canopy a simple marble slab in the floor immediately underneath covers the remains of Rodrigo Díaz de Vivar, el Cid Campeador, protagonist of the twelfth-century *Poema del Cid* and vassal of Alfonso VI of Castile and León, who exiled him to fame and fortune in Valencia, where he died in 1099 to become Spanish national hero number one. He is a comparative newcomer to this site. For over seven centuries after his death he lay with his wife in the monastery of San Pedro de Cardeña. Then came the Peninsular War. The French rifled the tomb, as was their wont, and took some of the relics. The rest were handed back to the populace by General Thibault in 1809. After the defeat of Napoleon these were recovered by the monks but with the expropriation of the monasteries in 1836 they were again brought to town and kept in the city hall for more than 80 years. In 1921 the then Archbishop offered his cathedral as 'the finest setting for the finest jewel' and on the seventh centenary of the founding of the church, el Cid and his wife, attended by Alfonso XIII and the highest dignitaries of the land, were resettled in their present resting place – minus one of the warrior's bones retained in a casket by the corporation.

To the west of the crossing is the **Coro** or choir, occupying two bays. The upper and lower stalls on gospel and epistle sides were made between 1505 and 1509 by the Burgundian Felipe de Vigarni assisted by Andrés de Nájera. The panels above the seats are carved in low relief in a transitional Gothic-Renaissance style – some of the scenes are noticeably flat with sharp facial profiles, while others are more rounded in form and agitated in feeling. The seats, back-rests and misericords are of walnut inlaid with grotesque scenes in paler wood. The archbishop's stall with the Rape of Europa was completed in 1583; the remaining stalls facing east were added in 1610. The organ on the epistle side was made in 1636 and the other in 1806. In the centre of the choir on a modern plinth lies the copper and gilt effigy of the co-founder, Bishop Maurice, who died in 1238. Pillow, mitre and other parts are enamelled in the Limousin style of about 1260. The **Capilla Mayor** or sanctuary to the east of the crossing has a retablo made by Rodrigo and Martín de la Haya between 1562 and 1580. The reverse face of the wall behind a high altar and giving on to an ambulatory is called the *trasaltar*. In this case it is carved with three stone panels by Felipe de Vigarni (there are five all told but the outer two are eighteenth-century). On the left of the scene showing Christ leaving the Holy City carrying the Cross is a mannered Renaissance pilaster, though the same panel includes a traditional piece of Gothic landscape carving in the top right corner. The damage to the other two panels is not due to human malevolence but to a disease of the soft Briviesca stone. Turning our backs on the Burgundian's work, we face the rounded arch and lavishly adorned entrance of the Constable's chapel. This opening provides the setting for a fine wrought-iron screen of 1522 by Cristóbal de Andino. By now the amiable sacristan has come with his ever-clinking bunch of keys and we are allowed in.

The **Capilla del Condestable** was added to the cathedral by Don Pedro Fernández de Velasco, Constable of Castile, and his wife Doña Mencia de Mendoza, daughter of the Marquis of Santillana. The interior was begun in 1482 and completed in 1491 by Simón de Colonia, who had succeeded his father as master of works. On the inside of the entrance piers are two delightful figures, one on each side, representing the Annunciation; below them are savage supporters holding shields. The first overall impression is of height and light. The vault is octagonal. The vaulting ribs intersect just above the vestigial capitals and soar up to burst into an eight-pointed star, whose central nexus of tracery is filled not with masonry but glass. There are vertical pairs of windows but these have not been run together as in the English Perpendicular style, which developed about the same time. The twelve main shafts are carved with canopied figures of the twelve apostles not far above their bases – all the stone figures are by the last great Gothic carver, Gil de Siloe. The lower wall panels bear the huge inclined shields of Velasco and Mendoza, which are repeated upright on a slightly smaller scale on the balustrade. This is an age of tireless heraldry.

The main altar retablo, made between 1523 and 1526, is a joint work by Felipe de Vigarni and Diego de Siloe, son of Gil, with colouring by León Picardo. The Gothic compartment formula has been rejected in favour of three main areas. A canopy with three scenes from the Passion extends over a recessed area, as it were a stage for the main scene, which is the Presentation in the Temple. The group of the Holy Family is by Diego de Siloe and that of the priests by the Burgundian. Underneath this is a predella, whose left-hand scene is a very beautiful Italianate Annunciation by Diego. The canopy is flanked by figures representing the Christian and Jewish Churches (the latter blindfolded) and the structure is topped off by a free-standing Cavalry. The design of the whole is bold and clear, while the figures have not yet fallen into the bad taste we shall find in the School of Valladolid. On the epistle side is a small Gothic retablo by Gil de Siloe, finished after his death by his son. Diego again collaborates with Vigarni in a Plateresque retablo on the gospel side. The walls of the chapel contain some fine tombs but one's attention is first claimed by the sepulchres of the founders facing the main altar. The unchipped Carrara marble, the firm property-owning visages, the relaxed hands, Doña Mencia's lap-dog, the two pairs of feet resting firmly on descriptive slabs, all combine to give an enviable impression of earthly substance and celestial peace. How different were the plain stone or wooden caskets of the early Castilian notables and kings! The author is unknown. The adjacent block of jasper weighing 40 tons was designed to take the tomb of the fourth Constable of the same line but remains unoccupied, as he is buried at Medina del Pomar.

Returning to the west end, let us now consider the side-chapels, starting on the epistle side. (Perhaps I should clarify here that the epistle side of a church is the right-hand side facing the altar and the gospel side is the left.) First comes the Capilla del Santísimo Cristo built in a wing of the old cloister. The much-venerated image is gruesome. Next is the tall **Capilla de la Presentación** occupying two chapel bays and built to designs by Felipe de Vigarni between 1519 and 1522. The octagonal lantern with Gothic tracery is raised high on double squinches at the four corners, an arrangement we shall see repeated elsewhere. The finely profiled tomb of the founder is by Vigarni himself. After this is the Capilla de San Juan de Sahagún, leading to the Relicario. Entering the south transept we come on the right to the **Capilla de la Visitación** by Juan de Colonia, who is buried in it with his wife under a slab near the entrance. Occupying the centre is the tomb of the founder, Bishop Alonso de Cartagena, by Gil de Siloe. In the rear wall there is an attractive relief of the Virgin sheltering the Carthusians under her mantle; beneath is the tomb of Garci Ruiz de la Mata, d. 1400. Across the transept from this chapel is the late thirteenth-century **Portal del Claustro** or cloister door. On the left jamb is a lovely two-figure Annunciation. The carved wooden doors are by Gil de Siloe – the two upper panels show Christ entering Jerusalem and Christ in Hades. Also opening off this transept is the seventeenth-century chapel of San Enrique. Entering the ambulatory, we come to the **Sacristía Nueva** of 1765 with an oval cupola supporting a hexagonal lantern. This is the head-quarters of the genial sacristan, Julián Pérez López, who holds all the keys of this kingdom. In the anteroom is a lighted brazier at hand-warming height, said not to have been let out for three centuries. Don Julián, who is also a poet, has some pleasant verses on this subject – and on others in connection with the cathedral.

A door leads from here into the **Claustro**, in fact the upper cloister. Built between 1290 and 1324, this now acts as a museum of sculpture. Immediately on our right, in the second arch of the north wing, are the delightful figures of Saint Ferdinand offering a nuptial ring to Beatrice of Swabia, who daintily extends her hand to receive it. In the fifth arch is the stone figure of Bishop Maurice, removed owing to the buffetings of time from the central pillar of the Puerta de Sarmental (his replacement there is a modern copy). Continuing to the left, we turn into the east wing, whose first arch contains the door of the **Capilla de San Juan Bautista** or **Nuevo Tesoro**, containing the Cathedral's collection of tapestries and vestments. In the next arch is the tomb of Gaspar de Illescas by Diego de Siloe (1529) and in the fourth the entrance to the **Capilla de Santa Catalina**, housing the rest of the *tesoro*. Spanish cathedral 'treasures' can be tedious, for the paintings are often of poor quality and church plate is not to everyone's taste. Here the walls are hung with standard portraits of bishops. There are six good gold-plated chalices, three Gothic and three Renaissance. Among the documents is the *carta de arras* or marriage contract of the Cid with Jimena, dated 1074. In the sixth arch of the same wing we find the **Capilla de Corpus Cristi**, which contains a chest known as El Cofre del Cid. This is one of the two chests, the story goes, that the Cid and Martín Antolínez filled with sand and stones and delivered to the Jews Raquel and Vidas as security for a loan of 600 gold marks. The occasion was the banishment of the Cid by Alfonso VI on suspicion that he had kept more than his due share of the tribute he was sent to collect from Seville. The author of the famous poem conveys through Martín Antolínez that the hero had never sullied his hands with ill-gotten gold and that his exile was really due to the machinations of his enemies. However, the Cid is astute enough – this side of his character is much admired – to allow the Jews to think the imputation true, ergo there must be illicit gains too heavy for him to take into exile. They agree not to open the chests for a year. By this time the Cid is well embarked on the successful campaign that led him to the conquest of Valencia. Alvar Fáñez is later sent to the monastery of Cardeña to bring his lord's wife and daughters safely to the conquered city. He delivers 500 marks to the abbot and spends another 500 on equipping the ladies for the journey but when the Jews apply to him for their due they are simply told by Alvar that he will bring the matter to the great man's attention. The poem never reverts to the subject. Popular opinion insists that the Cid redeemed his fraudulent pledge.

The staircase in this chapel leads up to the archive of Fray Martín de la Haya. Under the stairs is the door into the **Sala Capitular**, an unusually small chapter-house by the said Martín with Flemish tapestries and some paintings – the most attractive is a red-robed Virgin of the School of Memling. The ceiling shows continuing attachment to Moorish decoration. The third and fourth wings of the cloister contain a number of Gothic and Plateresque tombs; the best are to be found in the third, fourth and sixth arches on the south side and the second on the west. Stone and wood sculpture of varying interest is also displayed. The carvings of the four corners of the cloister itself should not be overlooked.

Returning to the ambulatory, we come to the last chapel on the epistle side, the large and luminous **Capilla de Santiago** built by Juan de Vallejo between 1525 and 1534. Divided only by a partition wall from the Baptist's chapel, where we saw the vestments, this is used as a parish church and nearly always open. Some of the monumental sculpture, notably the tomb of an abbot of San Quirce, is by Vallejo himself. Passing the Capilla del Condestable and following the ambulatory back towards the west, we pass three chapels not usually shown to the public. These are devoted to Saint Gregory, the Annunciation and the Nativity. The latter is a fusion of two older chapels with an oval dome and lantern by Martín de la Haya. We come next to a sepulchre in the ambulatory wall, that of Archdeacon Villegas by Simón de Colonia, after which we emerge into the north transept. On the right is the **Capilla de San Nicolás**, finished in 1230, the oldest in the cathedral. The transept is dominated by the famous **Escalera Dorada**, a double gilded iron staircase designed by Diego de Siloe in 1519 to connect the Puerta de la Coronería with the much lower transept floor. Every good Burgalese stoutly maintains that it served as model for the grand stairs of the Paris Opera, which resemble it not at all. After the transept the next chapel to the west is the **Capilla de la Concepción** by Simón de Colonia between 1477 and 1478, uniting two earlier chapels. In the centre is the Plateresque tomb of the founder, Bishop Luis Osorio de Acuna (d. 1495), executed by Diego de Siloe in 1519. The tomb of Archdeacon Bernardo Diez (d. 1492) is still totally Gothic. The big retablo of the genealogy of Christ is by Gil de Siloe. It is less tightly packed than some of his work and the family tree imparts a unity to the branches but the work suffers from a perfectly horrible job of glossy recolouring done in 1870. Next and last is the **Capilla de Santa Tecla** built on the site of no fewer than four earlier chapels by Alberto de Churriguera, younger brother of José, between 1731 and 1736. The retablo is a vulgar effusion of the taste of the time. In the triforium of the nave bay nearest this chapel is the **Papamoscas**, a grotesque painted mannikin whose right hand rings the clock tower bell on the hours; the quarters are rung by his secretary, a smaller figure beside him. This smacks of German humour and is probably a minor expression of nostalgia for their homeland on the part of the Colonias. The **Trascoro** or outer shell of the choir, round which we have circled, should finally be mentioned. It was ordered in 1646 and contains some canvases by Fray Juan Rizzi (c. 1659). Near the west end of the trascoro is an entirely functional floor grille, made in Paris. Through this hot air rises from the central heating system and on cold days the reverend canons can be seen to pause and warm their lower regions on this spot, while the warm current gently lifts and spreads their cassocks like budding wings which, when fully grown and spread, will waft them up to Heaven.

The parish churches of Burgos, the civil buildings and the museum can easily take up another couple of days, so I shall give preference to the three monastic foundations which no one should miss. The first is the **Real Monasterio de las Huelgas** 1½ km from the town centre – take the Valladolid road and follow the signs. *Huelgas* are industrial strikes in modern Spanish; in those days they meant leisure and the site was occupied by a royal country house. Here in 1187 Alfonso VIII and his Queen, Eleanor of England, founded a monastery for Cistercian nuns of noble blood, endowing it with great rents and privileges – the abbess had all the powers of a great feudal lord, including that of life and death. Visits are accompanied by one of the cultured young ladies trained by the Patrimonio Nacional, to whom I shall leave the detailed description. Church and tower are in the severe transitional Gothic style of the Cistercians. We enter by what was once a transept door. The full effect of the church is lost as nave and aisles are sealed off from the crossing by a partition decorated in the centre with a fresco of the battle of Las Navas de Tolosa (1212), by which Alfonso secured the main pass into Andalusia. The gospel side aisle is bare except for royal family tombs. Even royal remains were still consigned to plain caskets in the twelfth and thirteenth centuries. There is no question yet of elaborate effigies. There is hardly any carving except for the tiny scenes on the triangular ends of the coffin lids and the side panels of the little stone coffin of Leonor, daughter of the founders, who died at 11 months. A painted box was thought good enough for Fernando de la Cerda (d. 1275), son of Alfonso X. Crossing the Capilla de Ana de Austria, occupying the west end of the nave, we come to the epistle side aisle, called the Nave de San Juan with more plain tombs, mainly of noble abbesses and nuns – these were all whitewashed after their profanation by the French in the Peninsular War. We are finally allowed into the nave which is closed by a Renaissance retablo with a very charming Last Supper in a square recess. The retablo is crowned by an unusual free-standing Descent from the Cross of the thirteenth century. Facing this are the royal caskets, on crouching lions, of Alfonso VIII and Eleanor, flanked by those of Blanca, daughter of Alonso of Portugal and Berengaria, daughter of the founder and mother of Saint Ferdinand. Hers is the only adult coffin whose flanks and lid are fully carved with low-relief stone figures.

After the church comes the Gothic cloister, whose arcade has been walled in. Opening off this is the elegant **Sala Capitular**, whose capital blocks have never been carved. Among the 'treasures' are a Moorish standard taken at Las Navas and various pennants from Lepanto. There is also a wooden figure of Santiago, the patron saint of Spain, whose sword arm could be mechanically raised and lowered; his job was to knight monarchs who could not be dubbed by human hand. Also off the cloister is the **Museo de Telas**, the fabric museum, whose exhibits all come from the royal tombs opened by the French in search of gold and precious stones. There remain the delightful **Claustrillas**, a Romanesque cloister of the time of the founders with twinned columns topped by acanthus capitals so elongated that they resemble tall curling feathers. The **Capilla Mudéjar** in the style of the Almohad dynasty acts as a little museum of oddments, including items of Mudéjar carpentry.

From Las Huelgas the tower is visible of the **Hospital del Rey**, also founded by Alfonso VIII as a hostelry for pilgrims on the road to Compostela. This is easily reached on foot across the stretch of park called El Parral. The **Puerta de Romeros**, the forecourt and the atrium of the church all in the Renaissance style, have little to do with the pilgrim age but earlier times are recalled by the profusion of conches and a statue of Santiago on horseback, while even the low-relief warriors' heads sprout from conch-style medallions. Behind are two or three sprawling yards with low houses, which still give an idea of the pilgrims' lodging quarters.

A slightly longer excursion is necessary to the **Cartuja de Miraflores** and San Pedro de Cardeña. The first of these is reached by following the south bank of the river Arlanzón for some 3 km through the wooded area called El Paseo de la Quinta. This Carthusian convent was founded on the site of a hunting lodge by John II, father of Isabel the Catholic. The aisleless church is frankly disappointing; the later lining makes the Gothic vault appear to spring from a classical cornice running round the whole church – an unsuccessful combination. But the contents are of great interest. Following Carthusian custom, the church is divided into four zones. First comes a narthex or antechamber for the profane, followed by the lay brothers' choir with stalls in the Renaissance style by Simón de Bueras (1558). This leads into the priests' choir – here we find stalls of very delicate Gothic tracery with few figurative elements made about 1489 by Martín Sánchez, whose work we shall find again at Oña and in Santo Tomás of Avila. Finally we reach the sanctuary, which is remarkable for three major works by Gil de Siloe. John II – with his wife Isabel of Portugal – is the only monarch of the Trastamara line missing from the Capilla de Reyes Nuevos in Toledo Cathedral; the reason is that he had ordered for himself at Miraflores one of the most splendid Gothic tombs ever carved. Sadly, its perfection is marred by a good deal of minor damage. Coarser works may gain something from the buffets of history but here every nose or finger-tip lacking is to be regretted. The originality of the ground plan lies in the imposition of a diamond on a square. At the points of the diamond the evangelists recline at ease with their symbols and keep watch over the exquisite effigies of John and his wife, who are separated by a railing of crested tracery. There is a multitude of other figures, while lions both heraldic and natural gambol round the base.

Also by the genius Gil is the tomb surmounted by the kneeling figure of the Infante Don Alonso, brother of Isabel the Catholic, whose early death at seventeen opened the way for his sister to the throne. Some of the little angels of the canopy tumbling among the grape-clusters are almost devilish. Gothic carving has reached its highest pitch of ripeness and, dabbling with the revival of pagan themes, trembles on the brink of decadence – from which it is just restrained in this case by the precision of the master, who has included himself as an artisan with spectacles on nose and set-square in hand in the left-hand panel of the sarcophagus. Even after these works the great wooden, stuccoed, painted and gilded retablo might still be accounted Gil's masterpiece – if it were not so complex that it requires lingering study before it yields all its riches. In a preface to the 1908 Baedeker Professor Carl Justi, while on the subject of Gothic retablos, judges that 'an examination of the details is fatiguing; the artists have not divorced themselves from forms evolved for use in spaces of more modest dimensions; the desired amplitude is attained by the mere multiplication of units.' This is certainly true in many cases. Possibly it is true here, though the great central garland with the crucified Christ and the subsidiary garlands give the work a certain breadth of design; also there are such extenuating passages as the lovely sword-bearing Saint Catherine on the predella and the pelican in its pride savaging its breast to feed its young above the head of Christ, whose sacrifice this action symbolizes. And, then, when one thinks of the vulgar showmanship and flatulent mannerisms that are soon to accompany the clearer framework, larger figures and 'desired amplitude' of Renaissance and Baroque retablos, one sometimes yearns for the 'mere multiplication of units' – particularly when they are carved with the taste, feeling and loving care of execution that one can savour here.

It is 6 km from the Cartuja, taking the left fork after the village of Cardeñajimeno, to the **Monasterio de San Pedro de Cardeña**, already mentioned in connection with the Cid. This is where his wife Jimena lived under the protection of the monks during his exile and where she brought his body back from Valencia for burial, joining him five years later. The tall airy church of the fifteenth century, restored in 1950, incorporates the Romanesque tower that the Cid knew and one arm of the cloister preserves columns and capitals that were in position before his time. The warrior and his lady lay first in front of the high altar; then they were moved to the 'Chapel of Heroes' where they continued until their removal to the town. Despite the empty tomb I think one gets more of a feeling of the Cid and his times at Cardeña than in the richer setting of the Cathedral or from his romantic equestrian statue facing the bridge of San Pablo over the river. In these monuments the search for truth about the man has become subordinate to the myth-making necessities of a race.

The facts, as far as they are known, of the Cid's life are these. Rodrigo Díaz de Vivar was born not later than 1043 to a family of minor nobility. He is first mentioned in a charter of Ferdinand I in 1064. He then distinguished himself in the service of Ferdinand's son, Sancho of Castile, against Sancho of Navarre, gaining his title *el Campeador* in single-handed combat with the latter's champion. *El Cid* is simply a corruption of the Arabic for lord. Having assisted King Sancho in depriving his brother Alfonso of the throne of León, the Cid later forced Alfonso to swear he had 'neither art nor part' in Sancho's death in dubious circumstances under the walls of Zamora in 1072 (cf. p. 198). Alfonso's animosity was thus doubly assured. In 1074 the Cid married Jimena, daughter of the Count of Oviedo. When sent to collect tribute from Mutamid, the Moorish King of Seville, he helped this monarch to defeat Abdullah, King of Granada, in whose ranks were many Christian knights. Among those on the losing side was Count Garci Ordoñez, who later denounced the Cid to Alfonso for keeping back part of the Sevillian tribute. Whether done out of pique or on good grounds, this was sufficient to secure the warrior's banishment.

The Cid then became a pure soldier of fortune – Baedeker's description of him as 'a courageous but cruel and faithless condottiere' is probably not far off the mark – fighting under Christian and Moorish masters alike. For eight years he served Moktadir, Moorish King of Zaragoza. Even in the poem, which whitewashes its hero, one of his staunchest allies is Abengalón, Lord of Molina in Aragon. In 1094 after a siege of nine months he succeeded in taking Valencia from the Almorávides with an army of 7000 men, mainly Moors; the conditions of the surrender were in the main violated. Although the poem, written more than half a century after the events, stresses the Cid's ultimate loyalty to King Alfonso, there is no suggestion he should hand over Valencia to his royal master – on the contrary it is firmly stated that he has conquered it for himself and his family. And there are strong indications throughout the poem that he accepts the co-existence of the two faiths as inevitable, almost desirable. After all, if there were no Muslim presence in the peninsula, where would the source of honour and riches be? There is nothing to indicate that he was in any sense a crusader. In 1099 his favourite lieutenant, Alvar Fañez, was severely defeated by the Almorávides at Cuenca and in the same year the hero died. His widow managed to hold on to Valencia for another three years before abandoning it and taking her husband's body to Cardeña. An extraordinary footnote is provided by Philip II's earnest attempt to secure the canonisation of this great guerrilla leader, who burned churches and mosques with equal zest; this was not surprisingly rejected by the Vatican.

It remains to speak of Babieca, his horse. According to the cathedral sacristan, who got the story from an old inhabitant of the place, the Cid once went to Vivar, his ancestral property, to choose a horse. While he was there a great storm broke and all the horses on the common turned their rumps towards the driving wind and rain except one. 'Turn your tail like the rest, Babieca,' yelled the herdsman but the Cid said, 'If he can face a storm like this, he'll be all right in battle. I'll have him.' This is in direct contradiction to the poem, which specifically states that he won his mount in an encounter with the Moorish King of Seville and showed him off to Jimena during the celebrations of her arrival in Valencia. It is not beyond the bounds of possibility that there were several Babiecas, as men tend to get through war-horses rather quickly. Be that as it may, the Babieca of the time of the Cid's death was brought to Cardeña and in due course buried there. In 1951, at the instance of the Duke of Alba, a memorial stone was erected in the forecourt on the supposed site. It is inscribed with lines 3515 et seq. of the poem, in which the hero offers the animal to his King, who rejects the gift on the grounds that master and mount make an invincible pair against the infidel.

The city of Burgos to the north of the river can now be covered by a single itinerary, which can easily be broken and resumed at any point, for the distances are not great. Let us start at the **Puente de San Pablo**, adorned with eight modern statues of those closely associated with the Cid. They are, crossing from north to south on the right: Jimena with a dove; San Sisibuto, Abbot of Cardeña, Abengalón, Lord of Molina; Don Jerónimo, Bishop of Valencia. Recrossing from south to north, also on the right are: Alvar Fañez, the Cid's nephew; Martín Muñoz, Count of Coimbra; Martín Antolínez, who brought off the deal with the Jews, complete with one of the chests; and finally Diego Rodríguez, the hero's son, of whom we hear very little except that he was killed in battle at the age of twenty. The carving is in a chunky, simplistic style not much to be admired. Facing the bridge on the north is the bronze equestrian statue of the warrior with flowing beard, wind-tossed cloak, extended sword and straining horse. The eulogistic legend underneath is taken from an Arab historian.

Taking the street signposted to Santander and then the first on the right, we come to the **Casa del Cordón**, remarkable only for the Gothic façade with a hefty Franciscan girdle and tassel motif framing the main entrance. To the left of the door is a plaque whose inscription tells us that, in the house of the Constables of Castile, the Catholic Sovereigns received Christopher Columbus on his return from his second voyage to the New World, confirming him in all his privileges. This took place on April 23rd, 1497. Leaving this house on the left and taking Calle de la Puebla we come to the **Puerta de San Juan,** one of the gateways in the town walls. Beyond the gate a bridge takes us across the Vena, a tributary of the Arlanzón, to an open plaza on the left of which is the church of **San Lesmes** of the fourteenth and fifteenth centuries containing the sepulchre of this saint. On the opposite side is the 'Casa de la Cultura' with a late fifteenth-century doorway set in a modern institutional façade like an elaborate keyhole to a very plain box. Facing towards the bridge is the ruined monastery church of **San Juan**, through which we reach a sixteenth-century cloister, whose upper gallery contains a permanent exhibition of the works of Marcelo Santamaria, a Burgalese painter who died in 1952. Returning through the gate, we take Calle San Juan all the way to the Plaza de Alonso Martínez, where the Captain-General of the Region has his headquarters. From the corner formed by the grandly named one-star Hotel Norte y Londres, Calle San Lorenzo leads to the standard Baroque church devoted to Saint Lawrence. In this part of the town the older houses are encased by glassed-in balconies, usually running from the top to the bottom of the front, to capture the sun on the cold bright days of the long Burgos winter. Leaving the plaza, we take Calle Avellanos, at the end of which we turn right and immediately right again to find a flight of steps bordered by large urns leading up to the church of **San Gil**. This is of plain construction in the Burgalese Gothic style of the fourteenth century. The main features of interest are inside. Off the gospel side aisle we find the **Capilla de la Natividad** whose octagonal Gothic vault raised on fluted squinches is strongly reminiscent of that of La Presentación in the Cathedral. The tomb and kneeling effigy of Don Jerónimo de Castro were carved in 1556 by Juan de Vallejo. In the transept on this side is the **Capilla del Santísimo Cristo**, whose image was brought to Burgos in 1267; venerated by many as a superior Santísimo to the Cathedral's, it is drowned in a morbid purple artificial light inside a nineteenth-century gilt aedicule. The nave and aisles terminate in square-ended chapels. To the left of the sanctuary is the **Capilla de la Buena Mañana** with a small uncluttered retablo attributed to Gil de Siloe – the poorer churches could afford fewer figures, often with happier results. In the equivalent position on the epistle side is the better lit **Capilla de los Reyes** with a very similar retablo. The church is rich in interesting tombs, among them a number of effigies made of slate except for the marble faces, an innovation that appears to have been brought to Burgos by the Colonias.

Next to the church is the **Puerta de San Gil**, a gatehouse whose tunnel pierces the wall near the bottom of the steps. From this point Calle del Pilar leads back to the city centre but the steeply sloping Calle Hospital de los Ciegos presents more of a challenge. A little way up this on the right is a roughly-stepped path climbing to another gate, the **Puerta de San Esteban**. This area is not very well 'fixed-up' for tourists but it is worth the scramble. At the top we find the gatehouse, another tunnel supported in this case by four brick horseshoe arches and topped off by a brick gallery on the inner side and flanked by two stone towers. While churches went Gothic in the thirteenth and fourteenth centuries, fortifications and gates in particular often remained Mudéjar, using either pointed or horseshoe arches or a combination of both. From here part of the old wall stretches up the hill towards the remaining stumps of the castle towers. Skirting the base of the hill we follow a rough street slightly downwards towards the church of **San Esteban**, owner of a sturdy tower that overtops the cathedral spires when seen from the south. From the outside the fabric has a battered air. Against one flank cluster ramshackle houses and women come for their water to an old pump in front of these. The west door, handsome in its day, is badly damaged. Inside, however, all is in good trim. The west bay of the nave has a choir gallery with an openwork balustrade and corner tribunes like a pair of pulpits. The organ loft and tomb of the López de Gumiel family are by Nicolás de Vergara, an exponent of the precious early Plateresque style. On the epistle side are the rich monumental altar and tombs of Rodrigo de Frías and his wife, topped by a fine Flagellation of *c*. 1505–1510, possibly by Francisco de Colonia. By contrast, a modest well-designed double arch of *c*. 1570 with an altar in the left half and door in the right leads us out into the cloister. From San Esteban it is five minutes' walk up to the remnants of the castle, once the stronghold of the independent Count Fernán González. Gutted by fire in 1736, the fortifications were still sufficiently intact for the French to defend them successfully against the English in 1812. If the day is not too hot, the climb is worth while for the views over cathedral and city. The descent can then be made by stepped path leading to the **Arco de Fernán González**, a triumphal arch erected under Philip II to the founder of Castile. If the decision is against the climb, we continue downwards by Calle Pozo which brings us out under the north-west tower of the Cathedral. We can now visit the church of **San Nicolás** at the head of the ramp which rises from the Plaza de Santa Maria. (Climbers should also revert to this point.) In the wall facing the entrance are three tombs with slate figures of the Maluenda-Miranda family, all sheltered under an immensely wide canopy. The high altar retablo attributed to Simón de Colonia and Gil de Siloe is dedicated to the titular saint and includes scenes from his life among a profusion of other detail. Much worse lit than its fellow at Miraflores and more crowded, it fails to make the impact its admirable carving deserves and falls sadly into the category condemned in Baedeker.

Descending the ramp from San Nicolás and turning right at the bottom, we come to the street and church of **Santa Agueda**. With a single nave and a Plateresque tomb facing the entrance, this church is of little artistic interest but some fame as the place in which the Cid forced Alfonso VI to swear he had 'neither art nor part' in the death of his elder brother, King Sancho, in dubious circumstances under the walls of Zamora (see p. 198). By this death Alfonso, freed from exile in Toledo, gained Castile and León. When so required by the Cid (who had started his career in Sancho's service) he duly swore the oath of non-complicity but this according to the sacristan was 'the sardine that broke the donkey's back' and was more than enough, along with the imputation of fraud over the Sevillian tribute, to secure the Cid's exile. Skirting the west end of Santa Agueda, it is only a short way to the Arco de Fernán González, from which a walk leads west under the large modern seminary. A little before this on the left is an obelisk commemorating 'the modern Cid', Juan Martín Díez, el Empecinado, a famous guerrilla leader of the Peninsular War. Beneath the seminary terrace on the right we find the memorial erected in 1784 to mark the site of the Cid's town house. The inscription claims he was born here in 1026, though the more accepted date is 1043 and Vivar also claims him as her son. Hard by stands the **Puerta de San Martín**, another brick-vaulted tunnel with four horseshoe arches of the same period as the Puerta de San Esteban. From here we can either return to the cathedral or, passing through the gate, make our way south towards the pleasant Paseo de la Isla along the river. Following the north bank towards the east we eventually regain the Arco de Santa Maria. The **Paseo del Espolón**, which commences here, is always enjoyable in fine weather. Strolling along it towards the Puente de San Pablo, we find on the left an outlet formed by a triple arcade, which takes us under the unpretentious **Ayuntamiento** of 1788 into the Plaza Mayor, which is shaped like a pear and completely surrounded by a shopping arcade. Returning to the Espolón, we pass the Círculo de la Unión, the main club in a style resembling the Trocadero in London. The ladies in the windows are usually provided with coffee and cakes but the gentlemen sit for hours without anything, disdain for vulgar consumption written into every fold of their features. The larger-than-life statues of kings and saints along the river side of the walk, put up under Charles III, belong to the same series which graces some public walks in Madrid, rejected on grounds of weight from the balustrade of the royal palace.

Burgos on the cathedral side of the river has now been covered. Apart from the archaeological museum there is little of interest on the south bank. However, the three-star Hostal Asubio in Calle Carmen is a good place to stay (comfortable rooms, hot baths, ample parking, no restaurant) and anyone who puts up there must pass the **Instituto**, a girls' high school designed as a hospital and completed in 1565 by Juan de Vallejo. The other end of Calle Carmen is crossed by the railway tracks, beyond which on the left is the convent church of **Santa Dorotea** with a late Gothic tomb of the royal chaplain Alonso de Ortega (d. 1501) and a Plateresque one for the first Bishop of Almería by Nicolás de Vergara (1516). Passing the Instituto and turning right up Calle de la Concepcion, we find the sympathetic church of **Santos Cosmé y Damián** (that unbeatable team of miracle-making medicos) built between the thirteenth and fifteenth centuries with a later doorway by Vallejo.

The **Museo Arqueológico** is installed in the Casa de Miranda in the street of the same name. This house is a typical sixteenth-century mansion of the region with severe exterior and patio surrounded by lower and upper galleries. Both stages are supported on fluted columns with composite bracket-capitals, a peculiarity of Spanish Renaissance architecture. On the ground-floor, rooms I to III contain local findings of the Hispano-Roman period. The lower gallery contains more of this art along with shields and doorways from demolished houses in the town. Room V with a Gothic vault displays some important tombs, among them that of the kneeling Juan de Padilla, page to Isabel the Catholic, in alabaster by Gil de Siloe; also those of Maria Manuel by Simón de Colonia, of Gómez Manríquez and his wife by Francisco de Colonia and of Antonio Sarmental by Juan de Vallejo (1548). And the fourteenth-century walnut effigies, more than life size, of a knight and his lady are impressive. The staircase to the upper gallery is framed by a handsome Plateresque arch with angels swinging on swags in the archivolt. On the first floor room VII has a fine figured Arabic casket of 1026 bound in copper and enamel. Room VIII contains a copper altar front of the twelfth century from Santo Domingo de Silos – the semi-precious stones and some of the enamel plaques are missing. Room IX is devoted to Gothic stone-carving and room X to processional crosses. Rooms XI to XXII are occupied by a rather indifferent collection of painting, of which the leading lights are Pedro Berruguete, Lucás Jordán, Carducho, Mateo Cerezo and il Guercino. A primitive water-colour of Burgos, done in 1802, shows much of the castle still standing. On the topmost floor rooms XXII to XXVIII contain interesting items of Palaeontology, Bronze and Iron Age objects, Hispano-Roman artefacts, Visigothic and Mozarabic stone carving and (room XXVII) a good collection of late Roman bronze vessels, pottery and glass. Rooms XXX to XXXII exhibit modern and contemporary painting that need detain no one. Room XXXIII provides a progress report on the work of the team investigating the cave of Ojo de Guareña in the north of the province.

Burgos – Briviesca – Oña – Frías – Trespaderne – Medina del Pomar – Villarcayo – Valdenoceda – Vivar del Cid – Burgos

This excursion joins the route described on p. 109 from Bilbao to Villarcayo. We leave Burgos on NI for **Briviesca**, a quiet town, self-styled capital of the cereal region of the Bureba. The octagonal church of **Santa Clara** has a fine retablo in natural walnut begun by Diego Guillén in 1526. In the central panel is an ingenious representation of Jesse's tree. From here we take the road marked to Cornudilla and pause at the hamlet of Terrazos, whose sturdy little church on its cropped grass platform dominates the whole Bureba plain. Just beyond the next village, Los Barrios, stands a tiny Romanesque chapel, the apse of a once larger church with a belfry added at a later date. At Cornudilla we join N232, which leads to **Oña**, our main objective. This ancient town is built in a narrow cleft carrying the river Oca. A monastery was founded in 1011 by Sancho García, Count of Castile. Vestiges of the eleventh-century church are to be seen in the windows of the west façade, in front of which is a screen with niches containing curious truncated figures, the top halves of old sepulchral effigies turned into busts. A fifteenth-century Gothic-Mudéjar door opens into a narthex under the choir. The long nave contains restored murals of the thirteenth and fourteenth centuries, also a twelfth-century Crucifixion (following the norm in Romanesque carving, Christ's feet are nailed separately, not together), while in the first recess on the gospel side is the exquisite Italianate tomb of Bishop Pedro López de Mendoza of c. 1550. The ample crossing by Juan de Colonia, built between 1479 and 1495, spans a square of 20 m and contains an exceptional series of 100 choir stalls all of Gothic tracery without figures by the same Martín Sánchez we have met at Miraflores.

This remarkable church is also the pantheon of the early counts and kings of Castile. On the right of the high altar are the wooden coffins, some carved, others inlaid, of the grandchildren and great-grandchildren of Fernán González, whose independence from León became effective about 950. On the left nearest the outer wall lies the Infante García, son of Alfonso VII. Then come Doña Mayor, Queen of Castile, and her husband, Sancho the Great of Navarre, who died in 1035 having assembled an Empire only to leave Aragón to his son Ramiro, Navarre to his son García and Castile to his son Ferdinand. This process of accumulation of possessions followed by their dispersal in order to look after the family explains the thorny path to unity experienced by Christian Spain. Nearest the altar lies Sancho II of Castile, whose remains were brought from Zamora to Oña by the Cid before he exacted the famous oath of non-complicity in his brother's murder from Alfonso VI at Santa Agueda (see p. 130). Over these sepulchres are unique late Gothic baldachinos by Simón de Colonia with interior linings in the Moorish taste. The great cloister in the rich style of the turn of the century has corner groups of sculpture possibly by Felipe Vigarni and combines with the sacristy and chapter-house to provide the ideal setting for an embryo museum of painting and sculpture. One of the main exhibits is part of a Last Supper carved and painted in 1041 for the monks' refectory. Oña has a special genius loci; it is one of the most sacred shrines of Old Castile. One should not fail to notice also the fortified walls erected under Abbot Sancho (three of the twelve towers remain) as a result of the sacking of the place in 1367 by the troops of the Black Prince, who had sold his services to Peter the Cruel.

After temporarily restoring this extraordinary monarch, only to languish unpaid near Valladolid for four months of the hot Castilian summer, the Prince's disgruntled army pillaged its way back to France. Oña was one of the sufferers.

From here there is a direct road to Trespaderne and thus to Medina del Pomar but it is worth making the circuit via Barcina de los Montes to **Frías.** Little is left of the castle, one of the first *castillos* from which the name *Castilla*, Castile, derives. Only a single tower thrusts up from a natural outcrop like a hollow tooth that has resisted extraction. Below, the romantically sited town is skirted by a fringe of market gardens running down to the river Ebro, which is crossed by an old bridge with a fortified gatehouse on the town side. This river formed one of the earliest frontiers with the Moors. Crossing here, we soon come to a junction where we turn left to Trespaderne. The road then accompanies the railway via Moneo, with a pleasant parish church, to **Medina del Pomar,** whose castle is visible from some distance. Here the Hotel las Merindades does very well for a meal or even for the night. The older streets are enclosed by the remnants of the town wall and it is best to abandon the car and walk to the castle, which turns out to be a great double keep joined by a central block. Though certainly impressive, it is no more than a shell these days. Nearby is a good plain church of the sixteenth century with the tomb of the fourth Constable of Castile of the Velasco line. At 8 km is the trout-fishing centre of **Villarcayo,** architecturally uninteresting but agreeably situated in a plain ringed by hills. The traveller coming south will have noticed well before arrival at this point a sign reading **Merindad de Castilla la Vieja.** The Merindades, of which there are several, derive from the early judicial structure of the areas resettled by Christians as the Moors receded. The justices or magistrates were known as Merinos. They were much respected by the people and it almost seemed as if an independent judiciary was about to emerge. Two of the most famous early Merinos were Laín Calvo and Nuño Rasura whose statues are included in the Arco de Santa Maria in Burgos. In the event the rule of the count and later the king became paramount and the office died out. But it has important associations for many Spaniards with dreams of local autonomy and social justice. The official residence of the two judges of Castilla la Vieja was at Bisjueces, though the modern

Council of this Merindad (incorporating 33 villages) has its seat at Cigüenza, 2 km from Villarcayo. With the exception of the name it is now simply a rural municipality like any other.

Taking N232 south from Villarcayo we come to **Valdenoceda**, which has a restored square keep and a church with a Romanesque tower. Forking right here on C629, we climb steeply to the pass called El Puerto de la Mazorra, leaving the Ebro to curl away westwards through water-meadows under the massif of the Sierra de Tecla, whose flanks are streaked with undulating rock strata like the markings of some huge supine beast. From the top of the pass a desolate moor stretches for 30 km ahead. The road is marked by old stone pylons to show the way in heavy snows. Far over on the right rises the distant bulk of the Picos de Europa, where snow is almost perpetual; the horizon to the left is formed by the slightly lower but more imminent Sierra de la Demanda, usually white till well into the spring. The exit from the moor is through a narrow cleft called Peñahorada, soon after which we join the main road from Santander to Burgos. At 2 km on the left is the castle of Sotopalacios and a little farther on the rough turning, on the same side, to **Vivar del Cid**, a hamlet of thirty or so low square houses round a modern statue of the hero. This was the ancestral property of the Cid and his family, who also owned the mill and milling rights. Everyone here claims to be his descendant and even some of the humbler dwellings have armorial bearings over their doors. It is tempting to connect the neighbouring castle, which is an imposing pile, with the great warrior, but it was built long after his death.

Burgos – Palenzuela – Santa Maria del Campo – Lerma – Covarrubias – Santo Domingo de Silos – Salas de los Infantes – (San Pedro de Arlanza) – Quintanilla de las Viñas – (San Quirce) – Sarracín – Burgos

A rewarding circuit of the south of the province may be made leaving Burgos on N620 towards Valladolid. After some 30 km is the turning to Pampliega (2 km off the road) whose church rises most effectively above the village – owing to the clear air and remote horizons quite simple buildings often make an impression disproportionate to their interest from close up. At 48 km is the left-hand turning to **Palenzuela**, a very unspoilt mediaeval village overlooking the river Arlanza. In the sixteenth century the hall-church became popular in Spain. Based on the *lonjas* or secular exchanges of the Levant, these have aisles the same height as the nave. The parish church here is a good example with a Gothic vault springing from thick round columns with mouldings instead of capitals; among the contents are some curious retablos and Gothic and Plateresque tombs. The unusual holy water stoup near the west entrance is overhung by a conch forming a sort of grotto, crowned with three skulls on which two weary angels lean and sleep. The Ayuntamiento has an ancient belfry and there is a ruined fourteenth-century church near by. There are some stone buildings clustering round the main church but the houses are mainly of *adobe* with projecting first floors and eaves. During the Middle Ages the place was popular with the nobility of Burgos as a summer retreat. Descending to the river, we cross by a rebuilt mediaeval bridge whose 'spurs' or pointed flood-breaking buttresses point, curiously enough, downstream. From here C110 follows the river east to Peral de Arlanza. About 6 km beyond this a local road leads north to **Santa Maria del Campo**. This is a rough town with mud streets, yet it possesses a large ex-collegiate Gothic church with a rich Plateresque tower by Diego de Siloe and Juan de Salas topped by an octagonal upper stage. Inside, two building periods are apparent. The earlier nave has a choir occupying one bay with good non-figurative Gothic stalls possibly by Martín Sánchez, recalling those of Miraflores and Oña. The later and higher crossing and transepts continue the tradition of heads and figures on the capitals, unusual as late as the fifteenth century but inspired no doubt by the more primitive nave capitals. There are two fine Gothic tombs in the epistle side aisle and the pulpit has Gothic-Mudéjar plasterwork.

We now take the road running via Mahamud and Villahoz to rejoin the river at Tordómar. The churches of all these villages make a handsome impression; the latter also has an old bridge over the Arlanza. Continuing east along C110 we soon see **Lerma** cutting a fine figure on the skyline and shortly reach the main Burgos–Madrid road which passes under its walls. The **Colegiata** here is another, more luxurious hall-church (complete with ambulatory) combining large round columns topped by capitals of Ionic derivation with a shallow Gothic ribbed vault. The nave is lit by round-headed windows above a cornice. The scroll-capitals of the aisle pilasters running up to this are adorned with protruding winged putti, typical of the Renaissance style in Spain. Facing the high altar on the gospel side is the kneeling figure with bacculus and prie-dieu, all in bronze, by Pompeo Leoni, of Cristóbal Rojas y Sandóval, Archbishop of Seville, founder of the church and uncle of Philip III's favourite, the notorious Duke of Lerma, who ordered the monument to him. Gómez de Mora's palace for the Duke, built in 1605, is frankly a large dull barracks, whose only aesthetic contribution is the one made to the sky-line from a distance by its four corner towers. When its owner retired to it in 1618 he had been dismissed in favour of his son, the Duke of Uceda. On the King's death in 1621 Lerma was ordered to Tordesillas by the Count-Duke of Olivares, the new favourite. He died in 1625, despoiled of some but not all of his immense wealth, having taken the precaution before his fall of obtaining a cardinal's hat from Pope Paul V. His palace is now a tenement and the main entrance is occupied by a grocer's shop. Here everything is large – palace, plaza, colegiata – and everywhere there is physical and spiritual emptiness. The existence of several other churches of the same period does little to fill the vacuum. Lerma was built in all its essentials on the ill-gotten gains of one man and has had no real *raison d'être* since. At 4 km to the west on a local road is Ruyals de Agua whose very simple little Romanesque church has a transitional doorway with roughly carved capitals.

Leaving Lerma's hollow grandeurs, we turn north on the main road and almost at once rejoin C110, which now follows the north bank of the Arlanza past Puentedura, a picturesque village, to **Covarrubias**, the most attractive town in the whole region. Lying low along the banks of the river, its red roofs seem to grow out of the ruddy soil beneath and behind them. A good, solid, sixteenth-century gatehouse, which used to house the town hall and archive, leads into the quiet main plaza, in which is the comfortable Hotel Arlanza. Visible from the square is the **Torre de Doña Urraca**. This somewhat enig-matic tower, wider at the bottom than the top and recently restored, is pierced half-way up the south face by a little horseshoe doorway, which may be Visigothic. The corner windows and machicolated balconies, certainly of much later date, are covered by a tiled roof on wooden eaves. Facing this is the **Colegiata**, mainly of the fifteenth century on the site of earlier Visigothic and Romanesque buildings. The seventeenth-century organ is famed for its tone, which it is said to owe to its wooden pipes. The first chapel on the epistle side is by Juan de Colonia. Then comes the door to the sixteenth-century cloister, which is undistinguished except for the tomb of Christina of Norway who died in 1262 after four years of marriage to Philip, son of Ferdinand III the Saint and brother of Alfonso X the Learned. The tombs in this church cannot all be mentioned, for there are over forty of some merit. However, we cannot omit that of Fernán González, jutting into the sanctuary on the left of the high altar. The plain stone box resting on recumbent lions bears a simple inscription dated 1841, in which year it was brought to this place from the ruined monastery of San Pedro de Arlanza a few miles upstream. In the equivalent position on the other side lies his wife Doña Sancha, tenant of a very beautiful late Roman coffin carved with a patrician medallion of its two first occupants and arcadian scenes. The Romanesque lid belongs to the time of her death. In the wall above the Count is the tomb by Juan de Colonia of Abbot García Alonso, who was a great converter of Jews, among them Alonso de Cartagena who became a bishop and lies in the Capilla de la Visitación in Burgos Cathedral.

To the right of the sanctuary is a door leading via the one-time chapter-house to the **Sacristía**, where the museum is installed. The most vigorous of the paintings are by Alonso de Sedano and Pedro Berruguete – see the latter's scene of Saints Cosmó and Damían, grafting a black limb on to a white body. Among the manuscripts is a document of 950, itself of little note, subscribed in Latin: 'during the reign of King Ramiro in León and Count Fernán González in Castile . . .' The consensus of opinion is that the effective independence of Castile from León must have begun about this time. We also find the eleventh-century *Carta de Puebla*, which is a sort of charter of rights, and the document of 978 creating the Infantado de Covarrubias (a type of minor principality) in favour of Doña Urraca, grand-daughter of Fernán González, after her repudiation by Ordoño III of Léon to whom she had been married. It is her name that is attached to the tower. Leaving the sacristy, we enter the south aisle from the east end. Many of the tombs invite inspection but the pièce de résistance is the

Tríptico de Covarrubias by Gil de Siloe. The central panel
consists of a remarkable painted wood-carving of the Adoration of the Kings under gilded Gothic canopies. Everyone is
very serious indeed except the Child who stretches his hand
towards the golden cup. On the ground is a little dog whose
nose is pointed out of the composition towards the star. The
paintings on the sides of the doors are by Diego de la Cruz.
Before leaving the building one should note the hefty baptismal
font from the earlier Romanesque church. Covarrubias is a
good place to spend a night. The hotel food can be recommended.

The next port of call is the **Monasterio de Santo Domingo de
Silos** 17 km to the south-east near the weird gorge called the
Paso de la Yecla. This saint should not be confused with his
close neighbour Santo Domingo de Guzmán, founder of the
Dominicans, venerated 18 km farther south at Caleruega, nor
with Santo Domingo de la Calzada, whose cathedral church
gives its name to a town on the pilgrim route. Domingo of
Silos was born in 1000 and died in 1073. His church is no
longer in existence. The wonder of the place is the marvellous
Claustro, locally held to have been started in his lifetime though
there are grounds for belief that the first work was done
between 1085 and 1100. Visits lasting about three-quarters of
an hour are conducted by one of the Benedictine monks. We
are shown only the lower level of the two-tier cloister. From
the point of entry we find ourselves looking along the southern
arm. Attention quickly focuses on the corner pier whose west
face has a delicious scene of the Coronation of the Virgin in
the transitional Romanesque-Gothic style of the thirteenth
century; the south side of the same pier shows Jesse's Tree by
an earlier hand. Having learned that work by masters of three
different periods is discernible, we are side-tracked into the
pharmacy of 1705. Returning to the cloister, we continue up
the south wing, whose pairs of columns – almost joined – are
crowned by joint capitals notable for their twinned beasts and
curving forms. This is all the third master's work. At the next
angle begins the work of the first master of the end of the
eleventh century. The corner pier has on one face a remarkable
Ascension and on the other the Coming of the Holy Spirit.
This arm and most of the next – east and north respectively –
were the first built; the columns are farther apart than on the
south and slightly *bombé* with the result that the capitals

spring separately from them without merging at the base. Their motifs include lions, dragons and porfidions (mythical birds with two pairs of wings, one pair open, the other closed), all interlaced, usually back to back in positions of great intricacy, enmeshed too in a kind of strapwork reminiscent of Celtic book-bindings. On the right we pass arches opening into the chapter house in the process of restoration. The faces of the next corner pier represent the Entombment with the three weeping Marys and a moving Descent from the Cross, above which angels swing censers while others hold veils over the sun and moon. The work of the first master continues about two-thirds of the way along the north arm to a break in the arcading almost opposite the museum entrance. Beyond this the second master begins his labours with near-Persian formalism; some of the capitals recall the hypnotic arabesques of carpets and it has been suggested that Moorish craftsmen formed part of the team. Despite the change in the columns, the fourth corner pier is attributed by the monks still to the first master; its two scenes depict the Disciples at Emmaus with Christ dressed as a pilgrim to Compostela (an obvious anachronism) and the Doubt of Saint Thomas, particularly fine in its flat yet sophisticated handling. The second master's arcade continues round this corner to about the middle of the west arm, where number three takes over with a virtuoso centrepiece in which each of the four columns sidesteps on to its neighbour's base. Thus we return to the point where we came in.

En route we shall have been shepherded through the **Museum**, whose first room contains Gothic and Baroque sculpture. Beyond this is a long cellar containing the manuscripts; in case 6 the Mozarabic breviary and missal of the eleventh century incorporates some of the first paper used in Spain. Silos is thought to have continued using the Mozarabic rite – the form of service preserved by Christian communities under Muslim rule – until well into the fourteenth century. Among other exhibits a copper-gilt and enamel casket looks Limousin but there may have been an enamel workshop at Silos itself in the twelfth century. The saint's chalice of pale gold plate on silver with Mozarabic wire filigree is a major piece; so also is his paten. His walking-stick was mounted in silver in the eighteenth century. In the last glance round the cloister one should not neglect the wooden ceilings painted in the fourteenth century (except for the restoration on the north side). The corner low-reliefs and some of the capitals, which we so admire for the colour of their stone, were painted too. At the juncture of the east and north sides there is a large and rather alarming Romanesque Virgin in the Spaniards' favourite polychromed wood, who looks as if she could eat one up at a bite.

From Silos there is a good road to the village of Hacinas on N234. At 5 km is Salas de los Infantes, which is of little interest itself, though it is the point of departure for a fine scenic road over the Sierra de la Demanda to Nájera on the pilgrim route. Another 13 km bring us to Hortiguela from which C110 leads back to Covarrubias, passing the ruined **Monasterio de San Pedro de Arlanza**, the original resting place of Fernán González, beautifully situated on the banks of the river. Or continuing for 7 km beyond Hortiguela on N234 we find the turning to **Quintanilla de las Viñas** with a very interesting little church. A house in the village bears the placard *Turismo* and here one must stop to collect the guardian. Discovered only in 1927, this building was claimed as Visigothic and is still esteemed so locally. The argument for a date in the seventh century was based on similarities with San Pedro de la Nave (Campillo), which is now thought to date partly from the tenth century (cf. p. 204). Here only the square apse and transepts remain. One should walk first round the outside to see the horizontal carved stone courses decorated with peacocks, pheasants, guinea fowl and other birds framed in interlocking circles. Two of these run all round the fabric while a higher band on the end of the apse features bulls, griffins, panthers and lions. Inside, the transepts turn out to be little rooms with access by small rectangular doorways. The cupola of the sanctuary has fallen and been roughly roofed in but the sanctuary arch remains, an imposing horseshoe decorated on the west face with more interlocking circles framing flowers and birds. The imposts, resting on Roman columns, are carved in low relief; on the left angels support a figure representing the moon and on the right the sun. The decoration is certainly much richer and more varied than anything we shall see in the authenticated Visigothic church of San Juan de Baños (Palencia) and Bernard Bevan in his *History of Spanish Architecture* dates Quintanilla between 925 and 929.

Back on N234, half-way between Cubillos de Campos and

Hontoria de la Cantera, is an unmarked track to the right leading to the ruined **Monasterio de San Quirce** about 1½ km off the road. Anyone liking to combine a walk with some specific objective will find the eaves-brackets over the entrance and the intervening panels with the story of Cain and Abel of considerable interest. Just before the junction of N234 with N1 at Sarracín is the **Palacio de la Saldañuela**, right on the road. This is a sixteenth-century country house attached to an older tower. It is worth pausing to note the graceful exterior arcade with upper and lower galleries. And so to Burgos.

CHAPTER FOUR

The Pilgrim Route and Palencia

✣

Burgos – San Juan de Ortega – Burgos – Sasamón – Olmillos de Sasamón – Castrojeriz – Itero del Castillo – Frómista – (Támara) – Palencia

I have already mentioned the pilgrim route. This developed as a result of the supposed discovery of the remains of Saint James the Great near the place in Galicia now called Santiago de Compostela. A local pilgrimage existed as early as 884. A church was built and by 950 the shrine was attracting important contingents of pilgrims from France. This church was destroyed in 997 by the great Cordoban warrior Almanzor but when the holy site had again been made safe under Ramiro III the pilgrims began to flock there once more. The present cathedral was begun in 1078. The road to Santiago as far as Sahagún will form the northernmost limit of this book. But before setting off west from Burgos it is worth making a short journey east – 21 km on N120 for Logroño and then left through the village of Santovenia – to the church and shrine of **San Juan de Ortega**.

This saint, who lived from 1080 to 1163, was a disciple of Santo Domingo de la Calzada (to whom a cathedral church was erected some 70 km farther east) and like his teacher devoted himself to the protection of pilgrims on the route. His church became the last halt before Burgos. He is said to have designed himself the deeply embrasured windows of the main apse and was buried in a very fine Romanesque sarcophagus with carved lid and sides in the crypt. The rest of the church is thirteenth century. The gospel-side aspidal chapel has very well preserved carvings of the Annunciation, Visitation, Nativity and Annunciation to the Shepherds, all crowded on to three capitals. The monument with the saint's alabaster effigy under a Gothic baldachino belongs to the time of the Reyes Católicos. And there is a very sober, simple Castilian

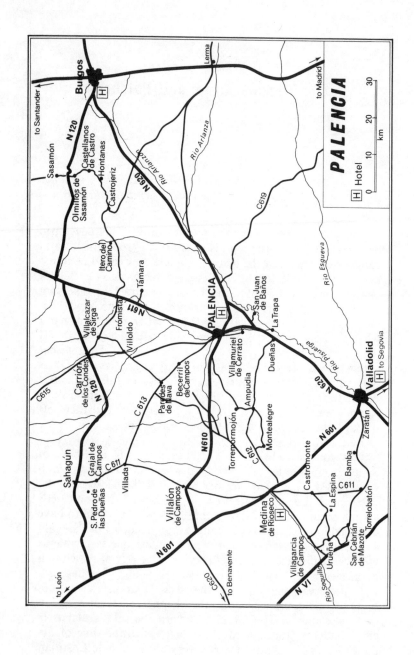

patio of the same period in the range of building once used for lodging and now forming part of a farm. There is still, however, an old and penurious caretaker-priest in residence, who appreciates a *donativo*. His big day is the very sympathetic *romería* or picnic-cum-pilgrimage with representatives from 24 pueblos, which takes place on June 2nd every year.

Returning to Burgos and leaving on N620 for Valladolid, we turn right after 6 km on N120 towards León. After 26 km we reach a cross-roads; turning right we come quickly to **Sasamón** with a large pilgrimage church, whose handsome thirteenth-century tower has a Renaissance upper stage. The nave is being restored and the entrance is by the south transept door, which is almost the split image of the Puerta de Sarmental at Burgos; in fact its warmer tone nearly gives it the advantage over its prototype. Returning to the cross-roads and continuing straight over N120 we find **Olmillos de Sasamón** with a ruined fifteenth-century castle and a plain sixteenth-century church. We now proceed via Castellanos de Castro and Hontanas to **Castrojériz**, an old town in very bad repair. But if the houses are falling apart some of the stone buildings still stand. The road passes under the Arco de San Antón, belonging to a ruined fourteenth-century monastery. Next, on the right, we find the substantial **Colegiata de Santa Maria del Manzano** dating from the thirteenth century onwards. The west doorway is in the transitional style with rather pretty statues of the Virgin and Saint John. The altars are Baroque and Rococo.

Climbing into the town, which is dominated by the *castro* or ruined castle, one should see the church of **Santo Domingo** whose sanctuary is lined with surprisingly sophisticated sixteenth-century tapestries of the seven liberal arts. From here one should walk through the main square with the town hall and ruins of San Esteban to the church of **San Juan** whose tower, which is Romanesque in the lower stages and transitional in the upper, is capped by fish-scale finials – this is a type of tile-hanging we shall find at Palencia and more prominently at Zamora and Salamanca. This ramshackle church has an unexpectedly fine early hall-church interior of the fourteenth century; the apse is of the same period as the tower. Despite its pointed arcade the cloister is essentially Romanesque in the pairing of its columns; the painted Mudéjar ceiling in bad repair is probably of the fourteenth century. When I murmured of a possible restoration of the cloister I received the reply that the congregation was composed of *gente a la antigua*, old style folk, who wouldn't want their church messed around by art experts.

From Castrojériz the route passes by Itero del Castillo with a keep and two churches, over a fine bridge spanning the river Pisuerga, into the modern province of Palencia and thus to **Frómista**, which is famous for the Romanesque church of **San Martín**, founded in 1066 by Doña Mayor, widow of Sancho the Great of Navarre, whose tomb we have seen at Oña. Rather over-restored in 1904, it is striking for its compactness, neatness and competence compared to some of the earnest, heavy-handed work one also finds at this period. The stone carvings have been the subject of much study. There are 315 exterior corbels, each one different. With four nave and aisle bays to the wider lantern bay, no extended transepts and three rounded apses, it is as neat and efficient within as without. The absence of clerestory windows is the only possible ground for formal criticism. The crossing, nave and aisle vault capitals are of the first order, tall and fully carved with themes usually involving beasts or birds locked back to back in insoluble struggle. The lower capitals facing the nave include strapwork and designs based on the acanthus. It is all, of course, very beautiful but somehow lacks presence, lacks an aura. Perhaps this is because services are no longer held and the church has become a 'museum' with an entrance fee, in which the only object on display is itself. Even the storks seem to feel this and avoid the place in case they should mess it up. I am glad San Martín has been preserved so zealously but I cannot like it as much as some inferior buildings such as the fifteenth-century Gothic church of **San Pedro** in the same town. From the outside, which looks on to the main road, one remarks the rough brick course between the top of the stone walls and the projecting eaves, which lends a loft- or barn-like look to the roofing – even at Avila Cathedral the same system can be observed over the vault. The grand porch has a curious brick Mudéjar cornice and eaves on Ionic capitals over a recessed Renaissance doorway. The tower – like all self-respecting towers in this region – supports a stork's nest. There is one other church, the late Gothic **Santa Maria del Castillo** with a retablo of 29 painted Hispano-Flemish panels under Gothic canopies. At Frómista we temporarily leave the pilgrim route and take N611, the main road from Santander, which runs straight down to Palencia. After 6 km we come to Piña de Campos, from where a road runs left to **Támara**, which preserves part of the thirteenth-century wall. The church of San Hipólito is a fine work of the fourteenth century, conceived on a grand scale. *Vaut le détour*. Returning to the main road, we continue to the provincial capital.

Palencia may not seem very prepossessing on first sight but it is worth penetrating the outer barrier of standard modern blocks. The old city is enclosed by a ring road. Attention to the signs marked to the Ayuntamiento and the Cathedral will bring one via the Avenida de José Antonio, a modern promenade with gardens, into Calle Mayor, the main shopping street, parts of which have arcaded pavements. Here any permitted parking place is good and the Plaza Mayor is best of all. The simplest approach to the **Cathedral** is by Calle Barrio y Mier, a short street fairly high up Calle Mayor on the left, which brings one out into the Plaza de la Inmaculada on the south side of the church. From here the building makes a somewhat dislocated impression with its solid tower and belfry (1428–1440), its spidery apse and long nave ending in a ponderous gable with rustic crockets. But the whole is very much helped by the sun, which gives the stone a warm golden glow. Circling the apse one notices the same fish-scale motif as at San Juan of Castrojériz, hung here like tiles above the apse and chapel windows. Among the mighty water-spouts, most of them improbable monsters, is one in the form of a human skeleton. Continuation round the outside yields little of interest. The north transept has a very decayed late Gothic door with panels of Plateresque detail, too pernickety to make an impression, in the tympanum. The south transept door has five better preserved archivolts but again the small low-relief scenes of Classical tinge in square coffered panels in the tympanum are of little effect.

The first stone was laid in 1321. The entrance is not by the transept door but by an additional doorway to the east of the tower. The first impression is one of darkness even for a Spanish cathedral. The ground-plan of this one takes the form of a cross of Lorraine and we are, in fact, in the shorter of two pairs of arms, whose crossing is lit only by two small windows above the triforium – there is no lantern. To the east, encircled by the ambulatory, is the **Capilla del Sagrario**, originally designed to house the high altar, which it no longer does. This is covered by a vaulted ceiling beneath the high windows of the apse, which further decreases the supply of light. On a shelf to the left of the Renaissance retablo attributed to Juan de Valmaseda is the simple wooden coffin with contemporary painted sides of Doña Urraca, wife of Sancho VI of Navarre, who died in 1189. On the same side, caged in a grille, is the attractive tomb in painted walnut of Doña Inés Osorio, who died in 1492.

Moving west from this first crossing we pass the flanks of the Capilla Mayor or sanctuary proper, added in the mid-fifteenth century, and reach the main crossing and transepts. A lantern is again lacking but the area is reasonably well lit by the windows over the triforium galleries. The vaults of crossing, sanctuary, transepts and to a lesser extent those of the nave are profusely adorned with *arandelas*, painted metal discs with coats of arms and emblems, instead of stone bosses. Behind the high altar is a very fine five-tier Renaissance **Retablo**, worthy of special remark. It was first commissioned from Felipe Vigarni by Bishop Diego Deza for the Capilla del Sagrario. His successor Bishop Fonseca, member of a family that delighted in opulence, having opted for a bigger and better sanctuary, required a larger retablo. The workshop of the Burgundian either couldn't or wouldn't produce enough additional figures and framework, so a happy solution was found by expanding the original construction to receive twelve beautifully painted panels by Juan de Flandes and a disciple. This measure had the pleasing result of relieving a threatened surfeit of Vigarni's niched figures (there are still 26 not counting the central scene) and letting air into the whole design, which is topped off by an effective Calvary by Juan de Valmaseda. The retablo is partly masked by a good wrought-iron screen by Cristóbal de Andino, the Burgalese master. Facing this is the choir, protected by another fine screen, finished in 1571. The lower stalls have backs carved in the non-figurative style of Martín Sánchez, but coarser; the canopies of the upper stalls are also Gothic, a bit impoverished, though the canopy of the episcopal stall is impressive for its height (7 m). On the gospel side is the very pretty organ by the Franciscan Domingo Aguire, who finished it in 1716.

The outer shell of the choir is richly decorated. Following

the north aisle westwards we pass under the painted organ loft, beneath which is a flamboyant Gothic canopy sheltering a Crucifixion called el Cristo de las Batallas. Then comes a delicately chiselled Plateresque altarpiece framing figures of Christ and the four evangelists by Vigarni, carved for the retablo mayor. Only when we have passed the choir casing do we emerge in the nave proper, three bays from the end. This was started about 1450 to designs by Bartolomé de Solórzano and finished in 1516. But our attention is distracted almost at once from the architecture by the trascoro by Simón de Colonia and Gil de Siloe. Combining Gothic niches and pinnacles with a Renaissance frieze, this is in the very lushest taste of the Catholic Sovereigns, whose emblems – the yoke and the arrows – occupy prominent places. Under the emblems and over the altar is a Flemish triptych showing the seven pains of the Virgin round a tall central panel, in which she is comforted by Saint John and Bishop Fonseca, who brought the work back from Flanders in 1505. Immediately in front of the trascoro are the steps leading down to the crypt. But before attending to any further details – and they beckon from all sides – let us pause and sit down here in the lightest part of the church and sum up impressions so far. The main weakness of the building is, I think, that in addition to the choir and sanctuary it has a third enclosed area in the shape of the Capilla del Sagrario, whose vaulted ceiling deprives it of any light from the high apse windows. Not even the newer crossing has been provided with a proper lantern. As a result of poor lighting much decoration that has been lavished on subsidiary surfaces can hardly be seen. On the credit side are the long wide aisles, from which one can appreciate the overall length of the building – it is well up in the first league here with over 400 feet. Then there are the clerestory windows of the nave with three lights each to the general advantage of visibility and the boldly pointed nave arches – one gets a bit tired of the flattened-out three- and four-centre arches that were becoming popular at this time.

We must now continue the circuit of the choir walls. Proceeding up the epistle side we pass a side altar by Diego de Siloe completed in 1534 with nine stone images by Juan de Riesga of Segovia. Next comes a five-panel Visitation in a flamboyant Gothic framework by the Maestro de los Reyes Católicos (badly lit). Crossing the main south transept we continue round the outer faces of the sanctuary. On the epistle side there is not much of interest. Turning the flat back of the high altar with a plain wall – there is no carved trasaltar here like at Burgos – we reach the richer side. In the first arched recess lies Dean Enríquez with his dog; then comes a very interesting panel by Alonso Berruguete, the sculptor, showing to a marked degree the influence of Michelangelo. After this are niches with figures of the two Saint Johns followed by the side altar of Santa Apolonia and finally the Gothic tomb of an abbot of Husillos.

So far the services of the sacristan, though proffered, have not been strictly necessary. Now they must be accepted if we are to see the cloister, 'treasure' and crypt. The cloister was built about 1520 by Juan Gil de Hontañón, whom we shall meet again at Salamanca and Segovia. It has been spoilt by the filling in of the arcade and now serves as part of the museum. Among the exhibits are tapestries and vestments, items of Roman archaeology including four columns with Ionic capitals from Husillos, a pretty Romanesque doorway and stone and wood carvings of varying interest. After the circuit we enter the **Antesala Capitular**, whose main exhibit is an early San Sebastián (*c.* 1580) by el Greco, done before he had developed his Toledan style. In the same room are two small panels by Pedro Berruguete and a Fifth Agony by Vigarni, another reject from the retablo mayor. In the **Sala Capitular** itself hang the best tapestries, very late fifteenth and early sixteenth century, ordered by Bishop Fonseca whose arms they incorporate. The 'treasure' housed in a chapel projecting from the west end of the church contains a large *custodia* by J. de Benavente (1585) – these elaborate monstrances carry the host through the streets on Corpus Christi day. There is the usual collection of chalices – including one given by Charles V to the chapter – but the item which most delights is a tiny pix, barely bigger than a cuff-link box, which looks Limousin though it may be a product of the workshop that is claimed to have existed at Silos in the twelfth century.

At last we are allowed into the **Crypt**. The steps down have an incongruous Plateresque lining. We first enter a vestibule with barrel vaulting springing almost from the floor; this tunnel is attributed to Doña Mayor's husband, Sancho the Great, who died in 1035, though it has also been dated as late as 1075. Beyond it is a much smaller chamber, the real kernel, at the end of which are three small horseshoe arches without central keystones – that is to say a stone has been dropped in on either side of the vertical line. These are supported by a pair of Roman columns with simplified acanthus capitals. On top of these are plain imposts carrying a stone shaped something like a squat spearhead, which launches the arch on both sides. This is a typical Visigothic arrangement and we are undoubtedly standing in a Visigothic structure, whose probable purpose was to house the remains of San Antolín, brought back from France by King Wamba in 673.

There remain only the side chapels. The epistle side aisle has none, owing to the adjoining cloister. On the epistle side of the ambulatory there are none of note. The axial chapel boasts a Baroque silver altar. The adjacent chapel on the gospel side contains the charming fourteenth-century alabaster *Virgen de la Blanca*. Next to this is the chapel of San Miguel with a retablo by Juan de Valmaseda. Between the north transept and the west end the first two chapels are of no interest. Of the remaining three those of San Ildefonso and San Gregorio have retablos by Valmaseda and the last – that of Santa Lucía – one of similar date by an unidentified artist. These are all decent works of the period.

The pleasantest part of Palencia lies along the banks of the river Carrión, visible from the west end of the Cathedral. Here an old bridge crosses the river to a tree-lined walk leading to 'the church beyond the river', now a cemetery. Following the river downstream on the town side we pass another bridge and taking the second turning on the left we come to the church of **San Miguel** whose handsome machicolated tower has exceptionally tall belfry windows. Nave construction lasted from the eleventh to thirteenth centuries. Interior arches are all pointed but the massive piers, each with twelve engaged columns, are of pure Romanesque stamp. This is one of the several churches claiming to have married the Cid and Jimena. Taking Calle Obispo Lozano and turning right we come to the Plaza de Isabel la Católica with the sixteenth-century façade of **Santa Maria de la Calle**; the rather successful Baroque retablo in natural wood enshrines the image of the Virgin, who is patroness of the city. Taking Calle General Franco from here and crossing Calle Mayor we reach the Diputación (County Hall), whose expanse of spotless white steps leads also to the **Museo Arqueólogico** – ground floor on the right. The Roman section is the strongest and includes some nice glass-ware, including glass liners for funerary urns. The Retablo of San Millán (c. 1400), from the village of Amusco, is well worth a look; altar paintings as early as this are rare in Spain. The backgrounds are of stamped gold leaf and the scenes of the saint's life are engagingly expressionist. Turning left out of the Diputación and following Calle Burgos, we find on the right the standard late-Gothic **Santa Clara**, founded by Alfonso Enríquez, admiral of Castile, who died in 1479. The comfortable sixteenth-century marble effigies of Beltrán de Guevara and Maria Fernández de Velasco, moved here in 1967, share a chapel with a venerated but gruesome recumbent Christ. Beyond this church on the same side rises the restored transitional tower of **San Lázaro**, said to have been founded as part of a leper hospital in 1090 by the Cid. It was rebuilt in 1505 and again in 1955–1959. Returning to the Diputación and turning right past the market we enter the Plaza Mayor, whose eastern arcade leads to **San Francisco** with an early Gothic atrium or porch under a simple belfry. The revamped interior is of no interest. The north end of Calle Mayor opens into the Plaza de Léon. A little beyond this on the left is the sprawling monastic church of **San Pablo**. On warm days the elders play a game of skittles under the apse wall adorned with Bishop Fonseca's arms. In the chapel of Dean Zapata on the epistle side is a Gothic retablo with a single scene, a Pieta to which Saint Anne adds her presence to those normally associated with the Virgin's mourning over her Son. The west front and belfry show the influence of the Escorial. For a night in Palencia there is a choice between two hotels, the Castilla la Vieja and the Rey Sancho de Castilla, both without restaurant.

Palencia – Villamuriel de Cerrato – San Juan de Baños – Dueñas – Ampudia – Torremormojón – Palencia

There is one short excursion from Palencia that is almost obligatory. The main objective is the Visigothic church of San Juan de Baños. Setting out on N611 for Valladolid, it is worth taking the turning after 8 km to **Villamuriel de Cerrato**, whose commanding church is a fine example of the 'transitional' style. Despite the pointed arches the Romanesque distribution remains and I personally think of the style as 'pointed Romanesque'. The Romanesque type and shape of capital has not yet been discarded either but the imaginative carving has gone; only vestigial acanthus leaves remain and no new decoration has been devised to supersede the old. The square apse and one corner of one transept have rounded turrets. The main tower is Romanesque with a Herreran top stage. The village has a long narrow old bridge over the Carrión – on which one is as likely as not to have to concede the right of way to a leisurely flock of sheep.

Returning to N611 and continuing south we very shortly find a left fork to Venta de Baños, a railway junction. Here we cross the tracks and follow the signs to Baños de Cerrato. A rough road leads to the church of **San Juan de Baños** on the far side of the village. This has been described as the most important Visigothic church still in existence in Spain – I overheard a Spanish pedagogue affirm to his unconvinced students that it was worth the whole cathedral of Seville. One's first impression is that it is very small, a mere chapel. Built in 661 by King Recceswinth in token of thanks for his cure of the stone in some nearby Roman baths, it consists on the inside of a nave and two aisles of four bays each ending in square apses. Attention immediately fixes on the eight Roman marble columns and the horseshoe shapes of the nave arches, aisle windows and the arch and vault of the sanctuary (the lateral apses have later Gothic vaults). Though the Moors are often credited with the introduction of the horseshoe arch into Spain, there is really no doubt, as is graphically illustrated here and in the crypt of Palencia, that a version of it existed well before the Moorish invasion of 711. But it is important to distinguish two main types. The one we see here is the 'modified' horseshoe, which is based (theoretically at least) on the intersections of three curves and had been used in Roman and Hispano-Roman decoration. On the other hand, the 'ultra-semicircular' horseshoe whose incurving arcs are simply the continuation of the circumference of a circle was indeed introduced by the Moors via Persia, Syria, and Coptic Egypt. And certainly the wide diffusion and continuing popularity of the horseshoe arch is due to them. Compared with the elegant proportions of San Juan de Baños, its decoration is impoverished. Star and helix are the main motifs on the sanctuary imposts. The Corinthian capitals are well-shaped but debased in detail. A rope-stitch pattern runs·in a band round the outer walls. The windows are framed on the outside by a rope-moulding and filled by stone lattice-work – a reproduction of what was common at the period. All in all, it does seem a far cry from this to the exotic friezes of Quintanilla de las Viñas (cf. p. 141).

A quick return can be made to Palencia but a more extended route of some interest can also be followed. Rejoining N620 and continuing towards Valladolid, we shortly find on the left the Monastery of San Isidro, locally known as **La Trapa**, founded in 911. This conserves its Romanesque bell-tower over the crossing and three parallel apses. One can only peer into the rebuilt nave through an iron railing just inside the west door, so it is hard to tell how much of the original structure remains at the east end. We come next to **Dueñas**. This is the little town where Ferdinand and Isabel first held humble court after their marriage in Valladolid in 1469. With part of its wall and two gates still intact, the place gives a tolerable idea of a small fortified villa in the fifteenth century. The main church, Nuestra Señora de la Asunción, with a rich Gothic retablo is completely restored inside, though the apse bears witness to its Romanesque origin particularly on the outside. The portico has a recessed flamboyant porch with five archivolts surmounted by a large decorative panel of heraldic beasts, tracery and shields. This is topped off by a coarse Renaissance balustrade. The lantern tower is of the late sixteenth century. From Dueñas a local road leads north-west to **Ampudia**, whose fifteenth-century castle shows scars from the *Comunero* rising of 1520. It is hard not to sympathise with this spontaneous rebellion of almost all the principal cities of Castile against the increasing power, tributary demands and foreign-born ministers of the Crown. The Comuneros were not Communists but Commoners, the town bourgeoisie supported by the small gentry and minor nobility and led by a gentleman, Juan de Padilla. The Count of Salvatierra, a sympathiser, was forced to yield Ampudia to troops loyal to Charles V. It was then retaken by the Commoners under Padilla but this hard-won success was all too temporary. The democratic aims of the junta cities had alienated the higher nobility, whose army retook Tordesillas and then defeated the Commoners at Villalar; Padilla was publicly executed the next day and the native plant of Spanish democracy, which had already put forth some sturdy branches, was torn up by the roots. These events constituted a turning point in Spanish history and it is interesting to speculate what course this would have taken if the towns had persuaded the first Habsburg to accept their legitimate demands. Ampudia also has a good Gothic church tower, reminiscent of Toledo Cathedral's and even more effective against the flat horizons. The rest of the buildings are of adobe. The whole castle hill is an abandoned warren of cave dwellings. It is 4 km only from here to **Torremormojón** with a twelfth-century fort, rectangular in plan and protected by three lines of defence. C611 now runs north-east to join N610 to Palencia.

Palencia – Becerril de Campos – Paredes de Nava – Villalcázar de Sirga – Carrión de los Condes – Sahagún – Villalón de Campos – Medina de Rioseco

The whole area between Palencia and Benavente bounded on the east by the river Carrión, on the north by the pilgrim route, on the west by the river Cea and on the south by the Duero is known as the Tierra de Campos, whose unofficial capital is at Medina de Rioseco. On our way north again to rejoin the pilgrim route at Villalcázar de Sirga we can take in two of the more interesting places of this region. Leaving Palencia on C613 we come first to **Becerril de Campos**, one of those slumbering, sprawling villages with yards and walls of sun-baked adobe, possessing – in this case – no fewer than five large churches, two of them completely ruinous. The churches have the monopoly of stone but this does not extend to the whole building for the top stages of the towers are almost invariably of brick. In these respects Becerril is similar to many other rural centres of population rising from the Castilian plains. However, it is also one of those selected for restoration by the authorities and may look quite different in five years' time. In the meanwhile, the keen ecclesiologist should, if necessary, force his way into **Santa Maria**, which has a very pretty painted wooden choir gallery in the Mudéjar taste, resting on three tiers of overlapping brackets.

The next town, **Paredes de Nava**, was the birthplace of the most famous decorator and sculptor of the Spanish Renaissance, Alonso Berruguete, whose death in 1561 is commemorated by a memorial slab in the parish church of **Santa Eulalia**.

The tower of this church combines Romanesque, early Gothic and Mudéjar work in the same structure. Inside, the two west nave bays have lower aisles; the building then blossoms into a hall-church without extended transepts. The retablo mayor, designed by Alonso Berruguete, incorporates six main panels and six in the predella by his father Pedro, taken from an earlier altar. The exhibition of single works of this type in museums often does not do them justice; the stamped gold may well seem a tiresome archaism. But there is no doubt that set in a retablo in a dark church with their strongly characterised features against smouldering gold backgrounds such panels make a fine showing, where subtler works would be lost. The carved Calvary on top is by Alonso, while the figures of Saints Peter and Paul are by his nephew Inocencio and that of the titular saint by his brother-in-law Esteban Jordán. These two were also responsible for the lateral retablos, though the Inmaculada in the one on the epistle side is by Gregorio Fernández. In the dependencies the parish priest has assembled an interesting collection, mainly of wood-carving, from this church and others no longer in use. His 'museum' is far more worthy of the name than many of cathedral rank. Among the most important pieces downstairs are early panels of the four evangelists with their symbols by Pedro Berruguete, a Flamboyant Gothic retablo whose predella may be by him, three wooden figures attributed to Gil de Siloe, two French fourteenth-century alabaster statuettes, works by Juan de Colonia and Juan de Valmaseda and a Saint Thomas in a red tunic by Alonso Berruguete. Upstairs we find the latter's *Virgen Guapa*, as she is known locally, with Michelangelesque face and parted lips; also a series (*127–139*) of small panels by the same artist of the life and martyrdom of Saint Lucy – there is something about these, a mystic intensity perhaps, that makes one think of William Blake. In the same room are two panels by Juan de Flandes earlier than those in Palencia cathedral.

We now take a local road from Paredes to Villoldo on C615, from where another local road leads north-west to **Villalcázar de Sirga**, at which point we rejoin the pilgrim route. Here is the thirteenth-century church of **Santa Maria la Blanca**, which belonged originally to a convent under the protection of the Templars. The tall porch contains two doorways. Over the main one, facing us, is a two-tier sculpted frieze depicting

Christ, the evangelical symbols and the apostles above and the Virgin and Child below with the Magi, Saint John, an archangel and the Magdalen. Inside, the church resembles Villamuriel in that the essential weightiness of the mature Romanesque style has not yet been overcome. There is a reduction in the size of the capitals and a greater reliance on floral decoration but the piers are still of tremendous girth, the walls very thick and the slit windows framed by two or three side columns, one in advance of the other, come straight from the Romanesque stable with no alteration except for the pointed arch. In the south transept under the rose-window are the thirteenth-century tombs of Saint Ferdinand's fifth son Philip (first married to Christina of Norway, cf. Covarrubias) and his second wife Leonor Ruiz de Castro. Her tomb is in almost perfect condition and much original painting remains – note the tall coif and bands under her chin and over her nose and mouth and the pomegranate clasped in her hands. Her husband lies with his sword and a falcon; at his feet are a hound and a hare. The sides of his sarcophagus are carved with mourning and burial scenes; at the foot the Infante's horse bears his master's shield upside down. The hieratic pose of the figures seems almost Egyptian yet the faces are extremely moving in their melancholy. These are among the finest painted stone sepulchres in Spain.

At 7 km is **Carrión de los Condes**, land and fief of those Infantes of Carrión who were married by Alfonso VI to the Cid's daughters, lived off their father-in-law's bounty in Valencia for two years, then stripped and abandoned their wives in the oak-grove of Corpes, where the ladies were rescued by the good Félix Muñoz. These matters occupy the second and third books of the *Poema del Cid*. The town is agreeably situated on the river Carrión. The church of **Santiago**, just off the plaza, has a brick tower and a Romanesque frieze over the door with Christ in Majesty surrounded by the symbols and flanked by the apostles, mostly decapitated. The charming figures of the archivolt representing trades and skills, including musicians, a cook, a scribe, a ruler, a prophet, a labourer and knights in combat are better preserved. This is one of those places where one realises the mediaeval world held little back and wore its heart upon its sleeve. Art is still responsive to feelings and phenomena. Its later uses for propaganda, glorification of secular rulers and idealisation of abstract virtues are still undreamed of in Romanesque sculpture. Then there is the church of **Santa Maria del Camino**, clumsy but endearing. Slightly pointed arches have been achieved at the expense of very heavy structure and huge piers. The gospel-side apse (opening into a later chapel) has traces of Romanesque painting. A chequer-pattern runs round the aisles. The pointed arches attempted have caused the walls to lean outwards, requiring the support of four hefty buttresses on the south side. These have been used to form a pleasing porch and there is an interesting doorway with imposts ending in pairs of ox-heads. But for all the blood and sweat of these poor stones little has been achieved in the Gothic direction. On the other bank of the river **San Zoilo** is now a seminary but application to the porter gains admission to the Renaissance cloister by Juan de Badajoz. Despite a wide repertoire of contemporary mannerisms this architect conserved a preference for the pointed arch in his cloisters and for ribbed vaults from whose intersections he hung extravagant adornments including outsize bosses with heads in medallions, slanted whorl-shaped pendants and shields. In a side chapel the porter shows us two Romanesque tombs containing, he claims, the mortal remains of those infamous Infantes of Carrión, Don Diego and Don Fernando.

After Carrión the route continues westwards by N120 across flat lands with the great Cantabrian mountain chain always on the right in the distance. Cervatos de la Cueza has a solitary brick tower with a pyramidal base and a large Baroque church, built mainly of adobe and now gaping open to the sky. The names are evocative of the pilgrim traffic. Santa Maria de las Tiendas is just a large farm corral – once a hospice? Across the road is an old dovecote. Perhaps fat pigeons for French pilgrims were bred here in the heyday of the route. Shepherds wearing blankets like plaids or hooded capes graze their sheep down to the roadside much as they did in those days. Terradilla de los Templarios is followed by San Nicolás del Real Camino and so we come to **Sahagún**, which – though much deteriorated – may legitimately claim to be the source of the brick church architecture that is the rule all over the Tierra de Campos, continuing southwards into the provinces of Segovia and Avila.

When the sovereigns of León and Castile sought help from the Benedictine monks of Cluny in developing the growing pilgrim trade, they opened the gates to a flood of French influence. A Frenchman, Bernard de Sédirac, became Abbot of Sahagún, which before long had 130 monasteries subject to its rule. On the recapture of Toledo from the Moors in 1085 Bernard became its first prelate and succeeded in getting thirteen of his compatriots nominated to Spanish sees. But neither military successes nor French architectural know-how could conjure stone out of the alternately muddy and dusty Leonese and Castilian plains. So brick became the vernacular and was used in all but the most important buildings. Another factor contributing to the adoption of brick was that the new Muslim vassals of the reconquered lands understood it. We have already used the term Mudéjar without discussing its origin. It was conjured up by José Amador de los Ríos out of the arabic word *mudijelat* (vassal), though it has since been used to describe quite indiscriminately not only works of art produced by Muslim subjects for Christians but also by converted Moors called *Moriscos* and even by Christians copying the Moorish style. To the first Mudéjares fell very naturally the crafts of masonry, plastering, carpentery and roof-making, in which they were experts, for their conquerors, who in any case lacked these skills, had their hands full with wars, civil and otherwise. The building trade including the construction of churches was left almost exclusively to the conquered race, giving rise to a brick and plaster hybrid architecture that was unique to Spain. The Moriscos, also practising the Mudéjar arts, virtually cornered the market in cloths, ivories, ceramics, metalwork, marquetry etc. until the end of the Reconquest, when the Christian Spaniards began to have more time to attend to such matters. Thus the term Morisco applied to the decorative arts is virtually synonymous with Mudéjar, though it cannot logically be applied after their vicious and stupid expulsion under Philip III in 1609. Even so, the patterns and motifs they had used continued to play an important part in Spanish decoration, while Mudéjar buildings have been put up in Seville as late as the present century.

According to Bernard Bevan the Mudéjar style makes its first appearance ever in Sahagún; basically it is an adaptation of the Romanesque into brick with certain Moorish embellishments. As almost nothing remains of the mighty monastery, we must turn to **San Lorenzo** for our first example. This church of the late twelfth century has a great brick tower composed of receding stages, which are decorated with both round and pointed blind arcades. But in the outside decoration of the main apse the horseshoe arch is lightly suggested, as if the masons were looking guardedly at their employers for approval of this departure from the Romanesque canon. In the earlier **San Tirso** (mentioned in 1123) the tower, apse and lateral portico have been rebuilt. The outside decoration is simpler than San Lorenzo's with regular recessed brick panels rising to the eaves of the apse. The tower appears to have had stone Romanesque columns and capitals in the first and second stage windows, while the base of the main apse is also of stone. The other churches of the town, made of large adobe blocks between uprights and horizontal courses of brick, are falling apart. Just outside the town on N620 is the **Santuario de la Peregrina**. Some attempts at early brick Gothic are to be found on the outside of this large semi-ruinous church but there are also recessed panels with a slight horseshoe tendency running the full height of the building and one cannot fail to notice the panel with four undisguised Moorish cusped arches. It almost looks as if the Mudéjar craftsmen didn't really like the Romanesque and Gothic designs they were shown and were unable to resist introducing, slyly at first, their own more congenial variants, which quickly found approval among their patrons. On the road to Mayorga de Campos 5 km out of Sahagún is the twelfth-century monastic church of **San Pedro de las Dueñas**, whose squat tower has *ajímez* windows with rounded arches on stone columns and horseshoe arches at the belfry stage. The apses are lined with stone on the inside and the stone capitals are in the best twinned-beast vein. This was an aristocratic foundation that could afford such luxuries. Even so, brick predominates.

Sahagún is the last point we touch on the pilgrim route. We must turn south before we are lured on to León and – who knows? – to Santiago de Compostela itself. But that is another story. Heading resolutely south on C611 we come after 6 km to **Grajal de Campos**, whose castle was built in the sixteenth-century with drum towers at the corners and walls sloping outwards to the bottom of the fosse. As it was designed to withstand artillery, good dressed stone was used instead of the more usual mixture of mud, pebbles and brick and the place is slightly reminiscent on a larger scale of the English Cinque Port fortifications. The village has a very large hall-church with round columns and a crumbling brick exterior. We continue through Villada on the same road to **Villalón de Campos** whose main church has vestiges of the pointed Romanesque period. In the same plaza is the *rollo*, a carved column on a platform from which edicts were given out; this one is in the Gothic-Renaissance style. The fate of the brick church of San Pedro hangs in the balance. Will they pull it down or not? The mayor says no – it is a monument; the priest says yes – it is dangerous; the baker says there are too many churches anyway. This town is representative of the region. The houses unashamedly reveal the wisps of chopped straw in the adobe blocks of which they are built; inside they are almost obsessively clean. All have stable yards. Not so long ago, said the priest, this was a cheerful place; many yokes of mules went out to plough the rich grain lands, each with a man in charge. As they ploughed, eight or ten yokes within shouting distance of one another, the men sang. They sang as they went out and they sang as they ploughed and they sang on the way back home. Now one man does the same work with a tractor and there is probably not another tractor within three or four kilometres. And this lonely tractor driver confesses that he is unhappy and afraid, because if he turns over there is not a soul to help him and he can be crushed or mangled by his machine with no one any the wiser; also he complains that the juddering of the machine is breaking up his bones. Certainly he never sings. And the population drops and drops. And the people now seem furtive, almost ashamed of their continuing existence on the land, while before they were proud of their pueblo and would dress themselves and their beasts up in great finery on high-days and holidays.

Another insistent feature of the Tierra de Campos is the great number of round or square pigeon-houses or dovecotes surrounding the towns and villages. Many of these were quite substantial buildings. but the majority are cracking into ruin. Time was, the priest went on, when everyone bred pigeons and fed them with grain. The saltpetre in their excrement was used in the manufacture of gunpowder and as a fertilizer on the land, while the birds themselves made a tasty dish. The nuns were the greatest dabs of all at baking pigeons in clay moulds, which they broke open before serving the succulent contents. But now there was only one landowner where there were eight before, artificial fertilisers had arrived and the Spaniards seemed to have lost their taste for pigeon, so no one bred them any more. Any traveller can confirm the priest's tale with his own eyes, for quite often elaborate pigeon-houses are tenanted only by swallows or the occasional stork who cannot find a vacant church tower and has had to come down in the world.

Not far from Villalón, on N601 from Valladolid to León, is a very similar town, Mayorga de Campos, with three brick towers and a view of the Piços de Europa, which are still snow-streaked as late as June. There is an interesting brick house across the street from the town hall. A very sturdy brick tower rises above the Hospital de San Lázaro, while brick continued to prove its adaptability in buildings of essentially Herreran inspiration like the convent of San Pedro Mártir in the same town. Villalón is, however, so representative of the area that the detour via Mayorga may well be rejected in favour of continuing south on C611 to **Medina de Rioseco**, an altogether more substantial place and unofficial capital of the Tierra de Campos. It was also the seat of the Enríquez family, hereditary admirals of Castile in the sixteenth century. Don Fernando Enríquez assisted Charles V in suppressing the Revolt of the Commoners in 1520–1521, receiving in return the dukedom of Medina de Rioseco. The town flourished and acquired some imposing stone churches. The hall-church of **Santa Maria de Mediavilla** is spacious and airy. The choir screen is by Cristóbal de Andino of Burgos and the retablo mayor by Esteban Jordán, c. 1590. To the left of the sanctuary is the **Capilla de Benavente** designed in 1543 by Jerónimo Corral of Villalpando with a retablo by illusionist Juan de Juni. By comparison with this orgiastic frenzy of stucco the work of Juan de Badajoz, which we saw at Carrión de los Condes and shall meet again, is a model of restraint. Yet, I must pause here before uttering a total and perhaps humour-less condemnation – the expressions of Jerónimo's lady caryatids facing the grille are after all rather amusing. And we who enjoy a lush and variegated countryside to rest our eyes on have an automatic tendency to find this sort of thing repulsive and in bad taste. But when we reach the bleak Tierra de Campos, where the majority of buildings are of adobe and even plain stone is a luxury and there is nothing to relieve the eye sometimes for miles but the dovecotes or the occasional repetitive brick arcade on the apse of a village church, it becomes at least possible to understand if not share the love of ornament that gripped these Renaissance decorators and found an outlet only when, as here, the bill could be footed by a rich patron. The other hall-church in the town dedicated to **Santiago**, is also interesting. Its eight fluted columns, traced by Rodrigo Gil de Hontañón, are of Gothic descent. The sanctuary and lateral chapels are of little depth and filled from floor to ceiling by their Baroque retablos. There is a dome over the crossing; the other bays are narrower and covered by transverse elliptical vaults, which were later decorated in the Baroque taste by Felipe Berrojo. Among the images are a Dolorosa by Juan de Juni and various works by Pedro Bolduque. The west front is in the severe post-Herreran style of the early seventeenth century.

Under the protection of the admirals the town developed industries and enjoyed a busy commercial life. The long narrow main street conserves the old shopping arcade on both sides throughout its length; some of the supports are formed by roughly shaved tree-trunks. The austere Herreran church of Santa Cruz rises near by. At the southern end of the street and on the edge of the town is the church of **San Francisco** with carved stone altars by Miguel de Espinosa and terracotta groups of San Sebastián and San Jerónimo by Juan de Juni. This was founded by the Admiral Don Fadrique and almost opposite is the three-star Hostal de los Almirantes, which does very well for a meal or a night. Parts of the city wall remain, including the **Puerta de Agujar**, which is reached by following the Ronda de Santa Ana from the hotel. A short excursion can be made along C612 for Palencia. At 11 km is the right-hand turning to **Montealegre**, whose business-like fifteenth-century castle in good condition has square towers at the corners and a round turret in the centre of each wall. From here it is 11 km via Valoria de Alcor to Ampudia. Those who did not take in this castle from Palencia may like to do so now, returning on C612 to Medina.

Medina de Rioseco – Castromonte – La Espina – Villagarcía de Campos – Urueña – San Cebrián de Mazote – Torrelobatón – Bamba – Valladolid

Only 38 km of good road (N601) separate Medina de Rioseco from Valladolid. But there is a very interesting circuit, including two of the rare Mozarabic churches in Spain, which can be taken by anyone with a few hours in hand. There is nowhere much to eat on route, so a picnic is advisable. Setting out on C611 for Tordesillas we reach Castromonte after 13 km and turn right for **La Espina**. Some 6 or 7 km bring us to the ex-Cistercian abbey of this name. Like Moreruela (Zamora) this was a sister house of Clairvaux. The nave has six bays to the crossing with massive Romanesque piers supporting pointed arches. The capitals are very simply carved; the vaults have pronounced ribs of square profile. The church is less magical than the ruined Moreruela and less pure than Valbuena de Duero (Valladolid), as the crossing and the sanctuary were completely rebuilt in the sixteenth century. The double cloister was added in the seventeenth; the most easterly court incorporates two sides of the old cloister and one of these opens into the Romanesque chapter house with nine vaulting bays resting on four low central columns with plain capitals. The church acquired a Baroque front in the same century as its new cloisters. The original lantern tower remains over the Gothic vault. From the remaining parts of the old south apse it would appear the eastern layout was square-ended.

A little farther on is a road junction. The left fork leads to our next destination, Urueña, but the road is bad and it is preferable to take the right fork to Villagarcía de Campos whose large red-brick Jesuit convent has a Herreran church. Following C519 south for some 3 km we can now turn left again for **Urueña.** This almost depopulated village is situated on a platform with wide-ranging views. The castle and walls are being virtually rebuilt at an expense and effort which seem somewhat misapplied when there are so many important buildings, monasteries in particular, crying out for attention. Descending into the valley on the south-east side we find a very compact little Romanesque basilica with octagonal tower, transepts, three semi-circular apses (there is a seventeenth-century addition to the main one) and outside decoration of Lombard bands. The inside is very plain with rounded arches rising directly from square pillars without capitals. The direct road from here to San Cebrián is in bad repair, so it is advisable to take the first right-hand turning, which brings us on to NVI. Some 3 km along this road in the direction of Valladolid is a left-hand turning with a good surface signposted to **San Cebrián de Mazote**. Of the churches actually built by Christian communities under Muslim rule there are only two known survivors: Barbastro (Huesca) and Melque (Toledo). All the other churches that we call Mozarabic were built or rebuilt from the end of the ninth century onwards by Christian refugees, whose artistic ideas derived from the Muslim culture they had left behind. The tenth-century church of San Cebrián is an important member of this group. Two handsome rows of marble columns divide the nave into five bays; these carry heavy pseudo-Corinthian capitals projecting horseshoe arches of the ultra-semicircular type. There are clerestory windows above the arcade and the nave is covered by its original painted wooden ceiling, recently revealed by the removal of a Baroque plaster ceiling underneath. But the finest effect of all is made by the large bold crossing arch, framing the much smaller but similarly shaped entrance to the sanctuary beyond. Of horseshoe ground plan inscribed in a rectangle, this is flanked by two rectangular apses, likewise introduced by horseshoe arches. This whole area is remarkably beautiful. Standing in the crossing one is suddenly struck by the fascinating process of reduction in size from the great triumphal arch via the smaller transept arches to the sanctuary recess, which reminds one irresistibly of the mihrab of a mosque – a clear sign of the nostalgia of its builders for the mixed culture that had rejected them. The vaults of the crossing and transepts are of the ridged domical or 'melon' type.

Continuing east on the local road from San Cebrián via Barruelo we strike C611 after 12 km and turning south immediately sight the great castle of **Torrelobatón**, square in plan with unusually high walls, round towers at three corners and the donjon on the fourth rising 45 m from the ground, itself reinforced by corner drums springing half-way up and by drum turrets in the middle of each face. This was one of the strongholds of the admirals of Castile and was defended in 1521 by a garrison of 600 infantry and 100 horse against an army of 6000 under Padilla, who reduced it after six days of fierce combat. It has recently been completely restored and relined inside by the Ministry of Agriculture to serve a more pacific purpose as a grain silo. From here a local road leads via Castrodeza to Bamba. First mentioned in 928, the church of **Santa Maria de Bamba** is less satisfactory as a whole than San Cebrián but none the less of great interest. The nave of four bays was rebuilt in the thirteenth century by the knights of Saint John and the roof is new. The rest is Mozarabic. As at San Cebrián the triumphal arch is much larger than the sanctuary arch and the vaulting compartment of the crossing is much higher than the others, permitting an east window above the sanctuary – which again resembles a mihrab. The main differences are that crossing, transepts and apses are all covered by individual barrel vaults running east-west and the horseshoe arches spring not from capitals but from rolled brackets on square pillars. It's a pity the knights were not content with the original nave. From here there is a good road to Zaratán where we emerge on N601 just outside Valladolid.

CHAPTER FIVE

Valladolid

Valladolid shares with Madrid the negative distinction of having no early history; it is first mentioned in the eleventh century. It made up for a slow start by becoming a popular royal residence and the meeting place of a number of cortes between the twelfth and sixteenth centuries. Isabel of Castile and Ferdinand of Aragón were married in the city and Philip II was born and baptised in it. Philip III's favourite, Lerma, succeeded in having the court removed from Madrid to Valladolid, a dubious blessing which lasted only six years. Then began a long decline until the city was recently taken over by modern light industry, owing presumably to its good communications network in flattish land not too far from Madrid. The population is now over 300,000. The old core along the south bank of the river Pisuerga is completely surrounded by high-rise flats. Traffic circulation is complicated. There are plenty of hotels from four stars to one. Simancas at 9 km on N620 to Salamanca offers two other lodging possibilities – the small Hotel La Barca with a good kitchen and a grander roadhouse, the Gran Parque. At 30 km is the Parador Nacional of Tordesillas.

I confess I was prejudiced against Valladolid for years and did no more than make day stabs at it from other places. When I was finally forced to tackle it properly, I found it less disagreeable than I had expected. This is always happening in Spain. Even the most unpromising towns usually have some saving grace, be it a fine church or a good bar or a local wit or simply the passing scene. Valladolid lacks none of these things. All the same, it is difficult to give a coherent account of a no longer coherent city. The Plaza Mayor, haunted by a vanishing race of bootblacks, is still in the traditional style with shopping arcades, though the large red brick Ayuntamiento is ugly. The older quarters have a street plan that is awkward without being charming and it is enclosed and often

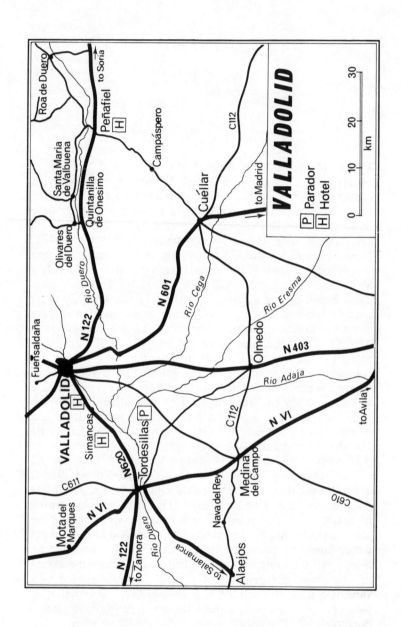

penetrated by buildings of appalling brashness. None of this is conducive to pleasant wandering. Normally one makes first for the cathedral, if there is one. Though this should not be missed, there is a strong case here for picking first on the Plaza de San Pablo, overlooked by the exuberant west front of this church (1486-1492), at the back of which is the even more extravagant **Colegio de San Gregorio** housing the important **Museo Nacional de Escultura**. Devoted mainly to religious imagery in the favourite polychromed wood, this is Valladolid's main attraction, what the Prado is to Madrid. The college itself was built between 1488 and 1496. The façade, sometimes described as Gothic-Plateresque, is in fact one of the last fantastic flourishes of the Isabelline-Gothic style and has more in common with the work of the wood-carvers of the great retablos than with that of any silversmith. One notes particularly the background patterns based on wickerwork or plaiting and the uprights resembling pollarded tree-trunks. Fleecy *maceros* or wild men are prominent as supporters of coats of arms. A large royal shield occupies the place of honour, supported by lions standing on the topmost branches of a tree from which hang the emblems of the monarchs and round whose base gambol naked children – not angels. Over the lintel Saint Gregory receives the offering of the college from its founder Bishop Alonso de Burgos. The architect of this extraordinary work was Juan Guas, though the carving is attributed to Gil de Siloe. The entrance court called the Patio de Estudiantes leads via a vestibule to the great patio with tall barley-sugar columns supporting segmental arches; over these runs a chain motif under the balustrade of the very richly decorated gallery stage; the whole is topped off by a frieze of the royal emblems.

Rooms I to III on the ground floor are devoted entirely to the sixteen-metre-high retablo made by Alonso Berruguete between 1526 and 1532 for the Valladolid church of San Benito – here dismantled and shown in its component parts. These include two painted panels and two grisailles which constituted a minor but essential element in the interplay of low relief, high relief, fully sculpted figures and architectural framework. A great wind seems to blow the robes and hair of some of the figures, particularly the smaller ones which occupied the lower places nearest the viewer. Higher up in the design they are larger and calmer, though the cloak of the

Virgin in the Calvary (room II) billows out in a great curved sweep, as if puffed by the same wind. This image comes constantly to mind in relation to Berruguete, to my mind the only inspired artist of the Spanish Renaissance – Italian-inspired certainly but inspired none the less with a universal view that required the whole to be always greater than the parts. Though it was a kind of Pandora's box that he opened, let us note that he is not all frenzy for frenzy's sake. In the absence of the wind, which sometimes drops, the robes fall straight from the body as in the case of the Sybils gazing upwards with their chins cupped in their hands (room II). He has his fine fling with anatomy in the small San Sebastián and with Abraham about to sacrifice Isaac (room III) but note also in the same room the posture of the Roman soldier leaning forward on his shield and balanced as precariously between wonder and derision as a baby between laughter and tears. This same soldier is shortly to become a grotesque 'baddie' – it happens in less than twenty years.

The main culprit was Juan de Juni, christened probably Jean de Joigny, who arrived in Valladolid from Champagne in about 1540 and became even more admired in Castile than Berruguete himself. In room XV upstairs we find his famous group of the Burial of Christ, made for the monastery of San Francisco of this city. The work is one of the first instances of Illusionism (what the Spaniards tend to call Naturalism or Realism). Eyes begin to glitter like glass eyes; the figure of Joseph of Arimathea on the left removing a thorn and holding it up to the public for inspection is a deliberate 'character' whose jutting underlip adds nothing to our understanding of anything except the carver's dexterity; throughout the composition there is a self-indulgent use of drapery for purely exhibitionistic purposes. Juni's bust of Saint Anne in the same room is a good example of Illusionism with its 'natural-istic' old woman's face and too perfect drapes falling as they never fall in nature. This trying to have it both ways is precisely where the false quantity lies. Unfortunately the School of Valladolid descends from Juni rather than from Berruguete, whose Mannerist tendencies never led him into – perhaps even saved him from – Illusionism. In his work teeth are barely indicated even in open mouths, eyes are conventionally shown, figures are subordinate to their role in the whole design and not allowed to make vulgar bids for individual attention like Juni's Joseph of Arimathea.

For the next major figure in the sequence we must go down again to room IV off the vestibule, devoted to Gregorio Fernández, who is thought to have come from Ponferrada and known to have lived in Valladolid until 1636. The greatest seventeenth-century luminary of the School, he continued and developed Juni's Illusionism. One should study carefully the *Cristo Yacente* or recumbent Christ, one of several attributed to him – one might almost call them his speciality – exhibited on its own beyond the main room. In this as in other 'important' works he introduces glass eyes, nails of leather, human teeth and even carves the tongue in the correct position in the half-open mouth. His Saint Theresa with raised eyes, open book and pen (1625) is anodyne and the large construction called the Virgin of Carmen delivering the scapulary to Saint Simon Stock is a bland thing with pretty angels playing instruments. But the Pieta with the two thieves formed part of a processional float and here he resorts to shock-tactics with the vicious slashes in the thieves' legs, quite out of line with the splendid conditions of their torsos. Here he is playing to the gallery on a public occasion. Rooms VI to VIII on the same floor contain more Holy Week floats. Fernández is represented by three, in which he follows Juni into the realm of caricature, endowing his 'baddies' too with enormous noses. However, strictures on grounds of taste are not very helpful in this sphere of imagery, which has elements of Punch and Judy and the carnival. Taking it in this sense, it is possible to enjoy Fernández's swaggering trumpeter on the float called *el Paso de la Verónica*.

Of the other rooms upstairs IX to XIV contain retablos and choir stalls – they were closed at the time of writing. Numbers XVI to XXII contain mainly standard works of the seventeenth century, though one should note the repentant Magdalen (1664) in room XXI by Pedro de Mena, 'the most spiritual exponent of the mysticism of the seventeenth century in Spanish imagery' according to the official guidebook. This may be so; he took over the eyes and teeth and nails from Gregorio Fernández but he also had a fine taut streak that raised him above his material. But he is an exception and these practices became widely exploited by lesser hands to give us such grand guignol stuff as the severed head of Saint

Paul in room XXVII by J. A. Villaabrille (1707). Rooms XXIII
to XXVI house the museum's collection of painting and
XXVIII to XXX contain Baroque and Neo-Classical carving
– these were also closed. For the end-products of the Valladolid
School of religious imagists we shall have to wait till we reach
Zamora, where an assemblage of tired scenes resembling
waxworks – helped out by such charming additions as human
hair, human finger-nails, real pincers and hammers and nails
and rope etc. – is on permanent display in the Holy Week
Museum.

It is a relief to take a long stride back in time. From the
Patio de Estudiantes a walk through the little garden leads
to the chapel by Juan Guas. The raised choir is extended on
one side by an organ loft in the form of one of his favourite
tribunes, sumptuously decorated. The arch that communicated
with the transept of San Pablo is blocked up and filled by the
marble tomb of a bishop of Tuy by Felipe Vigarni and his son
Gregorio. The high altar retablo, finished in 1526, is by Alonso
Berruguete and shows less of a sense of the whole than his
later work for San Benito; the colouring has been unpleasantly
retouched. On either side kneel bronze figures of the Duke and
Duchess of Lerma by Pompeo Leoni, cast by Juan de Arfe
and finished before 1608. These come from San Pablo next
door. Round the walls are painted wooden figures of the
Virgin and Child of the twelfth, thirteenth and fourteenth
centuries. Behind the choir staircase is the section devoted to
tombs. Such is the Spanish passion for polychromed wood
that the plain figures of the Count of Mogrovejo and his lady
in beautiful dark natural walnut are described as *madera en
blanco* as if they very much lacked something. There is a fine
skeleton figure of Death carrying a horn to blow up his flock;
it has been variously attributed to Juan de Valmaseda,
Gaspar Becerra and Juni. The choir contains the stalls from
the convent of San Francisco, Valladolid, carved by Pedro de
Sierra and delivered in 1735. Here we find ourselves at the very
end of the long flowering of choir-stall carving. All the low-
relief figures of the upper series – whether martyrs, bishops,
saints or a combination of all three – appear to be jigging a
Saint Vitus's dance, no longer blown on the wind but jerked
by strings.

Emerging from the museum, one notices on the left the
pleasant stone façade with Plateresque doorway of the Casa

del Sol. Walking back towards the Plaza de San Pablo one passes on the left the Gobierno Civil, previously a palace of the marquises of Villena. The first street on the left past this is Calle Fray Luis de Granada; a little way up on the right is the house where poet and playwright Zorrilla (1817–1899), author of the romantic verse play *Don Juan Tenorio*, was born. On the south side of the Plaza de San Pablo with entrance in Calle Angustias is the mansion in which Philip II was born. Mainly of brick with a corner window on the main floor of the tower, it now houses the Diputación. Facing the west front of the church is the dull ex-royal palace, now the seat of the captain-general of the region. Having taken these buildings in at a glance, we can address our attention to the façade of **San Pablo**, finished only three or four years before San Gregorio and almost as profusely decorated. But it is distinctly more normal in the substance and style of its decoration. Whereas San Gregorio is something of a phenomenon, work reminiscent of San Pablo was carried out at Salamanca some twenty years later. The scene over the doorway represents the Coronation of the Virgin. The prelate on the left, carved on an altogether larger scale than the divine personages, suspiciously resembles that magnificent Archbishop Fonseca whose tomb we shall find in the Ursuline convent of Salamanca; he was not one to take a back seat even in the company of the Holy Family; his shield of five stars also appears in the vast composition. The shields dated 1600 on the towers are identical on both sides and belong to Don Francisco Gómez de Sandóval y Rojas, Duque de Lerma, Marqués de Denia y de Zea etc. etc., another person disinclined to hide his light under a bushel. The interior of the church is plain by comparison except for the two facing transept doorways in the flamboyant taste, one of which opened into the chapel of San Gregorio. The apse is a septagon with tall narrow windows rising between the ribs of the vault. The lower part of the nave was refaced in the period of the Herreran dictatorship and a choir gallery added at the same time covering the three western bays.

Leaving the Plaza de San Pablo by Calle Angustias and turning left after the church of Las Angustias we reach the **Cathedral**. The foundations were laid in 1527 by Rodrigo Gil de Hontañón but construction was not begun until 1580 by Herrera then at the height of his success and on the point of completing his great work at the Escorial. Though not finished by him, the whole building at Valladolid is stamped with Herrera's personality. The lower part of the west front and the tower were finished according to his designs but the work above the balustrade, which was not carried out till 1735, is by Alberto de Churriguera. Strange bedfellows, one might think, but they go remarkably well together. Despite his deeply recessed central panel and the busy carving of the sun and moon under crowns, Alberto's idea of Spanish gravity was not so far removed from Herrera's after all. Inside, only four bays of the gigantic project were built. Had it been carried out as planned, the church would have been as long as Seville's and one of the largest in the Christian world. Even in its severely truncated form it is impressive enough with its huge square pillars, very shallow pilasters topped by deep Corinthian capitals and its pronounced cornice under rectangular windows which are set in semi-circular diaphragms. The crossing was never reached. The nave and side aisles are sealed by temporary apses, which became permanent. The retablo mayor is by Juni. In the context of this very decorous and frigid church his vulgarity, if one may be so bold as to call it such, is rather welcome.

To make way for the new wonder of the world that was to replace it most of the old collegiate church of Valladolid was pulled down. However, some dependencies were saved by the stoppage of the eastward march of the great work after 1668. In these the **Museo Diocesano** is installed. The first section occupies the old **Capilla de San Llorente**, which was rebuilt in about 1345 and covered by two domical vaults with Mudéjar plasterwork. Here we find Romanesque tombs and some fine Gothic doors from the earlier church. Off this opens the chapter house, 'an anodyne construction of the eighteenth century' as the catalogue admits, with a set of Rococo stalls. The next chapel, **Santo Tomás**, rebuilt in 1341, contains an attractive retablo devoted to Saint Anne and attributed to the Maestro de Gamonal. After this comes the **Capilla del Rincón del Claustro** whose best piece is the fine and moving Lament over the Dead Christ (*115*) of about 1500 by a sculptor very close in feeling to Gil de Siloe. The **Capilla de San Blas** of 1633 displays church plate. A vitrine in the base of the old tower contains the great four-tier silver monstrance by Juan de Arfe, third and last of his line, made between 1587 and 1590, in which changes are rung on the architectural orders. The lowest tier is a polygon in the Ionic mode; above this is a circle of Corinthian columns; next comes a hexagon in which Herrera is duly honoured and the whole is crowned by a little temple in the manner of Bramante. This is one of the best-arranged diocesan museums.

With due respect to local pride one should take with a pinch of salt the forty-odd buildings listed on the Tourist Office plan as worth a visit. In the immediate vicinity of the Cathedral rises **Santa Maria la Antigua** with an early Gothic interior and a slender Romanesque tower of the eleventh century; we shall not see a finer one until we come to San Esteban at Segovia. Las Angustias of the early seventeenth century contains Juni's Virgin of the Knives. San Martín with a thirteenth-century tower and the Iglesia de la Cruz contain works by Gregorio Fernández – but the imagists are much more easily seen and judged in the Sculpture Museum. El Salvador with a stone-based tower topped by two octagonal brick stages has two altarpiece panels by Quentin Metsys. I give no itinerary for these churches as they are all optional in my view with the exception of Santa Maria's tower, which it is impossible to miss.

To the south and east of the cathedral, however, there is a short itinerary of some interest. It begins in the **Plaza de la Universidad**. The university façade of 1715 is by Narciso and Antonio Tomé. Anyone who has seen Narciso's extravaganza known as the Transparente in Toledo Cathedral will be surprised by the sobriety of this work. There is a certain amount of agitated detail but the main accent is provided by two pairs of grand unadorned columns flanking the door. I sometimes think that the long shadow cast by Philip II and Herrera over Spanish architecture severely inhibited the natural development of Baroque in Spain. Though Baroque architects seem to feel driven into occasional explosions of frenzy inside their buildings, their exteriors remain solemn and heavy. There is nothing very extravagant even about the much-maligned Churrigueras except their altarpieces. In late Gothic and Plateresque buildings decoration moved cheerfully outwards from the retablos to the façades. With Herrera it was driven back in, to re-emerge only cautiously in the Baroque age. Following the Calle de Libreros we come next to some gardens with the **Colegio de Santa Cruz** on the left. This was built between 1480 and 1492 by Enrique de Egas, a key figure in the introduction of the Renaissance into Spain and author of the later Hospital de Santa Cruz at Toledo. The Plateresque doorway is finely chiselled but the façade has a hybrid look due to additions made under Charles V, possibly by Lorenzo Vázquez, in which the imperial and other shields are clumsily placed on a backing of lozenge-shaped stones as ineptly as weak lithographs on a strident wall-paper. Above, a heavy cornice and balustrade follow the projections of the buttresses, enclosing finials of Gothic stamp. Inside the porch is the entrance to the chapel with good Gothic doors. The first court has a ground level arcade and two upper galleries all with semicircular arches. This leads through a pleasant garden to a small Herreran court beyond. Taking Calle del Cardenal Mendoza along the south flank of the college, we enter Calle Colón with the **Museo de Colón** on the left. Installed in the much-rebuilt house where Columbus died in 1506, this museum is frankly disappointing and barely worth the entrance fee; the most interesting things are the wall plans of his voyages. Almost facing it is the church of La Magdalena whose façade bears a huge coat of arms described by Street as the 'ne plus ultra of heraldic absurdity'; at the back is the Convent of Las Huelgas Reales with a retablo by Gregorio Fernández. From La Magdalena, Calle Facultad de Medicina runs west to join Calle Membrilla, once inhabited by the gentry, with a few old houses still remaining. This debouches into Calle Duque de Lerma near the apse of Santa Maria la Antigua.

There remains the sector round the Plaza Mayor. Just to the south of this, a little way up Calle Santiago is the church of **Santiago**, whose nave has been given the Baroque treatment. The retablo mayor is Churrigueresque but the rear chapel on the epistle side contains an exciting small retablo by Alonso Berruguete, which should not be missed. The main scene is the Adoration of the Kings, who are blown in from both sides by Berruguete's mighty wind to the apparent consternation and even terror of some of their own retinue; this is in marked contrast to the repose of the central group, in which the elderly Saint Joseph has almost gone to sleep on his staff. From here Calle Zúñiga leads to the Plaza de Santa Ana, whose convent church contains three rather dull religious paintings by Goya, dated 1787. Calle San Lorenzo now leads past this saint's closed church to the gardens of the Plaza

del Poniente, at whose north-east corner is the large church of
San Benito, founded in 1388 and remodelled in 1500. The
two-storey portico is impressive. In the sanctuary with its tall
windows and slender finny vaulting reminiscent of San Pablo
stood Berruguete's great retablo, now in the Museum. The
house where he lived and worked forms the corner of Calle
Almirante with Calle San Benito. Near by is the church of
San Miguel with a recumbent Christ, one of the several either
made or inspired by Gregorio Fernández. Facing this is the
Palacio de Valverde with a façade restyled in 1763 and on the
other side of Calle Expósitos is the Palacio Fabio-Neli, which
houses the **Museo Provincial Arqueológico**. The Roman section on the first floor is much the best. There is an interesting
second-century portrait bust, which may be of Nero. The
standard tough-guy, stern citizen look has been dispensed
with and the face is extraordinarily naked and expressive. On
the other side of the same partition is a bronze head with a
disturbing satyr's smile. There is quite a large selection of
mosaics, mostly non-figurative. On the second floor is a
meagre Visigothic and Mozarabic section. The Mediaeval
section has nothing outstanding either, though the fourteenth-
century frescoes of the Magdalen and the Last Judgement
from San Pablo of Peñafiel (Valladolid) are interesting.

Finally, off Calle Miguel Iscar near the Plaza de Zorrilla,
there is the **Casa de Cervantes**, where the author lived between
1603 and 1606. This was bought for the nation by the Marquis
of la Vega-Inclán, who also presented the Museo Romántico
in Madrid and the Casa del Greco in Toledo. I personally find
the ghosts of great writers elusive, if not totally absent, in
these thoroughly restored and tidied quarters. The rooms in
this case are all on one floor and furnished as much as the
Casa de Lope de Vega in Madrid.

Eight kilometres to the north of Valladolid (take the road
for León and fork right immediately outside the town) is the
castle of **Fuensaldaña** built by Alfonso Pérez de Vivero, John
II's treasurer, who was thrown to his death from a tower by
the King's favourite Alvaro de Luna. Luna met his own fate by
public execution, forced on the King by the outraged nobility,
in Valladolid in 1453. Fuensaldaña is square with round
corner towers; the oblong donjon straddles the north wall,
projecting both into the patio and out beyond the rectangle.

This design was popular on flat surfaces where the plan was not dictated by the terrain.

Valladolid – Santa Maria de Valbuena – Peñafiel – (Roa de Duero) – Cúellar – Valladolid

The Portuguese Douro is known as the Duero in Spain. An excursion along this river valley to Peñafiel 55 km east of Valladolid is highly recommended. Leaving on N122, we follow this road as far as Quintanilla de Onésimo, where we cross the river to Olivares de Duero on the north bank. From here we pass through Valbuena de Duero to the modern village of San Bernardo clustering round the magnificent Cistercian abbey of **Santa Maria de Valbuena** about 1 km to the right of the road. This was founded about 1190 by Stephanie, grand-daughter of Pedro Ansúrez, the first recorded feudal lord of Valladolid. A quick walk round the outside reveals parallel apses and a ruined living block to the south of the church. A later block has been added on the west side and here the Archbishop of Valladolid very sensibly spends part of each summer. It is clear from the outset that the abbey was an important one; even so the interior of the church comes as a splendid surprise. The vaults of the four nave bays are quadripartite with strong ribs of square section – one of the Cistercian hallmarks. Each bay is marked off from the next by a pointed arch resting on twin columns applied to the huge square piers. The intrados of the arch is thus very wide, giving it the appearance of a short sector of pointed barrel vault between each quadripartite compartment. The crossing carries an octagonal cupola with a later brick lantern. The transepts with pointed barrel vaults give the church the form of a T and open up sufficient space for the five parallel apses. The grand scale of the church (unfortunately somewhat diminished by the fifteenth-century rear choir over the two western bays) is continued in the cloister with triplets of semicircular arches. The upper gallery is a sixteenth-century addition. The large refectory has a great pointed barrel vault worthy of comparison with Saint Philibert's at Tournus; the chapter-house vaults, again with square-section ribs, spring from three massive central columns. Other dependencies are ruinous but Cluny and Cîteaux themselves might well envy what is left.

This pleasant drive continues along the north bank of the river through Pesquera de Duero to **Peñafiel**, whose glinting whitish castle rising grimly on its ridge must, when new, have been a truly awe-inspiring reminder of feudal power to the labourer tilling the land along the river banks. It was built by the Infante Don Juan Manuel, grandson of Saint Ferdinand, nephew of Alfonso the Learned and author of *Conde Lucanor*, which preceded Boccaccio's *Decameron* by eight years. The fortifications, which occupy a long narrow platform, are 210 m long and only 20 m wide. They resemble the hull of a ship, square at the stern and pointed at the bow. The donjon added in the fifteenth century has the familiar shape of the flat-land castles (cf. Fuensaldaña) and straddles almost the whole width like a bridge, leaving only a narrow passage for circulation between itself and the north wall. There is a fine view from the prow over the town, which is built at the confluence with the Duero of the Duratón. Dropping down to the main square, we may leave the churches of San Miguel and Santa Maria, if not open, but on no account should **San Pablo** be missed. This was founded by Don Juan Manuel in 1324 and endowed with an unusually elaborate Mudéjar chevet, whose pointed windows framed in cusped horseshoe arches alternate with blind arches of similar pattern, while the upper stages of the buttresses are pierced to form open-sided niches or aedicules. This is all much more elaborate than anything we have seen in the region of Sahagún. The severe interior, showing Cistercian influence, has been plastered over. On the gospel side of the sanctuary is a Gothic-Renaissance chapel added in 1536, whose interior decoration is highly indicative of the hand of Juan de Badajoz (cf. Carrión de los Condes); unfortunately this has consumed, on the outside, one of the four perforated buttresses of the main apse. The frescoes remarked on in the archaeological museum of Valladolid came from this church. Near by is the Plaza del Coso, a square sanded area surrounded by houses with shuttered windows filling the whole façade in some cases; these served as boxes for the jousts and tourneys organised by the castle folk, who had to come down to plebeian level to find a flat space for their pastimes. This plaza still acts as the town's bull-ring. The two-star road-house inevitably called after Don Juan Manuel is very adequate for a meal or the night. Anyone who stays may like to make the side-trip to

Roa de Duero – 18 km east on N122 and then north – where Cardinal Cisneros died on his way north to meet the ungrateful Charles V. In the handsome four-bay hall-church the remnant of a good set of 'geometrical' Gothic choir stalls is arranged behind the high altar and one of the southern chapels contains two moving stone pietas.

The return to Valladolid via Cuéllar adds barely 30 km to the journey and is well worth while. Leaving Peñafiel on N122 westwards we find on the left the convent of Santa Clara, founded in 1604 by the Duchess of Osuna. The Baroque octagonal chapel is rather charming. A little beyond this on the left is our turning, which takes us across a stony waste to the large bleak village appropriately named Campáspero (Harshland). From here we come down into the mediaeval fortified villa of **Cuéllar**, which we enter by a shady alameda of old trees. At the road junction it is best to turn uphill to the great castle of the dukes of Albuquerque, built on the edge of the plateau before its plunge to the valley of the river Cega. The main entrance was by a gatehouse, now standing in isolation, with round-headed arches in the tunnel and unemphatic horseshoes on both faces. The south front of the castle, which dates in its essentials from the late fifteenth century, has triple brackets or corbels carrying the machicolated parapet out beyond the vertical of the wall; this faces across a rough football ground towards a ruined church. On the west side is a loggia added in the sixteenth century as part of the attempt to turn a stronghold into a palace. But no one can doubt that the massive north-west drum tower was built for serious defensive purposes and the grey stone of Campáspero gives the whole a forbidding look. To the east of the gatehouse, the other side of the main road, stands the church of **San Andrés** with a square grey tower and triple brick apse; the west front has vertical courses of slanted bricks over the door, unusual in this position. From this level we descend again by the same road and penetrate the town wall by the first archway on the right. Shortly the great Romanesque-Mudéjar apse of **San Esteban**, one of the finest in the region, rises above us. The decoration in five tiers combines blind arcades with both vertical and horizontal recessed panels. Calle Colegio and Calle San Julián both lead down to the small sloping Plaza Mayor, dominated by the Gothic church of San Miguel, whose two rear bays have received the Baroque treatment.

Just below this square is the little Plaza de Santa Maria, a pleasant corner with its rose garden overlooked by a brick tower.

Back on the main road and continuing down we come once more to the junction with the alameda on the left. The right fork marked to Arévalo takes us under the fortified apse of **San Pedro**. Turning right up the Avenida de Andrés Reguero Guajardo we come to **El Salvador** with a plain old tower and transitional belfry. The brick apse has been shored up at a later date by flying buttresses resting on the ground, a curious innovation. Clearly visible from here is **Santa Maria de la Cuesta**, whose tower rises bold and clear from the huddle of dwellings on its hill against a sky that is generally populated by great shoals of slow white clouds. At the southern limit of the town on the road to Segovia is the convent of Santa Cruz with a Renaissance doorway – one of the very few in a place whose whole character derives from the Middle Ages. This is a good point at which to pause and survey Cuéllar, which makes a brave showing indeed from this side. Much is ruinous, it is true, and more than half the churches are deconsecrated but Santa Maria and San Esteban and San Andrés and half a dozen more are still the undisputed masters of the skyline. And long, óh Cuéllar, may they so remain! From here it is 50 km on N601 to Valladolid.

Valladolid – Simancas – Tordesillas – Alaejos – Medina del Campo – Olmedo – (Valladolid) – Tordesillas

Leaving Valladolid on N620 for Tordesillas, we come after 9 km to the castle of **Simancas** rising proudly above the Pisuerga. An important battle was fought here in 939 as a result of which Ramiro II of León was able to gain control of Peñafiel, Cuéllar and Sepúlveda and reoccupy Salamanca. No part of the present structure, however, is earlier than the fifteenth century when the powerful Enríquez family (cf. Medina de Rioseco) began construction. Charles V then chose it as the strong-box for his archive and it is known now as the Archivo General de Simancas, the repository for all important and unimportant State documents from the time of the Reyes Católicos until 1808. Charles's archive is semi-circular, occupying half of one floor of one tower. Among its documents is a letter signed by the unfortunate Padilla in his capacity as Captain-General of the Commoners at Tordesillas on September 2nd, 1520, and the general sentence against the Commoners of Castile signed by Charles V on April 24th, 1521. One can also inspect the marriage contract of the future Philip II and Mary Tudor, signed at Westminster on March 6th, 1553. Not surprisingly the archive grew hugely under Philip, expanding into two very large rooms which still have their contemporary cupboards and shelves. Here also is that latter-day Domesday Book, the Catastro of the Marquis of Ensenada, in effect the first Spanish register of property, not compiled until the eighteenth century. On the ground floor is an exhibition of documents which include the marriage contract of Ferdinand and Isabel, the bull of Alexander VI conceding them the title of Reyes Católicos (1496), the official appointment of Columbus as admiral, the accounts of Gonzalo Fernández de Córdoba, 'the Great Captain' (which he was accused of fiddling), the order signed by Philip II founding the Escorial and the Peace of the Pyrenees signed by Louis XIV. Among many autograph letters are examples in the hands of Philip II, Don John of Austria, Ignatius Loyola, Alonso Berruguete, Saint Francis Borgia, Juan de Herrera, Titian, Cervantes, Velázquez, Quevedo and Góngora. It is interesting to note that the monarchs signed '*Yo el Rey*' (I the King) until Charles III discontinued the practice.

Simancas has a hall-church with Gothic vaulting rising from circular columns without capitals. The most interesting feature is the Romanesque tower round which the west end of the later church has been built. In the first storey of the tower is a small choir opening on to the nave. Below the village is an attractive old bridge over the Pisuerga.

Tordesillas sits up well on the north bank of the Duero, which is crossed by a mediaeval bridge whose level tilts up from the south bank to the north to meet the rise in the land. The main road skirts the town; a street clearly marked to the city centre runs straight to the pleasant Plaza Mayor. Here it is best to park and go down on foot to the **Convento de Santa Clara**, originally a palace built by Alfonso XI between 1340 and 1344 in the Mudéjar style, of which it is thus an earlier example than the Alcázar of Seville. Peter the Cruel ceded it in 1363 to his illegitimate daughters by Maria de Padilla, who turned it into a convent. The place is also strongly associated with that saddest of historical figures, Joan the Mad.

who was confined to it for most of the 49 years between her husband's death in 1506 and her own in 1555. The Patrimonio Nacional is in charge here and the visit must be accompanied. First we are shown the church, whose sanctuary is covered by a marvellous gilded artesonado ceiling with a honeycomb cornice above pictures of saints added later. This was Alfonso's throne room. On the epistle side of the church is a large two-bay chapel put up by John II's treasurer, the same Pérez de Vivero who was killed by Alvaro de Luna, about 1430. This contains alabaster tombs of the Saldaña family and a portable altar that belonged to Peter the Cruel. It was here that poor Joan lay for the first 22 years after her death until her removal with her husband to the Capilla Real at Granada. From the gospel side aisle a door leads to the present sacristy under a Gothic eight-ribbed cupola supported on beautifully-made Mudéjar brick squinches bridging the right angles of the walls. The window of the nun's choir at the rear of the nave is protected by a Romanesque grille. As always in convents one is conscious of a soft, rustling, withdrawn but not incurious life going on around one.

For the other parts of the convent on view we leave the church and return to the entrance court in which is a rect-angular doorway topped by two blind cusped arches on a central column. Over this is a delightful panel of Mudéjar tracery, which was originally tiled between the stone ara-besques. The door leads into a tiny vestibule with blind arches, Cufic inscriptions and a groined vault. From here we pass to the miniature Patio Arabe whose sides are composed of two pairs of horseshoe arches, facing each other and alternating with two pairs of split cusped arches (that is to say the prongs of the cusp are split to form a sort of mouth). This leads to the chapel of Alfonso XI, whose exquisite cupola is raised on squinches as in the sacristy. The lower part of the wall is decorated with blind arcading ingeniously combining the two shapes of arch introduced in the patio. This chamber contains various pieces of furniture including an organ, a brazier and a chest of Joan's; also other musical instruments, among them a clavichord of Charles V's with joyful panels on the inside of the lid representing a *fête champêtre* in a pavilion and gambols in the grounds outside.

On the same side of the town above the river is the stone Gothic church of **San Antolín** with a circular turret and brick tower. This is now a museum containing works by or attributed to Alonso Berruguete, Juan de Juni and Gregorio Fernández. These artists have been very amply discussed in Valladolid; the visit is worth while for anyone who wants to see more of their work. The carving called Nuestra Señora de la Guía over the high altar is said to have been taken by Pizarro to Peru and given by him to Queen Joan on his return. A plaque on an adjacent house commemorates the signing on this site on June 7th 1494, of the far-reaching treaty of Tordesillas whereby Spain and Portugal with the approval of Pope Alexander VI agreed on the lines of demarcation of their respective zones of conquest and christianisation in the New World. The remaining churches and convents are of no especial interest, though Santa Maria may be mentioned for its handsome Herreran tower, which dominates the town; the aisle walls and west front are also of stone but the nave translates the Herreran style into brick, proving once again the adaptability of this material. We have already remarked on the predominance of brick and the reason for it in the Tierra de Campos. Almost exactly the same applies to the area we are about to explore south of the Duero with the difference that the buildings are in the main later (and often more elaborate as we have just seen in Santa Clara) owing to the later arrival of the Reconquest. In order to avoid tiresome repetition, let us agree then that all the buildings mentioned in the rest of this chapter will be of brick unless stated otherwise.

Leaving Tordesillas on N620 for Salamanca we find the Parador Nacional just outside the town on the left. It is not a bad idea to book a room here for the same night – it is much more agreeable than the centre of Valladolid and will put us in a good position for the next day's itinerary. Another 27 km bring us to **Alaejos**, remarkable for the two great towers of its rival parish churches soaring up almost side by side from the plain. How, one wonders, could the basically horizontal life of the land, whose main ingredients are straw and dung and fowls and beasts, have run to these two extravagant vertical gestures, worthy of cathedrals? There is no answer except that Alaejos felt this need and built these towers. The lower of the two belongs to **Santa Maria**, which also has a lantern-cupola over the crossing. The interior of this is made of unpainted wood with Gothic and Renaissance motifs mixed. The sanctuary is covered by a very rich gilded and painted Mudéjar ceiling whose coffered panels are adorned with classical putti; the choir at the rear is in the same very charming hybrid style. The plaza of Alaejos is partly surrounded by arcaded walks and is dominated by the taller of the two towers, belonging to the simpler church of **San Pedro**.

Here we leave N120 and take C112 via Nava del Rey, whose sixteenth and seventeenth-century hall-church has a Baroque sacristy, to **Medina del Campo**, where Queen Isabel died. In her times this was the great mart and arsenal of Castile and is still the scene of the largest sheep market in Spain. It was here that she assembled supplies and mule trains for the support of the armies at the front during the final war of Granada. In the Revolt of the Commoners the town, which was largely of wood, was virtually destroyed by fire. Owing to the importance of its markets and fairs it rose again from its ashes. There must always have been a certain brashness and bustle in its character, which it preserves today with the aid of a busy railway junction. This, not the feeble trickle of the river Zapardiel, is its real lifeline. Above the station rises the **Castillo de la Mota** built after 1440 by the overmighty Fonsecas, who were dispossessed in 1473 by the town, which then presented it to Ferdinand and Isabel in 1475. The architects were Christian and the layout is Christian but the walls of compressed adobe packs and rubble dressed with narrow rose-coloured bricks are certainly of Mudéjar workmanship. The donjon, placed at a corner of the inner court, is unusually tall; the vaulting and brickwork of the two main chambers in this and the view from the top are worth the climb. The outer wall encloses vaulted passages on two levels running all round the fortification. The *aspilleras* or cross-bow slits are the only stone features of the building. Just for the record, Queen Isabel did not die in this castle, as is often claimed.

Descending to the river, we find the single-nave church of San Miguel whose Gothic sanctuary contains a seventeenth-century low-relief retablo. Crossing the bridge we come to the generously proportioned Plaza Mayor with arcaded side-walks. Most of one side is occupied by the ample **Colegiata de San Antolín**. Begun in 1503, this is a spacious hall-church of three bays, unfortunately obstructed by a very solid choir with stalls of little merit. The sanctuary contains an elaborate five-tier Renaissance retablo topped by a Calvary under a

Baldachino; the artists were Cornelius de Holanda, Joaquín de Troya and Juan Rodríguez. Built on to the west end at an acute angle is the **Capilla de Angustias** designed by Alberto Churriguera. On the same side as the church is the pleasant stone-faced town hall of 1656, perhaps inspired by Toledo's which it resembles, though on a smaller scale. The alternative term to Ayuntamiento, **Casas Consistoriales**, is used here. Next to it in the corner of the square is the quite modest house built over an arch, where Isabel the Catholic did die in 1504. Passing under this and continuing on the same axis we come to the **Hospital de Simón Ruiz**, the matching wings of whose façade give another example of the translation of the Herreran style into brick. From the north-east corner of the Plaza Mayor Calle Castro leads to the Plaza de la Cruz followed imme- diately by the Plaza de San Juan, out of which runs Calle Marqués de Ensenada. On the right is **Palacio de los Dueñas**, now a secondary school, built by the banking family of this name. The tower conserves military echoes and the great *zaguán* or porch leads to a Renaissance patio of fine propor- tions. Opposite is the **Convento de Agustinas Magdalenas**, begun in 1522 at the expense of the same family; the church is said to have an exceptional vault by Juan de Astorga which I was unable to see as the nuns, who belong to a closed order, were cleaning the floor. On the same side of the street as the palace is a Carmelite convent, Saint Theresa's second founda- tion. The other churches and convents of Medina are all of much the same period and much of a muchness. Beyond the town to the west is a house called the **Casa Blanca** built by Rodrigo de Dueñas between 1556 and 1563, which can only be reached with some difficulty via the *matadero* (slaughterhouse). This is one of that rare breed, the Spanish country house, and it is interesting to note its forbidding tower-like exterior, which does, however, conceal a central saloon rising the whole height of the building and elaborately decorated in stucco by the Corral family of Villalpando (cf. Medina de Ríoseco and Villalpando).

Twenty-one kilometres to the east of Medina del Campo on C112 lies Olmedo, immortalised in Lope de Vega's play *El Caballero de Olmedo*. The story is a very free adaptation of a murder that did take place on this road and is set by the author in the reign of John II. Both the King and the Constable, Alvaro de Luna, appear. The hero Don Alonso, known as the

Knight of Olmedo, goes to Medina for the fair. Here he is enraptured by the sight of Doña Inés and makes use of a bawd called Fabia to arrange a meeting. Inés reciprocates his passion but she has already been engaged for two years to a gentleman of Medina called Don Rodrigo. The rivalry becomes open. Don Alonso secures the approval of Don Pedro, Inés's father. The King and the Constable attend a bull-fight, at which the local Don Rodrigo disgraces himself and has to be rescued by the 'stranger' Don Alonso, who carried off all the honours of the day. That he should owe his life to his rival is too bitter a pill for Don Rodrigo to swallow. Don Alonso feels obliged to return the same night to Olmedo to reassure his ageing parents that he has survived the bull-fight unscathed. He is warned by Fabia and his servant not to go but insists. What can he have to fear from a gentleman whose life he has saved? In the meantime this same gentleman is plotting his murder. Don Alonso sets off alone on the road we are now following, flanked first by grain fields – brilliant with scarlet slashes of poppies in the spring. Then the sombre pine woods begin to draw closer and closer to the road. Fabia sends a messenger in the guise of a labourer to warn Alonso again with the lines: 'By night they killed/the Caballero/the pride of Medina/the flower of Olmedo.' Honour does not allow the threatened man to turn back. The labourer persists: 'Spirits counselled him/not to leave/and warned him not to go, /the Caballero,/the pride of Medina,/the flower of Olmedo.' With this haunting refrain in one's mind as dusk falls and thickens the shadows of the pines it is not difficult to imagine the mortal scuffle that ensues with Don Rodrigo's ambush. The murdered man's family and friends demand and obtain justice from the King. 'That is my calling,' says the weak monarch, for once rising to it. Don Rodrigo and his accomplice are executed.

The villain from Medina, the hero from Olmedo. It would not be quite fair to take this as a commentary on the character of the two places today. Even so, flourishing Medina is to my mind a much less attractive place than ruinous **Olmedo**, once known – its inhabitants proudly claim – as *la villa de los siete sietes*, the town of the seven sevens, from its seven churches, seven convents, seven squares, seven gates, seven fountains, seven noble houses and seven dependent villages. Little remains of any of this today. The south sector of the

walls, flanking the road from Medina, is the most complete
and there is a pleasant walk with shady trees along this
stretch. At the south-west corner is the church of **San Miguel**
protruding outwards from the wall. A section of the Romanesque apse is visible but the rest has been consumed by an
octagonal chapel of the eighteenth century. San Miguel is in
fact two churches in one. The old nave has a pointed barrel
vault. The altar is raised on a platform and on either side of it
are doors leading to balconies running round the inside walls
of the octagon. Beneath the altar are steps leading down to the
old barrel-vaulted crypt with a delightfully painted ceiling
which acts as passage to the octagon floor. Here is the shrine
of the Virgen de la Soterraña. Looking up, one finds oneself
under a cupola of 1746 with very pretty frescoes of Neapolitan
stamp which extend all over the walls. This Bourbon frolic
in the pink of condition comes as a real surprise in such a
crumbling mediaeval setting. At right angles to the west front
of San Miguel is a fairly well-preserved gate. The western
sector of the wall is very ruinous. Above it one can pick out
the shell of the once handsome tower of San Andrés. Nearby,
the very decayed church of San Juan has a curious apse and
belfry combined. There is also a church now used as a cinema;
the children were astonished when I suggested it had once been
a place of worship and even the older folk no longer remembered to which saint it had belonged. The north and east
sides of the town conserve only a few vestiges of the wall.

Let us return to the south side, where an arch facing the
Medina road leads to the narrow and irregular Plaza Mayor
with arcaded side-walks and a little rose garden. From the east
side a short street leads into a much larger and dustier plaza
on to which faces the church of **Santa Maria** with an atrium
on two sides. The interior has had a Baroque relining. The
retablo may have been designed by Berruguete but the paintings are not his. The sacristy is covered by an interesting
Mudéjar plaster ceiling. At the back of the nave is a curious
reliquary holder shaped like a large book-case, in which every
compartment is occupied by the bust of a named saint – 49
of them each with a little window in his chest intended to
display some relic of his person. 49 is clearly a mystic number
in Olmedo, for it is also the sum of the seven churches, seven
convents etc. Circling the apse of the church and noting the
slightly pyramidal tower with Romanesque belfry windows, one

should take the short walk to the **Convento de la Concepción** with a painted Mudéjar ceiling. The grille of the lower choir, behind which the nuns peer slyly up from their perpetual prayers and wait for the tinkle of your money in the poor-box, appears to be of Romanesque workmanship. The ribs of the Gothic sanctuary rest on brackets with brightly painted angels. The Baroque retablo contains a very swirling Inmaculada indeed and the altar was a riot of roses in June. One wonders why roses do so well on these windy dust-lashed plains.

Just to the north-west of Olmedo, approached by a dirt track off the Medina Road, lies the **Monasterio de la Mejorada**. In these flat lands a very slight advantage in height, as here, provides a splendid view over the granary of Castile, dotted and threaded with umbrella pines. The pretty chapel is almost derelict. Its altars and images have been removed to Valladolid but it conserves some fascinating Gothic-Mudéjar plaster-work over the tomb niches. A local road leads from Olmedo via Matapozuelos and Serrada direct to Tordesillas. The surface is likely to be rough and anyone with a sensitive vehicle may be well advised to return to Medina and take NVI north to the same destination. This excursion – excepting Simancas – may of course be made more speedily in reverse, leaving Valladolid on N403 for Madrid. But one misses the vicarious thrill of following in the doomed steps of Don Alonso, the pride of Medina, the flower of Olmedo.

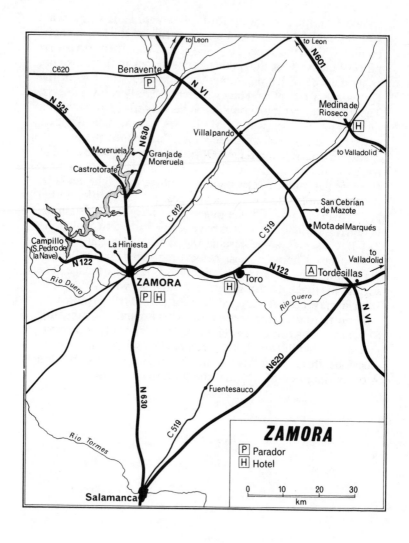

ZAMORA

P Parador
H Hotel

0   10   20   30
km

CHAPTER SIX

Zamora and Toro

✤

Tordesillas – Mota del Marqués – (San Cebrián de Mazote) –
Villalpando – Benavente – Castrotorafe – Zamora

Leaving Tordesillas on NVI to the north we come after 23 km
to **Mota del Marqués** the most remarkable feature on whose
castle hill is the large pebble advertisement, like a white horse
on the downs, for an aperitif called 'Cynar', the colour of
Coca-Cola and made from artichokes. I have virtuously
drunk this before midday under the impression it was non-
alcoholic. It is not and is even better with a dash of gin. The
hall-church is similar to that of Simancas, though the tower
is Herreran. Lower down is a small Renaissance palace with
upper and lower arcades round a three-sided courtyard; this
is now a convent. 6 km farther on is the turning to San
Cebrián de Mazote; anyone who has not visited this Mozarabic
church from Valladolid should repair the omission. Another
6 km brings us to Villardefrades whose ruined Baroque church
has curious oculi. Then comes **Villalpando**, rising out of a
land of mud-walled villages, abandoned pigeon-lofts, slow
sheep and aching distances. In addition to its grain silos,
which are such a feature of this area and look like castles
from a distance, this ancient bailiwick of the Templars conserves a number of towers from earlier times. After the dissolu-
tion of the order in 1341, it passed into the hands of the
powerful Velascos, constables of Castile, and became the
capital of a region known as Tierras del Condestable. Sectors
of the wall remain including the **Puerta de San Andrés,** a
serious-looking gatehouse with twin pointed arches on the
inside; the outer arch flanked by two drum towers was added
in the sixteenth century – over it is a panel with the arms of the
Velascos and of the town enclosed by a Franciscan girdle.
From this gate the Calle de la Amargura, the 'Street of Bitter-
ness', leads to the Plaza de San Nicolás with a rough tower of

stone, pebble-dash and brick and a long porch of vaguely
Mudéjar antecedents; the nearby San Pedro is of similar
construction. From the Plaza Mayor, with arcades on wooden
supports, Calle Dr Ballester Nieto leads to the restored triple
apse in the Romanesque-Mudéjar style of the twelfth century,
which is all that remains of **Santa Maria la Antigua** apart from
a massive shored-up belfry. The ruined stronghold of the
constables is on the left of the road to Medina de Rioseco.
Villalpando was the home of the Corral family, who carried out
the extravagant plasterwork of the Capilla de Benavente at
Medina de Ríoseco, where I confessed my personal dislike
for this sort of thing. But it was not all tasteless excess.
Francisco Corral, who translated the architectural works of
Serlio, was later to build the splendid staircase of the Alcázar
of Toledo and to design the great gilded grilles of the cathedral
sanctuary in that city.

The next important town on NVI – and on the westernmost
limit of the Tierra de Campos – is **Benavente**, one-time fief of
the powerful family of Pimentel, counts of Benavente. Built
on a slope, the place lacks a satisfactory centre but the
promenade on the west side is well situated on a terrace above
the plain and affords a good view over the valley of the Orbigo,
which runs into the Esla just south of the town. The western
horizon is formed by the first hummocks of oak-scrub that
roll away into Portugal, while to the north the Montes de
León are visible, still snow-streaked in May. At the south end
of the promenade the Torre del Caracol, only remaining
bastion of the Pimentels' castle, has become the nucleus of a
Parador of the M.I.T., useful for lunch or a night. Benavente
has two interesting churches. The first is **Santa Maria del
Azogue** with five splendid parallel apses of the late twelfth
century, crossing and transepts of the thirteenth and pointed
Romanesque (transitional) tower and nave. Against the piers
of the sanctuary are, on the gospel side, an angel and on the
epistle side a Virgin, both in painted stone of the fourteenth
century; together they form a delightful Annunciation. The
Romanesque transept doors have been preserved but the
west front dates from 1739. The other church, **San Juan del
Mercado**, just off the Plaza de España, was begun in 1182.
The fine south door retains traces of its original colouring and
the central apse has remnants of Romanesque frescoes. The
other religious and civil buildings are not of outstanding

interest and the town has been too indiscriminatingly developed to be pleasant for casual wandering. Of the two blights that affect Spanish towns, decay and development, the former is often preferable.

Returning 5 km along NVI we find N630 running south to Zamora. A little after Barcial del Barco with an octagonal belfry we come to Granja de Moreruela. Some 2 km beyond this is a turning on the right marked to the **Convento de Moreruela** at 3.7 km on a good dirt track. In much the same way that Alfonso VI had called in the Benedictines of Cluny, Alfonso VII the Emperor sent for reforming Cistercians from Clairvaux, who founded in 1131 their first monastery in Spain on the opposite side of the river to the present ruined buildings, which date from after 1169. Magical Moreruela shows that the rule of Cîteaux may have been severe but its architects still knew how to choose a beautiful, not to say a lush, site. Sadly, little remains of the nine-bay nave and aisles but the outer walls. However, the chevet is almost intact with its presbytery, ambulatory and seven apsidal chapels. The windows under the semi-cupola are rounded but the arcade separating the sanctuary from the ambulatory is severely pointed, while the ground plan of the radial chapels is also pointed, if only lightly so. The first Cistercian architects had abandoned the radial plan – no doubt because a profusion of chapels led to an excess of rich reliquaries and altar fittings – in favour of the simpler triapsidal plan. But happily this most graceful of all solutions for the east end of a great church made its reappearance in one of their own principal houses – Clairvaux – in 1174 and the notable example here on the banks of the river Esla must have begun to rise about the same time.

Some 9 or 10 km south of Granja de Moreruela is the village of Fontanillas de Castro. After a further 1 km we find on the right a track leading to all that is left of the villa and castle of **Castrotorafe**, which belonged to the order of Santiago and was of some importance in the Middle Ages owing to its bridge over the Esla. Its walls were pulled down on the order of Alfonso VII the Emperor in 1153 but seem to have been restored by Fernando II of Leon about 1176. During the war over the accession of Queen Isabel in 1475, the place was taken by the Portuguese, since when it has played no part in history.

The most important city on the Duero between its source

near Soria and its change of name at the Portuguese border is **Zamora**. This strong point on a bluff above the river was probably a settlement of the Vaccaei before it was overrun by the Carthaginians. The Romans left a fine bridge over the river. The place fell under Visigothic and later Moorish domination. During the eighth and ninth centuries – the early days of the Reconquest – the area immediately to the north of the Duero was a kind of no-man's-land; Zamora changed hands several times but as the enemy strongholds taken could seldom be held, its walls were no doubt demolished on each occasion by the successful side. In 893 a serious attempt at repopulation was made by Alfonso III of Asturias. The bishopric was established in 905. The Moors returned to the region in 939 and were defeated at Simancas; on their retreat they reoccupied Zamora but were swiftly dislodged. In the late tenth century came the terrifying raids of Almanzor, before which the principal Christian cities fell like corn under a scythe. But the crop was never gathered in, as the great marauder died in 1002. Having temporarily united the thrones of Castile and León by his marriage to the Leonese heiress Sancha, Ferdinand I ordered the reconstruction of the walls of Zamora, Toro, Benavente and other towns of importance. From this time Zamora became known as *la bien cercada*, 'the well-walled'. Though famous now for its Romanesque churches, the city retains a certain martial rawness; it is not a place of airs and graces.

The **Cathedral** near the west promontory of the walls is the earliest of the very interesting 'Zamoran' or 'Salmantine' group, which includes the collegiate church of Toro, the old cathedral of Salamanca, that of Ciudad Rodrigo and the sacristy of Plasencia. The most remarkable feature is the lantern-cupola, a variant of which is common to all these buildings other than Ciudad Rodrigo. On arrival at the north entrance one's first thought is one of regret that this remarkable construction with its tiles, hung like fish-scales, its spiny ribs, its corner turrets and intervening gables should be partly masked by the Herreran portico. It is not possible to walk all round the church and the three-quarter circuit involves the castle too. Contrary to our normal practice, let us therefore see the interior first.

Building took place between 1151 and 1174. There are only four bays to the crossing. Despite the pointed arches of the nave and over the aisles, the massive piers with engaged columns topped by castellated capitals are essentially Romanesque in inspiration. The main vaulting compartments are quadripartite between strong transverse arches, the transepts have slightly pointed barrel vaults and the building as a whole falls squarely into my category of pointed Romanesque. Over the crossing is the marvellous lantern, consisting of a circular drum, raised on pendentives and pierced by sixteen windows between short columns, from which spring the sixteen ribs of the dome. Mr Bernard Bevan in his *History of Spanish Architecture* has a fascinating passage on these lantern-cupolas, which are notable for a pronounced Byzantine quality, though their lineage has never been satisfactorily traced. It has been suggested that Don Jerónimo, the Cid's companion in arms, Bishop of Valencia and later of Zaragoza, brought the idea from his native Périgueux. But the stalwart bishop died in the year the cupola of Saint Front, Périgueux, was built and the cupola of Zamora was not in any case begun until some fifty years later. Sahagún has also been put forward as a source but little remains of the Cluniac abbey church there and it seems unlikely that there was ever a large stone cupola in the capital of brick. Gómez-Moreno favours the idea of a French architect who had worked under Norman influence in Sicily. Bevan prefers the theory that the prototype was the dome of the church of the Holy Sepulchre in Jerusalem, built on a Périgord pattern and consecrated in 1149, just two years before Zamora was begun. The corner turrets and gables, also the fish scales and the spiny ribs, all of Poitevin inspiration and absent in Jerusalem, were probably – according to this theory – afterthoughts during the course of building. Be all this as it may, we undoubtedly stand at Zamora under a very early, daring and beautiful lantern, which it will be interesting to compare with the others of the same group.

The original east end was triapsidal, opening directly from the crossing and transepts with no ambulatory. This was pulled down and rebuilt on a similar plan between 1496 and 1506 by the absentee Cardinal Bishop Menéndez Valdés, who also endowed the Cathedral with its splendid stalls and iron grilles. The high altar retablo of the eighteenth century is by the high priest of Neo-Classicism, Ventura Rodríguez. Both sanctuary and choir grilles are probably by Francisco Corral of Villalpando, who did such notable work at Toledo. The

Coro itself is really worthy of study. The finest late Gothic wood-carving in the land is to be found in these canonical reserves and I hope no one will protest that they are being led into dark corners for nothing. The polychrome tradition required by the public is disdained; the clergy does not need to have its scriptural i's dotted or t's crossed in the common way. Natural wood with no polish but that of slumberous heads or caressing hands comes into its own. The stalls at Zamora are from the workshop of Rodrigo Alemán, the master wood-carver of the end of the fifteenth century. The lower stage, as usual, is devoted to the prophets and kings of the Old Testament, while the upper stage depicts apostles and saints. A magnificent Christ presides over the bishop's stall. Under the banister leading up to this, on the right, are Adam and Eve with the serpent twined round the rail between them. The trascoro doors are beautifully carved with panels of the eight Sybils. Among the lady saints near the grille on the gospel side are the Magdalen, elegantly dressed as ever, Saint Lucy with her gouged-out eyes on a plate and Saint Polonia, patroness of dentists, with large pincers gripping an extracted tooth. But most remarkable are the banisters and some of the misericords with satirical carvings of monks and friars. A friar with a fox-mask preaches to a cluster of hens whose pullets he has just robbed and stuffed into his cowl – friars are also given asses', monkeys' and wolves' heads. On the hand-rail next to the grille on the gospel side is a much-caressed hand-rest representing a cowled wolf seizing a hen by the neck. Then there is a monk pulling a harrow on his hands and knees, whipped on by a seated nun. Several of the misericords, going even further and showing indecent sexual practices between monks and nuns, were nailed down by order of a recent bishop and remain invisible to laity and clergy alike. These malicious little scenes shed an interesting light on the poor relations between the often impoverished cathedral clergy and the rich monastic orders whose members – it was implied – led a self-indulgent life at the expense of the poor. The power and the glory have departed from the monasteries but arthritic hands still fondle these exquisite expressions of canonical spleen.

The remaining details of the interior are of less interest. To the left of the sanctuary is the altar of the much-venerated Virgen de la Calva, familiarly called 'the bald' because of her high forehead. The gospel-side **Capilla de San Pablo** has an agitated high-relief scene of this saint's conversion of the School of Gregorio Fernández. The central chapel of the west end gobbles up the original west doorway. Dedicated to **San Ildefonso**, it has a good grille in the style of Francisco Corral and contains a Gothic retablo by Fernando Gallego and some tombs of the Romero family. The tapestries represent the seven liberal arts, which were divided after the fashion of the schools of the Roman Empire into two groups: the quadrivium consisting of arithmetic, geometry, astronomy and music – and the trivium formed by grammar, logic and rhetoric. This trio was considered the least important part of the course, hence the modern word 'trivial'. Grammarians, logicians and orators, please note. The adjacent chapel devoted to Saint John the Baptist contains the sumptuous late Gothic tomb of Doctor Grado, whose very fragile tracery in good condition is reminiscent of Gil de Siloe at Miraflores. The doors leading from here to the chapter house are from the convent of Moreruela.

After the wooden-roofed cloister had burned down for the second time in 1591, Gómez de Mora, Herrera's follower, was called in to design the present stone cloister, of little charm but undoubted durability. He was also responsible for the ponderous north transept entrance we have remarked on, added presumably to satisfy his desire for uniformity in accordance with the dry tenets of the post-Escorial era. There is talk of now taking it down. The museum, housed in rooms off the cloister, has nothing of outstanding interest except some fine tapestries which are badly displayed on walls too small for them. The best is the fifteenth-century Coronation of Tarquin on the stairs; it has something of the clarity of a painting which is so often lost between the cartoon stage and the translation into thread. The pair illustrating the Parable of the Vineyard and the series of the War of Troy are also good.

Leaving the cloister and walking eastwards we observe that Bishop Menéndez Valdés's alterations present a standard Gothic exterior of the period with a decorated balustrade. Skirting this we come to the south transept door with its non-figurative archivolts, the inner of which is cusped on the lower edge; this scheme had considerable influence on other churches in the town and even farther afield. The niche to the right of the doorway has a very delicate carving of the Virgin and

Child with angels in the tympanum. Facing this doorway is the plain episcopal palace (now diocesan offices) with a grand entrance added by Bishop Cabanillas in 1762. We can continue no farther in this direction and must retrace our steps round the head of the church and past the north entrance. Leaving the rectangle of the cloister on our left, we pass under two arches into a pleasant garden called the Plaza del Castillo, in which archaeological specimens are distributed on the patches of lawn. A walk has been made along the battlements on the south side overlooking the Duero. From here there is an uninterrupted view of the cupola and of the great square tower; the latter with its three stages of windows beginning more than half-way up is sternly impressive. Following the battlements we come to the castle, protected by a fosse on the inner side and by its walls rising from the natural rock on the other flanks. The central court has been relined with modern buildings occupied by a trades school. Continuing along the perimeter of the garden we come to the Municipal Laboratory of 1911, equipped with a useful *evacuatorio público* or public loo. From here a short ramp descends to the **Portilla de la Traición**, by which according to an inscription on the outer face 'Bellido Dolfos, after treacherously killing Sancho II of Castile, re-entered the city, pursued by the Cid.'

Now, it is rather hard to be sure of all the details of this important episode in the shaky progress towards unity of Castile and León. Having brought the kingdoms together, Ferdinand I followed the usual self-defeating practice of dispersing them again on his death in 1065 between his children. To Sancho he left Castile, to Alfonso León, to García Galicia and to his daughters Urraca and Elvira the feudal lordships of Zamora and Toro respectively. Disagreements shortly arose between Sancho and Alfonso with the result that the latter was forced to flee and take refuge with the Moorish King of Toledo, where he stayed three years enjoying the most generous hospitality and garnering knowledge that was to be useful to him when he later captured this city. Either because the sisters supported the cause of their exiled brother or because he was simply greedy for their domains, Sancho then besieged Toro, which capitulated to him, and Zamora, which stood firm for Doña Urraca under the direction of a knight called Arias Gonzalo. During this siege Dolfos, described as a Lusitanian, committed the murder commemorated by the

inscription, thus causing great indignation among the be-
siegers and embarrassment among the besieged, because this
sort of thing was not done, or not done in this way. Whether
Dolfos was acting for Urraca or for Alfonso or simply on his
own initiative has never been established. The person who
stood to gain most from the regicide was undoubtedly Alfonso.
Advised by Urraca of the event, he returned from exile and
was proclaimed King of Castile, León, Zamora and Navarre,
though not – the story goes – before the Cid had extracted
from him the famous triple oath that he had had 'neither art
nor part' in his brother's death (see p. 130). Zamora, as we
shall see, disputes with Burgos the site of this event.

   If one cannot afford the Parador Nacional in the Plaza de
Cánovas, the Dos Infantas (no restaurant) is very adequate.
Sadly, the old, clean and cheap Hotel Suizo is no more.
From the Parador one must pass two churches to reach the
cathedral. The first of these, **La Magdalena**, is Romanesque
of the immediately post-cathedral period; the semi-circular
apse has four columns rising the whole way to the eaves with
a moulding running under the windows and over the columns,
while a higher moulding runs between column and column,
cutting into the windows at the springing of the arch. Inside,
the tall single nave, roofed in wood, leads to a barrel-vaulted
sanctuary ending in a four-ribbed semi-cupola. Unusual
baldachinos stand against the walls nearest the sanctuary;
next to the one on the gospel side is the very fine tomb of an
unidentified lady with castellated canopy and interesting
capitals. Not only do we find the usual pairings of birds and
sphynxes back to back but also some novel ramifications, in
which winged beasts and even human beings with intertwined
necks appear to be throttling each other to death in the most
elegant and ornamental fashion imaginable. Continuing towards the cathedral, we shortly come to **San Ildefonso,**
formerly San Pedro, reached through an archway on the left.
Little survives from its eleventh-century origin but the semi-
circular apse largely hidden by the sacristy and the blocked-
up south doorway derived from the south door of the
Cathedral. The wide fifteenth-century nave has had to be
supported by flying buttresses whose thrust is held by the
convent wall across the narrow cobbled Calle de San Pedro.
This church contains the remains of its titular saint.

   The other main church of this district is **Santa Maria la**

Nueva, which is reached by following the signs from the Plaza de Cánovas to the Museo de Semana Santa, in front of which the church stands. Begun at the east end before the cathedral, Santa Maria has a beautiful apse with five columns rising to support a blind arcade under the eaves. The capitals of the little columns are of almost Celtic intricacy and the pairs of birds pecking unfortunate humans on the skull should be observed. Inside, the original nave and aisle distribution has gone and we have a wide single nave on the lines of San Ildefonso, though not here coated with stucco. The apse is covered by a semi-cupola and lit by three slits corresponding to the window embrasures outside. The sanctuary contains a recumbent Christ by or after Gregorio Fernández and the altar is raised on what is claimed as a Visigothic capital, though it is hard to see the carving. In the sacristy there are remnants of Romanesque wall paintings.

The **Museo de Semana Santa**, in a modern building designed for the purpose, confronts us in no uncertain terms with the end-products of the Spanish Renaissance. Gothic wood-carvers frequently used symbols. They spared us the shock of gougings, flayings, trepannings, garrottings, stonings to death, disembowellings etc. The martyrs of the church placidly carried in their hands the instruments of their deaths – Saint Stephen his stones, Saint Sebastian his arrows, Saint Lucy her eyes, Saint Catherine her wheel. This was no longer good enough for Spain once the mastery of the figure for its own sake had penetrated the country. Alonso Berruguete, as we have seen at Valladolid, preserved much of the Italian pre-occupation with the ideal, but Spanish taste was better satisfied in the long run by Juan de Juni, who developed what I have called Illusionism – in which he was followed by Gregorio Fernández. The School of Seville also played an important part in fixing the public taste in this direction. Yet, worse was to come. The sixteenth and seventeenth centuries at least achieved a certain vitality through their enthusiasm for the new techniques and modes of expression and we noted in some cases an element of carnival caricature, which was not inappropriate to images carried in processions. But this first fine frenzy of the Illusionist tours de force – followed by the Baroque attempt to integrate sculpture fully with architecture – passed away, leaving only a spoiled public palate longing for further thrills, the type of faded thrill provided by the nineteenth- and twentieth-century imagists here in Zamora, most of whose work wobbles between the anodyne and the absurd. In the Way to Calvary (9) by Justo Fernández, the Roman soldiers wear the sort of armour one might give to a six-year-old child. The star of the show is Ramón Alvarez, whose tableaux are completed with real ropes, pincers, hammers, nails etc. His most admired work is the Spear-thrust (24), in which the Roman soldier who pierces Christ's side is mounted on a splendid horse and the thieves are crucified with nails too, not ropes. The Raising of the Cross (18) by Alvaro de la Iglesia also gives us a veritable hardware store of ropes and carpentry tools including a spade and a saw. One wonders sometimes if one is in the Chamber of Horrors or Disneyland. The two works deserving of most serious consideration due to their ferociously simplistic handling are numbers 11 and 18 by Mariano Benlliure.

Two walks will suffice for the remaining churches and civil buildings of Zamora. Running south out of the Plaza Mayor the steep Calle Balbornoz leads down towards the river. Near the bottom on the left we find **Santa Maria de la Horta** of the late twelfth century with finely corbelled eaves and an apse similar to La Magdalena's. This church is easily identifiable by the great brick chimney that rises above it. A little farther east is **Santo Tomé** of the early twelfth century with rectangular absidal chapels and outside decoration of chequered bands; the belfry was added in 1836. Returning to Calle Balbornoz we take Calle Zapatería running west to emerge in the picturesque Plaza de Santa Lucía. In front is the Palacio de Puñonrostro, whose doorway and coat of arms are framed by the Franciscan rope and tassel motif. On the right is **Santa Lucía** of the seventeenth century with a simple belfry suitable for storks; higher up the slope is **San Cipriano**, built in 1025 with rectangular apses like those of Santo Tomé. The mottled stone and tower crowned by a slate-hung witch's hat are very attractive. Continuing along Calle Zapatería we come to the north end of the old bridge over the Duero. Built in Roman times to connect Mérida with León, it has since been rebuilt with 'eyes', as the elliptical flood ducts in each of the piers are called. Following the river westwards we shortly reach the extramural quarter clustering round **San Claudio** of the early twelfth century, whose only door on the north side has archivolts decorated with beasts, flowers and human trades and skills in the Leonese tradition. Nearby are the ruins of mill houses built out over the river. Now the walls of the castle begin to curve round the promontory above us and the road describes a similar curve. On the left in the flat stretch between the city and the Duero stands the tiny chapel of **Santiago de los Caballeros**, which claims to be the true site of Alfonso VI's oath to the Cid. If this is anything more than a legend, Santa Agueda at Burgos seems the more likely candidate. We know that when Alfonso was recalled by his sister he hurried straight to Burgos. Also it is known that the Cid brought the late King Sancho's body back to Oña. With this duty accomplished, what more likely than for him to proceed to the capital, which was also his own residence, and demand Alfonso's assurance before swearing allegiance? Another Zamoran tradition holds more plausibly that the Cid was knighted by Fernando I in this chapel after completing the last part of his knightly training under Arias Gonzalo. From here we return to the main road and continue our circuit of the wall. No footwalk is provided for the pedestrian so we have to compete with the traffic and it is with some relief that we come eventually to a bit of garden on the right, from which a path leads up to the Portillo de la Traición, through which, like Bellido Dolfos and the Cid, we re-enter the city.

The Plaza Mayor is the best starting point for a tour of the northern and eastern sectors of Zamora. Above the Plaza itself the tower of **San Juan** rises out of a clutter of building on the west side. This church has a single-span vault on the scale of San Ildefonso and Santa Maria la Nueva with the important difference that the very wide arches run east-west, only one to each side, supporting the nave roof longitudinally instead of crosswise. This arrangement, which is repeated in a number of churches in the region, has the advantage of increasing the floor space by doing away with the normal nave piers and the disadvantage that it is seldom strong enough to carry a vault and usually requires a wooden ceiling. Unfortunately the underlying structure is obscured here by Baroque plaster-work – a criticism that applies to a number of Zamoran churches, including **San Vicente** (off the plaza) which has a south door resembling the cathedral's and a good 'transitional' tower. Not far from here is the twelfth-century **Puerta de Doña Urraca.** Built on living rock between two drum towers, this gate provides an opening in the north wall, which continues more or less uninterruptedly to the traitor's gate.

Three streets radiate eastwards from the Plaza Mayor to join the main traffic-bearing Avenida de José Antonio. Facing onto the northernmost of these, Calle San Torcuato, is the **Palacio de los Momos** with one of those favourite façades of the late Gothic period, long and low with a great semi-circular arched doorway, small windows on the ground floor and larger windows above with Gothic tracery and heraldry framed in rectangular mouldings. Now seat of the law courts, this palace was for many years a *posada*, the haunt of muleteers and gypsies and dealers and beggars. The façade still manages to exhale something of the splendours and squalors of the past. The middle of the three streets, Calle Santa Clara, leads to a square with the banks and the Gobierno Civil. A little farther along on the left is the late twelfth- and early thir-teenth-century **Santiago del Burgo** with rustic tower and square apse. The porch, blessed by the midday sun, is the haunt of all the black-bereted pensioners of the city, who gather there to cackle and munch and watch the motor-borne world go honking by. The nave is high in relation to its size with clerestory windows and a barrel vault over the two western bays, switching to a quadripartite vault nearer the sanctuary. The development of the acanthus leaf into a pro-nounced sinister beak with upper foliage resembling eyes is noticeable in some of the nave capitals. On the same side of the street is the Museo Provincial de Bellas Artes, which I am unable to describe, as I have always found it closed. By all accounts a rather modest light is hidden under this bushel. The southernmost street radiating from the Plaza Mayor is Calle San Andrés leading to the church of the same name with a seminary building attached to it in 1722. **San Andrés** is the largest of the single-nave wide-vault Zamoran churches. The span is so great that it embraces two parallel sanctuaries, neither of them mean in size and each with a large retablo. In the epistle-side chapel is the tomb with kneeling figure of Don Antonio de Sotelo, attributed to Pompeo Leoni; on the gospel side is that of Bishop Zapata. The wooden artesonado roof is interesting. The central portion is similar to those covering many secular halls of the sixteenth century but owing to the great width of the church lower sections of wooden barrel roofing are necessary on each side.

Under the northern walls of Zamora stretches the Bosque de Valorío, a pinewood popular for picnics on high-days and holidays. Through this winds the road to **La Hiniesta**, whose church has a grand recessed porch of the late thirteenth or early fourteenth century. The single nave is covered by a wide vault. There is an enjoyable fiesta here on May 22nd, when the streets are strewn with heather and bagpipes are played in honour of the Virgin.

At 20 km from Zamora is the fascinating little church of **San Pedro de la Nave**. Taking N122 from Portugal, we turn right after 12 km on the local road to the village of Campillo, to which the church was moved stone by stone between 1930 and 1932 from its original site, where it would have been lost under the new Esla reservoir. The church is claimed in its entirety as Visigothic of about 700 by some Spanish authorities, though dissenting foreign voices place it between 893 when Zamora was repopulated and 902. Bernard Bevan discerns two periods, the earlier comprising the sanctuary and all the decoration east of the crossing, which is of the crude Visigothic type whose motifs are wheels, stars, rosettes, crosses and helices. The arches throughout are of the Visigothic three-centred horseshoe variety. The aisles are separated from the crossing by pairs of horseshoe arches. There are barrel vaults over the sanctuary and its side chambers and a wooden roof over the nave and aisles. The outside fabric is of large stone blocks not matched but fitted together as in a dry-stone wall. They are much less homogeneous than those of Mozarabic churches such as Melque (Toledo). The ajimez windows have central columns with base and capital carved out of the same piece. The crosses, helices etc., on the outside are contained in simple non-interlocking circles.

So far, so good. There is nothing to cast doubt on a Visigothic origin. But then come the capitals of the crossing columns which, according to Bevan, 'are much superior to any absolutely authenticated Visigothic decoration'. These capitals have a curious trapezoidal shape. Among the themes, along with pecking birds and Christ and the Virgin, are Daniel in the lions' den and Abraham on the point of sacrificing Isaac, from which he is restrained by God's right hand plunging out of heaven. The imposts too are more sophisticated here with birds, human heads and bunches of grapes. On these grounds

Bevan deduces a reconstruction of about 900 and supports this view by pointing out – correctly – that the crossing arches do not really rest on their columns, which could have been added later. His suggestion is that there was a cupola over the crossing which collapsed during the Moorish occupation; the new capitals and columns were added to give additional support by the Christians who repopulated the area and rehabilitated the church. If this theory is correct, it has great bearing on the dating of Quintanilla de las Viñas (Burgos), which was given Visigothic rating on the grounds of the similarity between its carvings and these precise capitals at San Pedro. If the San Pedro capitals are not Visigothic, as seems likely, then nor is any part of Quintanilla. (cf. p. 141).

Zamora – Toro – Salamanca

After the capital the most interesting town in the province of Zamora and perhaps the pleasantest on the whole Duero is **Toro**, 33 km to the east on N122. Raised 100 m above a loop in the river, the little city enjoys an even more privileged position than either Tordesillas or Zamora and a wide view over the pines and poplars and grain lands to the south. Paradoxically, its loss of status as a provincial capital in 1833 (when it became part of the province of Zamora) has had long-term advantages. It has the layout of a considerable place, which was required by its previous importance, but has not been cursed by any of the present-day eyesores of provincial bureaucracy nor with a plague of banks.

Toro was repopulated by Christians in 910 and has been graced by many royal presences since then. Alfonso XI lived here with his son, later Saint Ferdinand, who was crowned here as King of León. The latter's wife, Beatrice of Swabia, died in the city. Maria of Portugal, wife of Peter the Cruel, was confined to it and her husband later captured it in his war with his half-brother, Henry of Trastamara, who chose it as the meeting place of his first cortes in 1369. John II, that indolent Trastamaran monarch, was born in Toro, held cortes in his birth-place in 1426 and 1442 and used it several times to meet the disgruntled opponents of his favourite, Alvaro de Luna. Isabel the Catholic was able to rally Toro to her side against her rival la Beltraneja; the battle of Toro (or Peleagonzalo) was decisive in that civil war. Less than 50 years later Toro was to declare itself totally against the Crown in the Revolt of the Commoners against Charles V. The ubiquitous Saint Theresa of Avila did not neglect to visit so important a town. In the next century it was the scene of the involuntary retirement of Philip IV's favourite, the Count-Duke of Olivares. If this all rather savours of name-dropping, it does serve to show that Toro has what Spaniards call *abolengo*, meaning a hoary ancestry.

A ring road flanks the town to the north. Off this a street leads to the centre via a plain gate erected under Philip III and dated 1602. To the right of the archway is an inscription carved in the stone. This tells us that the city had two fairs, one commencing on Saint Mary's day in August and ending on the fifth of September every year and the other lasting from ten days before Lent for twenty days; the royal licence for both of these was given by His Majesty on March 18th, 1600. The importance of these fairs, which often lasted a month and for which municipalities lobbied incessantly, was that the goods brought into and out of a city during these periods were exempt from the crippling royal taxes called *alcabala*, *peaje*, *portazgo*, etc. This is the true origin of Spanish fairs, which were not just fun-fairs and bull-fights as they are today but serious trading marts availing themselves of temporary tax exemption. It was a good way for the Crown to reward loyal or favoured cities . . . and later ask them for heavy subsidies out of the proceeds.

The first church on the right through this arch is devoted to our own Saint Thomas à Becket, known here as **Santo Tomás Cantuarense**. It has been much restored but is still impressive with its longitudinal arches on the Zamoran pattern. The sanctuary contains a fine Renaissance retablo in the style of Alonso Berruguete. Continuing up the street we come into the Plaza del Generalísimo with a wooden arcade on the north side. Facing this rises the **Torre del Reloj** begun in 1719 and attributed to Joaquín Churriguera. This handsome timepiece is pierced by an arch beyond which the road widens into the Puerta del Mercado. From here the famous collegiate church of golden stone is visible. Next, on the right, is the Plaza de España with the church of the **Santo Sepulcro** on the north side. Inside, there are three Romanesque-Mudéjar brick apses, only one of which has been freed of later accretions. There is a brick blind arcade along the north wall and the rear choir is raised above a wooden Mudéjar ceiling, which covers the first bay of the nave. The general structure is on the same principle as Saint Thomas's. On the other side of the square is the grave **Casa Consistorial** built on the orders of Charles III in 1778 by Ventura Rodríguez.

Thus we come to the splendid **Colegiata de Santa Maria la Mayor** built between 1160 and 1233 to a design based on the cathedral of Zamora. The view of the lantern, which with two tiers of windows outstrips Zamora, is unimpeded by any unfortunate additions. The four corner turrets are reminiscent of Zamora's but the gables are lacking. The normal tiled roof has a less exotic effect perhaps than the fish-scales and spiny ribs of the prototype but the original apses remain, giving us a very good idea of the appearance of the original east end of Zamora. The corbels are similar to those on Zamora's south face and the castellated capitals of the exterior apse columns are direct copies of those in the Zamoran nave. The north portico has four archivolts with musicians and angels and a cusped intrados, which is also carved with figures. The tower has a later top stage. Inside, we perceive at once that the building is shorter than the cathedral with only three bays to the crossing. It is also lighter, owing to the 32 windows of the lantern and the rose-windows, while the view is unimpeded to the sanctuary owing to the removal of the centrally placed choir (which lost its purpose once the church ceased to have a chapter). The piers are of huge girth, larger than their Zamoran equivalents. It appears from the untenanted columns that there was a radical change in the vaulting plan of the nave. What we have is a slightly pointed barrel vault instead of the quadripartite vaults that were presumably intended. The interior organisation of the apses again gives an excellent idea of what we should have found at Zamora, had it not been for the modernising tastes of Cardinal Menéndez Valdés. The slightly pointed sanctuary arch introduces a short stretch of barrel vaulting ending in a semi-cupola over a rose-window – a very successful arrangement. The Gothic tombs belong to members of the powerful Fonseca family. The sanctuary capitals are decorated with figures and beasts and one discerns among them Daniel and the lions.

The capitals become simpler and more schematic towards the west and one might be tempted to think that the enterprise was running out of steam, were it not for the overwhelming **Pórtico de la Gloria**, once the main entrance of the church but now enclosed by the ruined walls of the later church of Santo Tomé, added on in the fourteenth century and demolished in the eighteenth. This very fine painted stone doorway under a recessed arch seems to have been built between 1235 and 1240 and the story goes that Saint Ferdinand sent masons from Burgos for the purpose as a reward to Toro, which had been the first city to recognise him as King of León. An inscription above tells us that the paintwork of this 'retablo' was last re-touched in 1774, which shows of course that the Colegiata's door was used as Saint Thomas's retablo until that church was pulled down, owing its excellent state of conservation largely to this fact. The six archivolts contain angels, kings and prophets, martyrs, prelates, queens and crowned musicians. The outer rim depicts the Last Judgement – as usual the damned look no worse than the saved and who goes where seems to be as much a matter of chance as cutting a pack of cards. The crowning of the Virgin occupies the tympanum, the architrave underneath shows her 'transit' or death. The brackets supporting this on either side of the door represent angels and prophets. The *parteluz* dividing the doors reverts to the Virgin, here carrying the Child. Despite the pointed arch there is nothing 'transitional' here – or if there is, it is a transition that has become frozen on its first step towards the Gothic, for the whole distribution of this doorway is thoroughly and completely Romanesque.

Another church worth seeing is **San Lorenzo**. The key-holder of this (and of the Santo Sepulcro already mentioned) is none other than the priest of the Colegiata. San Lorenzo is built almost entirely of brick with two tiers of blind arcading circling the apse outside, tall Lombard bands running right up the outer walls and a brick belfry. The interior has a very attractive rear choir painted in bright simple colours; it is possible that this gallery was put together from the remnants of an earlier ceiling covering the same church. The original sanctuary arch is cut by a later Gothic vault. The retablo is by Fernando Gallego. The inside walls of the nave repeat the tall Lombard bands of the outside in a more deeply recessed version. Leaving the church we shortly reach a ruinous house of the dukes of Alba on the right. Turning left in front of this we come into the Paseo de San Francisco with the privately owned bull-ring built in 1828. It is rather difficult to see the ring except in festival times, because grass grows in the arena during the long rainy season and the grazing rights are held by a shepherd who also holds the only key. But the head waiter of the Hotel Don Juan II (a good place for a meal or the night) is usually able to fix a visit for anyone staying 24 hours. The covered upper and lower galleries, here all of wood, echo the design of the earlier and hallowed Ronda ring (1784).

The other things to see in Toro are not of vast interest but it is a tempting place to wander in, so they should be mentioned. If we return to the Torre del Reloj and turn left along the inner face of the old wall we come to the **Arco del Postigo** or postern gate and then to the ruined church of **San Pedro del Olmo** whose thirteenth-century brick apses have been preserved with some remnants of frescoes on the inside walls. The nearby Templar church of **San Salvador** has received the same treatment. Outside the wall beyond the church of La Trinidad are the remains of the **Palacio de Leyes**, which was the scene of a number of cortes in the Middle Ages. Only the doorway is left; the chain hanging over the lintel signifies that the building was visited by kings. On the outskirts, almost in the country, is the Dominican **Convento del Santo Espíritu**, where the alabaster sepulchre of Beatrice of Portugal, wife of Ferdinand IV of Castile, occupies the centre of the peaceful nuns' choir. The nave with a sixteenth-century wooden ceiling leads via a pointed arch to the sanctuary with a shallow and very pretty Mudéjar ceiling, painted in pale blue, coral and white with a coral frieze; from this dangle some meagre and incongruous little drawing-room chandeliers. Just beyond this convent is the shrine of **Nuestra Señora del Canto** on the very edge of the countryside. The brick churches of Toro are completed by the **Ermita de Santa Maria de la Vega**, founded in 1208, which lies about 1 km to the south among the market gardens that spread under the sandy eminence of the town. This is a good place for a picnic. If brick is becoming boring by now, it is right to remember that we are still on the southern fringe of the Tierra de Campos, where stone had to be brought from a distance and was a luxury. Even the dressed stone walls of the glorious Colegiata itself are not solid stone; the clean golden surfaces are made possible only by a core of *cal y canto*, a rough pebbly type of masonry.

From Toro C519 leads pleasantly but uneventfully via Fuentesaúco to Salamanca. Those who did not, while at Valladolid, take in the arrogant towers of Alaejos may prefer to take C112 to this town, where they join N620 for the university city.

CHAPTER SEVEN

Salamanca and Ciudad Rodrigo

✵

Salamanca is a name that arouses great expectations, not on the whole disappointed given the explosive phase of reconstruction that grips most of the old cities of Spain. The oldest surviving masonry belongs to that part of the Roman bridge – 15 arches of it – which stood up to the disastrous flooding of the river Tormes in 1626. This bridge was built to carry the road that linked Emerita Augusta (Mérida), capital of Lusitania, with Asturica Augusta (Astorga) – whose fortified camp like León's helped control the wild Astures. Certain dates there are none until 589 when Salamanca sent Bishop Eleuterio to the third Council of Toledo, which proves the place had been christianised by that year. In 712 it fell to Muza-ben-Nuseir, commander-in-chief of the Moorish invasion. Owing to its exposed position in the flat lands between the Duero and the Tagus it then changed hands with the usual frequency. Ordoño I of León took it in 863. Abdarraman III failed to take it in 938 before his defeat at Simancas but on his retreat he succeeded in entering the town, which suffered severely. Once again repopulated and twice sacked by Almanzor, it was not irrevocably secured for Christendom until 1085, the year of the reconquest of Toledo, when Alfonso VI charged his son-in-law Raymond of Burgundy with the rehabilitation. Walls and an alcázar were built – only to be demolished under Henry IV. The most important remaining bastion of 'Salmantica Fortis' is the old cathedral, most of which still stands.

Prior to 1230 Alfonso IX of León founded a school in emulation of the one set up by Alfonso VIII of Castile at Palencia; this was the germ of Salamanca's famous university. In the war of succession the town turned out for Isabel against her rival la Beltraneja and contributed to the victory of Toro. Under the Reyes Católicos it flourished, boasting 45 parishes, but it must have been of unhappy memory for the sovereigns whose only son Prince John died in 1497 while a student at the

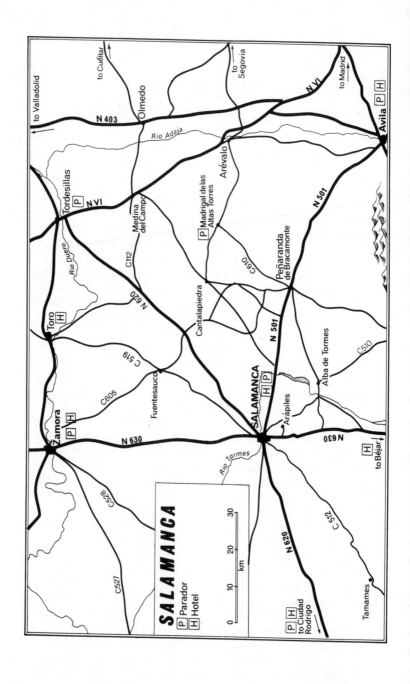

university. The municipality recognised Charles V as Charles I of Spain in 1517 but did not manage to prevent the Maldonados and other leading families from joining the Revolt of the Commoners, leading to severe reprisals in 1521. But this monarch was well received by the townsfolk in 1534 and it was at Salamanca that the future Philip II married his first wife Maria of Portugal. The flood that carried away half the bridge left the place desolate for nearly a century until it experienced a revival under the Bourbons. The Peninsular War brought fresh destruction. The licensed pillage of Napoleon's armies has left a vivid scar on the imagination of almost every major city in Spain. In Seville the villain was Soult, in Salamanca Leclerc . . . etc. But that is not to say that Wellington is popular, as we shall see when we come to his battlefield.

On July 18th, 1936, the Civil War broke out and Salamanca was from the outset in Nationalist territory. The Basque Rector of the University, Miguel de Unamuno, one of the most prolific – between 1880 and 1924 he wrote something like four thousand articles in addition to his major works – and tortured thinkers of the age, at first declared himself in favour of the military rising against the Republic. Later, in a clash with General Millán Astray, inventor of the famous slogan 'Long live Death!' he came out publicly against the Nationalists, by whom he was removed from his rectorship and confined to his house until his death on December 31st of the same year. But Salamanca as a whole accepted the new régime, acted as host to some of the government departments and thus did not suffer in the war. Since then the city has grown from 40,000 to 120,000 inhabitants, not without some unattractive results. All the same, the continuing expansion of its ancient university gives it a contemporary relevance lacked by such cities as Avila and Toledo.

At Salamanca one must start in the **Plaza Mayor**, whose sober Spanish Baroque style is given an agreeable warmth by the marvellous golden colour of the stone. The project was conceived during the visit of Philip V in 1710, though the work was not begun till 1728. The first designs were made by Alberto Churriguera, while José de Lara Churriguera and Nicolás Churriguera also played their part in building this great square, whose only possible rival is its drier namesake in Madrid, which preceded it by more than a century. The Churriguera

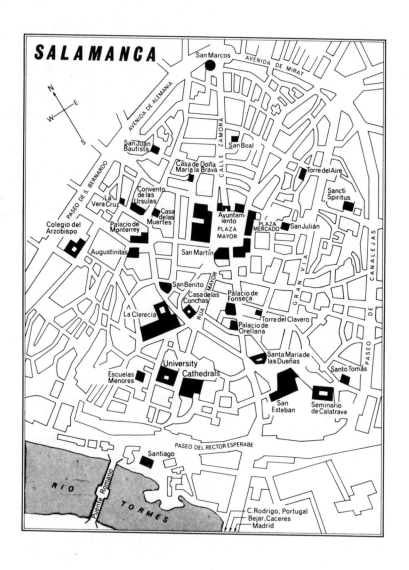

family came to fame as altarpiece-makers but, despite their reputation for extravagance, they did not in fact bring all the loaded ornament of their retablos to their outside surfaces when they graduated to architecture. Here they have doffed their caps in the direction of the Renaissance with the roundels of kings and heroes that decorate the south and east sides. Otherwise, the elevations are plain, except for that of the **Ayuntamiento** in the centre of the north side, whose slightly more florid façade with combined belfry and clock-tower is by Andrés García de Quiñones, the architect who completed the project in 1755. The warmth of the stone, the comfortable width of the arcades, the bustle of student life and the play of light and shade on the Ayuntamiento façade make this the most delightful square in Spain for a stroll followed by an aperitif at one of the many café tables with which it is lined.

Leaving by the south-west corner, we are confronted at once by the Romanesque doorway of the church of **San Martín**, recalling those of Zamora. Most of the outside of this building is encrusted with houses. The interior is in the pointed Romanesque style of the thirteenth century. From the south door, dated 1586, the Rua Mayor runs straight towards the massive cathedral tower. A little before this, set back on the right, is the tall Baroque façade of the Clerecía – we will return to this later. The Rua Mayor emerges in the Plaza de Anaya with the large Baroque college of this name, now the faculty of philosophy and letters, on the left. Facing this is the north side of the late Gothic cathedral, whose lantern was not completed till the eighteenth century. The sign at the bottom of the steps reads **Catedrales**, for there are indeed two of them. Climbing the steps, we come to the west front where the new cathedral was begun in 1512. Carved between 1513 and 1533, and thus later than the façades of Valladolid, the whole elevation is still in the exteriorised retablo tradition with its Calvary flanked by Saints Peter and Paul and its large high-relief scenes of the two Adorations over the doors. Though 'Gothic-Plateresque' is the term generally applied to stone-carving of this period in the Gothic taste, close inspection of the decorative bands reveal lurking beasts, monkeys, birds and human figures deeply carved at the artist's caprice and recalling the luxuriant Isabelline-Gothic foliage of Gil de Siloe, bravely putting forth its final shoots.

To the right of this entrance is the great square-based tower, which has an interesting history. Its core is formed by the tower of the old cathedral and its first stage is still occupied on the inside by a chapel with early frescoes. Rodrigo Gil de Hontañón, who took over the new cathedral works in 1512, disguised this old tower under a more fashionable casing. But the belfry, of wood still, was destroyed by lightning in 1705.

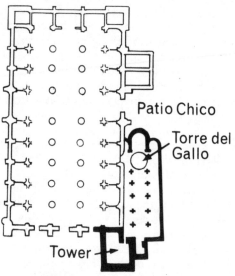

SALAMANCA CATHEDRAL
The old cathedral and tower shown in black

Rebuilding with a new lantern to designs by Pedro Ribera was completed in 1733. After this the whole structure began to give, presumably as a result of the additional weight. Alberto Churriguera took some measures of consolidation but they were insufficient. Matters were not helped by the Lisbon earthquake of 1755, after which the spire became twisted and cracks appeared in the walls, causing such consternation that the bishop moved his palace and the university seriously considered evacuation. In 1766 Ventura Rodríguez recommended demolition and presented a smug design of his own for two safe neat towers. But the people of Salamanca clung to their rickety old steeple and called in Baltasar Derrotón, who had shored up Córdoba after the same earthquake. He devised the solution of entirely encasing all the existing structure of whatever period in a strong plain strait-jacket of dressed stone. This was done and what we see is thus a real Chinese box of a tower within a tower within a tower.

On this side it is difficult to see much of the old cathedral and the best plan is to walk downwards from the tower and turn left up Calle Gibraltar, which leads to the Patio Chico under the south flank of the whole complex. First the lantern of the new cathedral soars into view. Then, as we get nearer the south door, the apses of the old church and the famous **Torre del Gallo** contribute their more sombre note. The latter is a lantern-cupola of the period of Zamora and Toro. With corner turrets, intervening gables and scaly tiles it most resembles Zamora, though the pitch of the roof is steeper here. As it is overshadowed by its later and larger neighbour, it is inevitably less impressive than the other members of the group. Even so, it asserts a potent presence against the flashier and more facile masonry all round it and we must, in any case, account it a mercy it has survived at all. We can now either enter the cathedral by the south door or continue the circuit by Calles San Vicente Ferrer and Silencio to re-emerge in the Plaza de Anaya near the north entrance, whose tympanum is carved with the Entry into Jerusalem.

By whichever door one enters, the first impression one receives on the inside is one of homogeneous grandeur. The piers rise from 'wicker-work' bases and, interrupted only by token capitals, exfoliate into a very graceful vault. There is an ample intake of light at three levels – from the clerestory, from the windows over the vestigial triforium balustrade and from the side chapels occupying the spaces between the buttresses. A gesture is made in the direction of the Renaissance by the medallions on either side of the clerestory windows, in the diaphragms of the nave arcade and in other parts of the church. Two nave bays are occupied by the choir. The transepts do not extend beyond the outer walls of the side chapels. The crossing is crowned and lit by the lantern put up between 1705 and 1733 by Joaquín Churriguera and Andrés García de Quiñones; the inside adornment of this is rather at odds with the rest of the building. In the sanctuary there is, for once, no retablo and the trasaltar has been prepared with virgin stone blocks for carving that was never carried out. The church is square-ended; the walk between the trasaltar and the three parallel east-end chapels returns one straight to the opposite aisle. I myself find this too abrupt and utilitarian an arrangement and long for a proper ambulatory such as we shall find at Segovia.

Entry to the old cathedral can only be achieved via the new, which has usurped higher ground. This is why the Torre del Gallo appears to such disadvantage from the outside and why we pass from the sixteenth century to the twelfth by a staircase that leads down from the first chapel on the epistle side of the main church. The contrast is remarkable. The five splendid, solemn nave bays of the **Catedral Vieja** are perhaps superior to those of Zamora and Toro. The carving of the capitals is certainly richer and more varied with its deeply and confidently incised foliage, human heads and twinned beasts – amongst the latter pairs of birds driving their beaks into human skulls. This cathedral was founded in 1102 during the bishopric of Jerónimo of Périgord, the Cid's companion-at-arms who had previously occupied the sees of Valencia and Zaragoza. It is not certain when building began but consecration is known to have taken place in 1160. The nave was originally intended for a barrel vault but a later master opted for the quadripartite system, whose ribs required additional support, giving rise to the large human and lions' faces on the brackets above the capitals. This is the direct opposite of the process that took place at Toro, where the quadripartite vaulting of the original plan was dropped in favour of the easier barrel vaulting. The Salamanca lantern, built probably between 1180 and 1200, is two-tiered with 32 lights as at Toro, though alternate windows have been blocked in the lower stage. The north transept and part of the north apse have been chopped off to make way for Big Sister but the south transept remains intact with its zig-zag vaulting ribs. This contains four fine Gothic tombs of canons with remnants of their original colouring and there is a fifth in the south apse. Salamanca is rich in painted stone sepulchres.

The semi-cupola of the sanctuary is decorated with a great fresco of the Last Judgement by Nicolás Florentino, under which is a marvellous **Retablo** of 55 painted wooden panels with scenes from the Life of Christ by the same master. This was ordered by Bishop Don Sancho of Castile and the contract signed in 1445, a year before the bishop's death. The elegant figures and delicate Italian colouring are in notable contrast with the harsh colours and bold or grotesque shapes of Castilian painting of this period. The Virgen de la Vega in the centre of the lowest row of panels is made of wood covered with copper, bronze and gold; the figures on her throne are enamelled and the eyes of mother and child alike consist of black pearls – how the guides love to recite these details! Among those buried in the sanctuary is Bishop Don Sancho, who lies appropriately close to his grand pictorial legacy. At the rear of the old cathedral in the base of the tower is the **Capilla de San Martín** with a retouched mural of 1262, whose lower border is painted to resemble a tapestry. The theme is the ever popular Last Judgement and the usual Romanesque blacks, ochres, whites and blue-greys predominate. The tomb of a bishop who died in 1339 preserves, like those in the transept, much of its original colouring.

The old cloister had to be largely rebuilt as a result of the Lisbon earthquake of 1755, which so shook the tower. Never re-vaulted, it is covered by a plain wooden ceiling. Parts of the Romanesque structure remain, however, and we are shown chapels that were used as class-rooms from about 1230 until the present university buildings were put up. The first of these is the **Capilla de Talavera** with a dome whose sixteen ribs, which do not meet at the centre, follow the practice of Moorish parallel vaults. As late as 1516 Doctor Talavera founded chaplaincies in order that the Mozarabic rite should be continued in his chapel. The carved and painted altarpiece is attributed to Pedro Berruguete. The **Capilla de Santa Bárbara** contains the tomb of Bishop Juan Lucero. At the foot of this is the chair on which candidates for doctorates in theology underwent their ordeal by questioning from the members of the tribunal seated on stone benches round the wall. The candidate might rest his feet on the stone feet of the bishop's effigy to derive inspiration from this august source. If he passed, he was carried out in triumph and great celebrations were organised, including a bull-fight. If he failed, he slunk out of the postern gate. Perhaps this was better than having to force a smile in answer to such condolences as, 'Bad luck, old man, better luck next time!' Next comes the **Museum** with interesting works by the Salmantine painter Fernando Gallego; this artist's macabre Triptych of Saint Catherine repays study. There is also a wood carving by Alonso Berruguete and an attractive high-relief panel of the seventeenth century representing the conversion of Saint Hubert, patron of the Chase, with the wondering animals standing around. Upstairs is a fine panel of Saint Michael by Juan de Flandes and the usual collection of church plate. The sophisticated Gothic-Renaissance **Capilla de Santa Catalina** has columns rising from brackets and splaying out in a way that almost seems to herald a fan-vault, though this supreme manifestation of Gothic never arrived in Castile. In this chapel is a metal cock (*gallo*) retired from duty on the Torre del Gallo, which acquired its name from these weathervanes. The thirteenth-century **Capilla de San Bartolomé** or de **Anaya** contains the magnificent tomb of Bishop Diego de Anaya, d. 1437, protected by an elaborate grille. There is also an attractive painted Morisco organ and loft.

Of the new cathedral chapels the following deserve brief mention. Leaving the old cathedral, the first on the right is the **Capilla Dorada** with 110 small polychrome wooden figures made by the sculptors of the west front for the then Archdeacon of Alba. The choir and pulpit are in the Gothic-Mudéjar taste. At the east end and facing the north aisle is the **Capilla de la Soledad**, whose virgin is by Mariano Benlliure (cf. Zamora). At the same end the **Capilla del Carmen** has a retablo by Joaquín Churriguera enshrining a small Byzantine crucifix said to have belonged to the Cid and to have been brought to Salamanca by Bishop Jerónimo. Here too are the battling bishop's remains in a rather unsuitable white Churrigueresque urn. Finally, the **Coro** should not be overlooked. The stalls are by Joaquín Churriguera, assisted by José de Lara Churriguera and Andrés Carnicero. The Gothic tradition of apostles and saints is preserved in the upper series, whose figures are finely carved with very crisp robes. The intermediary columns are decorated with amorini and the pinnacles with charming putti. By this period the misericords have become almost standardised, mostly taking the form of those wide-mouthed gargoyles one associates with fountains. But the carving in general shows none of the vulgar Mannerism of the early Spanish Renaissance and this choir, begun in 1724, does not dishonour its great Gothic predecessors. There are two organs, one of 1558 and the other of 1713.

After the cathedrals one should proceed via Calles Calderón and Libreros to the university. Approaching from any other direction, follow the signs marked **Universidad**. The entrance, generally acknowledged as the jewel of the Plateresque style, was begun before 1516 and finished in 1529. It is customary to distinguish three types of Plateresque, namely: Gothic motifs applied to Gothic buildings, Renaissance motifs applied to Gothic buildings and Renaissance motifs applied to Renaissance buildings. If these categories are accepted, the west front of the new cathedral falls into the first, while the university entrance is somewhere between the second and the third for it is an entirely Renaissance doorway from ground to balustrade applied to an earlier Gothic building. Whoever carried out the work came from or had been to Italy and paid little or no attention to the contemporary work in progress at the cathedral. Here the columns themselves are incised with very delicate low-relief designs; these and the pilasters appear not to vary between one side and the other but in fact there is considerable licence in their carving. The medallion heads are in pronounced Italian taste and the most important of them, depicting the Reyes Católicos, might almost be one of the bronze or lead medals fashionable at the time (cf. Museo Lázaro Galdiano, Madrid), so fine is the detail. The decoration of the lower panels is very tightly packed; the heraldic stage above introduces larger forms; higher up again is the bold stage of the papal panel and the whole is crowned by a yet more broadly handled balustrade. The execution is nowhere equalled in the whole of the Plateresque canon.

This entrance leads to the **Escuelas Mayores** begun in 1415. We have seen that the univeristy began its life in the cloister of the old cathedral. Saint Ferdinand and Alfonso X, the Learned, conceded privileges; so did popes, particularly that extraordinary figure Pedro de Luna, Cardinal of Aragón, later Benedict XIII, who founded yet a third papacy at Peñíscola after his expulsion from Avignon at the time of the schism. In the second half of the fourteenth century colleges began to be built, though they never developed the autonomy of their opposite numbers at Oxford and Cambridge. By the end of the sixteenth century the university had 8000 students and 70 chairs, and classes began at six in the morning. After a long decline numbers have risen again to 7000 but classes are more in line with office hours. Proceeding into the patio we find, in the upper gallery, our first example of the Salamantine or mixtilinear arcade, whose arches based on five intersecting circles are usually ascribed to Moorish influence. The chapel, rebuilt in 1776, contains the Virgin before which university members swore to defend the doctrine of the Immaculate Conception for over two centuries before its promulgation as a dogma by a tardy Vatican in the nineteenth century. The *paraninfo* or senate house, where doctorates and diplomas are awarded, is of no great interest but the *aula* or lecture hall of Fray Luis de León should not be missed. The benches and desks made from great tree trunks are original. The conical-hatted *cátedra* contains the pulpit, as it were, of the *catedrático* or professor with the seat of the *lector*, who read the texts to be discussed, underneath. Round the walls are bench seats for the servants of noble students and for the *licenciados*, those with masters' degrees. Fray Luis had the temerity to translate into Spanish a book of the Old Testament, the Song of Songs, for which he was imprisoned at the instance of the Inquisition for five years. When released, he resumed his chair and reverted in his opening lecture to the theme he had left in the air five years before with the celebrated words: 'As we were saying yesterday ...' In this hall sat most of the *esprits forts* of the Age of Gold, among them Calderón de la Barca and Cervantes. Nor should one forget dedicated souls like Father Vitoria, one of the founders of International Law – a subject that received great impetus from the discovery of the New World. Here it is not inappropriate to quote Doctor Johnson, who said, 'I love the University of Salamanca; for when the Spaniards were in doubt as to the lawfulness of their conquering America, the University of Salamanca gave it as their opinion that it was not lawful.' And Boswell adds, 'He spoke with great emotion.'

A staircase with a coffered ceiling and solid balustrade carved with grotesques and figures illustrating the labour and pleasures of country life leads to the gallery with the mixtilinear arches. From here there is a good view of the tower and lantern of the new cathedral rising beyond the university belfry. An inscription records that Alfonso the Learned established the library and stipulated in 1254 that it should have a professional librarian with a fixed salary, the first of his kind in Spain. The 60,000 'old' volumes are housed in handsome shelves from the Churriguera workshop. The manuscripts are kept in seventeenth-century shelves in a small room, which also houses the university chest – a strong-box whose five locks required the presence of all five key-holders to open it.

Mudéjar style, Military and Religious:

Top left, window of the ruined castle of Alvaro de Luna, Escalona;
right, tower once forming part of the town wall, Maqueda.
Below left, cusped and horseshoe arches on the apse of San Pablo, Peñafiel;
right, panel above the entrance to the convent of Santa Clara, Tordesillas.

San Pedro de la Nave (Zamora). Visigothic and Mozarabic elements are discernible. This trapezoidal capital probably belongs to the Mozarabic restoration of about 900.

The Salmantine lantern-cupolas:
The Cathedral of Zamora with the great tower on the left and the lantern in
the background.

Left, the cupola of the Colegiata of Toro and *right* the Torre del Gallo,
Salamanca.

Salmantine Baroque. The Ayuntamiento by Andrés García de Quiñones, finished in 1755.

The Renaissance in Salamanca. *Left,* detail with medallion heads in the patio of the Colegio del Arzobispo.
Right, detail of the University facade, 'generally acknowledged as the jewel of the Plateresque style'; the low-relief medallion depicts the Reyes Católicos looking distinctly satisfied with life.

Patio of the convent of Santa Maria de las Dueñas, Salamanca. 'The heavy arches of rounded profile recall the plain robust arcades of old Castilian mansions but the upper gallery bracket-capitals are alive with wildly contorted grotesques and figures, which lunge out so far that they almost meet to form a series of false arches.'

Panorama of Segovia with—reading from left to right—San Esteban, the Cathedral and the Alcázar.

Left, the Cathedral tower 'only lightly tethered to the Gothic age'.
Right, the Alcázar. 'The sharp west end, dividing those delightful streams, the Eresma and the Clamores, inevitably invites comparison with the prow of a ship.'

Piedrahita, Province of Avila. 'The town square is delightful with its plane trees round the parish church of Santa Maria la Mayor, whose squat old tower stands astride the crossing; in the south face there is a little ajimez window, which may be Visigothic . . .'

El Barco de Avila on the river Tormes.

Plasencia Cathedral, the high vault by Juan de Alava. '. . . nowhere did he produce such splendid vaults as at Plasencia.'

Facing the university entrance is a quadrangle presided over by a bronze statue of Luis de León. In the far left-hand corner is the gateway leading to the **Escuelas Menores**, which served from 1533 to 1934 as a secondary school preparing candidates for the university proper. Here again we find the mixtilinear arch, this time on stout circular columns round the pleasant patio. The arcade is topped by a balustrade in which Baroque urns alternate with Gothic finials and Renaissance grotesques; the combination is surprisingly successful. The **Salón de Latín** is covered by two quite separate artesonado ceilings, one painted and the other carved, both of the sixteenth century. The **Museum** has been specially made to take the great fresco done by Fernando Gallego in 1494 for the semi-cupola of the old chapel, which suffered severely in the Lisbon earthquake. The signs of the zodiac, the constellations and the four winds have been cleverly transferred to canvas and re-installed here in such a way as to preserve their original relationships. There are also some framed panels by Juan de Borgoña, whom we shall meet again at Toledo.

A feature of the whole university area that no one can fail to notice are the inscriptions in red ochre known as *vítores* on the walls of all the main buildings. These commemorate the doctorates of the learned and eulogise the achievements of prominent outsiders like General Franco and José Antonio Primo de Rivera. They are said to have originated with the bulls' blood inscriptions daubed on the walls after corridas held in honour of successful examinees. This has now become a tidy craft carried out with a stencil and even the bus and filling stations use it for their signs.

Leaving the university and continuing along Calle Libreros, we come to the immense Jesuit church of the **Clerecía**, which impresses by the sheer scale of its orders and decoration. But it is all much coarser than anything to be found in Gothic or Renaissance architecture. Here no longer are to be found the loving personal thrust of the chisel or the sly insertion of some favourite beast or jocular scene half obscured among the tendrils of an archivolt or pilaster. One might say there is no sense of humour. Artists are not encouraged to indulge personal idiosyncrasies. Everything is subordinate to a grand overall effect. And yet there is still no truly Baroque plastic treatment of the building as a whole. The project was conceived in 1610 when Philip III and Margarita of Austria made a visit to Salamanca. Plans were drawn up by Juan Gómez de Mora, nephew of Herrera's assistant Francisco de Mora, and the stern influence of the Escorial makes itself felt under the Baroque decorative motifs. The first stone was laid in 1627. In 1662 the cupola was covered but it was not until 1755 that the towers and belfry were completed by Andrés García de Quiñones, who was also responsible for the patio, now occupied by the 'Pontifical University'. This is grand enough in its way but heavy with the heaviness that we noted at Valladolid and from which Spanish architecture seldom if ever struggled free, even at the height of the Baroque period.

In front of the Clerecía is the **Casa de las Conchas**, finished in 1483 for Rodrigo Arias Maldonado, Chancellor of the order of Santiago. The conches with which the façade is studded proudly proclaim this coveted office. Over the doorway are the shields of the founder and the Reyes Católicos. Two of the main floor windows are mullioned and the others divided by ajimeces. In the patio we find an early version of the mixtilinear arch on square pillars. The gallery introduces a very flattened type of shouldered arch, while the balustrade of miniature columns is interlaced on the north and south sides with that wicker-work pattern so beloved by late fifteenth-century craftsmen – among whom it seems to have been a point of honour to demonstrate that they could produce this sort of effect in wood and stone (cf. Colegio de San Gregorio, Valladolid). A little way downhill from this house on the right is the **Plaza de San Benito**, which takes us back to the violent civil discords, based on less well-pondered points of honour, that had disturbed the peace of Salamanca throughout most of the fifteenth century. The parish church of San Benito in the centre of the little square gave its name to one of the bands of noble families whose energy was absorbed and whose blood spilt by a constant gang warfare arising usually out of absurd disputes. Burned down by the rival band of San Martín, the church was rebuilt about 1490 by Alonso de Fonseca, first of the two archbishops of this name whose works abound in the city. But the old houses of the factious Maldonado and Solís families remain and the little backwater is redolent of ancient feuds. Returning to the Clerecía and taking Calle Meléndez, it is only a short walk back to the Plaza Mayor.

The next itinerary embraces the south-east quarters of the

city. Again we start from the Plaza Mayor, this time taking
Calle San Pablo, which brings us shortly on the right to the
Palacio de Fonseca or **de la Salina**, built in 1538 by Alonso de
Fonseca II, Archbishop of Santiago and later of Toledo, son
of the rebuilder of San Benito. The patio is entered by a tall
portico of four arches opening onto a flight of steps. The
wooden gallery on the north side is supported by sixteen huge
stone brackets with tortured grotesque figures whose legs
dissolve into volutes. The second set of steps leading to the
main stairs rises under three unusually tall mixtilinear arches.
Though not large, this building is very gracious, more of a
palace and less of a fortress than Spanish mansions usually
are. A little farther down on the same side, facing the Plaza
de Colón, is the plain seventeenth-century **Palacio de Orellana**.
Like the Fonseca palace this has an exterior loggia on the
street but reverts to the older tradition of a corner tower. At
the north-east corner of the Plaza de Colón stands the **Torre
del Clavero**, whose square base generates an octagonal upper
stage decorated with an interlocking rope or net design. This
was built about 1480 for Francisco de Sotomayor, key-bearer
(*clavero*) of the order of Alcántara, and is still very much in
the fortified tradition. Near by is the adequate Hotel Clavero.
At the south-east corner of the plaza is the parish church of
San Pablo with a rusticated and pedimented façade and a
standard Baroque interior.

Bearing left round this church we are confronted by the
large monastic church of **San Esteban**, the most important in
Salamanca after the cathedrals. Building began in 1524 to
designs by Juan de Alava at the expense of Fray Juan de
Toledo, Bishop of Córdoba and son of the 'great' Duke of
Alba. The west entrance, set back under a huge recessed arch,
is in some ways more successful than the cathedral's. The
niches with canopies like stone monstrances are all tenanted.
The decoration of the pilasters places the work in the Plateresque sub-division of Renaissance ornament applied to Gothic
buildings. The fine central scene of the Stoning of Saint
Stephen over the door was not carried out till 1610 by an
Italian, Ceroni. At right angles to this façade is a long porch
of ten rounded arches with medallions and a balustrade. Let
into the wall is a plaque in memory of Fray Diego de Deza,
Columbus's advocate. Entering the monastery by a door in this
porch we come first to the **Claustro**, finished in 1544, by Juan

de Badajoz. The extravagant stucco bosses of his other cloisters (cf. Carrión de los Condes) are absent from the Gothic vault, rather to the advantage of the general effect. The rest of the decoration is fully Renaissance. The lower windows are unusual and elegant, each with three tall columns supporting an open fanlight of stone struts, while the upper gallery has round-headed windows between pilasters whose triple capitals are decorated with grotesques. To my mind this is his most successful work. The one-time chapter-house, now called the Theologians' Pantheon, contains the remains of the most illustrious Dominicans of the university under plain stone slabs in the floor. The present chapter-house is in the severe Spanish Baroque style. Beyond the stair-well is the sacristy, begun in 1627 by Juan Moreno and decorated with the painted shields of prelates. Under a Gothic vault the four flights of stairs rise to the gallery with pleasant views over the harmonious courtyard and the south side of the church. The choir, reached from this level, is reserved to the order.

The very large **Church** was designed by Juan de Alava, who became maestro mayor of the cathedral in 1531 and to whom we owe the marvellous vault at Plasencia, the finest late Gothic achievement in Spain. Here at San Esteban a reaction against the florid Gothic of the Reyes Católicos is evidenced by the wide relaxed vault, though a switch in the direction of the Renaissance, already heralded in the west front, is also apparent, particularly in the lantern which was not finished till the seventeenth century. The retablo mayor of 1693 is by José Benito Churriguera, founder of the family fortunes, faithfully and ponderously carrying out his task as master-builder of altar-pieces; the canvas of the Martyrdom of Saint Stephen is one of Claudio Coello's last works. The choir, raised on a great flattened arch and straddling nearly half the church, contains the tomb of Fray Juan's famous father, Don Fernando de Alvarez de Toledo y Pimentel, third Duke of Alba. Though this part is not on view, one cannot fail to notice from below the large mural on the west wall by Palomino, immodestly representing the Triumph of the Church through the good graces of the Dominican Order. Also in the part reserved to the monks is the Patio de Colón where Columbus held meetings with the savants of Salamanca and endeavoured to convince them of the feasibility of his proposals. The explorer first set foot in San Esteban in 1484 and the support of the Dominicans was indeed not to be despised. He received his first advance from the royal treasury three years later when virtually the whole income of the Crown was earmarked for the war effort against Granada.

From the porch of San Esteban there is a good view of the cathedrals and the towers of the Clerecía. Just across the cobbles and slightly to the right is the **Convento de Santa Maria de las Dueñas**, which one enters through a little garden and tiled hall to find a pleasant irregularly-shaped cloister. The heavy arches of rounded profile recall the plain robust arcades of old Castilian mansions but the upper gallery bracket-capitals are alive with wildly contorted grotesques and figures, which lunge out so far that they almost meet to form a series of false arches. In the gallery wall is a pretty Mudéjar door whose spandrels are inlaid with mosaic tiles. Returning to San Esteban and leaving it on the right we come to the **Seminario de Calatrava** built by Joaquín Churriguera in 1717. The dignified and reserved façade is Baroque in detail but not in feeling. The patio, modified in 1790, is positively stern. Almost facing the seminary is the church of **Santo Tomás Cantuarense**, a satisfying example of the pointed Romanesque style of about 1175. Continuing to the Paseo de Canalejas (a sector of the ring-road round the old city) and following this to the left for some distance we reach Calle Sancti Spíritus, also on the left, leading to the church of this name. What was once the choir at the west end has been switched round to become the **Capilla del Santísimo Cristo de los Milagros**, whose altar directly faces the high altar – outfaces it, one might say. This chapel with Mudéjar, Gothic and Renaissance elements and modern paintings of the Stations of the Cross is a good example of a Spanish jumble that somehow manages to achieve a kind of unity – perhaps simply because the faithful are blind to its defects. Following the slope downwards we come to the Gran Vía, where we turn right past the Tourist Office to the Plaza del Caudillo, which looks towards the Italianate Gothic mansion of the Fermoselle family. This once had four corner towers, of which only one remains, known as the **Torre del Aire**. Turning left along Calle Eloy Bullón we soon reach the Plaza de los Sesmeros with the robust old **Casa de la Tierra**, bought in 1713 as a meeting place for the *sesmeros* or mayors of the surrounding rural districts. This is a pleasant quiet corner to linger in under the lee of the church of San Julián before emerging into the Plaza del Mercado, whose west side is formed by an arcade from which buses leave and where gypsies, bootblacks, pig dealers, students and the picaresque world in general congregate. There are some cheap lively bars here. A flight of steps leads from the centre up to the more decorous Plaza Mayor.

There is a third itinerary that should not be missed. This time we leave the Plaza Mayor by the south-west corner, taking Calle Prior which leads to the Plaza de Monterrey. The **Palacio de Monterrey** was begun in 1539 to plans, it is claimed, by Rodrigo Gil de Hontañón and completed only on one side. It is the least successful of the Salmantine Renaissance palaces. Shields are tiresomely bent round the corners of the walls; above the loggia runs an overloaded balustrade. In the **Convento de las Agustinas**, opposite, the counts of Monterrey did better. The old convent of this order outside the walls was destroyed by the great flood of 1626. The new church was begun in 1636 at the expense of Gaspar de Acevedo y Zúñiga, Viceroy of Naples. His taste owes much to his Neapolitan posting. The style is a restrained and harmonious Baroque. Instead of elaborate retablos we find good pictures by Ribera (who lived and worked in Naples, it will be remembered) in elegant coloured marble frames over the five altars. The very dark background of the Adoration of the Shepherds on the epistle side was probably painted by Lucás Jordán to show off his master to good effect. In all these works Ribera displays his usual mastery of texture, composition, light and shade, which might have degenerated into a mere display of skills, had it not been for a tenacious and conscientious striving for excellence. The tombs with kneeling figures, also framed by coloured marbles, belong to M. de Fonseca y Zúñiga, Count of Monterrey and his wife, Doña Leonor, sister of the Count-Duke of Olivares.

Returning to the Plaza de Monterrey and leaving the palace on our left we shortly reach the pentagonal buttressed apse of the **Convento de las Ursulas**, rising above Vitorio Macho's bronze statue of Unamuno pacing – as was his wont – with hands clasped behind his back, hunched shoulders and questing beard, in endless colloquy with himself, his God and his fellow-men. Miguel de Unamuno (1864–1936) was rector of the university from 1901 to 1914 and from 1931 to 1936. His importance lies less in any single written work – the best known is *Del Sentimiento Trágico de la Vida en los Hombres y en los Pueblos* generally shortened in English to *The Tragic Sense of Life* – than in the way his own mental conflicts expressed and summarised those of the country as a whole. Despite his extreme subjectivity he thus became of national and even international significance. He was a Catholic who spent a lifetime trying to convince himself of the immortality of the soul. He approved of the great Spanish mystics but detested the vested interests of the Church. He was elected a Republican deputy to the cortes of 1931–1933 but was so appalled by the all too easy slide into crass materialism of simple people brought up in a ritualistic, authoritarian religion that he began to doubt the wisdom of teaching the workers to read and write. Progress was as bad as ultra-conservatism. He peddled such paradoxes and contradictions that he was seized and adopted by foreign intellectuals as an embodiment of the soul of Spain. But in one thing at least he was consistent and this was his constant, tireless soul-searching and striving for a reconciliation of opposites – which he knew in his heart would never be achieved. In this sense he was a heroic existentialist. In his last speech of all he made the proud claim, 'This is the temple of the intellect. And I am its high priest.' Salamanca produced or nurtured some great men and Unamuno's unfailing intellectual courage puts him well up in the class of Father Vitoria and Fray Luis de León.

An avenue of well-grown elms leads to the entrance of the Ursuline convent church, which contains the tomb by Diego de Siloe of its founder, Alonso de Fonseca I, Archbishop of Santiago and later of Seville, who also enjoyed the grandiose honorific 'Patriarch of Alexandria'. He died in 1512 and the alabaster casket with plaques and medallions was ordered by his son Alonso, who was to become Archbishop of Toledo. Against the wall is the sepulchre of the father's majordomo, a Quixotic figure in gentlemanly armour. The lower choir with two wooden ceilings – one of Italian Renaissance inspiration and one Mudéjar – houses a collection of paintings, among which are several panels with firm shapes and fierce hats by Juan de Borgoña from the original retablo of the church. Leaving Las Ursulas and realigning ourselves with Unamuno we find he is striding straight towards the **Casa de las Muertes,** so called from the four skulls carved under the upper window-sills. This façade with its sparingly distributed and finely wrought decoration was built by the second Archbishop Fonseca, who included a coped bust of his father in the centre of the composition. These Fonsecas built well and we shall shortly be able to admire the Archbishop of Toledo's impeccable taste on a larger scale. Unamuno sees none of this. He is chewing on sterner stuff.

Following the avenue of elms westwards we find on the right the church of **La Vera Cruz**. Once a synagogue, this was completely relined between 1713 and 1714 in the Churrigueresque taste. It contains images by Felipe del Corral and Gregorio Fernández. Skirting a public garden to the left we next come to the **Colegio del Arzobispo**, previously known as **Los Nobles Yrlandeses**. Put up between 1527 and 1528 (and now a university residence), this is the Archbishop of Toledo's finest building. The doorway successfully combines granite architectural members with sculpture in warm Salamantine stone. The wholly Renaissance patio – such was the all-embracing virtuosity of the day – was designed by the superb late Gothicist Juan de Alava; the work was carried out by Pedro de Ibarra. The lower arcade has fluted columns with double-order capitals from which spring rounded arches decorated with particularly fine medallion heads. The grand staircases – one on the east and the other on the west side – lead to the gallery which has candelabra columns between flattened arches. The juxtaposition of these two arcades is remarkably harmonious. The doorway to the chapel is more cluttered and bears the stamp of Alonso de Covarrubias. The single nave has a Gothic vault rising from sharply profiled column clusters without capitals. Here we must surely be back in the hands of Juan de Alava. The square lantern is reminiscent of San Esteban, though plainer and perhaps nearer what Alava intended in the larger church. In the sanctuary there is a beautiful retablo by Alonso Berruguete, in which not only the carved figures but also the painted panels and the framework are by Berruguete himself. This is one of the most graceful churches imaginable. It is not in use, so one may admire it without disturbing anyone's devotions. An inscription tells us that the founder, who chose his master-builders so well, died in 1534 at the age of 57.

We have now seen all the more important monuments of the city but the thorough traveller will find some evocative corners in the northern sector too. Leaving the Plaza Mayor by Calle

Consejo one soon reaches the Plaza de los Bandos on the left. The ex-Palacio de Solís, from which Philip II was married to Maria of Portugal, is now the telephone exchange. Across the square the Palacio de los Garci-Grande with a corner tribune-window over the street is now occupied by offices. In the south-west corner is the earlier **Casa de Doña Maria la Brava** with a doorway formed by the great radial slabs common in the fifteenth century. This lady, of the band of Santo Tomé, avenged the death of her two sons killed in a trivial quarrel over some game by girding on armour herself and pursuing the killers, whose heads she cut off and threw on to the graves of her dead sons. The name of the square commemorates such 'honourable' vendettas. Leaving by the north-west corner one reaches the Plaza de Santa Teresa with the plain old house where the tireless founder of convents stayed on her arrival in Salamanca in 1570. Just at the back of this is the Romanesque church of **San Juan Bautista**, which appears to be contemporary with Santo Tomás Cantuarense. Taking Calle de Zamora northwards from the Plaza de los Bandos for less than a hundred yards one finds on the right a short street leading into the Plaza de San Boal with two palaces, whose façades were stuccoed in the eighteenth century. The one now occupied by the Escuela de Comercio housed the Duke of Wellington during his brief stay in the city. At the junction of Calle de Zamora with the ring-road stands the interesting round church of **San Marcos**. Its circular shape leads one to suppose that it might be a Templar foundation but it turns out to be a 'regular' church inside with three parallel apses and a nave and two aisles. The central nave compartment is covered by a rectangular Mudéjar artesonado ceiling. The circular design was probably chosen for defensive reasons, as the building was put up in the twelfth century before the wall of Alfonso VII (whose line is followed by the ring-road) enclosed this area.

At the southernmost limit of the city outside the old walls is the completely rebuilt brick church of Santiago in the Romanesque-Mudéjar style of the eleventh century. The **Puente Romano** is best seen from the grass bank with poplars below this church. After the flood of 1626 it was half a century before the great bridge was fully restored. Under the trees there are a number of shanty bars where it is pleasant to sit and drink and watch the washing being spread out on the grass and the children paddling and the gypsies playing cards – allowing one's mind at the same time to wander back to the old world of the Tormes, on whose banks Lazarillo, the first *pícaro*, was born and the ducal house of Alba held court.

Salamanca – Alba de Tormes – Los Arápiles – Salamanca

For this excursion we set out on N501 for Avila, branching almost immediately right on C510, which we follow for 20 km to **Alba de Tormes**. This *villa ducal* owed its importance to the Alvarez de Toledo family, forebears of the present Duchess of Alba, and counted 22,000 inhabitants in its heyday. The dukedom was created in 1469 and is probably the best known of all the Spanish titles carrying grandeeship. (There are only some 300 out of a total of roughly 3000 titles to which this distinction is attached; the Duchess of Alba leads the league with 18 of them concentrated in her own person.) Pleasantly situated on the east bank of the river, Alba is also the burial place of Saint Theresa of Jesus, usually known abroad as Saint Theresa of Avila. In 1570 she founded one of her reformed Carmelite convents here and it was here in 1582 that she died. Her church is of no great artistic interest except for a relief of the Annunciation over the porch. Her uncorrupted remains are kept in an urn – given by Isabel Clara Eugenia, Philip II's daughter – over the high altar, except for her left arm and her heart, which are preserved as visible relics on the gospel and epistle sides of the altar respectively. Those of us who find the cult of relics distasteful should not forget that it gave rise to the building of all the finest pilgrimage churches of the Middle Ages. Theresa was briefly removed to her birthplace, Avila, after her death but successfully reclaimed by Alba. She was beatified in 1614 and canonised in 1622.

Nothing is left of the ducal fortress-palace except the **Torre de la Armería**, restored in 1961. A circular staircase leads to the main chamber on the first floor whose walls are covered with retouched sixteenth-century frescoes celebrating the third Duke's action under Charles V at the Battle of Mühlberg. Not far off is the church of **Santiago**, the oldest in the town; there are two brick belfries but the apses have been plastered over. Lower down in the Plaza Mayor is the twelfth-century church of **San Juan**, which has been almost rebuilt but still retains some interesting features. Of the three apses one is masked by later building. The central one has the normal blind arcades but the other is enriched by brick columns crowned by stone capitals – an unusual combination. The interior blind arcading uses shapes of distinctly Moorish inspiration. The high altar is surrounded by a magnificent and complete apóstolado in painted stone; the seated apostles are arranged on either side of Christ who is, as usual, larger than they. These figures are the true prototypes of the simplistic Romanesque-type figurines carved as souvenirs. It is exciting to find the real thing but a pity they were not left in their original positions round the walls of the epistle-side apse. The nave of this church is later and has longitudinal arches of the Zamoran type. Down by the river there is a 'beach' with a bar where one can lunch very agreeably if the week-ends are avoided.

From Alba a local road leads west via Valdemierque to join N630. Turning north at the junction and continuing until 7 km short of Salamanca we find the right-hand turning to **Los Arápiles**. These are two hillocks just to the east of the village of the same name and the battle of Salamanca is known to Spaniards as the battle of Los Arápiles. On the morning of July 22nd, 1812, both sides rushed for these heights, the Allies under Wellington gaining the northernmost and the French under Marmont the one to the south. The battle was decided in the afternoon by the brilliant charge of Anson's and Le Marchant's cavalry under Sir Stapleton Cotton. Wellington is severely criticised to this day by the Salmantines for his 'inexplicable' withdrawal after such a victory, permitting further pillage by the French of the university city. What is not taken into account is that the rout would have been far more complete if General Carlos de España had not, unknown to Wellington, evacuated the fort of Alba de Tormes, permitting the French to escape across the river. Nor is it remembered that Wellington advanced as far as Madrid and Burgos after the Salamanca campaign, with which the cortes – if not the Salmantines – were sufficiently satisfied to nominate him to the supreme command of the Spanish armies.

Salamanca – Ciudad Rodrigo – (Tamames) – Salamanca

For the benefit of those who plan to enter Portugal by N620 or have the time to make the 88 km journey – there is nothing of great interest en route – during their stay in Salamanca I must make some mention of **Ciudad Rodrigo**. This Spanish fortress on the river Agueda near the Portuguese border is named after Count Rodrigo González who founded it in the twelfth century on the remains of a Roman settlement of the province of Lusitania. The piers of the bridge are Roman. The **Cathedral** belongs to the Salmantine or Zamoran group. The south doorway is surmounted by a very fine apostolado, whose figures are quite undamaged. The old west entrance is masked by a tower added in the eighteenth century (and pitted by cannon-balls in 1812) but even in the dimness of the porch one can pick out the six archivolts enclosing the Coronation of the Virgin and, on either side of the doors, six apostles under whose feet are little canopies with tops carved to resemble the Torre del Gallo at Salamanca. Inside, however, no lantern has been attempted. The nave is of four bays, planned for a barrel vault but later converted to carry eight-ribbed cupolas resting on tall figures, some blowing trumpets. The crossing also has a domical vault. The columns and walls are of grey stone but a warmer stone from Salamanca has been used for the vaulting compartments, which were erected between 1212 and 1230. The aisle windows are in the pointed Romanesque style with outer archivolts cusped in the Zamoran manner. The sanctuary was rebuilt between 1538 and 1550. The **Coro** has a very fine set of stalls of about the same date as Zamora's and also probably from the workshop of Rodrigo Alemán. The panels above the upper series are carved with foliage enlivened by beasts and country labours. The hand-rests are all formed by the arched backs of animals stroked to great smoothness over the centuries. The misericords depict a medley of scenes, amongst them a bull teasing a dog, a monkey riding a dog and steering it by its ears, a bishop on all fours with animal hindquarters and tail and a cowled pig – presumably a monk or friar – playing a bagpipe. The **Claustro** is very peaceful with four tall cypresses soaring up from the garth. The western walk is the oldest with Romanesque capitals and columns supporting pointed windows divided into two or three lights; the southern walk follows on but the northern and eastern sides with four-light windows rising from basket-work bases were added by Pedro Güemes between 1525 and 1538.

The town is a delight to visit – it is one of the least spoilt in

Spain, The elongated plaza has a charming **Ayuntamiento** of the mid-sixteenth century with an external arcade and gallery ending in corner turrets. The large bishop's palace of 1790 has an invitingly cool courtyard. Many of the houses carry armorial bearings over their doors but it is less for the particular than for the general that it is so enjoyable to wander through the streets. In 1810 the place was taken by the French. Although 24 days had been calculated as the minimum required to reduce it by siege, Wellington, threatened by Marmont, made his famous assault on January 19th, 1812, after only twelve. A complete circuit of the walls can be made by a walk along the top and from this one can appreciate their strength. Though the fortifications are mediaeval on the side above the river Agueda, which also incorporates the keep, the other sectors were scientifically remade in the eighteenth century with proper gun positions and an outer fosse; their great width is shown by the tunnel gates that pierce them at several points. The assault was successful but not without the loss of 1300 men including Generals Craufurd and McKinnon.

Ciudad Rodrigo offers two good hotels, the Parador Nacional and the Conde Rodrigo, to travellers en route for Portugal or for Extremadura and Andalusia. The latter are catered for by a good road—C526—via Coria to Cáceres. Those returning to Salamanca may care to vary their journey by taking the local road from Valdecarpinteros on N620 to Tamames and continuing on the higher ground under the Sierra de la Peña de Francia to Vecinos, where they join C512 28 km short of the city.

Salamanca – Candelario – Béjar – (Plasencia)

The direct road south from Salamanca is N630 which soon rises into the mountains forming the south-western tip of the massif central. Just before Béjar a local road to the left leads up to **Candelario,** one of the strangest of Spanish mountain villages; the houses have half-doors like stables to prevent the children wandering out and falling into the foaming gutters, and the older women are remarkable for their peculiar hair style. **Béjar,** built on a narrow spine over the river Cuerpo de Hombre and under the Sierra de Béjar, is a pleasant hill town and the Hotel Colón is very adequate for a night. The long narrow Calle Mayor threads the old part almost from end to end, debouching in the Plaza Mayor under the castle, which now houses a secondary school. The church just beyond this, with a hefty square tower and Romanesque-Mudéjar apse, has an impressive coffered wooden barrel-vaulted ceiling, sustained on slightly pointed longitudinal arches. The smarter church of **Santiago** nearer the modern centre has a similar roofing system, which clearly recommended itself here owing to the abundance of timber in the foothills. From Béjar it is 59 km to **Plasencia** (see p. 297), the most south-westerly city dealt with in this book.

Salamanca – Peñaranda de Bracamonte – (Cantalapiedra) – Madrigal de las Altas Torres – Arévalo

Those of us remaining in central Spain now turn eastwards on N501. At 41 km is **Peñaranda de Bracamonte** with a large granite hall-church of the sixteenth century in the process of restoration. From here C610 leads north-west to Madrigal de las Altas Torres, birth-place of Isabel the Catholic. A detour can also be made on the local road north to **Cantalapiedra**. This village has an interesting parish church whose aisle walls are said to have belonged to a mosque – and it does appear that the brickwork and doors may well be Moorish rather than Mudéjar. The interior was rebuilt in the sixteenth century. A road leads due west from here to the town that enjoys not only the prettiest place name in Spain but also the most re-sounding title. Fully and correctly described it is **La muy Noble, Imperial y Coronada Villa de Madrigal de las Altas Torres**. After this fanfare the depopulated and semi-ruinous reality may disappoint on first sight. Apart from two grain silos the only high tower still standing belongs to the church of San Nicolás, visible from some distance. The adobe defensive walls, unusual in that they formed an exact circle of 677 m diameter, are very much deteriorated and of little visual appeal. But no one should lose heart. Entering by the restored Puerta de Cantalapiedra, the best thing is to follow the signs to the small – 8 rooms only – Parador of the M.I.T., from which we may set off on foot.

Turning right out of the door and continuing for a couple of hundred yards we come to the old hospital founded in 1443 by John II's first wife Maria, daughter of Ferdinand of

Antequera, King of Aragón. Her untimely death, followed by her daughter Catherine's, frustrated the first attempt to unite the two kingdoms. The hospital stands on the edge of a large open space (square or plaza has a connotation of activity quite lacking here), across which in a corner formed with the Civil Guard barracks is the entrance to the **Convento de Agustinas**. The forecourt, resembling a farmyard, is frequently crossed by women with jugs and cans who come to buy their milk from the nuns. The receptacles are placed on a wooden turn-table and returned full; the selling nun can be heard but not seen. By the turn-table is a bell for visitors. The invisible nun who answers will open communication with the words 'Ave Maria Purísima', to which the proper countersign is 'Sin Pecado Concebida' ... conceived without sin. The dogma of the Immaculate Conception of the Virgin is very dear to the Spanish heart. When these requisites have been complied with, we may state our business and will be admitted if the hour does not conflict with a religious office.

We have not been prepared by the humble entrance for the size of the cloister with arcade and gallery in the very plain Castilian style of the early fifteenth century. The atmosphere is one of space and peace. John II had little taste for government but a good instinct for places of repose. This was one of his favourite palaces and from it in 1447 he married his second wife, Isabel of Portugal, who was to give him a daughter, Isabel, born in this building. Later it passed into the hands of Charles V, who granted it in 1526 to the two illegitimate daughters of Ferdinand the Catholic for use as a convent. The nun on duty is a member of a closed order, which means she has probably seen less of the town than we have already. With enthusiasm untarnished by repetition she will tell us the history of the foundation as she conducts us through the ground-floor rooms. The most notable of these is the one-time royal reception chamber with an unpainted wooden ceiling, which has acted as refectory since the time of the foundation. The tables are raised on a narrow platform that runs all round the walls with benches on the wall side only; the pretty little pulpit is still used for readings during meals. The **Capilla Real** is separated by grilled windows from the church used by the nuns. It contains the stalls used by John II and his wife, their favourite altar and images, as personal as well-loved dolls, a Pieta given by Ferdinand the Catholic, figures of Saints Peter

and Paul by Alonso Berruguete and a large figure of Saint
Augustine, patron of the order, attributed to the same artist.
The Calvary group with robes in gold leaf is by Juan de Juni.
In the centre is a large medallioned plinth under which lie
Isabel of Portugal and one of the foundresses of the convent.
Through the grilles one can see the operational part of the
church which is Baroque.

The upper gallery is reached by a staircase rising under a
geometrical Mudéjar ceiling of unpainted wood. Opening off
the north side are the old royal chambers, which are of great
simplicity with their polished brick floors and whitewashed
walls, though certain 'museum' pieces have been added,
amongst these some inlaid caskets and a Mozarabic figure of
the Virgin painted in the cool ice-cream colours one associates
with Arabic plasterwork. The first anteroom has an attractive
painted plaster ceiling. The main parlour is pleasant but not
large with two balconies overlooking the convent garden. An
opening in the inner wall of this leads to the alcove in which
Isabel was born; a painted door with hinged panels looking
like a larder cupboard opens onto the service corridor. The
nun prattles sweetly on about the incalculable value of the
treasures under the care of the order. One is drawn from the
indifferent paintings to the windows, reflecting that in fact the
most valuable possessions the nuns have are the good plain
cloister and the vegetable garden cultivated in little patches
like allotments with bee-hives along one wall. This was the
first bit of the world the little princess saw. And beyond the
hortus conclusus stretches the great plain, the meseta, with its
harsh lands, clumps of pines and huge cloud-scapes, while
outside the palace gate were fortifications and streets of mud.
At the age of three Isabel was removed to the larger but not
essentially different villa of Arévalo. These were the places
and views that forged the sensibility of a woman of strong
will and great powers of endurance, who was to ride all over
the country, having her children as and where they came, in
fulfilment of her role as indefatigable quartermaster of her
husband's armies. One feels very close here to the source
of the traditional Spanish virtues – hardihood, asceticism,
piety.

In the centre of the town is the imposing brick church of
San Nicolás, whose tower we have already noted. Here John
married his second wife and Isabel was baptised. On slightly

higher ground is the church of Santa Maria del Castillo with a Romanesque-Mudéjar apse. The Parador of Madrigal is a good base for anyone who did not visit Medina del Campo and Olmedo from Valladolid. And 29 km west of Madrigal – a short day's mule ride – lies **Arévalo**, one of the most important centres of architecture in brick. The church of San Salvador strikes the key-note on the way in and no sooner do we arrive in the large irregular arcaded Plaza de José Antonio than we find the Baroque-cloaked church of **Santo Domingo** with a brick Romanesque apse. Walking to the narrower end of this plaza we find on the right a rebuilt gatehouse leading into the Plaza del Generalísimo Franco with an arcaded pavement on two sides. From here the Calle Santa Maria leads to the tower of **Santa Maria** straddling the street by means of a tunnel with a pointed barrel vault. This tower, like others in the town, is built of rough mortared stone between brick courses. Inside the church there is a Morisco ceiling under the choir and over the rear bay of the nave. The sanctuary walls retain some traces of Romanesque frescoes. Facing Santa Maria across the dusty **Plaza de la Villa** – the earliest town centre with arcaded sidewalks supported on wooden columns – is the church of **San Martín** with two great square towers and a late Romanesque porch with worn capitals on unusually tall slender columns on the south side. Returning to Santa Maria and continuing through the tunnel we emerge eventually in front of the pentagonal castle, which rises on a rubbish-strewn bluff over the river Adaja. In the great donjon, rect-angular on the inside and semi-circular where it protrudes beyond the wall are the rooms which provided Isabel as a girl with higher and wider views of her future kingdom than the more domestic balconies of Madrigal. Like Torrelobatón this castle has become a grain silo of the Ministry of Agriculture.

Just outside the town on the road to La Nava de Arévalo are the remains of what must have been the finest brick church of them all, known as **La Lugareja**. Only the three apses, north transept and lantern tower still stand. Blind arcades run the whole height of the apses. In the noble lantern only one window is opened in each face, negating – one would have thought – the purpose of this structural feat. The visitor should be warned that Arévalo is fiendishly cold in winter and fiendishly hot in summer; dust is blown into one's face by a cold wind or a hot wind according to season. The drink is brandy in the winter and iced brandy in the summer. But the bitter burning place should not be missed. The Hostal del Comercio specialises in sucking pig. And the town is circled on the west by NVI allowing a quick run north to Medina del Campo and placing us equally well for our approach to Segovia.

CHAPTER EIGHT

Segovia

✤

Arévalo – Coca – Santa Maria la Real de Nieva – Segovia

Ideally we should plan our day to reach Segovia in the evening and catch the setting sun on the golden stone of the cathedral. The direct route from Arévalo is by C605, which crosses NVI and N403 and passes through Santa Maria la Real de Nieva. But let us assume that time permits us to leave C605 at the intersection with N403 and follow this north for about 7 km until we find the local road on the right leading to **Coca**, whose rose-brick castle, built for the first of the two Fonseca archbishops, represents the last decadent flowering of the Mudéjar tradition of fortifications. Despite obvious affinities with the slightly earlier Castillo de la Mota and a fierce appearance, Coca is largely a fake, for the walls are of *mampostería* – cemented mud and rubble – coated with plaster to hold the delicate bricks in place. The main deterrent is the very deep fosse with brick sides, which gives the castle the air of a fantastic island in the middle of a dried-up lake. The plan of the inner fort reflects the outer walls with the exception of the donjon, which is square with circular turrets running the whole height. The battlements conceal an upper walk behind the merlons, which were tortured into a kind of brick topiary of varying shapes, now mainly weathered away. It seems probable that the core consisted of a luxurious Renaissance patio, since disappeared. The interior has been entirely relined to house a Forestry Commission school.

From here it is 16 km via Nava de la Asunción to **Santa Maria la Real de Nieva** whose parish church belonged to a convent founded by Henry III and his wife, Catherine of Lancaster. The north door has some good carving, notably in the outermost archivolt with the dead bursting from their tombs. But the main feature of interest is the unusual cloister which, though built at the end of the fourteenth century,

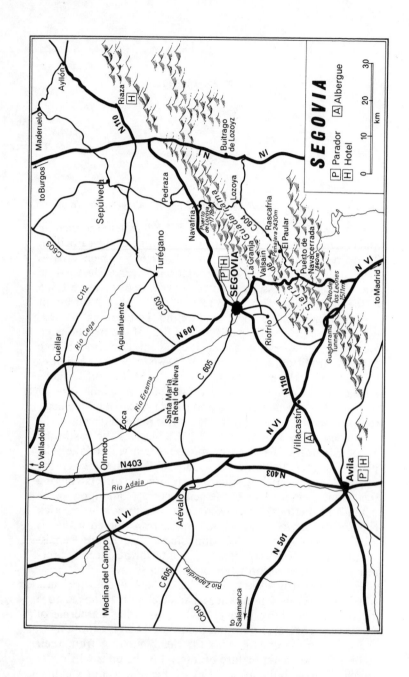

shows a pronounced archaic reversion to the Romanesque. Some of the carving is straight heraldic – the shield quartering the lions of England with the castle of Castile is supported by angels (no less!) – but we also find animals with intertwined necks (clumsily done, for this kind of Celtic skill had been lost) alternating with more successful scenes of boar, bear and wolf hunting and country labours. There is a charming Flight into Egypt near the entrance from the church.

Approached from any direction **Segovia** is still a satisfyingly compact city, whose golden stone cathedral tower is in complete command of the skyline. Coming from Santa Maria we get the best view of all with not only the cathedral but also the spire of San Esteban and many other worthy buildings alternately rising and dipping below the smooth crouching bulk of the Sierra de Guadarrama. A few kilometres short of the city we are offered a choice of access for the road bifurcates; the left branch leads into Segovia past the sanctuary of the Virgen de la Fuencisla, skirts the dramatic promontory of the Alcázar to the north, crosses the pleasant stream of the Eresma and follows the northern walls to arrive under the famous aqueduct in the Plaza del Azoguejo. The right or southern branch is less leafy and charming but provides very fine views of the cathedral before bringing us likewise to the same point under the aqueduct.

From here a road climbs steeply into the town, passing between the houses of the Marquises of Moya and Lozoya, where the gate of San Juan stood till 1886, and continues almost straight to the Plaza Mayor, arcaded on the sides occupied by the Ayuntamiento and the Teatro Juan Bravo and opening on the west to the pinnacled chevet of the cathedral. The best places to stay are the modern Parador Nacional with views of the Old City or the Hotel Acueducto very near the Roman aqueduct. The latter is better placed for nocturnal rambles in the heart of Segovia.

The **Cathedral** is the last complete Gothic church of the first rank in Spain. Designs were submitted in 1522 by Juan Gil de Hontañón to replace the old cathedral near the Alcázar which had been badly damaged in the Revolt of the Commoners. Work began in 1525 closely following the plan of Salamanca, which the same master had commenced in 1513, and was largely completed by his son Rodrigo. It is hardly surprising that the building seems only lightly tethered

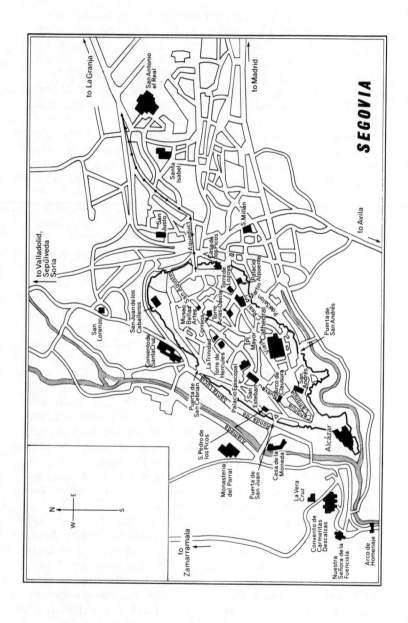

SEGOVIA

to La Granja

to Madrid

to Avila

to Valladolid,
Sepúlveda
Soria

San Antonio
el Real

Santa
Isabel

San
Justo

S. Millán

Casa de
los Picos

Aqueduct

San
Lorenzo

San Juan de los
Caballeros

Palacio
Alpuente

Museo
Bellas
Artes

Torre de
Arias Dávila

Torre del
Lozoya

Convento de
Santa Cruz

Correos

Pl.
Mayor

Calle Real

Calle Martin

La Trinidad

Torre de
Hercules

Cathedral

Puerta de
San Andrés

Puerta de
San Cebrián

Palacio Episcopal

San
Esteban

Arco de
Clausura

San
Andrés

Alcázar

S. Pedro de
los Picos

Casa de la
Moneda

Monasterio
del Parral

Puerta de
San Juan

La Vera
Cruz

Convento de
Carmelitas
Descalzas

Nuestra
Señora de la
Fuencisla

Arco de
Homenaje

to
Zamarramala

N
W — E
S

to the Gothic age when we recall that Rodrigo also built the highly successful university façade of Alcalá de Henares in the Renaissance style. A quick walk round the outside will show there is hardly any external sculpture except for some shields and the lions on short columns guarding the forecourt. The doors of the west front are framed in plain flattened arches, themselves enclosed in simple rectangular mouldings. After Rodrigo's death the crossing was covered with an Escorial-type cupola and when the spire of the great tower fell in 1614 it was replaced by a similar cupola reducing the height from 105 to 88 m. The chevet with its flying buttresses and many finials is described by Richard Ford as 'over-crocketed', a criticism that may have occurred to him precisely because of the uncluttered elegance of the rest. All in all, it can be accounted one of the great homogeneous cathedrals of Europe, almost reminding one in its consistency of the Early English Salisbury.

Entering by the **Puerta de San Frutos** in the north transept we find ourselves in a large church giving an immediate impression of well-ordered calm, of resolution rather than aspiration. There are five nave bays with aisles and side chapels. As usual in Spanish churches there is a very definite delineation of the bays. In earlier cathedrals like Zamora, where the Romanesque style is still the prisoner of square bays, this effect is produced by structural considerations. Gothic developments in France, Germany and England tended to minimise if not eliminate the compartment-quality of the bay. In Spain continuance of this long after the structural problems that produced it had been overcome seems a matter of taste arising from a special Spanish characteristic – the addiction to clear-cut cubic scaffolding at once creating a confining space. You can't let the inner space run away with you, the architects seem to say, so you must make strong open-ended boxes for it. Here it is very beautifully done. There are pronounced horizontal string-courses. The vertical shafts have tiny capitals like wreaths or coronets. There is a vestigial triforium incorporated in the lower part of the area belonging to the clerestory windows; in the transepts, which do not protrude from the flanks of the building, the triforium is carried on as a tribune gallery. The ambulatory with seven radial chapels is a distinct improvement on Salamanca.

Turning to the fixtures and fittings, the Baroque grilles of sanctuary and choir were forged in 1733. The retablo mayor (1768–1775) is by Francisco Sabatini. The choir stalls of the second half of the fifteenth century were brought from the old cathedral. The choir walls and the trascoro of 1784 are by Ventura Rodríguez. 'The worst work we have in the cathedral,' complained the sacristan, 'though now I am going to show you something else which is really bad.' He led me to the chapel immediately to the right of the Puerta de San Frutos, called **Capilla de la Piedad**, containing Juan de Juni's Retablo de la Piedad dated 1571. Here the great Illusionist excels himself; the Roman soldier with the spear wears a hideous grin, while his companion who drove in the nails is weeping over his hammer. I was puzzled the sacristan should not like a work so much in the Spanish taste and was about to say as much when I saw a sly smile spreading over his face and realised he had been teasing me and it was really his pride and joy. In this chapel there is also a painted triptych of the same subject by Ambrosio Benson, a follower of Gerard David's, who is well represented in the Prado. Benson flourished between 1521 and 1550, yet this work shows little Renaissance influence. The white drapes are modelled on Rogier van der Weyden; in one of the side panels Saint Michael sports rose-coloured wings. The Gothic world still holds its own. The **Capilla de la Concepción** in the same aisle has a grille made of woods brought from the Indies. The second chapel off the south aisle, counting from the west, contains one of Gregorio Fernández's recumbent figures of the dead Christ; I do not know how many he produced but this was his most popular subject. In the fourth chapel off the south aisle, **Capilla de Santiago**, is a good retablo carved by Pedro Bolduque and painted by Alonso de Herrera in 1595. The portrait of the founder is by Pantoja de la Cruz. In the **Antesacristía** is the prized Cristo de Lozoya, a Baroque image by Manuel Pereyra (d. 1667) set in an Art Nouveau tiled framework by the ceramist Daniel Zuloaga. The **Capilla del Sagrario** by José Benito Churriguera reveals the founder of the much maligned dynasty as a serious, one might almost say stodgy, decorator. The retablo is highly decorated without any dramatic movement of surfaces or levels.

Just as the choir stalls were brought from the old cathedral, so was the Gothic *Virgen del Perdón* presiding over the inner side of the main west door. But the most important contribution from this source was the entire **Claustro**, first erected by the Fleming Juan Guas and moved to its new site by Juan de Campero in 1524–1525. This is entered through a fine fifteenth-century iron screen by Fray Juan de Segovia. Immediately on the right are the tombs of Covarrubias, confessor of el Greco and Raimundo Losado (d. 1288), confessor of Saint Ferdinand. Guas is sometimes a bit indigestible but his strong sense of design is usually sufficient to control his love of ornament. Here the windows of the arcade onto the garden contain excellent decorated tracery supported on slender stem-like columns. It is rare enough that a master-builder is paid the posthumous compliment of the removal of his work stone by stone to another place; in this case it is well-deserved.

The cathedral **Museum** is installed in the base of the tower. It is hung with Gobelin tapestries of the eighteenth century and contains one work each by Pedro Berruguete and Ambrosio Benson. In the centre is the tomb of the Infante Don Pedro, little son of Henry II of Trastamara, who was carelessly dropped by his nurse from a balcony of the Alcázar when he was two years old. The **Sala Capitular** has an impressive artesonado ceiling of the seventeenth century in white and gold – the gold leaf is original. It is hung with Flemish tapestries of the same period from cartoons by Rubens; the clear ample compositions and muted blues, greys and beiges are most agreeable. The staircase, also hung with tapestries signed by the Van Brustrom brothers, leads to the **Archivo**, which contains a good collection of early printed books. Some of the manuscripts deserve inspection, amongst them a document with the resolutions of a council held at Peñafiel in 1302 by the archbishop of Toledo and the bishops of Palencia, Segovia, Osma, Sigüenza and Cuenca to discuss the defence of 'the legitimately acquired privileges' of their churches and chapters against 'the excesses and abuses of the kings of Castile and León'. The seals of the six bishops are affixed.

Before leaving the cloister we should pause just inside the door back into the church to pick out the plain stone slab that commemorates Rodrigo Gil de Hontañón, who died on May 31st, 1577, when the main fabric of the cathedral was all but finished; the same inscription also notes that the first stone was laid on June 18th, 1525. A few slabs away lies Rodrigo's father. It is very meet and fitting that they should rest here in Juan Guas's cloister. Between the three of them they covered and contributed largely to a great age of Spanish building, during which the Gothic-Renaissance struggle was resolved in the latter's favour but not without some remarkable compromises on the way.

A proper appreciation of intramural Segovia requires two days and the itineraries should be carried out on foot. The first leads from the Plaza del Azoguejo to the Alcázar and the second does the reverse by a different route. A good day is then needed for the very interesting churches and convents outside the walls.

Let us start with the **Aqueduct**, the largest and most complete piece of Roman building left in Spain, generally thought to date from the time of Augustus and to have been restored under Trajan (98–117). The structure is entirely of granite blocks without mortar or clamps. The total length is about 900 yards, for 300 of which it consists of two tiers reaching a height of 94 feet. In the centre is a raised section of stonework designed to carry an inscription, which is missing, though the holes for the pins of the bronze letters remain. In 1071 35 arches were destroyed by the Moors and it was not until 1483 that a monk of El Parral was commissioned by Isabel the Catholic to restore them to their original state. It may seem surprising that so imposing a monument should exist in splendid isolation, for though Roman stones have been identified in the city walls, there are no signs of a theatre, amphitheatre or any other of the appurtenances of Roman civilisation. The answer seems to be that Segovia was simply a military post whose job was to keep the tribes in order. As such, one of its first requirements would have been water, which was accordingly brought with characteristic thoroughness across the valley from the melting snows of the Sierra de Fuenfría. During the great period of the cloth industry little factories grew up under the aqueduct's vast granite wing, drawing their water from the top by pipes called *cervatanas*. The inevitable filtration damaged the fabric and produced cascades of icicles in the hard winters. These were removed in the eighteenth century after the industry's collapse but the cluster of buildings between the legs of the great water-bridge remained, leaving only the two central arches for wheeled traffic. Then in 1806 the wife of the Swedish ambassador, staying at La Granja, took the recommended drive one day to the charming city of Segovia. Her coachman misjudged the clearance and the carriage overturned, causing the distinguished lady – who was pregnant – to miscarry. All the houses blocking the arches were swiftly torn down by royal order. The mediaeval aspect is preserved in the etchings of Gustave Doré and a painting in the Museo de Bellas Artes.

The main shopping street, Calle Real, rises steeply from the Azoguejo towards the north-west and breaches the old wall by the **Casa de los Picos,** built possibly by Juan Guas for Pedro López de Ayala, Count of Fuensalida; the *picos* are the pyramidal points into which all the stones of the façade are shaped and these certainly recall Guas's use of diamond-faceted stones at Manzanares el Real (Madrid). Calle Real – this is actually a popular compendium term for four streets, namely Cervantes, Juan Bravo, San Martín and Isabel la Católica, joined head to tail like caterpillars – now leads past the **Palacio de los Condes de Alpuente,** set back in a little plaza on the left. This is worth remarking for its two elegant Gothic windows and the esgrafiado plasterwork with a regular moulded pattern covering its façade. Local authorities suggest that this system of decoration, which is peculiar to Segovia, originated in the custom of early builders to whitewash the layers of mortar between uncut stones, producing a crazy-paving effect that was later sophisticated in the way we see. Whatever its origin, it has been so enthusiastically seized on by restorers and pastiche-builders that it has become something of a cliché. At the back of this palace in a cul-de-sac is the old **Alhóndiga** or wheat exchange. Returning to Calle Real, we come next to the Plaza de San Martín, popularly called de las Sirenas owing to the Neo-Classical sphynxes that were set to guard the statue of Juan Bravo when the square was done up in 1840. He was the Segovian leader in the Revolt of the Commoners and it is interesting to note that, even under Franco, these men were still revered as heroes and honoured with street names. We have a strong democratic tradition in these parts,' I was told by the mayor of a small town in the region.

The Plaza de San Martín is grouped round a series of steps rising towards the north. To the right of the Commoner's monument, as we climb, is the great keep of the **Torre de Lozoya,** also with esgrafiado surface decoration. The salient top storey projects on corbels and the whole is a good example of the semi-fortified town houses from which feuding nobles would make sallies against their neighbours. Two small palaces in the granite Plateresque style complete this side. Down on Calle Real is a Gothic house with an upper loggia; nineteenth-century Liberals identified this as Juan Bravo's birth-place – which is now thought to have been higher up the street on the site of the Hotel Las Sirenas.

In the centre of the plaza is the parish church of **San Martín,** which provides a fitting introduction to Segovian Romanesque. This is mostly of the thirteenth century and lacks the heavy grandeur of the great twelfth-century churches of Zamora, Salamanca and Toro. However, it derives a special graciousness from the arcaded porches common to nearly all the churches, one of which runs round three sides of the present building. The arches spring from pairs of columns with twinned capitals as in a cloister. The capitals are of great height and bulk in relation to the columns and carry a wealth of carved descriptive scenes and fabulous figures, including pairs of birds facing each other on a background of formalised acanthus leaves with their claws resting on the rim of the column and sirens with female heads and bodies and the wings of birds of prey. These porches were not purely decorative but served a purpose as the meeting places of guilds and brotherhoods; even the town council might meet in one or other of the church porticoes. The west doorway here is sustained by two saints who are not merely set in niches but actually form the upper parts of the columns. On the outside wall of the central apse, looking towards Juan Bravo, is a good statue of Saint Martin with pastoral staff, cap and halo and dexter hand raised in benediction. The interior of the church is a sad commentary on the fate of many of its kind. In a politer age the original capitals and carvings were chipped away to permit a Baroque face-lift. Later zealots for restoration chipped the stucco off and laid bare the ravages underneath. Though it is good to see buildings as they were built, it is sometimes kinder to leave them alone.

Almost opposite the church the Bajada de la Luna (at whose bottom stood the old Puerta de la Luna) leads to the Paseo del Salón with good views to the south of the city; this was a favourite walk of Isabel II, whose reign ended in 1868 to the sound of General Prim's slogan 'No more Bourbons!' The houses lining it are built on the foundations of the wall and incorporate two semi-circular towers. At the farther end of the walk is another alley called the Bajada del Sol, where stood the Puerta del Sol, unnecessarily removed at the same time as its sister, the Moon Gate. Returning to Calle Real where we left it, we find on the right a robust building of the early seventeenth century which was the municipal prison and now contains the library and archive. A little way up on the left is a doorway with the inscription Corpus Cristi over the door; this was a synagogue which became a church in 1410 and was largely destroyed by fire in 1899. The last stretch of Calle Real debouches into the **Plaza Mayor**, which is still a very decent city centre. The Ayuntamiento of the seventeenth century is yet another instance of the influence of the Escorial on Spanish civil architecture. On the opposite side, partly obscured by buildings against its flank is the severe late Gothic church of **San Miguel**, finished in 1558 probably by workmen from the cathedral. Three of the statues from an earlier church, including that of the patron saint, have been incorporated in the west front.

Christian Segovia, like all Castilian cities, sheltered three communities: Christian, Jewish and Moorish. The last seems to have lived outside the walls but the Judería or Jewish quarter lay within, between the apse of the cathedral and the Puerta de San Andrés. The Christians were distributed in three main districts, those of the nobility, the clergy and the merchants. Leaving the Plaza Mayor and passing the north side of the cathedral we enter the Barrio de los Canónigos or clerical quarter. Opposite the north transept is the Renaissance Palacio del Marqués del Arco, given by Philip II to the Segovian Cardinal Espinosa. Then comes the Carmelite convent founded by Saint Theresa. Farther down on the left is the pleasant Plaza de la Merced with the twelfth-century Romanesque church of **San Andrés**, completely revamped inside and now remarkable only for its fine brick tower. From here the constantly narrowing Canonjía Nueva leads us down to the platform, on which the old cathedral stood, in front of the **Alcázar.**

We are now confronted by the most dramatically sited of all Spanish royal fortress-palaces. The platform narrows to a promontory, which is fully occupied from side to side by the improbable castle whose walls are almost flush with the rock.

The sharp western end, dividing those delightful streams the Eresma and the Clamores, inevitably invites comparison with the prow of a ship, while the high crenellated and corbelled donjon facing us may be likened to a poop or bridge. The steep slate roofs with dormer windows and the witches' hats on the round towers and turrets are forms of head-dress worn by no self-respecting Spanish castle in its heyday. Yet, these additions – the former due to Philip II and the latter to the restoration after the great fire of 1862 – give it the memorable silhouette by which it is known the world over. The walls have an esgrafiado pattern of contiguous circles picked out with small lumps of *escoria* or coke, something like currants, at the four points where each circle rubs shoulders with its neighbours. With due respect to the local theory (see p. 249) I think this is more likely to have been inspired by the Gothic-Mudéjar plasterwork that adorned the interiors of the Alcázar and other important buildings. Decorative motifs in Spain usually start on the inside before finding a way out.

The building was commenced by Alfonso VI on the site – according to the nineteenth-century antiquarian Sr Avrial – of one of three fortresses erected by 'Hercules the Egyptian, Son of Osiris Pharaoh, King of Egypt'. This remarkable personage is also credited with the foundation of the city in 1706 BC. The same chronology dates the Creation of the World in 2500 BC, so even Archbishop Ussher must have turned in his grave! Alfonso X made important additions but the present shape is mainly owed to the Trastamara dynasty. On the death of Henry IV in 1474 Isabel was supported by the Segovians in her claim to the throne and on December 13th of that year she proceeded in state from the Alcázar and was proclaimed Queen from the church of San Miguel. The resistance of the fortress to the Commoners' rising under Juan Bravo was rewarded by handsome royal expenditure on the fabric in the reigns of Charles V and Philip II but the building was almost gutted by the fire of 1862 and the restoration which still continues is largely based on the painstaking drawings made about 1844 by Sr Avrial.

Entering by the drawbridge, we pass through the base of the donjon into the Herreran Patio de Armas. On the right is the door to the **Sala del Palacio Mayor**, devoted to a permanent exhibition of suits of armour. This was the main room of the old palace; the ajimez windows with curious

frescoes in their embrasures gave on to a wooden gallery before the construction by the Trastamaras of the parallel Sala
de la Galera. We now proceed through a small chamber on the
right with a fireplace into the **Sala del Solio** or Throne Room,
built in 1456 for Henry IV by Xadel, a Moor. The decoration,
much-restored, is Gothic-Mudéjar. The ceiling of the correct
period was brought from Urones de Castroponce after the
fire. This room opens into the great **Sala de la Galera** whose
windows give on to the refreshing prospect of the Eresma
valley. This was built in 1412 on the orders of Catherine of
Lancaster, by then widow of Henry III and regent during the
infancy of their son John II. There is a fine artesonado ceiling
with an upper honeycomb Mudéjar frieze and a lower stucco
frieze with heraldry. Next comes the **Sala de las Piñas** of 1451;
the Gothic plaster frieze is original on the north-west and
south-west sides. From here we are conducted into a room
fitted up as a bedchamber, where Ferdinand VII slept in 1817,
using the Sala de las Piñas as his study. These rooms would all
have had tiled dados and been furnished with the richest wall-
hangings, settees, cushions and other luxuries appropriate to
a dynasty that affected Moorish dress.

Recrossing the Sala del Palacio Mayor we now return to
the Patio de Armas, from which an attendant puts us on our
way to the **Capilla**, whose ceiling was also destroyed and replaced by another brought from Cedillo de la Torre. The main
works of art are: the fifteenth-century retablo of the School of
Pedro Berruguete, the Adoration of the Kings by Bartolomé
Carducho and a Flemish triptych depicting Santiago in his
usual Spanish role as scourge of the Moors. The adjacent
Tocador de la Reina overlooking the Eresma has a slanted
opening focused on the chapel altar; it is conceivable that this
is the first instance of the arrangement for viewing the sacrament from a sick-bed later adopted by Charles V at Yuste and
Philip II at the Escorial. The anonymous portrait of Isabel the
Catholic shows a plain queen with long nose, stubborn chin
and pale blue eyes. In the barrel-vaulted **Sala del Cordón**
Alfonso the Learned is supposed to have doubted the sun's
movement round the earth (one version) or to have said that
if he had been present at the Creation he would have been
able to advise God how to order things better (another
version); whichever his blasphemy was, it was rewarded by
thunder and lightning and even his innocent Queen's head-

dress was burned. On the following day he publicly retracted his words and ordered that Saint Francis's girdle should form part of the decoration of this room, which it does to this day. Like the Sala del Cordón the **Sala de los Reyes** was almost entirely destroyed in the fire. Begun by Alfonso the Learned and finished in 1596 by Philip II, its most remarkable feature consisted in the polychrome wood figures of the sovereigns of Asturias, León and León-Castile from Pelayo in 716 to Joan the Mad who died in 1555. The recarving of this series, which also includes the Cid and Fernán González, is still in progress and was again made possible only by the pre-fire drawings of Avrial. It was here under the gaze of all his predecessors that Philip married his fourth wife, Anne of Austria.

After visiting these rooms we emerge on to the terrace, from which there is a good view to the north over the Huerto del Rey (the wooded slope immediately under the walls) and the bosky walk along the Eresma called the Alameda del Parral. Close to the river is the Monastery of El Parral and higher up the slope the twelve-sided Templar church of Vera Cruz. On the horizon is the village of Zamarramala. The terrace leads to the **Sala de Armas**. The sixteenth-century armour is characterised by sockets for the bases of the long lances then in use and by a raised half-collar protecting the left side of the throat. Pikes have rear spurs under the spear-head enabling the infantrymen to hook the armour-joints of the cavalry and bring them crashing to earth. In a side chamber there are some coffers with fantastically complicated locks. The Spaniards have always enjoyed locks and all that goes with them; even today no Spanish dame worth her salt is without a good jangling bunch of keys.

I suggest we return to the Alcázar to commence our tour of the northern parts of the city. This zone, comprising the rest of the clerical district and all of the Barrio de los Caballeros, makes pleasant walking, as there is very little traffic. Descending by the street to the left of Canonjía Vieja we come to the **Puerta de Santiago,** one of the seven gates of the mediaeval city, with a round-headed portcullis arch introduced by pointed horseshoe arches. Keeping to the inside of the wall, we shortly come upon the charming little Romanesque church of **San Pedro de los Picos**, closed and very likely for sale; the purchase of a church is not as far-fetched as it sounds, for we shall come across two in Segovia used for secular purposes. Climbing from here we pass the Hospital de la Misericordia on the left with an entrance of 1678 and bearing right we come steeply into the Plaza de San Esteban. This can also be reached on the flat simply by taking Canonjía Vieja from the Alcázar and passing under the **Puerta de la Claustra**, one of three gates of the old canonical precinct, to emerge at the same point.

The church of **San Esteban** dominates the square. The interior has received the Baroque treatment but the porch remains much as it was and the capitals like those of San Martín are worth inspection. The tower, however, is the thing. Despite extensive repairs at various times it preserves the splendid proportions of a five-stage design raised on, roughly, a double cube of plain masonry. The first two decorated stages have pairs of blind windows, the third is the belfry, the fourth repeats the belfry stage while the fifth has triplets of windows. When Avrial drew this tower in the eighteen-forties, it had an Escorial-type spire. It has now, I think, been improved by the substitution of a sharp pyramidal slate spire, which from certain viewpoints outside the walls raises it above the tower of the cathedral. Across the triangular plaza, and forming an acute angle with the axis of the church, stretches the long grey front of the episcopal palace in what local historians call the granite-Plateresque style, though this is something of a contradiction in terms, as the coarseness of the stone does not permit the mannered and delicate type of decoration we normally associate with Plateresque.

We now walk a few yards up Calle de Desamparados, leading out of the west side of the square, to a house set back behind a little garden on the right, next to the Capilla de San Juan de Dios; this used to be a *pensión* and here Antonio Machado (1875–1939) lodged during the twelve years he spent in Segovia as Professor of French. Machado, though an Andalusian born in Seville, is the poet who has best understood and rendered the gaunt beauties and traditional austerities of Castile. His finest collection of work is the superb *Campos de Castilla*, first published in 1912 and mainly written while he was teaching in Soria (see p. 387), where he married his young wife, Leonor. She died of tuberculosis in 1911 after only two years of marriage and Machado left shortly afterwards, never to return. During his subsequent appointments in Baeza, Segovia and Madrid he continued to write but he never surpassed the poems inspired by the Sorian landscape and the river Duero. During the Civil War he was a supporter of the Republic and he died in 1939 in Colliure in the South of France after escaping from Barcelona with his aged mother, who followed him a few days later to the grave. His room is reverently shown by the family that looked after 'Don Antonio'; it is preserved just as it was in his day with his iron bed, round work table and paraffin stove.

Next we take the street leading from the east end or apex of the Plaza de San Esteban which brings us, bearing left, to the Romanesque church of San Quirce, which now acts as the lecture hall of the Universidad Popular de Segovia. Facing the north side of this is the one-time Capuchin convent with a doorway of 1637 and fine marble shields of the founders on the façade. Continuation eastwards leads eventually to the deconsecrated and unused Romanesque church of San Nicolás with pleasant views over the Eresma. Rather before this on the right is a rough flight of steps leading into a crooked alley skirting the back of the church of **La Trinidad**. This church has an arcaded portico on two sides. The single nave ends in a semi-circular apse decorated on the inside by blind arches on double columns. The slightly pointed arches of the crossing carry the tower. The Capilla de los de Campo contains some good tombs. The little Plaza de la Trinidad is dominated by the great fortified house of the Portocarrero and Arias de la Hoz families, which became in 1513 the Convent of Santo Domingo el Real. The massive corbelled tower, dating from about 1200, is known as the **Torre de Hércules** (cf. the legend of 'Hercules the Egyptian'). Continuing eastwards from this plaza and taking the second turning right we emerge in the large Plaza de los Huertos, where the Thursday markets take place. This has been officially renamed after Doctor Andrés Fernández de Laguna, whose statue occupies the centre. Dr Laguna, who died in 1560, was a famous practitioner of his day, acting as personal physician to Charles V, whom he failed to cure of gout, and to Popes Paul III and Julian III, who loaded him with earthly honours. Presiding over his square is the strong machicolated and merlon-topped tower of the Arias-Dávila family, which is all that remains of their great mansion. This with the towers of Lozoya and Hércules completes the trio of secular keeps that act as a cruder foil to the more graceful towers of the churches.

We are now well into the Barrio de los Caballeros, which occupies the north-eastern bluff of the city. Taking Calle San Agustín past the post office we come to the modest Casa del Hidalgo housing the **Museo Provincial de Bellas Artes**. At the top of the stairs are two paintings of the aqueduct. In the eastern view by Avrial the bases of the central arches are hidden by the houses surrounding the church of San Justo; the western view would appear to be earlier and shows the medley of buildings right up against the pillars, amongst them the church of Santa Columba, which was pulled down in the clearance. Sections of the sixteenth-century retablo of this church are distributed about the museum. The capacious fireplace with ingle-nook seats in the kitchen-dining-room has a pleasant farmhouse air. Calle San Agustín continues into the Plaza del Conde de Cheste, surrounded by rather grander houses whose doorways are all formed by great radial slabs, usually framed in a rectangular label and surmounted by a coat of arms. The left of the plaza as we enter is taken up by the Casa de los Maldonado; on the right following the pavement of the street is the Palacio de Quintanar with perhaps the best doorway; opposite this is the Palacio del Conde de Cheste. At the far end on the left is the Casa del Marqués de Lozoya facing the large Palacio de Moya, also known as the Casa de Segovia, on the other side of the street. The walls present a riot of esgrafiado decoration ranging from the crazy-paving to the regular variety, with and without 'currants'.

From this square the street dividing the Cheste and Lozoya mansions leads into the Plaza de San Juan, now officially called after Diego de Colmenares, author of a history of Segovia and from 1617 until his death in 1651 parish priest of the delightful church of **San Juan de los Caballeros**. The long open space between the houses and the church was the jousting field of the Segovian gentry, where they also performed such exercises as galloping with bamboo canes in order to pierce and carry off small beribboned rings (*sortijas*) strung on a line; this practice is still continued by countrymen on mules and mares in the *carreras de cinta* (ribbon races) of country festivals. Dating from the end of the eleventh century, San Juan is the oldest of the Segovian Romanesque churches. Its nave and aisles end in three parallel apses; the semi-circular arches of the nave are supported on strong round columns. In the Capilla de Nobles Linajes are the tombs of the Segovian leaders who played a prominent part in the capture of Madrid. In 1905 the building was bought by the potter Daniel Zuloaga who used the whole church as workshop and exhibition area. The present **Museo Zuloaga** occupies only the porch, which has been walled in. In addition to the usual ceramic objects Daniel and his children made tile-pictures large and small. There is a big Art Nouveau panel by Daniel of peacocks, urns and fountains at La Granja; in other works pre-Raphaelite treatments of the figure are supplemented by Renaissance decorative motifs. The family as a whole injected a high degree of artistic self-consciousness into craft techniques; the results have a period charm but the smaller products, like the plates with Don Quixote and Sancho Panza, are the undoubted forerunners of some very debased tourist souvenirs.

Returning to the Plaza del Conde de Cheste, we cross the road and take the street to the right of the Moya palace, which leads past the church of San Sebastián to the Plaza del Avendaño. A passage runs from here to what was one of the *postigos* or postern gates of the city, affording a good view of the aqueduct from the upper level. This stands at the head of a flight of steps which brings us down once more to the Plaza del Azoguejo. It may now seem time to try the Segovian k'itchen, which is based on the *horno de asar*, really a bread oven with a shallow brick vault, fuelled by wood. The specialities are sucking pig, lamb, partridges, hare and other game but the whole piglet, not more than 40 days old, is the most renowned of these. One Cándido, who goes by the grand title of Maestro Mesonero de Castilla, is the acknowledged high priest but he has been spoiled by success and is only affable to celebrities. His restaurant is handy, as it is almost under the piers of the bridge but there are several others that provide essentially the same food and drink at lower prices. The wines of the region are of low alcoholic content and never reserved as vintages; the product of the last crop is drunk fresh as a *mosto*, or must.

The Azoguejo, as usual, is the best starting point for a tour outside the walls. The convents and churches to the north and north-west of the city are so thick on the ground that they have been described as a 'spiritual rampart.' A little way along the road to Valladolid on the left is a broad track leading down to the Barrio de San Lorenzo, whose brick houses with exposed wood frames and overhanging upper storeys make a nice village atmosphere. The twelfth-century Romanesque church of **San Lorenzo** has a brick tower of four stages on a stone base, an arcaded porch and a pretty apse. From the plaza an unmade road leads to the **Convento de Santa Cruz** (which can also be reached more directly by the Ronda de Santa Lucía from the Azoguejo). This was built near a cave inhabited by Santo Domingo de Guzmán, otherwise Saint Dominic, founder of the Dominican order in the thirteenth century. During the priorate of Fray Tomás de Torquemada, later first Inquisitor-General of Castile, it was rebuilt at the cost of Ferdinand and Isabel, whose motto *Tanto monta* ... *Monta tanto* repeated forwards and backwards runs all along a frieze on the south side under the roof; on the north side is the slogan *Isabel como Fernando*. Both emphasise the parity of Aragón and Castile, though Ferdinand was never more than King-Consort in his wife's domains. The entrance to the church is a fine example of the Flamboyant Gothic style of Juan Guas. The interior has four very strongly delineated bays to the crossing, which is supported on round columns. In the garden below the main buildings is Saint Dominic's cave, now a chapel containing a polychrome wood figure of the saint. In 1574 Saint Theresa spent four hours here in a state of ecstasy. When she came out, she told the brothers that their founder had appeared to her and they had conversed and the figure was an excellent likeness of him.

Drivers will have to continue down the Ronda de Santa Lucía under the walls and past the Puerta de Santiago until they find a sharp right turn, which takes them past the **Casa de la Moneda**, founded by Alfonso VII and rebuilt by Henry IV in 1455. It was fitted with German machinery in 1586 by Philip II and all the national coinage was struck here until 1730 when the mint was moved to Madrid. The road now crosses a bridge to the **Monasterio del Parral**. Those of us on foot can take an even prettier way down from Santa Cruz through market gardens to a footbridge over the Eresma, which brings us into the leafy Alameda del Parral, once the fashionable parade of carriage folk and pedestrians and one of the pleasantest walks in the world, happily unsurfaced and neglected by a motoring age. At the far end of this we join the road to the partly ruinous monastic buildings, whose vines and gardens were once celebrated by the proverb *Las huertas del Parral, paraíso terrenal* – the Parral's orchards, earthly paradise. The Jeronymite order founded in 1373 is unusual in that it is confined to the Iberian peninsula and that an application to extend it into Italy was turned down. However, it enjoyed the special favour of the Trastamaran kings. John I contributed to the endowment of Lupiana (Guadalajara), Henry III to Guadalupe (Cáceres) and Henry IV to El Parral and San Jerónimo in Madrid. After the *desamortización* of 1835 by Mendizábal's government, forcing the sale of monastic lands to relieve the treasury, El Parral like many other foundations stood empty for decades and was roofless when reclaimed; even now the large complex is tended by only eight monks. The church has been restored by Bellas Artes and the doorways, chapels, recesses and tombs stand out almost like exhibits from the walls, which have been picked back to brick. The building was begun in 1459 and strong evidences of the architectural personality of Juan Guas are visible throughout, notably in the unfinished west front and the luscious sacristy door, which can only have been built by the author of the cathedral cloister. There is a single nave with shallow side-chapels. The arms of the transepts are short and well-lit. The fine five-tier Plateresque retablo, finished in 1528, is flanked by two lateral tombs in the same style, almost retablos in themselves; these are carved in alabaster with some colouring added – the yellow ochre is particularly effective – and contain the remains of Juan de Pacheco, Marquis of Villena, and Maria Portocarrero his wife. Villena, who enjoyed the Grand Mastership of Santiago, was childhood companion and later favourite of the weak Segovia-loving Henry IV, whom he dragged off in 1474 in order that Henry should present him with the feudal lordship of Trujillo in Extremadura but the castle resisted and the King became ill and returned to Madrid where he died, followed not much later by Villena. Among other interesting memorials in the church are those of Villena's daughter, the Countess of Medellín, and a plaque in the north transept to Don Diego López Pacheco, who died *'en la jornada de Ynglaterra Año de 1588'*, in other words the Great Armada.

The motorist must recross the river from El Parral and branch right and right again over yet another bridge, the Puente Castellano, to reach the **Convento de Carmelitas Descalzas** on the edge of a large grove of eucalyptus trees. The pedestrian

may reach the same place by continuing along the north bank
of the river. This convent contains the remains of Saint John
of the Cross in a chapel founded for him in 1618. In 1927 the
excessive veneration of his admirers removed his bones from
their simple tomb under the floor to an urn of chocolate-
coloured marble under a pompous catafalque. This timid
saint, tiny of stature, described affectionately by Saint Theresa
as *medio fraile* – merely half a monk – has also been called
el doctor extático. The interest of his exquisite lyric poetry is if
anything heightened by the application of the vocabulary of
profane love to mystical experience.

Architecturally the most interesting monument in the area is
undoubtedly the church of **La Vera Cruz**, which is reached by
a short walk up the road to Zamarramala. Founded in 1208 by
the Knights Templar, this is a twelve-sided polygon with a
square tower attached. The interior consists of a circular ambulatory round a central core of two floors, the upper of which is
reached by a double staircase facing the west door and lit by
eight apertures in the metre-thick walls – it also has a window
looking directly onto the high altar in the apse below. The
lower chamber or crypt is inspired, after the fashion of these
churches, by the Holy Sepulchre. It is worth climbing the
tower for the very fine view of San Esteban and the cathedral
asserting their verticality in contrast with the heavy mass of the
Guadarrama.

On the other side of the eucalyptus grove to the Carmelite
convent is another church, standing under a cliff called the
Peñas Grajeras. This is the sanctuary built between 1597 and
1613 for the patroness of Segovia, **Nuestra Señora de la
Fuencisla**. The legend has it that this image, buried during the
Moorish occupation and later installed in the old cathedral,
was called upon by a virtuous Jewess named Esther, who had
been falsely accused of infidelity with a Christian and sentenced
by her own people to be flung off the cliff. The Virgin brought
her safely to ground, the Jewess was converted, a shrine was
begun and when it was ready the Virgin was moved to the site
of her miracle. The Baroque **Arco de Homenaje** just beyond,
supported by impassive caryatids, was built in 1704. Passing
through this we come to a left fork which crosses the river and
climbs the long slope of the Cuesta de los Hoyos following the
rivulet of the Clamores. The route affords good views of the
southern walls, which can be re-entered by the Puerta de San

Andrés under the cathedral. Or we can continue on the road until it straightens out between the walls and the Cerro de la Piedad, a flat-topped mound with a number of memorial crosses. Bearing left along Calle Caballares and Calle del Carmen we return to the aqueduct, having completed the circuit of the city.

Another half-day is required for the visit of the eastern outskirts. As usual it is best to start from the aqueduct, taking Avenida Fernández Ladreda, which is signposted to Madrid. Half-way along this on the right stands the church of **San Millán**, the most perfect example of Segovian Romanesque. It is said to owe its foundation to a successful expedition by Fernán González in 923, though it is doubtful if the Christians of this period could have established a strong enough post to permit the building of a church outside its walls and no part of the present building seems older than the twelfth century. There are long lateral porches on the north and south sides, and the body of the church consists of nave and two aisles ending in semi-circular apses. The nave capitals are remarkable for their sculpted scenes, which include the Adoration of the Kings and the Flight into Egypt along with lions and centaurs. The crossing vault raised on conch-shaped squinches is a legacy of the Moorish Caliphal style developed at Córdoba. In the porches there are some beautiful bird capitals of the sort we have already noted in the later San Martín. The restored tower has horseshoe windows in the upper two stages, though these were not there in 1844. The somewhat fussy slate spire is the only thing at variance with the spacious bold design of the church and the intricate but never cluttered stone carving.

Crossing the Avenida and walking a little way back towards the aqueduct, we find Calle San Clemente on the right leading to the church of the same name. Restorations have left little Romanesque work but the squat tower is attractive. Continuing south-east we reach the Plaza de Santa Eulalia, which preserves old arcaded houses on two sides; number ten with a typical radial entrance was the house of Buitrago, one of Juan Bravo's companions in the Commoners' Revolt. Turning left here we shortly come to the convent of Santa Isabel, whose late Gothic chapel (about 1560) contains a fine iron screen from the old cathedral by Fray Francisco de Salamanca.

From here it is but a brief, if dusty, walk slightly uphill to
the **Convento de San Antonio el Real.**

Artistically, this convent, which began life towards the
middle of the fifteenth century as a country house of Henry
IV, is perhaps the most interesting element in the 'spiritual
rampart' surrounding the city. Henry had built it during
his father's reign and after his accession gave it to reforming
Franciscans, who ceded it to their female branch, the Poor
Clares. After various changes of tenancy the nuns are once
again Franciscans. The church entrance is Flamboyant Gothic
of the period immediately preceding Juan Guas; the convent
entrance is Plateresque with praying figures of Ferdinand and
Isabel. The nave of the church was discreetly plastered and
given a classical cornice in 1730. The magnificent Mudéjar
ceiling over the presbytery, very similar to the one built for
Alfonso XI more than a century earlier at Tordesillas (Valladolid), shows the persistence of this style at its highest level
of excellence right through the Trastamaran period; like its
prototype it is shaped like an *artesa* with the west end, facing
the nave, missing. A Baroque frame in the nave displays (unfortunately behind glass) a notable Golgotha or Calvary with
many figures in high and low relief made of polychromed
wood in Utrecht about 1470.

To the right of the chancel steps is a door into the sacristy
in which we find another door with a bell. Through this we are
admitted to the **Claustro,** which is the glory of the foundation.
The enclosed walk is covered by a painted Mudéjar ceiling
with pendent bosses at the corners; the tracery of the windows,
filled in to preserve the sisters from the cold, is Gothic. There
are three Dutch terracotta triptychs of the fifteenth century
and enjoyable Baroque figures of Saint Roch with the dog that
brought him bread after his expulsion from the town of
Piacenza and of Saint Anthony the Abbot, patron of animals,
with a little pig. In France Saint Anthony's hospitallers kept
pigs and these were allowed free scavenging in the gutters by
royal order; they wore bells to identify them. The refectory
with a plain beamed roof has an interesting pulpit with Mudéjar
designs and some very sweet primitive frescoes, possibly by
the nuns themselves. The **Sala del Rey,** once the parlour of
Prince Henry's country house, has a delightful ceiling of beams
painted with floral motifs in gay, fresh colours; the panels in
between contain geometrical designs that seem to foreshadow

esgrafiado decoration. There is a medley of furniture and the room is hung with carpets from Cuenca. The **Sala de la Reina** is now the chapter-house and it would be hard to imagine a prettier setting for the solemn conclaves of the sisters, which take place under an unusually low-pitched octagonal Mudéjar ceiling with pendants and golden stars and shields.

From the number of references I have made to the Trastamaras it will be apparent that Segovia was particularly associated with this dynasty, not the most successful in Spanish history until we come to Isabel the Catholic. The ruthlessness of Henry II, the founder, served him in the murder of his half-brother Peter the Cruel in 1369 but did not enable him to control the nobles who had supported him. John I's claim to Portugal was put out of court by his defeat at Aljubarrota in 1385. Henry III, known as 'the Ailing', married John of Gaunt's daughter Catherine of Lancaster and the Portuguese claim was again pressed without success. There was little further reconquest on the frontier with Granada. John II's long reign (1406–1454) was largely dominated by the able but unscrupulous Alvaro de Luna. His successor Henry IV was deposed in effigy at Avila in 1465 and then went back on the agreement he had signed disinheriting his supposed daughter la Beltraneja in favour of his sister Isabel. On the credit side, John II patronised poets and was no mean troubadour and dancer himself, while Henry IV's works at the Alcázar, El Parral and San Antonio el Real show him to have been a judicious prince in matters of taste. Brought up at Segovia from the age of four and made its feudal lord at fourteen, he always referred to 'my Segovia' and was known as *el Rey Segoviano*. He granted tax privileges to the town and allowed two tax-free fairs a year lasting thirty days each. Despite its shortcomings the Segovians have some reason for their affection for the Trastamara line.

The convent entrance is not far off the main road from Segovia to La Granja. Striking this and turning downhill, we soon find on the left the first arches of the aqueduct, built here of uneven blocks of stone. A couple of hundred yards farther down is the church of San Salvador with a four-stage tower whose windows have been blocked up. A little below this is **San Justo** with a charming two-tier tower crowned by a stork's nest. The sanctuary arch is painted with a Romanesque geometrical border in yellow, orange and black, framing a fresco of the Saviour in the single apse. These paintings have recently been much over-restored. The only part of the church with any sign of luxury is the Capilla del Cristo de los Gascones, the local patron saint of lawyers. From San Justo there is an easy descent to the Azoguejo. Though there are some walks and buildings left out of this account, I shall make no more Segovian recommendations. Whoever is captivated by the city will discover them himself, while they are superfluous for those who would be quickly on their way.

Segovia – La Granja – Valsaín – Riofrío – Segovia

Leaving Segovia on N601 we come after 11 km to the most attractive of all Spanish royal palaces, **La Granja.** The Trastamaras built a hunting lodge here and a shrine to San Ildefonso administered by the Jeronymite monks of El Parral, who added a farm (*granja*). The Habsburgs did not delight to honour the place, preferring the neighbouring site of Valsaín. Philip V thus found almost virgin ground for the implementation of his own ideas. The palace that arose has been called 'the first great building of the Spanish Bourbon dynasty'. The dates are 1719 to 1739. The first architect was Theodore Ardemans and the south-east court with its slate-hung spires overhung by the dome and lantern of the collegiate church still shows signs of the Escorial influence Philip was trying to escape. Between 1735 and 1739 the King employed the Italian architects Juvara and Sacchetti to remodel the garden front, which they did with great success. Giant orders run the whole height of the two-storey façade, whose central triad has a panel rising above the balustrade – which cleverly incorporates the attic windows. There is no rusticated basement as in the palace at Madrid by the same designers and the result is at once imposing and domestic, as one can walk straight out of the ground-floor windows into the gardens. These were designed by the Frenchman Boutelou and made between 1727 and 1743. The hand of Philip's second wife Isabel Farnese is discernible, specially in the bronze fountains by disciples of René Carlier, which have been judged superior to those of Versailles. The main waterworks occupy a slope rising gently to an artificial lake called El Mar, which is hidden in the pinewoods under the great mountain wall of Peñalara. The site is one in which human artifice and natural beauty join hands to achieve a happy graduation from rugged sierra through natural wood and formal garden to grand country house.

Inside, La Granja does not fall short of that luxury which the outside leads us to expect. It would be tedious to describe every room on view but the nine rooms en suite on the ground floor have the same general characteristics, the most notable of which are the shallow domical vaults with circular paintings and the lovely chandeliers made at the palace's own glass factory, which occupied a building beyond the cavalry barracks. The French-inspired furniture mostly belongs to the reign of Charles IV. The dining room has benches shaped like gondolas and canvases by Philip's dull court painter Van Loo. The throne room has very handsome lamps and mirrors. The only room with a fireplace is the royal study – smokeless braziers were probably preferred to smoky fires for the sake of the natural silk wall hangings (unfortunately destroyed by a fire in 1918 and replaced by paper). Altogether, there is no doubt that the combination of Farnese and Bourbon tastes gave rise to a luxury hitherto undreamed of in Spain, leading to a pronounced rift between court art and architecture and popular – or even noble – taste. Gone was the time when an Alvaro de Luna or an Archbishop Fonseca could outface his monarch in terms of wealth and show. La Granja, the Palacio de Oriente, Aranjuez – the so-called Sitios Reales – are buildings completely removed from the realm of normal dwellings and immensely different in spirit from the sober Habsburg style, which had been generally adopted through the whole field of civil and domestic architecture. No contemporary magnates tried to ape the first Bourbons and where there was an eighteenth-century building boom, as for example in Salamanca, the style favoured was a revival of Renaissance Plateresque. The streams were not to join again until the middle of the nineteenth century when the dim, bourgeois taste of Isabel II found acceptance among all classes.

La Granja has another great attraction consisting of the collection of tapestries in the **Museo de Tapices**, which contains some of the finest hangings in the very extensive royal collection, said to measure 14 km in length. The first room gives us sixteenth-century Flemish works. Romulus founds Rome and dictates laws to burghers in furred gowns. Here also begins the series devoted to Cyrus of Persia, continued in the next room. Room three is mainly devoted to the great series of Honours and Virtues woven in Brussels from cartoons by Bernard Van Orley with its huge cast of characters drawn from Classical mythology, Roman history, the Old Testament, saints, kings and heroes. Such a curious medley can never have been conceived before or since and a prolonged contemplation of it leaves one almost dazed. The end wall nearest the entrance is occupied by the oldest piece in the museum, a fifteenth-century Flemish tapestry of Saint Jerome praying, surrounded by wondering animals; facing this at the other end is the Miraculous Draught after Raphael. The rest of the collection is by no means an anticlimax. In the fifth room we find two very delightful tapestries of the Creation with splendid animals and birds. In one of these God finally produces Adam in front of the astonished beasts; the leopard has severe doubts about the wisdom of it all. There is also a very pleasant set of monkeys playing in decorative bower-like structures. The sixth room contains works from cartoons by Bayeu and Goya along with rustic junketings after Teniers. The seventh, a long room like the fifth, shows famous matriarchs on the end walls and the five Triumphs of Petrarch on the long side. Downstairs are more Flemish tapestries and more Spanish works of the eighteenth century.

Continuing 3 km south we come to **Valsaín**, where the Trastamaras had another hunting lodge and a kind of zoo for their collection of wild animals. Philip II brought the architectural canon of the Escorial to the place. The last Habsburg, Charles II, watched this building burn shortly before his own death in 1700. Even though Philip V preferred La Granja for his ·palace, Valsaín is very special. The Trastamaras had an unbeatable instinct for a good site. The valley has a floor of open sheep pasture, through which the delightful Eresma runs, tamed but not dulled after its first bold leaps down the slopes of Peñalara. This was the royal park, an ideal area for coursing or chasing or tilting. Little remains of the burned palace except one corner of the façade. Many of the granite columns and capitals have been removed for humbler purposes such as small bridges and byres. Modest farmyards nestle in the corners of the ruinous courtyards and stables, while turkeys and geese lord it on the green where huntsmen, courtiers and pages trod.

This area boasts yet another royal residence. Returning to La Granja and continuing about 3 km towards Segovia we find on the left a local road signposted to **Riofrío**. This runs past an army camp, across N603 and under a railway before emerging near the palace built in 1751 by Ravaglio, a disciple of Sacchetti's, for Isabel Farnese, by then a widow. It is a large rectangular building plastered in pink standing somewhat gauntly in a deerpark. The chapel is oval with balconies for the family to hear mass. The grand staircase divides, leading to a reception room in the middle of the two flights. After Isabel's death the place seems to have remained unloved until taken up by Isabel II and her husband Don Francisco de Asís, whose bedroom and study are shown. The furnishings have a flavour of carpet chairs and slippers and Alfonso XII's study even has curtains of carpet material. Despite these homely touches, melancholy prevails. The building has recently been given a fillip by the installation of the **Museo de Cacería**, which will be found interesting by keen shots.

Segovia – Sotosalbos – Navafría – Lozoya – (El Paular) – Puerto de Navacerrada – (Valsaín) – (La Granja) – Segovia

The main objects of this excursion are to see something of the Sierra de Guadarrama and to visit the monastery of El Paular, if this has not already been taken in from Madrid. Setting out on N110 for Soria, we find after 18 km on the left the very decrepit little village of **Sotosalbos** whose Romanesque church follows the Segovian plan with a long wide porch and very squat tower. 11 km farther on is the turning to Navafría, from which an unsurfaced but adequate road winds right up through pine woods to the Puerto de Lozoya at 1778 m to descend equally steeply to the town of Lozoya in the river valley on the other side. If there is snow, it is better to continue on N110 to join NI, taking this south past Buitrago de Lozoya (Madrid) and entering the Lozoya valley from the far end on C604, which brings us to the same point. The next village up the valley is Rascafría and a little beyond this on the right is the very sympathetic **Monasterio de El Paular** with the magnificent painted alabaster retablo referred to in the excursion from Madrid (see p. 103). The air up here is extremely bracing and a picnic on the river bank with plenty of red wine has much to be said for it. The road climbs steeply via Puerto de los

Cotos (1830 m) to Puerto de Navacerrada (1860 m), the highest pass in the Guadarrama, from which N601 runs down to Segovia via Valsaín and La Granja.

Segovia – Pedraza – Riaza – Ayllón – Maderuelo – Sepúlveda – Turégano – Aguilafuente – Segovia

This excursion has two variants, a shorter and a longer. By the first we cut from Pedraza via Castilnovo to Sepúlveda, leaving Riaza, Ayllón and Maderuelo for another occasion.

Starting again on N110 for Soria we find after 32 km a left-hand turning, which passes the recently restored Romanesque Nuestra Señora de la Vega with interesting carved capitals in the porch, before reaching **Pedraza**, a dramatically situated mediaeval villa that well repays a visit. In the Plaza Mayor the first floors of the houses, overhanging the arcaded sidewalks, are supported by an assortment of pillars, some of which dispense with capitals in favour of simple wooden brackets. The town hall has an upper gallery of very flattened arches overlooking the square. The adjacent church of San Juan Bautista retains a fine Romanesque tower with a two-tier belfry. The castle is a private residence of the Zuloaga family. There is a good Government 'Hostería for lunch. Anyone opting for the shorter variant will take the road from here via La Velilla and La Matilla to Sepúlveda. Just before this route crosses C112 the castle of Castilnovo rises among trees and meadows on the right. It is not open to the public but even from the road one can distinguish an interesting example of Mudéjar military architecture; this was one of the many acquisitions of the Marquis of Villena.

Those of us who have opted for the longer circuit return from Pedraza to N110 and continue to **Riaza** on the far side of NI. This pleasant little town has an almost circular plaza completely surrounded by low buildings projecting over the pavement. The Hotel La Trucha is very adequate for lunch or for the night and can be borne in mind as a useful half-way house between Burgos and Madrid. From here N110 runs through a rusty plain with a profusion of russet oak-scrub and the final spurs and folds of the massif central on the right to **Ayllón**, an old walled stronghold with a porticoed plaza and a watch-tower on a ridge. It also contains a little rustic palace to which the great Alvaro de Luna was once confined. The massive slabs of the entrance in the Segovian style are framed by the Franciscan girdle. The house is privately owned but can be visited in the summer. We now take C114 for Aranda de Duero through a countryside in which the women still wash their clothes in the streams and the men stop work to watch a passing car. After 15 km a bridge on the left leads to **Maderuelo**, almost undistinguishable at first from an outcrop of rock above the eroded ashen earth and the brown waters of the Embalse de Linares curling round its base. The church is remarkably sympathetic. The Baroque stucco sanctuary with plaster putti sitting on the cornice combines successfully – perhaps because there is something fresh in its exuberance – with the simple wooden roof, gallery, floorboards and pews of the primitive structure. There are several interesting altarpieces and some good tombs. The interesting Romanesque murals displayed in the mock-chapel off the lobby numbered LI in the Prado came from a ruined chapel beyond the river. From Maderuelo a local road leads, partly following the main north-south railway, to Boceguillas where we recross NI and take the road for **Sepúlveda**.

This is one of those small Castilian towns that provide the nearest approach to an unsullied contact with the past, now that the provincial capitals have all to a greater or lesser extent surrendered to development. Built on a bluff above the confluence of the rivers Caslilla and Duratón, it was captured by the Christians after the battle of Simancas in 939 – though Almanzor was able to make himself temporarily master of the place in 986. The town's most treasured possession (deposited at Santo Domingo de Silos) is the Romance Latin *Fuero Breve* granted by Alfonso VI in 1076. This is of great importance, as it became the model for many other fueros granted by the Castilian kings in order to encourage the repopulation of reconquered areas. In effect, Sepúlveda became a little republic accountable only to the monarch. Gentlemen were given extensive privileges and even commoners might with impunity kill any strangers who dared to till their land and imprison those who shot their game. Any breaking of the rules was treated very seriously indeed. Moorish and Jewish communities were allowed to exist but if a male of either race was found with a Christian woman, he was cast off a high rock and she was burned alive. The town declined after the twelfth century but remained jealous of its rights. The fuero was confirmed in 1305 by a lavish document issued by Ferdinand IV at Medina del Campo. When Henry IV wished to present the feudal lordship to the Marquis of Villena, the Sepulvedans rose in arms and prevented the favourite's entry. The town thus avoided the classical type of feudal servitude, claims the town clerk. May be. But as the contractual relationship between a hard-pressed Crown and the new frontiersmen diminished in importance – by 1085 Sepúlveda was well behind the 'lines' – royal respect for the fuero also diminished. Though confirmed and reconfirmed by every monarch down to Charles IV, by the time of the Reyes Católicos the privileges had become almost meaningless. The rulers of the mediaeval period were by necessity almost 'constitutional'. After the unification of the country by Ferdinand and Isabel they became 'absolute'. The last shot in the clash between the power of the towns and of the Crown was fired in the rising of the Commoners of 1520–1521 – unsuccessfully, as we have seen, for the Commons.

Climbing the slope to the centre we pass the Casas Consistoriales, a respectable nineteenth-century town hall, in which one can usually see the fuero of Ferdinand IV during office hours. Continuing upwards we reach the elongated **Plaza Mayor**, once an extramural market. On the west side rises the remnant of the twelfth-century castle, modified in the eighteenth with a balcony from which the corporation could watch bull-fights. The main churches are all Romanesque. Above the castle, occupying the highest position within the walls, is **El Salvador** of the end of the eleventh century. Sepulvedan Romanesque is mostly older than Segovian and here we find a precursor of the Segovian porches with stubby columns carrying totally disproportionate capitals like large inverted cones. The carving of these has little to do with Christian symbolism or hagiography – it is probable the craftsmen, whether Christian or Morisco, were not very well versed in such matters. But their work has a crude vigour that is pleasing. There is a fine apse with columns running from ground to eaves in the Zamoran manner. The upper stage of the sturdy tower has ajimez windows. All the elements of this church contribute to a satisfying whole. Lower down is **San Justo**, the preferred burial place of noble families; the triapsidal crypt contains a beautiful thirteenth-century stone high-relief of the Virgin and Child on the epistle side of the altar. Beyond the west end of the plaza stands **San Bartolomé**, a simple structure of the end of the eleventh or early twelfth century. A little outside the town on a platform above the rivers is the sanctuary of **Nuestra Señora de la Peña**, whose tower was finished in 1144. The tympanum of the entrance inside the porch is more richly carved than usual in the area. **San Frutos** down by the river Duratón dates like El Salvador from the late eleventh century. The main door with a cusped intrados opens into a porch whose arcade has been walled in; the carvings on the frieze between the corbels are varied and interesting. All these churches belong to the most vigorous age of Sepulvedan history. The domestic architecture, mostly of the late Gothic and Renaissance periods, is rich in heraldry but by this time the long decline had set in. The local nobility maintained some kind of social life spiced with gossip and lawsuits throughout the eighteenth century, but the Peninsular War and the insecurity of the times drove them away to the bigger cities and the shutters were closed in the little palaces, generally for good.

From Sepúlveda the local road via Consuegra joins C603 to **Turégano**, another attractive mediaeval villa with an elongated plaza and a combined church and castle, which was one of the seats of the bishops of Segovia. C603 continues to join N601 near Segovia. A detour can also be made from Turégano on a local road running north-west to **Aguilafuente** with a brick Romanesque parish church that has been well restored by the present incumbent and a castle with a motif of interlocking chains round the windows. A couple of kilometres to the south is an excavation where an extensive Visigothic necropolis has been discovered on the site of a Roman villa. The road via Aldea Real joins N601 from Cuéllar to Segovia.

Segovia – Villacastín – Avila

Between Segovia and Avila the half-way house is **Villacastín** on NVI from Madrid to La Coruña. The grand sixteenth-century hall church with a Herreran exterior stands up well on a shelf above the road. The tower is unfinished. Inside, Gothic rib vaulting springs from piers with applied Classical pilasters. There is an imposing polychrome retablo but it is the delightful painted pulpit that catches the eye. The Capilla de la Purísima with an elegant cupola contains the tombs of the Tóvar family. Shortly after Villacastín N501 crosses into the province of Avila.

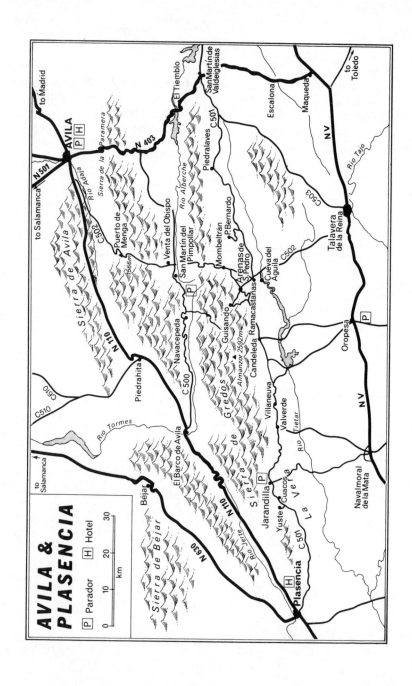

CHAPTER NINE

Avila and the Five Rivers

.✤.

At 1133 m above sea-level Avila is the highest provincial capital in Spain. It is situated on a wind-swept moor under the northern slopes of the Sierra de la Paramera – which is one of the bastions of the great south-westerly extension of the Guadarrama known as the Sierra de Gredos. Approaching on N501 from Villacastín, we cross the moorland, which is strewn with huge boulders, sometimes so improbably tilted that we are tempted to imagine some Cyclopean Stonehenge. These give the landscape an immensely primitive look. The few human habitations are crabbed and wretched by comparison with this splendid litter of Nature. Within the borders of the province one finds the most beautiful mountain scenery in Castile. In these mountains four rivers are born: the Tormes rising under the peak of Almanzor and winding northwards through Alba and Salamanca to join the Duero; the Alberche rising in the same valley and describing a great curve eastwards via San Martín de Valdeiglesias to join the Tagus near Talavera; the Tiétar rising under the southern slopes of the Sierra de Gredos to feed the Tagus at the Embalse de Torrejón; and last but not least in terms of beauty the Jerte, which rises not far from El Barco de Avila, just over the pass of Tornavaca, and runs down the lovely valley between the Sierra de Gredos and the Sierra de Béjar, passing under the walls of Plasencia to join forces with the Alagón, another Tagus tributary. Something will be seen of all these rivers and the settlements they have attracted but first we must consider the Adaja, stemming from the gentler Sierra de Avila and running north past Arévalo to join the Duero, for it is on this less picturesque stream that the famous walled city is built.

The enciente with its 88 towers and nine gates, the most complete in Europe, is certainly spectacular though one can detect a good deal of rebuilding in the upper stages, especially of the merlons, which give it a rather theatrical aspect. None the less, the *abulenses* reject with scorn any comparison with Carcassonne, which is a 'new' construction dreamed up by the Gothicising zeal of Viollet-le-Duc. Raymond of Burgundy here as at Salamanca was charged with the repopulation of the area by his father-in-law Alfonso VI, whose capture of Toledo in 1085 virtually secured for Christendom all the land north of the Tagus. Even so, it seems to have been thought prudent to establish a second line of defence on the axis Salamanca–Avila–Segovia. Quite what Count Raymond found when he arrived with gentlemen and craftsmen from Galicia, Asturias, León and Burgos – attracted by the many privileges and tax exemptions offered to repopulators – is uncertain. There had been a Celtiberian settlement and a Roman fort. Any Visigothic presence must have been a poor one, for there are no archaeological traces of this period in the walls, while those of earlier periods abound. And – perhaps because there was nothing much to take or destroy – the Moors seem to have passed it by.

Once the site was selected as a Christian strong-point fortifications were undertaken with great speed and efficiency. The vicious raids of Almanzor in the previous century cannot yet have been forgotten. The walls were begun in 1090 and finished in 1099. To carry out this project in so short a time it has been calculated that some 1900 men were employed daily. The result is not typically Spanish, in fact it is unique in Spain. As designers there are records of one Casandro, a Roman, and Florín de Pituenga, possibly Florian de Ponthieu. Nowhere else are there so many *cubos*, towers rounded on the outer face and rectangular at the rear, seen so close together. This is quite contrary to the Moorish tradition of wall-building, which the Christians largely took over for military purposes. And the main gates here, formed by prominent cubos linked by bridging arches, do not resemble any Moorish gatehouse in the peninsula. But there are traces of Mudéjar brickwork on the north side, which seem to indicate that some Moriscos at least were employed. The most impressive single feature of the whole enceinte – and of the same period – is the great semi-circular fortified apse of the cathedral, which projects beyond the eastern stretch of the wall where the land is flattest and the defences were most vulnerable. On this side also are the two strongest gates, those of San Vicente and the

Alcázar; the second of these was rebuilt in 1596 along with the Alcázar itself, of which nothing remains.

A little to the right of the apse is an arch in the wall which leads the pedestrian (but not the motorist, for the traffic is one-way in the opposite direction) into the old town under the north side of the **Cathedral**. The transept on this side has a fine rose-window and a charming brick loft with projecting tiled eaves runs along the top of the walls. The thirteenth-century portico was transferred from the narthex to its present position by Juan Guas in 1458; the carving of the archivolts, tympanum and figures is very deteriorated. We now emerge under the west front with its granite north tower of forbidding stamp, whose fellow on the south side was never completed. Both towers have a repetitive decoration of small salient hemispheres reminiscent of studs in a door or helmet or piece of armour. The main west door is flanked by grotesque figures called *maceros* (in English 'woodwoses' or 'green men'); it had plain archivolts until some unsuitable amorini and floral motifs were added in 1779. Above the door is a curious screen which partly obscures the west window. Where the stonework ends, one again notices the cathedral's brick loft with its faintly countrified air. In fact, it has two facets, one rustic and unsophisticated, the other martial and grim; neither is much affected by subsequent attempts at prettification.

Entering the cathedral by the west door we find ourselves standing in what was a narthex between two lateral chapels without grilles occupying the bases of the towers; these were used in early times by those preparing for conversion and this area was divided from the main body of the church by the doorway later moved by Juan Guas to the north side. Passing into the nave proper, which consists of four bays, one is immediately struck by the quantity of light admitted by the plain glass windows. The triforium has been suppressed in favour of a lower window area under the clerestory. However, the logical development of joining these has not been carried out, the tracery is somewhat coarse and the lower parts of the window openings are filled in with stone blocks. Avila, to be fair, lost most of its stained glass in the Lisbon earthquake and, had this been in place, our critical faculties would probably have been surrendered to the magic of colour. As it is, the plain panes are left rather defenceless. From this part of the church we get a good view along the main axis, though a tying

arch topped by a stone crucifix over the trascoro frets the eye
of the profane seeking aesthetic rather than religious thrills.

Chronology now urges us to the earliest part of the church
at the east end. The apse, whose fortified exterior we have
already seen, was begun in 1091 by one Alvar García. Work
was abandoned 16 years later and little more was done until a
certain Fruchel became master of the works in the time of
Alfonso VIII. To this master we owe our first sensation of
delight, for the stern machicolated bulwark is found to encase
a double ambulatory, which was vaulted in a curious mottled
stone about 1200. The ground plan of this is irregular; the
distance of the columns from the sanctuary piers is more or less
constant but the outer walk between these columns and the
radial chapels varies considerably in width. John Harvey in
his *Cathedrals of Spain* comments that 'the slim shafts, which
encircle the apse, based upon the ambulatory of St Denis,
have an endearing quality of youthfulness like the hesitant
legs of a colt.' This is very apt – though there is nothing
hesitant about the presbytery and sanctuary with their two
tiers of narrow windows whose *ajimeces* show a distinct horseshoe tendency. And here the remaining glass, mostly of the
fifteenth and sixteenth centuries, begins to make an impact
which extends to the transepts and the north – but not the
south – rose-window. Pleasure is unfortunately lessened in
this area of the church by the disconcerting switch from
mottled stone to granite and by an excessive picking out of the
pointing, to say nothing of the piecemeal painting of some of
the architectural members. The crossing, which is the same
height as the nave and transepts, was vaulted between 1312
and 1355. The two longitudinal arches which tie the crossing
piers also rather offend the eye on their upward sweep. A sum-
mary of the average person's impressions to date will probably
combine admiration for structural innovations – this church
has certainly taken the plunge into Gothic and can no longer
be described as 'transitional' – with irritation at so much
variation of building materials and so many changes of plan,
which all combine to produce a rather restless effect.

On the smaller scale of church furniture and fittings Avila
contains some notable things. The Gothic **Retablo Mayor** includes ten predella panels by Pedro Berruguete with characteristic golden haloes; among the larger scenes the Agony in
the Garden and the Flagellation are by the same artist, who

died in 1504. Juan de Borgoña, whose use of gold is less fierce, contributes the Annunciation and the Birth on the gospel side and the Descent into Limbo, the Transfiguration and the Presentation on the epistle side; the remaining panels are by other hands. The Renaissance alabaster ciborium in the centre is by Vasco de la Zarza. A pleasant exception to the rule is the absence of any screen between this retablo and the viewer. The **Coro** shelters behind a brass grille by those doughty metal-workers Fray Francisco de Salamanca and Fray Juan de Avila. The stalls of 1536–1547 are by Cornelis, a Dutchman, assisted by Spanish carvers. The lower series abandon the Gothic tradition of Old Testament scenes to present various martyrdoms, among them Saint Lawrence actually on his gridiron, Saint Sebastian being shot and Saint Stephen being stoned. These happenings are reported directly but the upper stalls with pilasters and canopies in the Renaissance style curiously enough revert to the symbolic treatment of martyrdom, whereby the same victims in perfect health hold the instruments of their deaths in their hands in marked contrast to the agonies they suffer immediately below. Considering their late date this is a good set of stalls, displaying Dutch reversionary tendencies towards the late lamented Gothic world. The trascoro facing the west door has charming high-relief stone panels of the childhood of Christ by Juan Rodríguez and Lucás Giraldo (1536).

The aisle side-chapels contain little of interest. In the north transept is a retablo devoted to San Antolín by Isidoro Villoldo (1551). Backing on to the north-east pier of the crossing is an alabaster altarpiece devoted to Saint Catherine – this is probably by Vasco de la Zarza and Juan Rodríguez (c. 1524). The iron pulpit on this side is by Llorente de Avila (1520). Against the south-east crossing pier is a similar altar to Saint Catherine's of slightly later date; the adjacent pulpit is of Gothic tracery on a Renaissance stem. The south transept connects by an open arcade with the Capilla de San Ildefonso; in this area there are several good Gothic tombs, including that of Don Pedro de Valderrábano with a page asleep on his master's helmet.

In the ambulatory we note that the shallow radial chapels are scooped out of the thickness of the wall and not enclosed by grilles. Opposite the axial chapel on the wall of the trasaltar is the Renaissance sepulchre of Bishop Alonso de Madrigal, known from his dark skin as el Tostado. He was author of 54 books and is shown writing at his desk. His short stature gave rise to the following incident. When he presented himself before Pope Eugenius IV, the pontiff believing the bishop to be on his knees, told him to rise. Affronted, el Tostado answered that he was already on his feet and added sharply, gesturing from his eye-brows to his hair-line, 'A man's stature is measured from here to here!' The bishop died in 1445. The tomb, made some 70 years later, is so finely executed that it has been attributed to Domenico Fancelli, author of the tombs of the Reyes Católicos in Granada and their son Prince John at Santo Tomás here in Avila. The panels on either side are inferior work. On the epistle side of the ambulatory is a door leading to the Capilla del Santísimo and to the street just south of the great apse. The next door leads to the **Sacristía** with an octagonal vault of the sixteenth century. The alabaster retablo by Vasco de la Zarza and Nicolás Villoldo is of good quality and this is true of most of the work of these and other Renaissance enthusiasts in the cathedral – though it is fortunate for the general character of the church that their contribution is confined to the smaller-scale items. The museum in the Capilla del Cardenal has a rather poor collection; the best pieces are the three delicate little painted alabaster reliefs, said to be English of the fifteenth century, representing the Adoration of the Kings, the Ascension of the Virgin and the Crucifixion of Christ between the knees of the Father with two kneeling angels holding chalices to catch the blood. The cloister is plain work of the fourteenth and fifteenth centuries; the arcade is walled in and it is used as a storehouse for Holy Week floats.

After the cathedral the most important churches of Avila lie outside the walls. Foremost among them is **San Vicente**, a Romanesque building of great assurance compared to the 'coltish' Cathedral. Here we find the maturity of an old style expressed in all its splendour in the golden stone that is appropriate to a golden age of Spanish building – an age Spaniards were profoundly reluctant to leave in pursuit of the new-fangled pointed style. The church is devoted to Saint Vincent and his sisters, Saints Sabina and Cristeta, all martyred together in 306. It was begun in the twelfth century in sandstone with a filling of rubble masonry. The magnificent west front has a great double doorway recessed under a pointed arch, which joins the two towers; a narthex is thus formed with flanking chapels outside the doors for aspiring converts, who were not admitted to the nave or aisles. This arrangement was later copied at the cathedral. The scenes in the twin tympana represent the Parable of the Rich Man's table and the Death of Lazarus. The lintels are supported by brackets shaped like bulls in the centre and lions on the jambs – which are carved with figures of Saints Peter and Paul. The other apostles converse in pairs. The north tower was completed in 1440 with curious inverted belfry windows and a gabled silhouette, all decorated with the strings of small stone hemispheres we have already noticed on the cathedral. The incomplete south tower was restored in 1849. The south wall has a marvellous wealth of animal heads and floral designs between the corbels. The figures flanking the south door, though of the Romanesque period, have been inserted later. The long porch on granite columns belongs to the fourteenth century. The tall triple apse is supremely elegant, the best of its kind in Castile, with slender engaged columns rising from base to eaves; between these are two series of windows, the lower of which correspond to the crypt and the upper to the sanctuary level. The granite sacristy protruding from the north side is an addition of 1477. The granite buttresses belong to this period too.

The inside of the church is as impressive as the outside. The aisles are covered with brick groin vaults, the crossing is barrel-vaulted, while the nave vault is quadripartite with pronounced ribs – note the slanting of the pilasters to launch these firmly on the right trajectory. There is a proper triforium and a tribune gallery at the rear links the towers. The piers have an assortment of differently-shaped bases; both by such irregularities and by its grand scale San Vicente avoids the too perfect preciosity of San Martín at Frómista (Palencia). However, idiosyncrasies are carried a little far by the deplorable imitation of the mottled stone of the cathedral painted onto the walls of the lateral chapels and by the smothering of some of the best capitals (north apse chapel) in gold paint.

The most important single object in the church is the tomb of Saint Vincent and his sisters, which fills the entrance to the south transept. This great Romanesque sarcophagus of the twelfth century was also painted and gilded in accordance with the practice of the time but has lost most of its colour. The excellent carving round the casket is beginning to develop

in the Gothic direction – see particularly the fine Adoration of
the Kings on the end facing the altar. This monument was
taken over in the fifteenth century by the nobles of Avila,
who endowed it with its strange almost Chinese baldachino,
decorated it with their shields and used it as a touchstone for
their oaths. It was also used by accused persons and litigators
to swear their statements where evidence was lacking and it
was widely believed that whoever swore falsely would see the
arm he had placed on the tomb dry up and wither away. The
crypt contains a Virgin venerated by Saint Ferdinand. This is
still popularly believed to have been carved by Nicodemus,
painted by Saint Luke and brought to Avila by Saint Peter –
no one is the least shaken in this conviction by the fact that
three-dimensional images were prohibited among the early
Christians. San Vicente remains an extremely popular church
among the abulenses. Even the new car-owning middle class
is drawn by a well-thundered diatribe against the Consumer
Society. The text of a sermon I heard was the Eye of the
Needle. Not for nothing are the rich man at his table and
Lazarus rising from his tomb carved over the west front.

Just below San Vicente on the north side rises the tower of
San Andrés, a church of the same period, open only on
Sunday afternoons for mass and during the Semana Polifónica
de Avila in July, when it is used for certain concerts. The lateral
apses do not share a common wall with the main apse, which
is rather unusual. The windows admit little light and this gives
an added luminosity to the sanctuary, whose barrel vault leads
into a perfect semi-cupola above three windows. The wall
leans out a little and the sanctuary arch, flattened round the
centre, has as a result a faintly Visigothic look. In general,
however, this is a very harmonious church.

Yet another extramural church belonging to this period is
San Pedro facing the Puerta del Alcázar across the Plaza del
Mercado Grande. Though begun a little before San Vicente,
it has a slightly greater ogival tendency. The west front was
restored in the fourteenth century – hence the granite columns
framing the rose-window. The triple apse is similar to San
Vicente's but neither so tall nor so impressive, as there is no
crypt. The transepts are pronounced. A rustic tower with
brick-topped belfry occupies the corner between the north
transept and the north apse. The lantern, completed in the
late fourteenth century, is best appreciated from the south

side. The nave arcades are formed by rounded arches rising from very massive pillars on round plinths of granite. Both aisle and nave vaults are of warm sandstone. The north apse has some very fine capitals with leopards, winged lions, four-legged birds, doves, storks and animals with human heads – these have all been picked out in gold as at San Vicente and here too the absurdity of painting the walls to resemble the mottled stone of the cathedral has been indulged in. Backing onto the piers of the presbytery arch are two Plateresque wooden altars in imitation of those carved in alabaster in the cathedral. This is a handsome church, less rich in external sculpture than San Vicente but in other respects yielding little to its more famous neighbour.

We have now seen the main Romanesque monuments of Avila. They are distinguished by the warm colour of their sandstone, which is sometimes combined with granite in the main architectural members. Chronologically they fall mostly between the earliest Zamoran Romanesque and the thirteenth-century churches of Segovia. The height of the city and the cold winds militated against the lateral porches common in Segovia and Sepúlveda – San Vicente's is an afterthought. Nevertheless, the three churches we have studied are on an ampler scale than their fellows in the more northerly towns, always excepting those of cathedral or collegiate status. The main influence seems to be Burgundian and the narthex of San Vicente has something in common with those of Vézelay and Autun. The west front system of a narthex set back under an arch joining two towers was adopted and gothicised in the cathedral.

Also outside the city walls is the **Monasterio de Santo Tomás**. Taking Calle Gabriel y Galán from the Plaza del Ejercito (behind San Pedro) and turning first right along the Paseo de Alféreces Provisionales, we come to this very large palace-monastery built between 1483 and 1493. The first Inquisitor-General, Torquemada, played a part in its founding; Ferdinand and Isabel contributed; so did heretics and Jews with their confiscated goods. The tribunal of the Inquisition had its seat here for six years and the monarchs used it as a summer residence. The west entrance continues in the tower and narthex tradition. There is a pomegranate frieze over the archivolts and above the doorway. This was the time of the great euphoria when the precious fruit, symbol of Granada, was ripe to drop into Castilian hands. Possibly it had dropped by the time the doorway was completed. The hemispherical decoration derived from the cathedral – which I shall call the ball motif from now on – is general throughout the building. The suggestion that this too was inspired by the pomegranate seems improbable as it was in use before Granada was even a gleam in the eye of the Christian kingdom.

The monastery has three cloisters. The first is the small plain **Claustro del Noviciado**, which leads to the larger and grander **Claustro del Silencio** with a Gothic vault springing from brackets. The gallery has fancy shouldered arches of five centres decorated with the ball motif; the panels of the solid balustrade are carved alternately with the emblems of the monarchs and the shield of the Dominican order represented twice with the pomegranate in between. Next comes the largest of all, the **Claustro de Reyes**, round which were the royal quarters. The semi-circular arcade is trimmed with the ball motif, though the shouldered arches above are not. From this cloister a door leads into the large **Church** near the east end. The wide vault springs from clusters of columns over which a moulding runs on to form a cornice. The sanctuary, raised most unusually on a gallery, has a retablo representing scenes from the life of Saint Thomas Aquinas; the retouched lower panels are by Pedro Berruguete. In the centre of the nave below this is the moving alabaster tomb by Domenico di Alessandro Fancelli of Prince John, who died in 1497 while still a student at Salamanca. The young prince, simply dressed with a page-boy haircut, lies sculpted on the lid with hands reposing on his sword – on either side is a discarded glove.

In the side-chapels on the gospel side are the tombs of Hernán Nuñez de Arnalte, one of the founders, and of the Prince's governess Doña Juana Velázquez de la Torre and her husband – though in the style of Fancelli these are probably by a local hand. The raised **Coro** at the rear is reached from the gallery of the Claustro de Reyes. The very fine Gothic stalls are of the 'geometrical' type by Martín Sánchez (cf. Miraflores and Oña), though unicorns, dragons, eagles and the devil can be detected lurking in the formalised foliage. The misericords, out of respect no doubt for the royal patrons, are not carved with the usual ribald or grotesque scenes. Next to the railing overlooking the nave and facing each other are the splendid royal stalls under fretted canopies, each carved with the arrows and the yoke under the joint shield of Aragón and Castile. The pomegranate is also frequent in these stalls. In a series of rooms reached from the same gallery the monks have installed their **Museo Oriental**. This collection has been built up over four centuries by Dominican missionaries to China, Japan and Vietnam.

One cannot spend long in Avila without becoming aware of the pervasive presence of Saint Theresa. Her mortal remains lie at Alba de Tormes – with what deep resentment Avila must have let them go! – but to the *Abulenses* she is still *their* saint and they don't even bother to specify her by name. She is simply *la Santa*. Just inside the south wall and facing the gate that is called after her stands the **Convento de Carmelitas Descalzas**, whose church was built between 1631 and 1636 on the site of the house where Theresa was born – of a good family of Jewish origin – in 1515. The façade stems from Herrera with some Baroque elements. The interior is standard work of the period, now painted in clinical white and cream with polished marble flooring. The retablo shows the saint being invested with a golden collar by the Virgin and Saint Joseph. Among the images in the side-chapels are Christ at the Column and Saint John of the Cross with pen and book, both by Gregorio Fernández. A door from the left transept leads down into a tiny bit of the garden in which Theresa played as a child; it is now rather dank and gloomy with privet hedges. Outside there is a small museum of relics, in which Saint John of the Cross is included, with a souvenir shop and lavatories – the Theresan cult is well organised in this respect. Facing this is the mansion built in 1541 by Blasco Núñez Vela, first Viceroy of Peru, now the Palacio de Justicia. The severe granite patio well illustrates the gravity of domestic architecture in Avila.

If we follow Theresa's career in chronological order, we should go next to the **Convento de la Encarnación** outside the walls on the north side and easily visible from the terrace of San Vicente. Following the slope that descends from the Puerta de San Vicente, we quickly spot the stone-based tower with two Mudéjar brick upper stages belonging to the Ermita de San Martín. Turning right past this chapel (which faces the humble Ermita de Santa Maria de la Cabeza across the road) we soon reach the convent, inaugurated in 1515. Theresa joined the Carmelite order here in 1537 and the place became her base for 30 years – for three of these she was prioress. Between 1562 and her death in 1582 she thoroughly reformed the order and founded 18 convents under the reformed rule, ranging from Burgos to Granada. A Theresan museum has been installed here (as in most places she was closely connected with); this contains among other mementoes an interesting little drawing by Saint John of the Cross of Christ crucified, seen from above left. A window opens onto a mock-up of the cell Theresa occupied as prioress – one remarks her wooden pillow.

Theresa's first foundation was in Avila itself. Known as the **Convento de San José** or **de las Madres**, it is reached by circling the church of San Pedro and taking Calle San Juan de la Cruz. The convent came into being in 1532, though Francisco de Mora's church was not finished till 1610. Beside this there is yet another Theresan museum, thoughtfully provided with the usual lavatories. In vitrine 2 are the musical instruments – drums, flutes, a tambourine – used by the saint and her nuns at Christmas; Theresa was the drummer. In vitrine 6 is a canvas of Saint Francis of Assisi attributed to Zurbarán and a Christ at the Column by Alonso Cano. The **Museo Provincial** also contains statues and portraits of *la Santa*. Just beyond the cathedral apse on the right, Calle Los Leales leads to the church of Santo Tomás el Viejo with a Romanesque portico. On the left is the granite **Casa de los Deanes**, which houses the museum. In the second room is a triptych with the Descent, Entombment and Resurrection all included in the central panel; this is attributed to Memling (*c.* 1430–1495) though the outer panels and some parts of the main panel are distinctly inferior to the rest. In the third and fourth rooms are several examples of that most prized of all pieces of Spanish furniture, the *bargueño* with its many drawers and secret compartment organised in a framework of Renaissance architecture; the name comes from Bargas in the province of Toledo which specialised in this type of chest.

Making now for the Tourist Office, facing the west front of the cathedral, and taking the first right after this, Calle de los Reyes Católicos, we come to Avila's rather disappointing Plaza Mayor. This is of brick on a stone arcade with the stone-faced Ayuntamiento of 1865 on the north side and on the south the sixteenth-century church of San Juan, whose brick tower was rebuilt and lowered in 1732 and again in 1918. Leaving by the

north-west exit into Plaza Zurraguín and following Calle
Bracamonte we come to the **Capilla de Mosén Rubí** attached to
a Dominican convent school. This church consists of two very
distinct halves. A Renaissance portico flanked by pairs of
columns admits us to a nave of only one bay under an elegant
shallow vault; this is barely more than an antechamber opening
into the much taller east end with a very gracious Gothic vault
springing from the four columns of the crossing. In front of
the high altar is the sepulchre of Doña Maria de Herrera (d.
1516) who endowed the church and placed it under the protection of the influential Bracamonte family of French Jewish
origin; given the late date it is not likely the building was ever
used as a synagogue.

No particular itinerary need be recommended for the rest
of intramural Avila. It is a pleasant place to wander in and
some sector or other of the wall is visible from almost every
point. The majority of the *mansiones* shown on the excellent
plan issued by the Tourist Office are still in private hands; only
those that have been converted to public uses can normally be
visited. These include the old episcopal palace facing the
north flank of the cathedral (Post Office), the Palacio de
Valderrabános by the west front of the cathedral (luxury
hotel), the Palacio de Benávites (Parador Nacional) and
the Palacio de los Núñez Vela already mentioned (Palacio de
Justicia). The Casa de Polentinos, beyond the Plaza Mayor via
Calle de Villespín, contains a Renaissance patio with combined
bracket-capitals supporting lintels instead of arches after the
manner of the Casa de Miranda at Burgos. Among the houses
that can only be seen from the outside are those of the Velada
family, looking on to the north tower of the cathedral, of the
Verdugos with a façade of large granite blocks (the seat of an
insurance company) and of the Aguilas – these are all in the
north-east corner of the walls. Against the south wall is the
fortress-like Palacio de los Dávila with its huge round-headed
doorways of large radial slabs. Near this, in the Plaza General
Mola, is the square Torreón de los Guzmanes, a great brutal
keep, overlooking a modern monument to the gentle Saint
John of the Cross. By contrast, the western half of the walled
area is very rustic and peaceful with sloping streets flanked by
humble one- or two-storey houses, into which sheep and other
animals are still driven at night. The chief, in fact the only,

church of this village-like district is the very simple Romanesque **Capilla de San Esteban**.

The major churches and convents we have seen outside the
walls are supplemented by others of lesser importance, not
all of which can be mentioned. Anyone walking in the garden
under the south wall will notice the octagonal tower that rises
from the church of **Santiago**, into whose granite structure the
yellow stone of an earlier and smaller Romanesque church
has been incorporated. A little above this to the east is the
firmly walled Convento de Nuestra Señora de Gracia, where
the future Saint Theresa was sent to school in 1531. The steps
leading upwards under the convent walls level out near the
south-east angle of the town wall, opposite which is the church
of La Magdalena with a Romanesque entrance. A few paces
farther along on the left is the Puerta del Alcázar. The area once
occupied by the Alcázar itself is now the Plaza de Calvo Sotelo,
dominated by the pompous façade of the Bank of Spain.
Across the Plaza del Mercado Grande a battered church may
be noticed facing the south flank of San Pedro; this is Santa
Maria la Antigua, from whose apse Calle Gabriel y Galán
leads to three more religious foundations. The first is the
Convento de Gordillas, followed by the Ermita del Cristo de
la Luz founded in 1467. Last and most important is the
Convento de Santa Ana founded in 1330 and containing the
tomb of Bishop Sancho Dávila, tutor of the child King
Alfonso XI; Isabel the Catholic spent some of her childhood
here and so did Philip II. The above are optional – one may or
may not come across them in one's wanderings – but there is
another extramural church on the north side that should not
be missed. This is the **Capilla de San Segundo** right down on
the river Adaja under the north-west corner of the wall. It is
partly hidden in a grove of poplars and not easily distinguish-
able from the road. The surroundings are particularly pleasant;
cows graze the grass, nibble the poplar shoots and rub their
noses on the church door. The Romanesque portico leads
into a curious little church of trapezoidal shape, the gospel-
side aisle being much wider than its fellow. The nave is covered
by an artesonado ceiling of the sixteenth century. The capitals
of the pillars supporting the irregular sanctuary arch are
carved with primitive beasts and figures. In marked contrast
to all this is the sixteenth-century kneeling monument to the
saint, attributed by Baedeker to Alonso Berruguete and by

the custodian – with more probability – to Juan de Juni. Here in this very simple setting are all the tricks of the Master Illusionist – the mitred head cocked to the left, the praying hands to the right, the wrinkled gloves, the chunky folds. This sumptuous figure of the Spanish High Renaissance represents the humble missionary who is popularly supposed to have brought Christianity to Avila as early as the first century AD – one would of course expect Avila to be well in the van in this respect.

Continuing under the walls and following the signpost to Toledo one soon passes on the left the golden stone Romanesque church of San Nicolás, almost entirely relined with Baroque plasterwork. A little farther on, the Toledo road forks left round the modern bluish-brick Plaza de Toros, which I personally rather admire, though I have yet to see a corrida in it. It is certainly much to be preferred to the vaguely Moorish arenas put up over most of Spain in the nineteenth century. About 1 km beyond this is a good bar called El Rancho, where they serve delicious lamb cutlets. Another 3 or 4 km bring one to the **Ermita de la Virgen de Sonsoles**, whose spacious shady precinct is provided with stone benches and tables for picnickers, a fresh-water fountain and lavatories. The fifteenth-century chapel, restored in 1561, is linked to the curate's house by an arch carrying the belfry. This is a windy place with a good view over Avila from the south.

I spoke at the beginning of this chapter of the beauties of the surrounding province. After the capital – the highest and breeziest and still one of the least spoilt in Spain – my plan is to lure the reader to the cathedral city of Plasencia, to which two main routes with several possible variants can be followed. The first and most direct is by N110 from Avila via Piedrahita and El Barco de Avila direct to Plasencia. Two variants of this offer themselves only 6 km along N110, from which point we can make a detour via the Parador de Gredos, rejoining N110 at El Barco, or cross right over the range to join the second main route at Arenas de San Pedro. If it is decided to leave the Sierra de Gredos and Plasencia for another trip, N403 may be taken leading direct from Avila to Toledo. Or this road may be left at San Martín de Valdeiglesias in order to follow C501 via Arenas de San Pedro and Jarandilla (for the monastery of Yuste) to Plasencia – which should not incidentally be confused with Palencia, capital of the province bordering Burgos

on the west. I will describe these routes in the order I have
stated them above.

Avila – Piedrahita – El Barco de Avila – Plasencia

This road follows the valley of the Adaja, which rises just to
the east of the mountain pass of Villatoro; we cross this at
1356 m before descending to **Piedrahita,** which is pleasantly
situated in the valley that divides the Sierra de Avila from the
Sierra de Gredos. Here the dukes of Alba built themselves a
rather charmless eighteenth-century 'bungalow' palace in a
lovely position under the Gredos foothills, near an abandoned
Dominican monastery. The town square is delightful with its
plane trees round the parish church of Santa Maria la Mayor,
whose squat old tower stands astride the crossing; in the
south face there is a little ajimez window, which may be Visigothic, under the three round-headed belfry windows. Inside,
the retablo de Santa Ana is attributed to Pedro Berruguete.
At 21 km from here we come to **El Barco de Avila** on the river
Tormes. This is another agreeable town with a fifteenth-
century castle that follows the standard rectangular design of
the period with rounded corner towers; the donjon straddles
the wall, though here it presents its narrowest face to the
attacker, and not its longest as at Fuensaldaña (Valladolid).
The west wall has windows overlooking the Tormes, which is
crossed a little higher upstream by an old hump-backed
bridge with spur-shaped piers. In the streets one notices the
use of tiles hung on side walls and even on fronts, as at Béjar.
The fourteenth-century parish church owes certain mannerisms
– such as the dummy machicolations over the south door and
the use of the ball motif – to Avila Cathedral. The road rises
from El Barco to the Puerto de Tornavaca at 1283 m, after
which it enters a series of tight downward curves at the head
of the very beautiful valley of the Jerte. The flanks of the
Montes Tras la Sierra on the right and the Sierra de Gredos
on the left rise from steep russet woods. Immediately below
the pass there is a mesh of narrow terraces cultivated with
vegetables and fruit trees, including some oranges. As the
valley opens out, the narrow floor is divided by neat dry stone
walls into hundreds of little meadows, grazed by black cattle.
Each meadow has one or two haystacks supported on a central
pole and surrounded by a low stone wall to prevent the

animals from nibbling their reserves away. Poplars, small oaks, olives and minute vineyards add to the variety. The almond and fruit blossoms in the spring are so breath-taking that the susceptible driver may be well advised to take a less stunning route. The road follows the river closely to Plasencia.

Avila – Puerto de Menga – Venta del Obispo – Parador Nacional de Gredos – Navacepeda – El Barco de Avila

This variant of the previous route affords natural rather than architectural thrills. Following N110 for only 6 km we find C502 on the left, which climbs to the Puerto de Menga at 1566 m. The landscape is one of small hillside grain fields surrounded by stone walls and ploughed by oxen. Great slabs and mounds of stone break the surface of the earth. The churches are very low and modest with porches to catch the sun. Storks occupy the belfries and crickets set up a disproportionate din in the grass. Snow lingers into June on the higher slopes. Beyond the pass is Venta del Obispo and 2 km beyond this C500 branches west towards the Parador. To the left of the road, a little beyond San Martín del Pimpollar, rises the river Alberche. Then comes the Parador de Gredos, one of the first of the national network, built of grey stone with a slate mansard roof and overlooking a wide, leafy, highland valley – across which rears up Almanzor, at 2592 m the highest of the Gredos peaks. From Hoyos del Espino a few kilometres farther on a local road branches left to cross the new-born Tormes by the Puente del Duque on its way up to an 'Alpine Club' right under the peak. The pines along the banks of this almost Scottish stream provide good shade for a picnic and a siesta. The whole of this high mountain valley is very beautiful and breathless and still; the only sound apart from that of a very occasional car is made by the axes of the foresters trimming and clearing the trees. C502 continues along the north bank of the Tormes through pleasant villages such as Navacepeda to rejoin N110 at El Barco de Avila.

Avila – Puerto de Menga – Venta del Obispo – Mombeltrán – Arenas de San Pedro

This route is identical with the previous one as far as Venta del Obispo but the right branch along C500 is not taken. C502 continues south to the Puerto del Pico, which it crosses at 1352 m. I shall never forget the effect this drive had on me the first time I came to Spain in 1948. We had slept the night at the Parador de Gredos. As we breasted the top, it seemed to me the whole world, the universe almost, was at my feet. Of course this impression was produced only by the valleys of the Tiétar and beyond this, with intervening hills, of the Tagus but for someone brought up between London and the Home Counties with the odd holiday in Scotland it was a revelation. A few kilometres below the pass lies **Mombeltrán** with a square fourteenth-century castle of the dukes of Albuquerque. This has drum towers at the corners; the machicolated parapets are carved with crude conches and trefoils. The parish church is built in the rather heavy version of the French ogival style that penetrated these remote mountain regions. The raised choir at the rear is reached by a grand staircase more appropriate to a castle. The wide arch carrying the organ loft is supported on pillars with applied columns twisted in the 'Solomonic' shape, which resembles barley-sugar spirals. There are some good grilles and pleasant tile-pictures from Talavera or Puente del Arzobispo. Most of the houses conserve their projecting eaves and wooden balconies. From Mombeltrán C502 continues south to join C501 at Ramacastañas, though a right fork 8 km before the junction leads direct to the main town of the area, Arenas de San Pedro.

Avila – El Tiemblo – Toros de Guisando – San Martín de Valdeiglesias – Escalona – Maqueda – Toledo

We leave Avila on N403, the direct road to Toledo. Soon we begin to climb on to the desolate moorland of the Sierra de la Paramera, which we cross at 1395 m. Here again is the great litter of huge rocks like gigantic pebbles, which we noted lower down on the road from Villacastín. After the pass the road descends to the valley of the Alberche, which it crosses at the foot of the Embalse de Burguillo. A little south of the river is the village of **El Tiemblo** with a neat little Baroque church, rather self-conscious and solemn like a bumpkin in fashionable clothes. It is worth making the short detour from El Tiemblo to see the famous **Toros de Guisando**. There are other examples of this breed of ancient stone animals at Avila, Salamanca, Ciudad Rodrigo and elsewhere but their greatest concentration – four in a row – is here. No one has ever given a copper-bottomed explanation of their origin, though in view of their wide dispersal and their number – a hundred years ago some 70 were traced and a recent count yielded 30 – the most acceptable seems to be that they marked the territorial limits of a pre-Roman Celtiberian tribe. The four on the present site witnessed the celebrated meeting on September 19th, 1468 – subsequently dishonoured on his death in 1474 – at which Henry IV acknowledged his sister Isabel as heiress of the kingdoms of Castile and León. More recently they have been adopted as mascots by the Ministry of Information and Tourism, which awards a silver or brass plaque engraved with their most untaurine silhouettes to deserving restaurants. The next town to the south of El Tiemblo on N403 is **San Martín de Valdeiglesias**, pleasantly situated in a vale of small villages and fruit trees and overlooked on all sides (but not oppressively) by large wooded hills. Beyond these to the west the snow-streaked massif of Gredos is visible. On the edge of the town is a small ivy-hung but rather bogus-looking castle popular with film-makers. On the southern side of the unpretentious Plaza Real of 1834 is the unfinished parish church, consisting only of sanctuary, crossing and transepts. Inside, there is a good Baroque retablo in plain unpainted wood.

Continuing 25 km to the south we come to **Escalona** with a large and very ruined castle built for Alvaro de Luna and stoutly defended by his widow after his execution in 1453. In its day it is said to have surpassed in magnificence the royal Alcázar of Segovia. The outer court is now a rough football ground; the inner court or palace still shows vestiges of Gothic elegance. Most of the construction is of rubble masonry faced with one layer of stone but the window embrasures and the vaulting of the passages are made of slender bricks of delicate Morisco workmanship. From these ruins there is a fine view over the wide sandy bed of the Alberche. A pleasant arcaded plaza forms the town centre. N403 now runs down to **Maqueda**, which is dominated by a restored fourteenth-century fortress with Mudéjar brickwork under the merlons and a good machicolated gallery over the main entrance – this is now a Civil Guard barracks and cannot be visited. Other features of interest are a bold upstanding tower, rounded on the outer face and rectangular at the rear, with rubble masonry between courses of bricks placed vertically – this formed part of the wall – and the entrance to the parish church, unusually reached by a stone-walled tunnel with a brick vault over a shallow flight of steps, leading to a stone horseshoe arch, which frames the church door. This probably belonged to a gatehouse in the wall and the stone arch may be of Moorish construction. Just south of Maqueda N403 crosses NV, the Madrid–Extremadura road, and continues through flatter lands via Torrijos (see next chapter) to Toledo.

Avila – El Tiemblo – San Martín de Valdeiglesias – Ramacastañas – Arenas de San Pedro – Candeleda – Villanueva de la Vera – Jarandilla – Yuste – Plasencia

This route like the last starts on N403, which we leave at San Martín de Valdeiglesias to follow C501 westwards along the valley of the Tiétar, claimed as the 'Andalusia of Avila' on the grounds of its oranges and olives. Certainly the countryside is extremely pretty and so are its villages. Piedralaves has houses with the regional wooden balconies and wide eaves – under which garlic and red peppers and tomatoes are hung in the best of all larders, the fresh air. Pedro Bernardo, a little off the road to the north, has charming terraced streets on a steep slope; only the church belfry breaks the earth-hugging line of roofs and chimneys. 4 km beyond Ramacastañas is the **Cueva del Aguila**: a shallow hill has become almost hollow, apparently as a result of a schism some 8 or 10 million years ago, which produced a sinking of the lower rock. The fault thus created has been busy 'growing' stalactites and stalagmites and other calcinous formations ever since. Some weird Bosch-like shapes are to be seen, electrically lit in several colours. There are no wall paintings and the cave would seem to have been uninhabited in prehistoric times. C501 continues from Ramacastañas to **Arenas de San Pedro**, another agreeable little town with a Roman bridge over the river. The shell of the castle with its round corner towers and rectangular donjon is impressive. There is also a hall-church with an elegant interior. San Pedro de Alcántara, after whom the place is named, lived here and is commemorated by a chapel, shrine and monastery a few kilometres to the north. From Arenas a short detour leads up to Guisando, a sweet village nestling under the peak of La Mira. The descent to rejoin C501 affords enormous views of the river, of the Embalse de Rosarito, of the larger and more distant Embalse de Valdecañas and of the hills of Toledo and Extremadura.

The next village on the route is **Candeleda** with some delightful streets; it is worth stopping for a drink and a stroll here. We now enter the district called La Vera, meaning literally the bank or verge and applied here to the southern slopes of the Sierra de Gredos running down to the Tiétar. These are scoured with snow-ducts called *gargantas* – throats – and most of the villages have open channels of sparkling water running beside their streets to feed their pumps and irrigate their orchards. **Villanueva de la Vera** may be remarked for its tradition of weather-boarding. **Valverde de la Vera** has a nice old church whose very flattened arches are decorated with the ball motif we saw so much of in Avila. Then comes **Jarandilla de la Vera**. When Charles V resigned the Empire in 1555, he was in Brussels. He took ship to Laredo near Santander and then had himself carried half across Spain by litter (owing to his severe gout) to this little town, where he stayed for some months in the castle of the Count of Oropesa, while modest quarters were being built for him at the neighbouring monastery of Yuste, which had been selected for his retirement. The castle, which has become a Parador, is a good place to spend the night; adequate food and lodging can be found more cheaply at the Hostal Cristina. The turning for the monastery is a little farther along C501 just after the village of Cuacos. A 2 km climb through woods mainly of oak-scrub brings us to the Emperor's retreat.

The Jeronymite order, it may be remembered, was founded in 1373 and never spread beyond the borders of Spain. In Charles's time the community at **Yuste** numbered some 70 monks. The church belongs to the late fifteenth century. Charles had four simple rooms added to its south flank. This annexe, now rather incongruously dignified by the title 'palace', is of brick with a porch supported on granite columns and approached by a ramp, which enabled the crippled monarch to mount and dismount within a few yards of his quarters. The first room on the right off the passage is the despacho or study, whose walls are hung with the black drapery Charles adopted on the death of his long-lived mother, poor Joan the Mad, which also took place in 1555, the year he came to Yuste. There is a writing desk with a red

velvet cloth near the fireplace. The only concession to comfort
was the installation of a good fireplace in each of the four
rooms. Off the study are a mirador and gallery, from which
Charles would fish for captive tench in the fish-pond immediately underneath – there is also a fine view from here of the
valley of La Vera. The next room on this side is the dining-
room with a simple trestle table and Charles's invalid chair
with adjustable back and leg-rests. Crossing the passage, we
enter the alcoba or bedroom, also hung in black. A pair of
doors open to reveal the church altar; the floor is a little lower
than the sanctuary and the opening is so slanted that it was
possible for the invalid to watch celebrations of the mass from
his bed. This device was later to be adopted by Philip II at
the Escorial. From the alcoba we pass to the guard-room, containing the litter in which Charles was carried from Laredo in
order to avoid the intolerable jolting of a carriage. This
vehicle, if such it can be called, is a curious cross between a
pram, a trunk and a coffin. In the sides of the canopy are
leather window-flaps and there is a leather windscreen too,
so that the traveller could completely seal himself off from
bad weather. The only reminder of the imperial splendours
we associate with the chastiser of the Commons and the victor
of Mühlberg and Tunis is the bronze bust in the porch, which
is cast in the heroic Renaissance mould. An inscription on the
wall above tells us that the Emperor was sitting in this very
place when the ague seized him on August 31st, 1558; less
than a month later he was dead.

The church, shown by one of the few remaining monks, is
plain Gothic with a raised rear choir projecting over the two
west bays. The retablo is by Herrera el Viejo (1576–1656).
In the predella are the four Fathers of the Latin Church. Both
cloisters are still forbidden territory to the profane and may
only be seen from their entrances. The smaller of the two is
late fifteenth century with flattened arches at both levels.
The larger, restored after serious damage in the Peninsular
War, is in an undecorated Renaissance style with semi-
circular arches rising from heavy Ionic capitals and a flattened
arcade round the gallery above. From the sacristy we descend
to the crypt. Charles ordered in his will that his body should
be laid here under the high altar in such a way that any priest
celebrating mass would be standing directly over his head and
chest. This was done and the body remained in this position

in its lead-lined coffin (which is preseryed) until it was removed by Philip II to the Escorial 16 years after his father's death.

From Yuste the road winds down to **Plasencia** on the river Jerte. I include this Extremaduran city, as it is on the road to Andalusia from both Salamanca and Avila and thus a natural stage for many motorists. Also, the new cathedral is intimately linked with the late Gothic work at Salamanca and Segovia, while the chapter house of the old cathedral belongs to the Salmantine or Zamoran group we have also studied. But space obliges me to restrict myself to these churches, leaving the other major buildings and the surrounding area for another hand and another work. Once one has penetrated the high-rise fringe, one finds that Plasencia is an extremely civilised city, which has taken the very sensible measure of banning traffic from its Plaza Mayor and the seven or eight narrow streets that debouch into this engagingly irregular town centre, one of the most agreeable in Spain.

The **Cathedral** complex rises above the south rampart and is approached through an arch in the wall on the right of the Cáceres road (N630). At first sight it may seem to present a confusing hotchpotch of styles, causing a certain bewilderment, not to say frustration, in the visitor. The sacristan claims with some pride that it is 'complicated'. It is not so really, if it is understood from the outset that the new cathedral is not built alongside the old as at Salamanca but was designed to gobble it up entirely. This did not happen because the new building ran out of steam and money and a considerable part of the old was therefore spared. There is happily no attempt to make an awkward sort of synthesis of the two parts – they are firmly treated as two separate churches, albeit with communicating doors. It is a curious fact that some cathedrals belong to the 'outside first' category and others to the 'inside first'. Plasencia is essentially one of the latter. Though it would be tidy to start chronologically, pedantry can go too far. We are naturally drawn first to the Plateresque façade of the north transept, which leads into the breath-taking half church whose foundations were laid by Enrique de Egas about 1498. The main credit, however, belongs to Juan de Alava, who joined the team in 1513 in conjunction with Francisco de Colonia and became sole master from 1522 till his death in 1537. Alava, as we have seen, was architect of the Colegio del

Arzobispo and of San Esteban at Salamanca and also master of the cathedral works in that city from 1531, but nowhere did he produce such splendid vaults as here at Plasencia. The sanctuary belongs to the period of his collaboration with Colonia but the transepts and the first and only bay of the nave and aisles are his alone. The two sanctuary piers retain vestigial capitals but those of the choir exfoliate into the vault without check. Under the windows runs a balustrade of Renaissance influence; there is also a sparing use of medallion heads round the upper walls. The foot-rests of the niches applied to the piers rise from the same curiously jointed columnettes (almost resembling drain-pipes) that we saw on the west front of Salamanca Cathedral. Yet, none of these details, whether slanted towards Gothic tradition or Renaissance innovation, detract from the great sweep up to the high vault, whose curving ribs swing triumphantly across the divisions of the bays. By comparison one finds it hard to pay too much attention to the large retablo with figures by Gregorio Fernández or the lateral Churrigueresque altars or to the tomb of Bishop Ponce de León on the gospel side of the presbytery or to the niggly Plateresque door on the epistle side or even to the Gothic Virgin in the ciborium. The architect has stolen the show.

A doorway at the rear of the gospel-side aisle leads back into the older church by an unusual passage with chapels on the right between the buttresses. The pier bases, similar to those of the new section, are clear evidence of the plan, never completed, to extend the new cathedral by four or possibly five bays towards the west. Walking down this false aisle, we

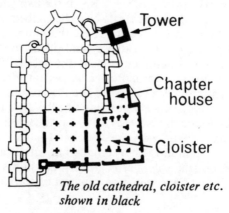

The old cathedral, cloister etc. shown in black

turn at the bottom into the **Catedral Vieja** proper, built between 1320 and 1400. Four nave bays remain. They are of fine proportions but sad aspect owing to their dreary coating of white and grey washes. The capitals and bosses are interestingly carved in a somewhat archaic mode and each vaulting compartment is unusually decorated between the ribs with a carved beast or human head. Crossing to the epistle side and leaving by a door in the south wall we enter the **Claustro**, which is small but of great character. It is said to have been built by two hands in the early fifteenth century. If this is so, the north walk is archaic indeed with its paired columns and tall Romanesque-type capitals supporting double pointed windows. The other sides have been given larger pointed openings which lack columns or tracery. From the west walk we look across the little garden to a small scaly spire strongly reminiscent of the Torre del Gallo at Salamanca; this one is called the **Torre del Melón**, owing to an odd topknot shaped like a melon, and it covers the chapter-house. Continuing to the right, we get a charming view of the old cathedral, the belfries and the storks that inhabit them. In the east walk we cannot but pause before the massive corner of undressed masonry which the new building here advances into the cloister, encroaching on but not quite preventing circulation and narrowly missing the chapter-house itself. When we enter this, we find ourselves under the last of the great series of Salmantine or Zamoran lantern-cupolas, built about 1250. This appears to be more pointed than its predecessors and the dome with sixteen ribs rises from squinches instead of pendentives. The windows are blocked on the north side by the advancing wall of the new church and some have been filled in on the east so the lantern is deprived of much of its light. All the same, it is a worthy member of a great series and it is something of a miracle it has survived at all.

We now take the cloister door leading back into the new cathedral, once more receiving the full impact of the great design – or as full a one as can be got of a work that can never be seen from a proper distance. The **Coro**, occupying the only nave bay, is worthily furnished with stalls from the workshop of Rodrigo Alemán. Instead of the more usual figures in relief the traditional saints and martyrs are shown in flat marquetry panels above the upper stalls, while the lower panels are abstract. Above the seats at both levels runs a carved frieze of biblical scenes, some sadly deteriorated or even missing. The misericords are beautifully carved with country and grotesque scenes; the one beneath the bishop's stall shows a craftsman toiling at his workbench – very likely Master Rodrigo himself.

Leaving the church, we can now make more sense of the outside. The Plateresque north transept façade, impressive enough in its way, is academic compared to Alava's great portico for San Esteban, Salamanca. It would appear to have been built after his death, most probably by the sophisticated Alonso de Covarrubias, the Lutyens of his day. Inspiration declines even more as we walk west. The buttresses containing the chapels we saw on the inside are in an uneasy compromise style. Turning the corner, we find ourselves facing the original west front with a Romanesque doorway of five plain archivolts. We can go no farther in this direction, for buildings hem us in. Standing back, we notice that there seems to be no serious tower. There are two belfries certainly but where is the tower? Whoever heard of a cathedral without a tower? To get the answer we must retrace our steps and make the circuit of the chevet – and there on the south side above the modern motor road we finally track down the squat tower of the old cathedral with 'transitional' windows, still firmly in place under the fancy finials of its later neighbour. Plasencia cathedral is a strange place, full of surprises. It is a nice question whether one is glad the new church got no further or whether one would prefer to see Juan de Alava's work majestically finished. Providing the fascinating commentary that it does on more than three centuries of Castilian church architecture, there is a strong case for preferring it as it is.

Plasencia – Toledo

Plasencia stands at the south-west limit of this book. From here we make for Toledo. Those who reach Plasencia by N110 from Avila may like to work east again on C501 (my last route in reverse) to San Martín de Valdeiglesias, where they can join N403 for Toledo. A faster way is to leave C501 at Jarandilla, whence a local road runs south, crossing the Tiétar, to join NV at Navalmoral de la Mata. From here it is a quick run through Oropesa and Talavera de la Reina (both described in the next chapter) to Toledo.

CHAPTER TEN

Toledo

✿

Of Roman, Visigothic and Moorish Toledo little remains above ground. The city as we see it is almost entirely post-Reconquest. But its physiognomy, particularly its street plan and its noticeable lack of a good town centre, owes a great deal to its Arab past. Civil wars during the period of the Caliphate and the degeneration of this into petty kingdoms produced in the fortifications and fortresses and palaces, according to a local historian, 'a veritable Penelope's shroud, which was woven and unwoven with frequency though never in the same form.' For more than a century after the Reconquest – from the entry of Alfonso VI in 1085 to the battle of Las Navas de Tolosa in 1212 – the city remained on a semi-war footing, requiring constant repairs of the walls and towers. Then came the surge of religious building of the thirteenth, fourteenth and fifteenth centuries. The secular area became more and more confined by the churches and convents that hemmed it in and expansion outwards was prevented by the fortifications. Eventually things came to such a pass that both Church and State had to take notice of the matter. Alfonso X prohibited the building of any more monasteries or churches without royal licence. Archbishop Mendoza constantly refused permission for any more religious building inside or outside the city. Charles V ordered no more religious building without permission of the prelate. None of these measures seems to have had much effect. The city council approved and put into practice a scheme for buying property for secular purposes but this had little success either and was unpopular as it led to a rise in taxes.

It should now be clear that it was the combination of the earlier Moorish network with the later encroachment on habitable land by the religious orders that led to most of the features we find charming in Toledo today, such as the covered passages known as *cobertizos* and the salient upper stories or *saledizos.* But by shutting out the light and air these bred sickness and were less well viewed in their day. Alfonso X made an order prohibiting manure and garbage in the streets, to little avail. In vain did the urban police try to keep *animales inmundos* (unclean animals) off the public thoroughfares. And it was not until September 1502 that Ferdinand the Catholic approved an order for the stone paving of the streets and the installation of a drainage system. Despite the zeal of the municipality in putting this into effect, it came too late. For Toledo was entering on its long decline. In 1560 Philip II made a brief stay in the city but finding the arrogance of the Toledan clergy little to his liking, he moved the court in the next year to Madrid.

If we approach on N403 we pass the large Hospital de Afuera or de Cardenal Tavera (which I shall leave for the present) before joining the road from Madrid just outside the **Puerta Nueva de Visagra**. Motorists are advised to park their cars in this area for the moment and continue on foot. The north face of the gatehouse carries a huge shield of Charles V's armorial bearings between drum-shaped towers. Walking through the arch we find a small court with a bust of the Emperor enclosed on the far side by an inner gate with square towers and tiled spires. This is all by Alonso de Covarrubias. To the left of the gate and severed from it by a break for motor traffic, stretch some 200 yards of Arab wall with remnants of three towers. To the right the wall is pierced by an arch, also for traffic, and continues for a much greater distance. In this section is the ninth-century Arab **Puerta Antigua de Visagra**, through which Alfonso VI entered the city with the Cid. Stubby pillars with crude capitals rest on massive stone masonry; above is a blind arcade combining the pointed and the ultra-semicircular horseshoe shapes. This leads straight to the Mudéjar brick church of **Santiago del Arrabal** built in Alfonso VI's reign and much restored. The exterior decoration is extremely variegated, incorporating rounded, pointed and cusped arches. The free-standing tower with ajimez windows belongs to an earlier mosque. Inside, the nave arches are pointed with little tongues protruding at the springing, nostalgic reminders probably of the incurving horseshoe. It was from here that the intolerant Saint Vincent Ferrer went forth in 1405 at the head of the rabble he had roused to throw the Jews out of their synagogue (now Santa Maria la Blanca).

A steep slope climbs from here to the **Puerta del Sol**, a sophisticated Mudéjar structure of the fourteenth century, whose outer and portcullis arches are pointed, while the other two are ultra-semicircular. The mutilated medallion with the sun and moon shows the Virgin investing Saint Ildefonso with the chasuble – this popular local miracle is also commemorated in the cathedral. Beyond this gate Calle de Carretas climbs through the mediaeval Puerta de Alarcones towards the Plaza de Zocodover, the nearest thing Toledo boasts to a city forum, but it is worth making for a flight of steps slightly downhill from the Puerta del Sol leading up to yet another gate, the **Puerta de Valmardén**, which belonged to the Visigothic wall of King Wamba. Just through this is the delightful little **Ermita del Cristo de la Luz**, a tiny square mosque of three bays on each side built in 922; a brick Mudéjar sanctuary has been added at a later date and on a higher level. Each of the nine vaulting compartments is different from the others and the centre one higher than the rest; ingenious variations are played on a theme of ribbed and domed vaults. Legend has it that on the entry of Alfonso VI his horse (one version) or the Cid's (another version) knelt in front of the mosque and refused to go on. The King had the place searched and a wall opened, in which a niche was revealed with a candle still burning from the Visigothic church on the same ·ite; this had therefore stayed alight for 365 years and Alfonso ordered the first mass of the Reconquest to be said here. The old custodian also gleefully shows the room above the Puerta del Sol with machicolated openings for boiling oil, lead etc.

The motorist will now do well to return to his vehicle and drive up to Zocodover, from which signs will direct him along Calle del Comercio to the cathedral. Those of us on foot will – taking it easily – reach the same point by climbing Calle Cristo de la Luz and asking if we get lost. The street plan of Toledo is so intricate that in default of a sign – and these are quite plentiful – one must be prepared to ask one's way. Once in Calle del Comercio it is easy going and we descend Calle Arco del Palacio under an arch to emerge in the Plaza del Ayuntamiento with the episcopal palace on the right and the **Cathedral**, seat of the Primate of Spain, on the left. The church was begun at the east end in the early thirteenth century. The lower part of the west front now facing us was built by Alvar Martínez between 1418 and 1444. The central door is called the Puerta del Perdón. The tympanum shows the imposition of the chasuble on Saint Ildefonso, the popular Toledan miracle which has already appeared on the Puerta del Sol and which is supposed to have taken place at a spot we shall see inside the cathedral. To the south or right is the Puerta de Escribanos and to the north or left the Puerta de la Torre. Last Supper figures in Plateresque stall-type niches occupy the stage above the portico. The great rose-window thirty feet in diameter is partly masked by two slanted arches carrying a prow-shaped balustrade with urns – this part of the work was begun by J. B. Monegro in 1606. The whole is capped by a pediment of 1787. To the left rises the great north-west tower. The lower stage is by Juan Alfonso and belongs to the early fifteenth century; it was carried up higher by Alvar Martínez between 1425 and 1440 and crowned with its superb finials and triple-coroneted spire by Hanequín de Egas in the years 1448–1452. The front was planned for two towers and it is perhaps as well that the second was never fully completed, for two soaring spires would have been one too many for the enclosed space and the cramped effect of the west porches would have been increased. In the event, the south tower did not rise above the lowest stage and the cupola added by el Greco's son J. M. Theotocopouli provides a sufficient but not excessive foil for its taller and grander neighbour.

At right angles to this west front is the façade and terrace of the **Ayuntamiento**, one of the most agreeable town-halls in Spain. Despite the Escorial-type spires with dormer windows it has none of the usual Herreran grimness. Round-headed windows with grilles between Doric columns on the ground floor – the designs were Herrera's carried out by Nicolás de Vergara – are matched on the first floor by gracious French windows between Ionic columns by J. M. Theotocopouli, who was responsible for the towers also. The building was completed in 1618. Refreshment may well be required at this point and can be taken at a bar called 'La Burgalesa' which is easily picked out just below the parapet of the bit of municipal garden stretching under the town-hall front. Anyone speaking Spanish will find that the owner, Villegas, is a wag. With him we can fortify ourselves for the glories of Toledo, which are still ahead with their attendant tourist-traps like a great host with its swarm of parasites.

Now let us enter the church. Passing the base of the tower

we find on the right the **Puerta del Mollete** which leads via the large and rather dull cloister of 1389–1425 to the **Puerta de la Presentación**, outside which tickets are sold for the dependencies. Inside, a tenebrous grandeur reigns. With 446 feet this cathedral is very nearly as long as Seville's. Moving eastwards, while we accustom our eyes to the dim light, we come eventually to a double ambulatory with radial chapels. This, the earliest part of the building, was begun in 1226. The inner ambulatory piers are surmounted by a triforium gallery, whose twin-columned cusped arches show Moorish influence. But the eye is distracted almost at once from such details by the extraordinary confection on the trascoro wall known as the **Transparente** and described in Baedeker (1908) as 'a barbaric but extraordinarily well executed fricassée de marbre'. Finished by Narciso Tomé in 1732, it is the latest major feature of the cathedral but since it is so obtrusive we will deal with it here. Basically we are confronted by a large and very extreme example of a Rococo altarpiece. Forms run and slip like ice-cream somehow desperately gelled by art. The far-flung extremities of the swirling design are drawn together by gilt shafts of sun and this gilding is repeated in the column-flutings, capitals, wings, shields, cardinals' hats and other decorative props. Such is the frigid ebullience of the whole that the edges, if such they can be called, overflow and congeal almost like chocolate on top of the Gothic carving of the trascoro. In order to light this extravaganza one of the triforium galleries and one compartment of the ambulatory vault have been destroyed to make a skylight, in which high and low relief give way to frescoes in no less frenzied a vein. Whatever one may think of all this, it is undoubtedly the best place in the church to consult one's guidebook without ruining one's eyes.

Back to the structure proper. Passing to one or other of the transepts we see they have a triforium along their east walls, occupying the equivalent space that is devoted to the lower parts of the windows in the nave. The acanthus leaf decoration of the east end capitals is carried right through to the west end, which was not completed until about 1400 – though the leaves become more naturalistic towards the west. The huge twelve-shafted nave piers have rectangular bases raised on a sort of bench seat. Simple six-ribbed vaulting compartments cover the strongly emphasised bays. The stained glass of the nave windows is Flemish and Dutch of the fifteenth and sixteenth centuries; the aisle windows were designed by the Vergara family (*c.* 1560).

In Spanish cathedrals it is usually difficult to resist for very long the lure of the sanctuary and Toledo is no exception. The ticket to visit the dependencies includes the **Capilla Mayor** and the rich grille by Francisco Corral de Villalpando (1548) is open during visiting hours. The retablo mayor, a fabulous dolls' house of many mansions, contains fourteen main scenes from the New Testament with flanking figures and a crowded predella. As usual, the higher the figures the larger they are, in order to preserve the illusion of consistency in size. The work, carried out between 1502 and 1504, contains carvings by Enrique de Egas, Pedro Gumiel and Felipe Vigarni. The framework and niches are still fully Gothic and populated with actors who are all given personal characteristics. The relation of the ideal to the individual was the essence of mediaeval sculpture, especially in Spain. Godhead, suffering, martyrdom and rejoicing are depicted in essentially human terms. Despite its date and some Renaissance influence this retablo is still mediaeval in feeling.

On the gospel side of the high altar are the tombs of Alfonso VII (d. 1134) and the Infante Don Pedro de Aguilar and on the epistle side those of Sancho III the Desired (d. 1158) and Sancho IV the Brave (d. 1295) – all under great crowned shields in superbly crested flamboyant Gothic niches by Diego Copin (1507). The piers on either side of the altar steps are encrusted with sculpture. On the left pier are figures of Alfonso VIII and the shepherd Martín Alhaga, who guided the King along a difficult mountain path, enabling him to win the decisive battle of Las Navas de Tolosa in 1212. On the right pier, equally prominent, is the Alfaqui Abu Walid, who mediated between Alfonso and Bishop Bernard after the latter had done his best to dishonour the royal pledge to act as 'king of the two religions'. On the epistle side is the monumental tomb completed by Miguel de Florencia in 1509 to house the remains of Cardinal P. González de Mendoza, who had died in 1495. The rear or ambulatory face of this is carved with a medallion of the Holy Cross held by Saint Helen by Alonso de Covarrubias. In order to make way for this grandiose sepulchre the whole Gothic screen between the pier of the altar steps and the pier of the crossing was pulled down – its fellow, exquisitely delicate with saints and finials, remains intact on the other side.

Facing the Capilla Mayor behind a fine screen of 1548 is the **Coro**, occupying two bays of the nave. Though many Anglicans and some Catholics complain of the siting of Spanish choirs there is no doubt it is cosier for the clergy. 'Even with a choir in the middle,' I was told by a parish priest who came to walk in the cathedral daily, 'thousands of people can fit into a large church like this and anyway it only happens on feast days and holidays. But the canons have to use the place day in, day out and they need a smaller and more intimate area. Why, there is a cathedral somewhere in Galicia, I forget which, where they actually removed the choir and there was too much space and nobody was happy. Believe me, there is a necessary sense of enclosure and intimacy for a chapter which transcends aesthetic considerations.' And whatever the affront to architecture there is no doubt that these enclosed choirs – as we have already seen at Zamora, Salamanca and Ciudad Rodrigo – gave rise to some of the finest carving in the land. The Toledo stalls are magnificent. The lower series, consisting of 54 stalls, was carried out between 1489 and 1495 by Rodrigo Alemán. The misericords are highly original but it is the panels above each seat that are so riveting. These represent scenes of the taking of walled towns and strong points during the final war of Granada, which lasted from 1483 to 1492; most of the place names are incised in their respective panels and those that are not can usually be deduced from other evidence. Any knowledge of these campaigns will confirm that the carvings bear an astonishingly accurate relation to the events. It would perhaps be too much to describe Rodrigo as a 'war artist' and there is no record that he ever went to the front but returning troops and released prisoners would have been able to relate episodes to him as he worked, while it is to be supposed that the monarchs themselves and the Cardinal would have kept a watchful eye on the recording of exploits for posterity. Thus, where Ferdinand was present he is shown and when he was accompanied by Isabel or Cardinal Mendoza they are shown too; if the place in question was taken by a lesser person – as at Alhama de Granada captured in a famous action by Rodrigo Ponce de León, Duke of Arcos – the King is absent. Also, details of the engagement – whether the place was taken by assault with ladders or burnt or peaceably surrendered – are recorded faithfully in the panel. I strongly recommend a close look at these fascinating carvings. The choir light is not of the best and a torch is a help.

The *sillería alta* or upper series was commissioned in 1539. Felipe Vigarni and Alonso Berruguete agreed to complete the work in three years at 150 ducats a stall. The backrests, like Rodrigo's of walnut, are inlaid with marquetry designs and each stall has a canopy supported by jasper columns with alabaster bases and capitals – above are low-relief alabaster panels of the patriarchs. The 35 stalls on the gospel side are by the rampant Berruguete, whose work is full of Renaissance dynamism and flowing motion; the 35 on the epistle side are by the slightly worn Vigarni whose carving is more Gothic in feeling and a little stiffer. Each artist worked his own side both in wood and stone. The large alabaster group of the Transfiguration under a bronze canopy over the archiepiscopal throne is by Berruguete. The throne itself was awarded to Vigarni but he died in harness in 1542 and it was completed by his colleague, though the alabaster plaque is by Felipe's brother, Gregorio. On the floor of the choir are two long lecterns with Doric entablatures by the Vergaras and a central lectern, eagle-shaped, by Vicente Salinas (1646). On the free-standing altar is the delicious Virgen de la Blanca, a thirteenth-century figure in polychromed alabaster, whose smiling face along with the Child's has turned a pale coffee colour with time. The trascoro or walls surrounding the choir are decorated with a blind arcade of 52 columns of Toledan jasper, topped by fine Gothic stone-carvings in niches of about 1380 – the same sculptor did the figures we shall see over the Puerta del Reloj. The capitals are decorated with sphinxes and winged men, lions and dogs, echoing Romanesque tradition. In the centre of the rear wall facing the great west door is a medallion by Alonso Berruguete of God the Father, flanked by statues of Innocence and Guilt by N. Vergara (*c.* 1550).

Along with the choir and other dependencies the **Sacristía** also figures on our ticket. Entered from the gospel side of the ambulatory, this was built by N. Vergara the younger between 1592 and 1616 and contains the chapter's collection of paintings. El Greco's *Apostolado* or set of the twelve apostles and the Saviour is earlier than the series we shall see at the Casa del Greco. The debt of Cézanne to this painter has been

remarked on by others. In the picture of Saint James the Less
– if one half closes one's eyes with this in mind – the greens,
browns and greys of Mont Ste. Victoire will overcome the
presence of the apostle. The famous *Expolio*, in which Christ's
robe is about to be ripped from him, is an early work painted
between 1577 and 1579. The accusing figure with the stabbing
finger is one of the most haunting in the whole of the artist's
canon.

Here it is worth briefly considering el Greco's career. Born
in Crete in the fifteen-forties (the date is not certain; the Prado
has opted for 1541), he reached Rome in 1570, having already
studied in Venice under Titian. He seems to have entered
Spain in 1577, attracted by the prospect of participating in the
decoration of the Escorial and the hope of an appointment as
painter to the King. Having whetted Philip's appetite with a
smaller version of the *Expolio*, he obtained a commission for
the work known as *El Sueño de Felipe II* (Escorial). But the
King's dislike of the later large Saint Maurice and the Theban
Legion put an end to the relationship. Henceforth el Greco
confined himself to his base in Toledo and earned his living
as a popular religious painter. This involved repeating whole
series of his productions – which may go some way to explain-
ing his unevenness. The most important part of his work in
Spain is to be found here in Toledo (cathedral, church of
Santo Tomé, Casa del Greco, Museo de Santa Cruz and
Hospital de Tavera), at Illescas (Hospital de la Caridad), in
Madrid (the Prado) and at the Escorial.

Other noteworthy pictures in the sacristy include two
Adorations by Pedro de Orrente, Saint Sebastian and Christ
on the Cross by el Greco's pupil Luis Tristán, the sexually
beautiful Saint John the Baptist by Caravaggio, the cool and
competent Holy Family by Van Dyck and one of Goya's
better religious works, the Taking of Jesus. There is also a
very fine triptych by Juan de Borgoña of the Last Supper
flanked by Saints Ildefonso and Barbara; the usual 'family
photo' design is dropped in favour of an interesting vertical
group built up in the central panel. Borgoña is a good clean
painter using a cool palette and showing restraint with the
rather murky gold affected by his immediate predecessors
such as Pedro Berruguete. In the smaller room are works by
Giovanni Bellini, the Bassanos, Van Dyck, Velázquez and
Mengs. El Greco's Saint Francis is not exciting and Goya's

Cardinal Bourbon is strictly in his duty style. There is also a collection of vestments. Off the main sacristy is a passage leading to the **Ochavo**, a chapel to which it is planned to move the Treasure; at present it contains *el Guión*, the famous cross that Cardinal Mendoza planted on the heights of the Alhambra, when Granada finally fell in 1492.

Leaving the sacristy and continuing round the ambulatory we find on the left the entrance to the **Capilla de Reyes Nuevos**, to which the ticket also gains admittance. This was finished by Covarrubias in 1534 in a hybrid Gothic-Renaissance style as a resting place for the monarchs of the House of Trastamara, who had previously lain in the north aisle. It led to the architect's appointment as master of the cathedral works in succession to Enrique de Egas. On the gospel side lie Henry II (d. 1379) and his wife Joan (d. 1381); flanking the altar are John I (d. 1390) and his wife Leonora (d. 1381) and on the epistle side are Henry III (d. 1406) and his wife 'Catalina de Alencastre', otherwise John of Gaunt's daughter Catherine of Lancaster, who died in Valladolid in 1418 and was brought to Toledo in the following year. It is immediately noticeable that the effigies are older than their setting; the marble faces are fine and calm, the robes and drapes almost straight. Catherine of Lancaster with an angel at her head, gilt missal in her hand and lap dog at her feet appears to lie in the deepest peace. So also does the black-bearded, sword-bearing fratricide, founder of the dynasty. John II (d. 1454), buried as we know at the Cartuja de Miraflores, is represented here by a kneeling figure in polychromed wood by that able all-rounder Juan de Borgoña.

Continuing round the ambulatory we come next to the **Capilla de Santiago**, built in 1435 at the expense of Alvaro de Luna. His tomb and his wife's, commissioned by their daughter from Pablo Ortiz in 1488, occupy the centre in front of the altar. Other family tombs are set in the walls. The present descendants of the powerful favourite are still buried in the crypt. At the head of the ambulatory is the **Capilla de San Ildefonso** with a number of interesting tombs, amongst them that of Iñigo López Carillo de Mendoza, Viceroy of Sardinia, who was killed at the siege of Granada in 1491. Both these chapels are usually locked and application to visit them – and the Capilla Mozárabe – should be made to the sacristan (tip 25 pesetas). Passing the little Capilla de la

Trinidad, we come next to the chapter house, which figures on
our ticket as **Sala Capitular**. The antechamber door is set in a
flamboyant Gothic frame by Diego Copin (1510), while
Mudéjar plasterwork incorporating conches and pine cones
surrounds the door into the main chamber, which was built
by Pedro Gumiel and Enrique de Egas between 1504 and
1512. The painted artesonado ceiling begun by Diego López
de Arenas of Seville and finished by F. de Lara in 1508 ingeniously combines Moorish geometry with Renaissance
coffering. There is an arresting fresco of the Last Judgement
by Juan de Borgoña, who also manages to make a pleasing
decorative frieze out of his hack commission to paint 'portraits'
of all the bishops of Toledo from Saint Eugene (d. 103) down
to the great politicos, Pedro González de Mendoza (d. 1495)
and F. Jiménez de Cisneros (d. 1517). After his death the
series was continued from the life by contemporary artists.
Goya again plays safe with Ludovicus Cardinalis de Borbon
(d. 1823). Petrus Cardinalis de Inguanzo (d. 1836) by Vicente
López is extravagantly extolled by the guides but its horrible,
crinkly, gloved hands give me a shiver of repulsion.

Walking west from the chapter house we pass the Puerta de
los Leones facing the crossing (there are no extended transepts)
with good Renaissance carved doors and the family tree of
the Virgin in the tympanum. Next to this is the huge fresco
called the Cristobalón, 46 feet high, restored in 1638. This
giant Saint Christopher is of no artistic merit but we cannot
complain, as he is designed for our safe-conduct when we
leave the church. The **Capilla de San Eugenio** next to the
enormous talisman has a grille by Enrique de Egas and a
statue of the saint by Diego Copin (1517) in the altarpiece by
Juan de Borgoña (1516). Notice the Mudéjar tomb of Fernán
Gudiel (d. 1278). We now proceed to the **Capilla Mozárabe** –
another requiring the services of the sacristan – in the base of
the south-west tower. This was built by Enrique de Egas in
1504 for Cardinal Jiménez de Cisneros and contains frescoes
by Juan de Borgoña commemorating the capture of Oran, at
which the Cardinal was present. The main scene shows the
storming of the town. On the left the Cardinal is shown em-
barking at Cartagena and on the right disembarking at Mers-
el-Kebir. The octagonal lantern on squinches by J. de Arteaga
and F. Vergara (1519) is covered by the cupola we noticed on
the outside, added by J. M. Theotocopouli in 1626.

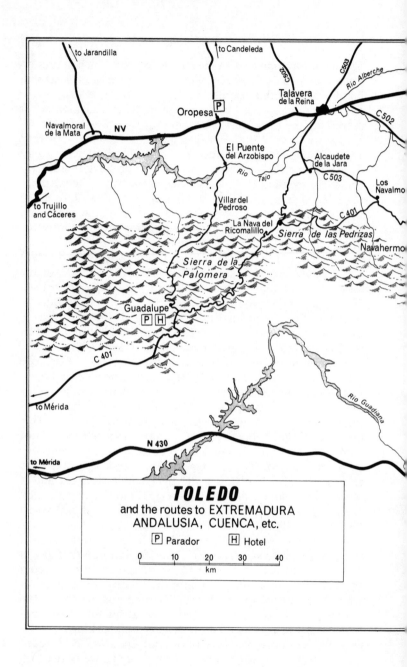

TOLEDO
and the routes to EXTREMADURA
ANDALUSIA, CUENCA, etc.

P Parador   H Hotel

0   10   20   30   40
km

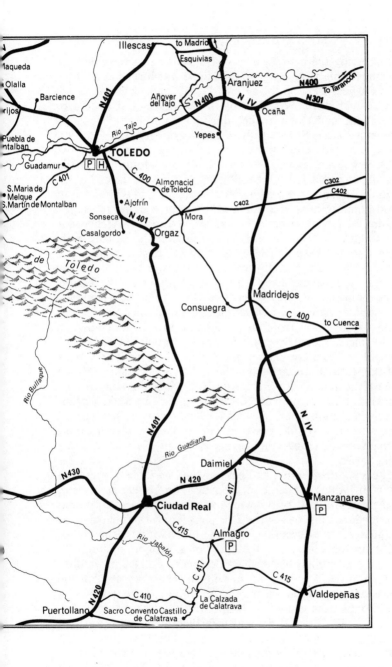

Crossing the church, it is worth pausing to read the self-confident inscription above this door, which runs as follows: 'In the year 1492 on the second day of January Granada was taken with all its Kingdom by the Monarchs our Lord Don Fernando and Doña Ysabel, during the archbishopric of the Most Reverend Sr Don Pedro González de Mendoza, Cardinal of Spain. This same year at the end of the month of June all the Jews were expelled from all the Kingdoms of Castile, Aragón and Sicily. In the following year, 93, at the end of the month of January were finished the repairs and whitewashing and pointing of all the vaults of this church under the supervision of Don Francisco Fernández de Cuenca, Archdeacon of Calatrava.' What immense satisfaction the worthy archdeacon must have derived when this was freshly painted up! In the base of the north-west or main tower we find the last of the dependencies to which the ticket admits us, the **Tesoro**. The main exhibit, the masterpiece of the gold and silversmith Enrique de Arfe, is a monster Gothic monstrance consisting – one may overhear from the guides who love such details – of 5,500 pieces secured by 24,000 screws. Though the framework is Gothic there are Plateresque panels in the base and many of the statuettes derive from the Italian Renaissance. This is one of the first of a long line made by Enrique, his son Antonio and his grandson Juan to meet the requirements of the Corpus Christi ceremony, during which the host is still carried through the streets, a fragile passenger in its large and immensely ornate container, accompanied by religious, civil and military dignitaries.

Leaving the treasure and passing the Puerta de la Presentación (by which we came in) we reach the **Capilla de Nuestra Señora la Antigua**, before which war banners used to be consecrated. Against one of the aisle piers facing this chapel is the **Capilla de la Descensión**, a pyramidal Gothic structure of 1601 on the site of the high altar of a Visigothic church to which the Virgin is held to have descended on December 18th, 666, to invest Saint Ildefonso with his chasuble. Part of the old stone altar table on which she stood for this purpose is let into the back wall of the chapel and greatly venerated. The large **Capilla de San Pedro** a little farther on is used as a parish church. Here mass is said every morning according to the Mozarabic rite, pending the restoration of the Capilla Mozárabe, where this normally takes place. This rite, which was preserved by the Christians under Moorish domination and differs from the Latin in 13 points, is also used in the parishes of San Marcos and Santa Justa but nowhere else now in Spain.

We can return to the cloister either by the Puerta de la Presentación or by the **Puerta de Santa Catalina** immediately to the west of the Capilla de San Pedro. In order to climb the tower it is necessary to walk out again into the Calle del Arco del Palacio. Passing under the arch over the street and bearing right round the cloister wall, we soon find a door with the notice *a las Campanas*. From here a staircase takes us up to the cloister gallery, humanised by dwellings and family washing; another set of stairs leads to the belfry. Views of the biscuit-coloured roofs, the Ayuntamiento, Alcázar and countryside reward the climber – also of the layout, cupolas and buttresses of the church, difficult to envisage from underneath.

If we leave the church by the **Puerta del Reloj** just to the east of the Capilla de San Pedro we find on the outer face carving by the late fourteenth-century master of the trascoro; here he has produced four horizontal bands decorated with figures, all contained within the semi-circle of the tympanum. Taking the first right out of the narrow Calle de la Feria we come to the Plaza Mayor, site of the market and the Teatro Rojas. Toledo's lack of a real centre is jointly made good by this square, providing food and entertainment, the Plaza del Ayuntamiento, seat of local government, civil and religious, and Zocodover which specialises in cafés and central government offices (the proximity is perhaps no coincidence). From the Plaza Mayor, Calle Sixto Ramón Parra leads south under the chevet of the cathedral which is masked by the sacristy block, chapels and chapter house – only the distant views, particularly from the Parador, reveal it in its entirety. The second turning on the left reveals the Gothic entrance of the **Posada de la Hermandad**, over which two stone crossbowmen support a wooden coat of arms flanked by the arrows and the yoke. The Santa Hermandad or Holy Brotherhood was founded by Saint Ferdinand after the capture of Córdoba and Seville to police the lines of access between Andalusia and the centre of the country. It operated in *cuadrillas* of four men on the highways, and drovers' tracks, mainly in the regions of Talavera, Toledo and Ciudad Real. Disbanded by Isabel the Catholic, who found that by her time it looked after its own interests more than anyone else's, it is considered by many to be the spiritual, if not the direct, ancestor of the Civil Guard, which was established by the González Bravo in 1844. Hugging the cathedral wall, we now enter Calle de la Puerta Llana under the south side of the great mass. The first entrance is the **Puerta de los Leones** of 1460 by Hanequín de Egas and Juan Alemán (who carved the figures); the upper carvings in elliptical panels were added in the eighteenth century. The great bronze doors – whose inner woodwork faces we have already seen – are by Francisco Corral de Villalpando and were made between 1545 and 1550. Next comes the **Puerta Llana**, a standard Neo-Classical entrance built in 1800 and so called as it is the only one of the eight cathedral doorways without any steps. Thus we return to the bar of 'La Burgalesa' where further stimulus may well be required and a decision can be taken about lunch or dinner. In Calle Nueva just off Calle del Comercio is the sound cheap Restaurante Río. Down on the Paseo de Recaredo near the Puerta Antigua de Visagra is the more expensive but good Hostal del Cardenal. And there is the Parador on the other side of the river, which is also the best place to put up. Partridges in season are the speciality of the region and there is a good strong local red wine from Yepes.

The western and south-western quarters of the city contain a galaxy of good things which deserve at least half a day. This is the area most exploited by souvenir-sellers but they are not a sufficient deterrent to keep one away from the monuments. Leaving the cathedral square between the episcopal palace and the Ayuntamiento, we take the narrow partly-covered Pasadizo del Ayuntamiento to emerge in a small plaza; from here we take Calle San Salvador leading us to a junction of several streets at the head of the Calle Santo Tomé, which we follow to the church of **Santo Tomé** a bit farther along on the left. The pretty Mudéjar tower has brown and green glazed ceramic columns set into the brickwork of the upper stage. The interior has been revamped in standard Baroque and the church's fame rests on its possession of one of el Greco's best-known paintings, the Burial of the Count of Orgaz, painted in 1586. Though the Count who had rebuilt the church died in 1323, he and his mourners are shown in the dress of el Greco's day. The faces of the mourners are portraits of prominent

Toledans of the time including the artist himself. The figures holding the dead man are Saint Augustine and the young Saint Stephen (above whose head el Greco's face appears). The small boy in the foreground is the painter's son Jorge Manuel and the signature is on the handkerchief protruding from the lad's pocket. This is a two-tier composition in which the heavenly and terrestrial spheres are demarcated by the line of human heads but drawn together by the brilliant use of colour.

We now take the alley descending along the flank of the church, which brings us out onto a platform in front of the **Palacio de Fuensalida** built about 1440 for Pedro López de Ayala, Mayor of Toledo and first Count of Fuensalida. The very plain front has a Gothic entrance opening into a handsome *zaguán* from which a flight of stairs rises to the very splendid and expertly restored patio, whose west windows offer a good view over the old Jewish quarter to the slopes across the Tagus. The heavy wooden beams of the gallery rest on sixteen strong, square pillars with pared edges – a favourite Mudéjar effect; similar columns on a smaller scale support the gallery roof. Ogival windows are combined with Mudéjar friezes. The place is used by the Ministry of Education as a conference centre and the accommodation upstairs is closed to the public. However, the exercise of a little charm on the young lady attendant will secure removal of the rope from the bottom of the staircase; the three-flight ascent under a coffered ceiling is lit from the gallery by two shallow Plateresque arches whose columns are joined by a Gothic balustrade. Throughout the building there is an unusually happy mixture of the Mudéjar, Gothic and Plateresque styles. One room downstairs is furnished in period and contains a good fifteenth-century Flemish tapestry of a castle and grounds. Charles V stayed here in 1547 and here in 1539 his Queen, Isabel of Portugal, died at the age of 36.

At the rear of the palace across a garden is the museum called the **Taller del Moro**. Originally part of a palatial building of the fourteenth century, this was later used as a *taller* or workshop by masons employed on the Cathedral. The long high chamber and the subsidiary rooms at either end all have artesonado ceilings. The Mudéjar plasterwork is interesting for the protruding features which appear to be pine-cones and the upper frieze is diversified by another fruit resembling a custard apple. The objects on display include examples of

Mudéjar carpentry of the fourteenth and fifteenth centuries – note particularly the modillions or brackets used for supporting galleries or eaves; some of these have curious fins and eyes recalling Nordic decoration. There is also a collection of tiles – and one bilingual inscription on stone in Latin and Arabic of the twelfth century.

We now continue downhill to the **Casa del Greco** – though there is considerable doubt that the rooms we are shown are those in which the artist lived and worked. The facts are that the buildings on this site belonged to Samuel Ha-Levi, treasurer of Peter the Cruel, and much later passed into the possession of the Marquis of Villena. It is known that the painter lived at one time in *las casas del Marqués de Villena*. At the beginning of this century the Marquis of La Vega-Inclán bought the present building – the rest of the block had been destroyed – and restored it as a typical house of the sixteenth century, incorporating some vestiges of plaster-work from Ha-Levi's house. Both house and garden are charming. The museum proper occupies an annexe. Downstairs are works by Valdés Leal, Carreño, Zurbarán (represented by the Tears of Saint Peter and a small Cistercian Martyr with lovely sculpting of the yellowish-white habit), Herrera el Viejo and Luis Tristán, whose Saint Dominic holds a length of chain in his hand, while his dog holds a candle in its mouth in order to enable its master to flagellate himself more efficiently. Also downstairs in a chapel-like room is el Greco's Saint Bernard, painted in 1603. The saint is shown with three rejected mitres on the ground and the plaque on the frame quotes the verse of the Marquis of Santillana on the subject – which may be rendered as follows:

> No dignities did undermine
> the strong walls of your sanctity.
> Sienna, Ferrara and Urbino know it well.
> Their rich mitres did nothing tell
> against your vow of poverty.

El Greco's *Apostolado* is upstairs. This is his last version of the famous series. Carmines, blues, greens and yellows predominate with the occasional brilliant jab of orange – as on the left arm of Saint Thomas. Saint Bartholomew is painted with a splendid yellowy robe. Saint Andrew is unfinished and so are the hands of Saint James the Great and Saint Matthew.

Saint John, as usual, is a sinister-looking young man with a baby dragon in his cup. These are all bolder in colour and freer in handling than the earlier cathedral set, though the Saviour himself with his direct disconcerting gaze and dexter hand raised in benediction has an almost Byzantine quality.

Leaving the Casa del Greco and continuing down the same narrow street, we shortly reach the **Sinagoga del Tránsito**, built between 1360 and 1366 by the Samuel Ha-Levi already mentioned. The ex-synagogue consists of a large chamber with a restored artesonado ceiling. Fretted windows in cusped arches circle the walls above an exquisite floral plasterwork frieze with the shields of Castile and León between bands with Hebrew inscriptions celebrating the founder and the kings of Spain. In the wall containing the entrance is a gallery or tribune with wooden lattice-work, from behind which women were able to attend services. Beneath are a doorway and a tomb in the Plateresque style – the building was made over to the knights of Calatrava after the expulsion of the Jews. Later it was consecrated to the death (Tránsito) of the Virgin. In an adjacent room a small **Museo Sefardi** has been installed. There is an interesting map showing all the Jewish communities in mediaeval Spain.

At the bottom of the slope we have followed all the way from Santo Tomé runs the wide Calle Reyes Católicos. Turning right along this, we soon reach another one-time synagogue, probably of the thirteenth century, now known as **Santa Maria la Blanca**, from which the Jews were ejected in 1405 by the ferocious Saint Vincent Ferrer at the head of the rabble he had roused and led from Santiago del Arrabal. In 1550 it became an 'asylum for penitent Magdalens' (Baedeker) – the Spanish guidebook confines itself to the discreet *monasterio de religiosas*. By 1600 it was simply an oratory and remained as such until commandeered as a barracks in 1791 'owing to lack of houses'. In 1798 an enlightened general repaired it and turned it into a quartermaster's store in order that it should not be put to worse uses. It is now a very beautiful and peaceful place, and given its chequered history it is surprising it has not suffered greater damage. Twenty-four columns in four rows and four engaged columns at each end support horseshoe arches which rest on remarkable capitals derived from the acanthus but extruding the sort of pine-cone we have already noted in the later Taller del Moro.

Close inspection shows that many of these have been broken off – whether by not so penitent Magdalens or licentious soldiery is uncertain. But the overall harmonious effect remains. There are conch-shaped sanctuaries at the end of the two inner aisles while the nave leads to an altar under a fluted dome on conch-shaped pendentives. The conch motif is repeated below the frieze over the arches and it is worth remarking how widely this is used not only in Christian architecture but also in Muslim and Jewish.

From Santa Maria la Blanca, small, delicate and private, the next step – only a few minutes' walk in physical terms – is gigantic. Calle Reyes Católicos leads straight to the magnificent convent church of **San Juan de los Reyes** founded in 1476 by Ferdinand and Isabel who intended it as their resting place. But the surrender of Granada in 1492 was an event of such outstanding importance that it could only be fitly marked by a change in the burial plans of the joint monarchs and the Capilla Real in that city, by Enrique Egas, became their mausoleum. In the meantime, at Toledo, the Flemish Guas had almost completed his masterpiece. His delight in decoration was always underpinned by very strong structural features (cf. Convento de Santa Cruz and El Parral, Segovia), including massive circular columns and the strong demarcation between bay and bay and between arch and clerestory. Possibly shortage of funds had something to do with the relative sobriety of his Segovian churches. Here in San Juan de los Reyes the plan is similar to that of other Guas churches; there are four nave bays with side chapels but no aisles and a raised choir occupies the rear bay at gallery level. But the whole is enormously enriched. The piers have clusters of shafts and flamboyant niches with figures. The moulding between arcade and clerestory has become a fully fledged cornice with crested tracery. The crossing carries a lantern with windows and the north-west and south-west piers burgeon out into tribunes (like theatre boxes) for the royal founders – F for Fernando and Y for Ysabel are carved on all the stone panels of these. The interior walls of the unextended transepts each carry six stone-carved versions of the same coat of arms, León and Castile quartering Aragón, supported by huge single-headed eagles wearing haloes and all looking towards the altar, so that those on the west walls look straight ahead but those on the north and south walls have to twist their necks. This same achievement, eight or nine feet high, is repeated twelve times in all between the two transepts.

The **Claustro** has gracious arches with decorated tracery carrying a gallery of shouldered arches with a Mudéjar ceiling incorporating the devices of Castile and León, the pomegranate of Granada, the arrow and the yoke and the initials F and Y. At the corners flattened arches under the ceiling support crouched and snarling plaster lions over the motto *Tanto Monta* permutated forwards and backwards. This device meaning 'Tantamount' was designed to emphasise the equal status of the Reyes Católicos, though Ferdinand, King of Aragón in his own right, was never more than King-Consort in Castile. A lighter note is provided by the water-spouts; among the traditional gargoyles are some amusing variations. Over the monastery entrance is a decorated cross in the tympanum under a pelican in her pride and over a skull and crossbones. On either side of this are the founders, Ferdinand looking up and Isabel modestly down. The remaining exterior figures are heralds in tabards and the walls of the building are hung with chains struck from the limbs of Christians made captive during the war of Granada. The main church entrance was completed by Covarrubias after Guas's death. With so much heraldry and so many emblems it might all have become a great bore. However, Guas is never boring because his basic constructional solutions are always stimulating and his inventions arresting. A lesser man could well have turned San Juan de los Reyes into something pompous and frigid, whereas it is delightful despite the propaganda. The Fleming did his masters proud. Even if they had failed to take Granada, they would not have lacked a noble resting place. From here we can either drop down to the Puente de San Martín and cross the river, rejoin the Paseo de Recaredo under the walls via the Puerta del Cambrón or retrace our steps to the centre. The **Museo Victorio Macho** off Calle Reyes Católicos is not really worth a visit, as his work is better seen in public places. If he had had his way, colossal heroic statues would have been as frequent on the hill-tops of Castile as the great black bull advertising Osborne brandy.

Another important building started a little later than San Juan de los Reyes and easily accessible through the horseshoe arch on the east side of Zocodover is the **Hospital de Santa Cruz**, conceived by Cardinal Mendoza and built between

1494 and 1515 by Enrique de Egas. As the Cardinal died in 1495, his plans had to be put into effect for him by Queen Isabel. The ex-hospital is shaped like a huge cross with four equal arms on two floors meeting at a central crossing lit by a lantern. During the Civil War the building was occupied by Republican troops, who set up a mortar at the east end of the façade to assist the siege of the Alcázar just above. The Plateresque entrance, the windows and grilles and stonework of the façade suffered from enemy fire but the main damage was caused by a Republican plane which dropped its bombs in error on the lantern and destroyed it – there is a rather inferior replacement now. 'They didn't dare fly low enough to lay their eggs properly,' I was told by a veteran of the winning side. The one-time wards now house the **Museo Provincial**. On the ground floor it is really the furniture that steals the show. The most interesting paintings are the triptych and five panels from Alvaro de Luna's castle of Escalona (*1507* to *1511*) and a tiny diptych with portraits of the six children of Joan the Mad and Philip the Fair (*1644*). At the end of the arm facing the entrance is the great blue standard of the Holy League that was hoisted on the galley of Don John of Austria at the battle of Lepanto along with a smaller pennant from the same vessel. Piped music of the sixteenth and seventeenth centuries helps to put one in the right mood.

Upstairs are works by el Greco. There is a smaller version of the *Expolio* (*1300*). The Assumption on the end wall is a very busy and brilliant work painted three months before his death. Saint James the Apostle with an orange robe belongs to his early post-Titian period. The Apparition of Christ to his Mother (*1296*) is a very beautiful work, also in his earlier and stiffer manner. The Saint Joseph and Child, signed, with a view of Toledo and angels tumbling upside down is delightful. The Coronation of the Virgin (*1677*) is a successful middle period visionary composition. Saints Peter and Ildefonso are copies of the same subjects at the Escorial. On the same floor are works by Pedro de Orrente, Ribera, Juan de Mena and the end of the western arm is taken up by a retablo by Alonso Berruguete. Juan de Arfe contributes an elegant processional monstrance. At the end of the south arm is a room over the main entrance with a Crucifixion (*1829*) by Goya and two attractive works – note the musical instruments and interlocking haloes – by the fifteenth-century Master of

Sigena (*1628* and *1629*). A staircase leads down from here into the grand Plateresque patio round which the archaeological department of the museum is installed. The Roman section has a brilliant circular mosaic floor of fishing scenes from the meadows called La Vega just outside the city walls and another large floor with a scintillating centre. The Moorish occupation is represented by inscribed burial columns, capitals, carved wooden epitaphs and little oil-lamps with longer lips than the Roman variety. Ceramic well-heads were also popular. The Mudéjar style provides an assortment of carpentry, plaster-work, more well-heads, pitchers and ceramic fragments. A grand staircase with a Mudéjar ceiling leads to the gallery off which are rooms containing local iron and glass ware, also ceramic work from the sixteenth to nineteenth centuries made at the two centres of production in the province, Talavera de la Reina and Puente del Arzobispo.

Rising grimly above the Hospital de Santa Cruz is the vaunted **Alcázar**, which is most easily reached by returning to Zocodover and taking the Cuesta del Alcázar. The huge building is a reconstruction of reconstructions. A Roman fort gave way to a Visigothic citadel. After Alfonso VI's capture of the city, the Cid – it is said – was installed as first Alcaide. Saint Ferdinand, Alfonso the Learned, John II, Ferdinand and Isabel, Charles V and Philip II all contributed to its gradual conversion from fortress to palace. It was burned in 1710 during the War of the Spanish Succession. It was restored between 1772 and 1775 by Cardinal Lorenzana. It was burned again by the French in the Peninsular War. It was 'a miserable skeleton' in 1862. Then it was pieced together again and became the Spanish Sandhurst. As such during the Civil War of 1936–1939 it resisted a siege of two months by Government troops who held the rest of the town and repeatedly claimed the Alcázar had fallen or was about to fall, but it hadn't and didn't and the siege was raised by General Varela on September 28th, 1936. By this time it was in ruins again. All the outer faces have now been restored. The north front is a life-size copy of the façade of Enrique de Egas incorporating heraldic sculpture by Alonso Berruguete and Juan de Mena. The east front embodying part of Alfonso X's wall had to be built up again almost from ground level. The new south façade repeats Herrera's designs. The west, built under Ferdinand and Isabel, was and remains rather dull. Because of its size and Escorial-type spires the Alcázar is impressive from a distance, though its uncompromising bulk has none of the fairy-castle quality of its opposite number at Segovia.

Both the lower ground floor and the piano nobile have been devoted to the **Museo del Asedio** perpetuating the memory of the last siege. Under the double flight of stairs is the pantheon of the 104 defenders who died out of the 1197 officers and men, 106 militia and 538 non-combatants of the garrison. In the patio most of the spandrels and capitals are newly carved and a heroic bronze group after Pompeo Leoni, representing Charles V trampling a chained enemy, occupies the centre. Francisco Corral's grand staircase had to be totally rebuilt. On the first floor one can visit Colonel – later General – Moscardó's office in the south front. The wooden floor is pitted and the ceiling tattered by a grenade that sailed in through the window one morning, wounding various members of the staff but not the commandant himself. On the wall is a transcript in many languages, including Arabic and Hebrew, of the telephone conversation held on July 23rd, 1936, between the commandant, the chief of the Republican militia, and the commandant's son Luis, who had fallen into the enemy's hands. The militia chief demands the surrender of the Alcázar within 10 minutes or Luis will be shot. Luis comes on the line and confirms this will be so if his father does not surrender. Moscardó says, 'Then commend your soul to God, shout "Long live Spain!" and die like a patriot.' Luis answers, 'A big kiss, Father.' And the latter replies, 'A big kiss, my son.' After all, Spain does not change much under the skin. This immediately calls to mind the almost identical action of Guzmán el Bueno in similar circumstances at Tarifa in 1294.

By now the main monuments inside the walls have been seen but there are one or two strolls that can be recommended to anyone determined to see Toledo thoroughly. Starting uphill from the little Ermita del Cristo de la Luz just above the Puerta del Sol, we soon find the steep Cuesta de Carmelitas Descalzas; a sharp right turn again at the top of this brings us into the Plaza de Carmelitas with a severe Herreran church. Leaving this on the right we continue between high walls into a district of cobertizos carrying religious buildings over the narrow public alleys. Here we are in conventual Toledo, very quiet, perhaps a little grim, but totally free of the tedious souvenir shops that proliferate round the more glamorous monuments. The Cobertizo de Santo Domingo leads to the Plaza de Santo Domingo el Real, whose church has a four-columned portico. This was the favourite square of the Romantic poet Gustavo Adolfo Bécquer (1836–1870), who loved to roam these backwaters by night with his painter brother, indulging in moon-chilled *frissons* of delight; he is commemorated by two plaques on the convent wall. Calle de los Buzones now leads to the Plaza de la Merced which is over-powered by the Diputación Provincial, remarkable only for its size. Passing quickly on we soon reach a cobbled slope on the left leading to the restored church of Santo Domingo el Antiguo with a brick Mudéjar entrance and pointed horse-shoe arches in the belfry windows. Skirting this to the left we find a plaque on a ruined house in Calle Santo Domingo to the effect that the famous poet Garcilaso de la Vega was born on this spot in 1503. A climb to the left brings us out into the sprawling Plaza de Padilla, named after the gallant commander-in-chief of the rising of the Commons of Castile in 1520–1521. Leaving by Calle Esteban Illán we find at number 11 the **Casa de Mesa**, whose main room has a mag-nificent artesonado ceiling in the form of a barrel vault of several inclined planes without cross-beams. There is also some very delicate Mudéjar plasterwork and a dado of *cuerda seca* tiles. Retracing our steps a little we find the narrow Calle San Román on the left, which widens out under the tower of the thirteenth-century Mudéjar church of **San Román** with a nave of three bays supported by horseshoe arches resting on columns of Visigothic origin. On the walls are some interesting late Romanesque frescoes. The presbytery cupola was rebuilt by Covarrubias. This church has recently been turned into a **Museo Visigótico**. Round the walls are displayed fragments of funerary inscriptions, capitals, imposts, little window columns etc. Maltese Cross and wheel patterns or rosettes in-scribed in circles are the most common decorative motifs. The cases in the centre hold bronze objects, brooches, fibulas and other personal effects found in sepulchres. Both church itself and museum deserve a visit. Back to back with San Román is the church of San Pedro Mártir – large, Neo-Classical and uninteresting except for some tombs moved from Santo Domingo el Antiguo and other churches. Continuing along Calle San Román under the bulky church of San Ildefonso, we reach the Plaza del Padre Juan with a view of the cathedral and Alcázar. Callejón de Jesús y Maria and Calle de la Trinidad return us to the Ayuntamiento.

Anyone who would like to see a district that has really not been tidied up for tourists at all should try the semi-ruinous Barrio de Candelaria on the brink of the river. Starting from the Plaza Mayor and passing the Posada de la Hermandad, we follow Calle Sixto Ramón Parra to the Plaza de San Justo, which provides a good view of the cathedral chevet. Circling the church we find the ruined late Gothic portico of San Juan de la Penitencia. Continuing our descent we come to the church of San Lucás with a restored Mudéjar tower, from which there is another good view of the Alcázar and cathedral. San Lucás also presides over a God-given rubbish tip into the Tagus. On the river's edge under the frowning seminary is a small waterside community with a hundred yards of muddy beach. From San Lucás it is possible to steer a tortuous course via San Pablo and San Lorenzo to the Calle de Pozo Amargo. A side street leaving this climbs again to the church of **San Andrés** with a Gothic apse in the Avila style, Mudéjar nave and tower and a later belfry. This is just beginning to be smartened up. The Travesía de San Andrés leads to the Plaza de Santa Isabel. On the left is all that remains – a Gothic entrance with three shields – of an Alcázar of Peter the Cruel. It is worth going into **Santa Isabel** to see the particularly fine artesonado ceiling. Continuing along the street, we emerge once more in the Plaza del Ayuntamiento just by the bar of 'La Burgalesa' – which may provide a welcome halt after a rather rough walk.

The time has come to move outside the city walls. The first visit is certainly deserved by the **Hospital de Tavera**, which we passed on the way in. This is just beyond the Puerta Nueva de Visagra on the road from Madrid and was built for Cardinal Juan de Tavera, who died in 1561, by Bartolomé de Bustamente with decorations by Alonso Berruguete. Through the porch we reach a double patio divided by an arcade leading from the main entrance to the large chapel; the doorway and the tomb of the founder are by Berruguete. The chapel also houses the family mausoleum of the dukes of Medinaceli. The lower order of the patio is Doric supporting an Ionic gallery above.

The rooms surrounding the western half of the patio con-

tain a collection of art and furniture belonging to the dukes
of Lerma. On the first floor is a long parlour among whose
pictures is a very delightful brown and rose Zurbarán of the
then Duke of Medinaceli – it is rather in the vein of his female
saints in fashionable clothes. There is also a little model of a
naked man with one arm raised said to have come from el
Greco's studio; its proportions are conventional except for
the length of the arms and the large hands. On the same floor
are one of el Greco's versions of the Tears of Saint Peter, a
Saint Francis kneeling before a skull and crucifix, and the large
Baptism of Christ by Saint John, claimed to be his last work.
Elements of many previous pictures appear and all his palette.
The red-robed Magdalen is ready with a pale blue towel, while
the green-robed angel on the left with the piquant face is
hailing the heavenly host in a charmingly familiar way – she
and the dove draw the two spheres together. The robes of the
angel at the top right have high-lighted folds like zig-zag lightning and God the Father with the orb on his knees is robed
in white. In short, all the tricks in one glorious package. In a
smaller chamber are works by Tintoretto and Lucás Jordán,
also two impressive portraits of the Marquis of Las Navas
and his lady by Antonio Moro. The Master of Brussels of
the fifteenth century has a curious picture on an easel of a
shipwreck in which a detachment of devils has taken over the
ship. Downstairs, in the first chamber, one's attention is immediately drawn by a magnificent dining-table on three
columns with a top made of a single slab of walnut about
20 feet long. The portraits are of Isabel Clara Eugenia by
Coello, of Mariana of Austria by Carreño and of Cardinal
Tavera by Luis Tristán. The long room on this floor contains
the hospital archive and some huge leather-bound volumes of
Gregorian chant. Among the pictures are Ribera's Philosopher
– whose thoughts so overheated his head that water had to
be poured on his cranium – and el Greco's Holy Family in
orange, blue, yellow and carmine from his first Spanish
period. This makes a very popular post-card owing to the
outrageously pretty rendering of the Virgin. In a smaller
room, tucked away and only coyly revealed, is Ribera's
Bearded Woman. This bombshell is surrounded by blameless
views of Naples, Venice etc. in the style of Canaletto.

From the Puerta Nueva de Visagra the Paseo de Recaredo
– signposted to the Puente San Martín and Navahermosa –

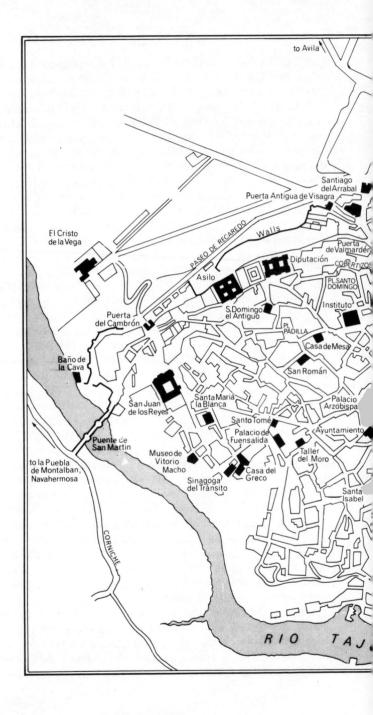

to Avila

Santiago
del Arrabal
Puerta Antigua de Visagra

El Cristo
de la Vega

PASEO DE RECAREDO   Walls

Puerta
de Valmardén

Diputación   COBERTIZOS

Asilo

PL.SANTO
DOMINGO

Puerta
del Cambrón

S.Domingo
el Antiguo

Instituto

PL
PADILLA

Baño de
la Cava

Casa de Mesa

San Román

San Juan
de los Reyes

Santa María
la Blanca

Palacio
Arzobispa

Santo Tomé

to la Puebla
de Montalban,
Navahermosa

Puente de
San Martín

Palacio de
Fuensalida

Ayuntamiento

Museo de
Vitorio
Macho

Taller
del Moro

Sinagoga
del Tránsito

Casa del
Greco

Santa
Isabel

CORNICHE

RIO   TAJ

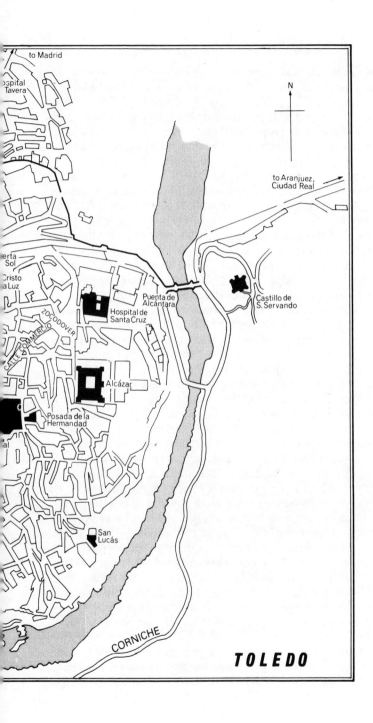

to Madrid

N

to Aranjuez,
Ciudad Real

Hospital
Tavera

erta
Sol

Cristo
a Luz

ZOCODOVER

CATLE COMMERCIO

Puenta de
Alcántara

Hospital de
Santa Cruz

Castillo de
S. Servando

Alcázar

Posada de la
Hermandad

al

San
Lucás

CORNICHE

TOLEDO

leads under the walls, with the ungainly Diputación and the lunatic asylum towering above, to the **Puerta de Cambrón**, one of the gates of King Wamba's wall rebuilt by Alfonso VI in 1102 and restored in 1576 with four brick towers and a tribune gallery facing west. Immediately opposite is a dust track leading down to the church of **El Cristo de la Vega** on the site of the former Visigothic basilica of Santa Leocadia (whose remains had to be smuggled to Oviedo when Toledo fell to the Moors). A single fluted column from this period stands in the garden. From here one can walk to the so-called **Baño de la Cava** on the river's edge. This is not a bath at all but the remnant of the gatehouse of a bridge destroyed by flood in 1203, part of whose masonry has fallen forward into the water. It provides a good view of the **Puente San Martín**, a fine mediaeval bridge built for Alfonso X and renewed in 1390 by Archbishop Tenorio after the damage it received in the civil war between Peter the Cruel and Henry of Trastamara. This has a gatehouse on the far bank with pointed and horseshoe arches; the opposite number on the town side was restored under Charles II in 1690. Above the bridge the river runs through a gorge; below it becomes a wide mill-race before meandering west through softer lands.

It is possible to continue the circuit of the city by the south bank route called the Ronda de Toledo, about 4 km in all from bridge to bridge, but the road is narrow and traffic makes it unpleasant for walking, so it is best covered by car. All along this corniche there are parking bays. Half-way round is a right-hand turning leading to the discreet modern Parador Nacional, which lies about half a kilometre off the circuit. Its drive affords the best views of all of the city and quite often, on winter mornings in particular, the cathedral and Alcázar appear to float on a bed of cloud that fills the Tagus gorge and blots out the lower town. Returning to the corniche and continuing along it we gradually come down to a modern motor bridge which leads back to the town centre. But it is worth continuing a few hundred yards on the south side to the **Puente de Alcántara**, closed to traffic. This was built by the Arabs in 866 – in 1257 it was largely carried away by a flood and rebuilt on the orders of Alfonso X. It was again repaired during Archbishop Tenorio's thorough overhaul of the defences. Here the gatehouse on the city side is Mudéjar; the outer gate is a purely decorative arch put up in the eighteenth century. Immediately above this bridge on the other side is the **Castillo de San Servando** erected by Alfonso VI to house a monastery and defend the city. Repaired like the bridges by Archbishop Tenorio, it is now a school but one can drive up for the view and it is a good place to turn for the run back across the river to the centre.

For anyone who decides to make Toledo a centre for touring there are a number of interesting local excursions. But it will also be a turning point for many travellers. Some may wish to head north via Madrid, others to continue west to Extremadura and Portugal, while others yet will want to make for Andalusia. I shall follow up the excursions by briefly outlining these alternatives and the best routes for their accomplishment. At the same time, I hope I shall still have some companions who will continue with me on the last stage of this book covering the fascinating but less-known provinces of Cuenca, Guadalajara and Soria.

Toledo – Illescas – (Madrid) – Esquivias – (Aranjuez) – Yepes – Mora – Orgaz – San Pedro de la Mata – Ajofrín – Toledo

Illescas, a dusty town on N401, was the old half-way stage between Toledo and Madrid. The **Hospital de la Caridad** founded about 1500 by Cardinal Cisneros has five paintings by el Greco in the church. The work in the aisle called the Virgin of Charity sheltering the Spanish Nobility includes the painter's son, now a man, in the foreground with his father behind him. Saint Ildefonso, second Archbishop of Toledo, he of the chasuble, is shown in black and white sixteenth-century dress at a writing table covered with crimson velvet – in this picture the artist is really in vein and it is one of the best of his early period. In a side chapel are a round canvas of the Nativity, notable for Saint Joseph's amazement and the great thrust of the ox's horn, a round Annunciation and an oval Coronation of the Virgin by the Holy Trinity. Illescas also has a fine Mudéjar parish church tower of five stages. The road leads straight on to Madrid but those still based on Toledo should turn right to **Esquivias,** 9 km to the east. This is a bleak little town with a wooden-galleried Ayuntamiento. In the plain parish church Miguel de Cervantes was married in 1584. Whoever did not visit Aranjuez from Madrid may now like to take the local road which joins NIV at Seseña just north of the royal pleasure ground. The rest of us turn south to Añover del Tajo from which we descend and cross the river, continuing over N400 on a local road to **Yepes**, a mediaeval villa given by Alfonso VII to the 'Mitre of Toledo' in whose hands it remained until the reign of Philip II. He managed to get Pope Gregory XIII's approval for its return to its own citizens in 1576. Before the chapter lost the lordship it had approved the building of a **Colegiata** of noble proportions on the hall-church plan whose piers are adorned with Ionic pilasters giving birth to a late Gothic vault. Licence was given for the work to begin by Archbishop Fonseca in 1532 and it was finished in 1552. There are some excellent grilles by Domingo de Céspedes and the retablo contains six paintings by Luis Tristán.

A local road leads south-west from here to **Mora de Toledo**, whose ruined castle (at 3 km on C402 to Tembleque) is none of your fancy castles built to impress the neighbours but a genuine keep, narrow as the spine on which it is reared and something like a keyhole in plan. Anyone who climbs up – it is a ten-minute scramble from the road – will command a view of much of New Castile. Though the olive is popularly associated with Andalusia, it begins here and the groves marshalled with military precision stretch away to the horizon. C402 leads westwards from Mora to **Orgaz**, an agreeable little town with wide streets and low houses and an arcaded sidewalk in the Plaza Mayor, which is dominated by the impressive parish church begun in 1741 and left incomplete in 1762 without the south tower, crossing or sanctuary. Even so, it is a fine solid example of Spanish provincial Baroque. There is also a small Roman bridge and a mediaeval castle, once the seat of that count whose burial is the subject of el Greco's famous painting in Santo Tomé. N401 now leads north to Toledo. From Sonseca there is a dust road to Casalgordo with the very early church of **San Pedro de la Mata** (not, confusingly, to be found at La Mata to the west of Toledo). For the key Tía Maxima must be found and I have never been lucky as she takes lunch to her husband in the fields and does not return till late afternoon. But the evening should find her at home. In the official inventory of monuments the church is attributed to the seventh century; it has a rectangular apse and the imposts inside are said to be of great interest. The next village on N401 after

Sonseca, **Ajofrín,** has a late Mudéjar church tower; it also boasts a fine parish pump of 1624 with four spouts – the women take their pitchers to the water in little racks pushed like wheelbarrows. The return to Toledo provides good views of the city as the road winds down to the river.

Toledo – Guadamur – Santa Maria de Melque – La Puebla de Montalbán – Toledo

This is a pleasant journey for a winter afternoon or a summer evening. Leaving Toledo by the Puente San Martín, we take C401 signposted to Navahermosa. After 12 km there is a right-hand turning to **Guadamur.** The compact little castle was built, like the Palacio de Fuensalida, for Pedro López de Ayala. The straight staircase occupying the width of the fabric rises under a coffered ceiling to a pretty double arch on black columns. The saloon has a flat painted ceiling of beams and panels – all the Mudéjar woodwork on this floor is original. The so-called Mozarabic Room – really Morisco – has very charming painted stucco decoration with Hebrew inscriptions. This is one of the few 'Castles in Spain' anyone might – not so idly – dream of inhabiting. Returning to the road and continuing 9 km beyond Gálvez we turn right on C403 to San Martín de Montalbán. About 5 km past the village and a hundred yards or so before an isolated croft on the right of the road is a dust track which ends after some 2 km in a group of farm buildings – out of which rises the semi-ruinous Mozarabic church of **Santa Maria de Melque.** This has a cruciform plan and the whole is made of remarkably large blocks of unmortared stone rounded on the outside corners. Unexaggerated horseshoe arches at the crossing are carried on massive round columns made of great stone slabs like millstones piled one on top of the other. Not only the majority of the arches are of horseshoe shape but so too is the ground-plan of the apse. The church has been claimed as Visigothic – it will be remembered that the three-centred horseshoe was used as early as the seventh century – but the balance of expert opinion is that Melque belongs to the late ninth or early tenth century and is one of the only two known examples – the other is Barbastro (Huesca) – of a Christian basilica built on Muslim soil and under Muslim rule *before* the general exodus northwards of refugees who were to

found such churches as San Cebrián de Mazote and Santa
Maria de Bamba (Valladolid) in Christian territory. The
tower was probably added as an observation post by the
Templars some two centuries later. Preliminary excavations
seem to show that a considerable Christian community
flourished here throughout the Moorish rule in the region.
It is a rather magical place.

C403 continues – with a rough but passable surface – to **La
Puebla de Montalbán,** a pleasant old town with a good Plaza
Mayor; the parish church with a four-bay nave of granite
Renaissance arches is covered by a handsome artesonado
ceiling. From here we can follow the Tagus valley back to
Toledo through some of the richest land in the province. The
route is lovely in the evening when the dying light somehow
intensifies the earth colours of the undulating landscape and
the greens – which always seem to grow more vivid towards
dusk.

*Toledo – Barcience – Torrijos – Talavera de la Reina – Oropesa
– El Puente del Arzobispo – Guadalupe – (Extremadura) –
Navahermosa – Toledo*

If this complete circuit is followed, it is wise to plan a night
at Guadalupe. Leaving Toledo on N403, the Avila road, we
find a little after Rielves a dust track on the right leading to the
village and castle of **Barcience,** which is visible from some
distance. This was built about 1440; the elegant window ribs
and remnants of stone window seats bear witness to gracious
living but the place is little more than a shell and though finely
situated with good views of the Sierra de Gredos does not
merit a detour unless it coincides with plans for a picnic lunch.
The next town is **Torrijos,** whose late fifteenth-century
Colegiata has a very tall airy nave and vault and a good
retablo in the style of Diego de Siloe in the Capilla de San
Blas. The most interesting feature of the church, however, is
the west front portal, dated 1510, which has been attributed
to Covarrubias – though this seems unlikely even as a prentice
work of so sophisticated and self-conscious an architect, for
it has an ebullience and naïveté that almost seem to prefigure
Mexican Baroque. Columns have been incorporated from a
mosque and delicate capitals of the period of the Caliphate
have been used upside down as bases for them – a solecism

Covarrubias would never have committed. The whole looks more like an early provincial effort by local builders in the fashionable Plateresque style.

Immediately after Torrijos we take a left fork via Alcabón to Santa Olalla on NV and continue on this to **Talavera de la Reina**, so called as it became from the time of Alfonso XI the hereditary portion of the queens of Castile. The bridge of 35 arches across the Tagus dates from the fifteenth century. On the left of the road driving in stands the large **Ermita de Santa Maria del Prado** facing a wide public walk bordering the road. Lining the porch and most of the interior walls is an attractive series of seventeenth-century tile-pictures in a naïve Baroque style with pleasant landscape backgrounds. The dados are all blue and white but the pictures include green and yellow too. Subjects include the Genealogy of Christ on the epistle side, the Passion on the gospel side and the Temptations of Saint Anthony the Abbot just inside the entrance. Sadly Talavera, the Caesobriga of the Romans, has been swamped by modern building but the **Colegiata** in the Plaza del Ayuntamiento is worth a look for its Gothic-Mudéjar rose-window, so is the small Mudéjar brick church of **Santiago** with a brick-ribbed rose-window in the east face (which is supported by buttresses springing from the house opposite). This well illustrates the versatility of the material in Morisco hands. The **Arco de San Pedro** was a gate in the Roman wall, of which some sectors remain. Outside the town on July 27th and 28th, 1809, Wellington and Cuesta gained their rather costly victory over King Joseph, Jourdan and Victor.

Continuing west on NV we come next to **Oropesa**, whose castle, once a frontier fort, was rebult by the Alvarez de Toledo family in the early fifteenth century. Fernando, first Count of Oropesa, fought on the wrong side in the war over Queen Isabel's succession but the order that his castle should be razed to the ground was never carried out. In the long run it was the French who did the most damage and only an eye-catching shell is left. The later barrack-like block along the west side of the forecourt has become a useful Parador of the M.I.T. The parish church is Herreran with a Gothic tower and some Plateresque windows. From Oropesa the main road continues west to Mérida for Portugal or Andalusia. But a tempting variant is offered by the local road over the Sierra de la Palomera to Guadalupe. The first village is **El Puente**

del Arzobispo with a fine mediaeval bridge over the Tagus. A pleasantly simple place with cows mooing in the houses, it once rivalled Talavera as a centre of ceramic production and there are still some potteries. Crossing the river we find after 9 km a left-hand fork to Villar del Pedroso from which the road winds for 62 km over the sierra to descend on **Guadalupe**.

Like the more modest Yuste this great fortress-palace-monastery (a combination to which Spanish monarchs were addicted) is situated in pleasant foothills whose slopes are covered by woods and market gardens and overhung by a high peak, in this case Villuerca (1607 m). The village is a delightful medley of low houses, porticoed streets, stable-type front doors and overhanging upper storeys on rough-hewn beams. Considering that this place is the seat of the famous black Virgen de la Hispanidad, declared senior Virgin of the Hispanic world in 1928, there are remarkably few souvenir-shops and the life of the inhabitants of the mediaeval houses and their animals continues naturally enough. The monastery was sequestrated like all its fellows in 1836 and the Jeronymite monks turned out at bayonet point. In 1908 it was reoccupied, this time by Franciscans. They bought out the private owners who had turned the place into a tenement house and now run a hostelry with about 100 beds in the Patio Gótico and do a thriving business in weddings and wedding breakfasts. Getting married at Guadalupe is widely believed to assure fertility. There is also the Hostal Zurbarán, a Parador collaborating with the national network.

State restoration of the large complex of buildings and the monks' initiative have made Guadalupe one of the better pre-served monasteries; royal endowments and gifts have made it one of the richest. Starting life as a mere hermitage, it attained monastic status in 1300 following a miracle of the Virgin. Alfonso XI won the battle of El Salado in 1340, having first commended himself to the Virgin of Guadalupe, whom he duly rewarded. The magnificent **Church** of the second half of the fourteenth century is open at all normal times. The wide cornice running all round the inside was turned into a gallery by the addition of the elegant iron railing made between 1510 and 1514 by that great team, Fray Francisco de Salamanca and Fray Juan de Avila. It is a pity the vaulting ribs have been masked by Baroque decoration attributed to Lara Churriguera, though the Baroque stalls in the raised choir are a good set. The rest of the complex requires a ticket. A very fine double Plateresque doorway leads to the Mudéjar **Claustro**. The lower arcade of horseshoe arches supports a gallery stage in the ratio of one arch below to two above. This relationship is constant but the arches on the south and east sides are pointed horseshoes, while those on the other sides vary and some are ultra-semicircular. The enchanting **Templete** or pavilion in the centre is a jewel of the Gothic-Mudéjar style with unusual garlanded capitals; the gabled three-tier upper stage is of brick framing tiled panels. The whole thing is rather improbable and extremely pretty. The cloister garden also affords a view of the rose-window with fine-spun tracery of distinctly Muslim flavour – this is probably an earlier example than Talavera's.

The **Museo de Bordados** or needlework museum installed in the old refectory is worth a visit. The most famous exhibit called the Frontal de Enrique II (No. 61) is an altar-front showing types of clothing of the period with sharp folds and elegant design. The **Sala Capitular** contains 86 illustrated choir-chant books. There is also a small Goya called Confession in the Prison and a triptych attributed to Isaac Isembrandt. The **Sacristía** begun in 1638 by an anonymous monk is claimed as the most beautiful in Spain. The cupboards and mirrors form part of a total design which incorporates eight portraits by Zurbarán of brethren of the community. These confirm, if confirmation were required, his great mastery over whites and yellows; their frames are identical with those of the windows in the facing wall. Also by Zurbarán is a small Apotheosis of Saint Jerome, which the monks call his 'pearl'. A chapel decorated with Renaissance frescoes contains relics and reliquaries, a garment embroidered for the Virgin by Philip II's daughter, Isabel Clara Eugenia, and the crown made for the Virgin's imperial coronation in 1928 (see p. 336).

Finally we are admitted to the **Camarín de la Virgen** in an equivalent position behind the high altar to the 'Transparente' at El Paular (Madrid) but in more pleasing taste. Built between 1688 and 1696 by Francisco Rodríguez and decorated with frescoes by Lucás Jordán alternating with polychrome figures in niches of biblical matriarchs, this rich but well-balanced chamber is no more than the anteroom to the little recess behind the altar, which contains a gyrating niche made in this century. When the enamels of the rear of this have been explained by the eager monk, he turns it round and the Virgin now faces back into her dressing-room. She is not of course 'black' but coffee-coloured. She is dressed in pink robes which one is invited to kiss after paying one's respects by prayer. No one knows how old she is or where she came from and this confers a potent aura of mystery on her. I retired from her presence quite involuntarily impressed. From Guadalupe it is a pleasant drive back to Toledo on C401 and C503 via La Nava del Ricomalillo, Alcaudete de la Jara and Navahermosa.

Toledo – Orgaz – Ciudad Real – Almagro – La Calzada de Calatrava – (Andalusia)

N401 is a good, almost traffic-free route to take from Toledo for Andalusia. It joins the main road NIV between Andújar and Córdoba and the drive through this empty quarter (which provides the best boar-shooting in Spain) is rather exhilarating. Ciudad Real itself is not up to much. The quite decent Plaza Mayor has been spoiled by modern buiding and the cathedral is little more than a large respectable parish church. But the detour on C425 to **Almagro** is highly recommended. Once a possession of the powerful military order of Calatrava, it is now perhaps the best preserved town of the Renaissance period in Spain with a large and very charming Plaza Mayor, sixteenth-century theatre and interesting university and religious buildings. A Parador has recently been opened. From here C417 leads south to **La Calzada de Calatrava** and 7 km south of this on CR504 is the ruined 'Sacred Convent-Castle' of Calatrava, originally the seat of the knightly order and one of the most exposed strong points on the whole Reconquest frontier. From Calzada C410 rejoins N420 for the south at Puertollano.

Toledo – Mora – Consuegra – Madridejos – (Andalusia) – (Cuenca etc.)

C400 leads south-east passing under the ruins of the castle of Almonacid to Mora, already described in the first excursion from Toledo. A little after Mora we are told we are entering La Mancha – which comes from an Arabic word meaning the dry land. The next town is **Consuegra**, a dusty place of brick

churches and convents under a long ridge with ruins of a
fourteenth-century castle. Perched on the same spine are
seven or eight resuscitated windmills. When I enquired if they
were still used, I was told they had been rebuilt 'as a luxury'.
This would surely have amused Cervantes. Three km to the
south of Consuegra are some Roman ponds, where Trajan is
claimed to have bathed. Another 6 km bring us to **Madridejos**
with a five-bay hall-church devoted to El Salvador. The vault
rises from circular columns who capitals are adorned with
giant Ionic scrolls. Immediately to the east of the town runs
the main north-south NIV from Madrid to Andalusia. In the
next chapter I propose to take those who are still with me on
a north-easterly sweep to Cuenca.

CHAPTER ELEVEN

Cuenca and Guadalajara

✣

Madridejos – Alcázar de San Juan – Campo de Criptana – Toboso – Venta de Don Quijote – Mota del Cuervo – Belmonte – (Villaescusa de Haro) – San Clemente – Honrubia – La Almarcha – Cuenca

The route I have chosen now enters a region much less well known than the cities and provinces so far described and consisting of the eastern parts of New and Old Castile bordering on Aragón. It is a region with much to recommend it both in buildings and scenery, while the lack of exploitation makes itself agreeably felt in noticeably lower prices for lodgings and meals. At first the prospect is perhaps a little bleak, for we are still in La Mancha, the dry land, the land of the *noria* or water wheel. There are no surface springs, so a well is dug down to the level of the water table and a chain of small containers is wound up to the surface by a capstan turned by a blinkered mule or donkey plodding round and round and round, as each container tips its contents into the irrigation channel before going down for more. The whole process is a living symbol of monotony and acceptance, the sturdy acceptance of the peasant and the dumb acceptance of the beast. And what on earth would a gentleman do here but read ... and read ... and read? How appropriate it is that La Mancha should have been chosen by Cervantes as the seeding ground of Don Quijote's preposterous delusions.

From Madridejos C400 leads to **Alcázar de San Juan**, a railway junction with unswept streets and half-finished buildings near a stagnant lake. There is a handsome tower called after Don John of Austria, which has been rather overrestored. The nearby church of Santa Maria is built of the same reddish stone and so is the larger and later Trinidad, in which Herreran and Baroque elements are mixed. **Campo de Criptana**, 7 km farther on, sports like Consuegra a skyline of rebuilt windmills whose sails never turn. The now open struts of these were covered with canvas; the poles that protrude like stiff pigtails from the flattish conical roofs almost to the ground are called the rudders and by them the roofs are, or were, turned so that the sails should face the wind. A little beyond Campo de Criptana a local road on the left leads to **El Toboso**, home of Don Quijote's Dulcinea and now a neat, self-conscious village. The four-bay hall-church of Santiago, low and wide, is unexpectedly impressive. The circular columns and late Gothic vault and rear choir would have been familiar to Cervantes who – like Shakespeare – died in 1616, though the crossing, sanctuary and tower are of later date. Outside the Convento de la Concepción is a rose-garden presided over by the brooding statue of a local worthy with the charming legend: *España fue su Dulcinea*. In El Toboso they sweep the streets on principle, even when a high wind makes mockery of their efforts. From here a local road leads to **Venta de Don Quijote** on N301 from Madrid to Albacete. This is simply a range of buildings with tile-pictures on the outer walls implying that here stood the inn Don Quijote mistook for a castle and in which he was knighted by the inn-keeper. Nine km nearer Madrid is Quintanar de la Orden, which has little to say for itself, so it is best to head south-east as far as Mota del Cuervo, where N301 meets N420 to Cuenca.

Now the landscape becomes less monotonous. At 16 km we come to **Belmonte**, a mediaeval township that belonged to the Marquis of Villena, Henry IV's omnivorous favourite (cf. El Parral, Segovia), who built the castle on an elegantly symmetrical plan with a triangular patio de armas inside a variation on the theme of a hexagon. Although contemporary with the Fonseca showpiece at Coca (Segovia), it is solidly made of stone. There is a low outer wall pierced by a drawbridge gate on the north-east side. A walk along the top of the inner wall leads to the guardroom, occupying the upper stage of the donjon (which has no other entrance); from here a staircase leads down to the prison and beneath this again is the dungeon proper, accessible only by a hole in its ceiling – from which it is claimed no prisoner ever emerged alive. The triangular patio unfortunately has an ugly brick lining on two sides, added by the Empress Eugènie, Spanish wife of Napoleon III, presumably in order to conserve warmth in the previously open galleries. But these retain their original Mudéjar ceilings in pale pine, while the main reception chamber has a noble artesonado in the same wood with coloured panels in orange, yellow and blue.

The doorways and embrasures are carved with bold and effective Flamboyant Gothic tracery and there is an interesting stone carved frieze running round the walls. The ex-chapel has another good ceiling – shallow squinch-arches transform the quadrilateral into an octagon, above which two tiers of friezes under a galaxy of stalactites cleverly launch another octagon at odds with the one below. Off the upper gallery is the Marquis's bedroom with the most ingenious, if pointless, ceiling of all. This is made of walnut and incorporates a mechanism that permitted it to gyrate. The creakings of this contraption were counteracted by the tinkling of a myriad of tiny bells attached to the mobile canopy. But Don Juan de Pacheco's thoughts were not all devoted to such elaborate toys. If a king's head lies uneasy, even more so does a favourite's. From one corner of the room a very practical-looking spiral staircase leads right down to the basement from which escape could be made in emergency. Under the castle walls a slope studded with umbrella pines runs down towards the town. This open space is enclosed by the town wall, of which long stretches remain including three of the five gates – the Puerta de Chinchilla being the best preserved of these.

The most remarkable building in the town is the **Colegiata**, a fourteenth-century church on Romanesque foundations, improved and extended by the Marquis. A frequent decorative motif is the conch of Santiago superimposed on the arms of the cross of Calatrava, in both of which privileged military orders the related Pacheco and Téllez Girón families occupied powerful positions. The elegant nine-sided apse, which is higher than the older nave, is one of the Marquis's additions; it contains some good alabaster tombs. The Gothic choir stalls finely carved with biblical scenes were bought by the canons of Belmonte (the church acquired collegiate status in 1459) from the chapter of Cuenca Cathedral. Cuenca, as we shall see, came off worst in the deal. The high altar was made in 1619 and gilded in 1667. The side-chapels contain some good Renaissance retablos, notably one devoted to the Virgin in high and low relief in the family chapel of Fray Luis de León, the great Salmantine theologian, who was born at Belmonte. On the gospel side is the chapel of the Espinosas.

The shield of this family – a thorn-tree (*espino*) clutched by a female bear (*osa*) is remarkably similar to the shield of Madrid. An Espinosa was *corregidor* (chief magistrate) of Madrid before its elevation to capital rank and it is at least possible he gave his arms to the Villa. At any rate this theory is more probable than some others advanced. The west entrance of the church again bears the stamp of the Marquis's taste. Nearby are the ruins of a palace that belonged to the Infante Juan Manuel, builder of Peñafiel (Valladolid). 6 km to the northeast of Belmonte on N420 lies **Villaescusa de Haro**. The parish church here is reputed to have an exceptionally fine Gothic retablo protected by an equally remarkable grille but as the priest will trust the key to no one else and serves other parishes in addition to visiting his family in yet another town the odds are rather heavily loaded against admittance. I was twice unlucky.

One can of course continue to Cuenca on N420 via La Almarcha. However, there is another town that belonged like Belmonte to the extensive Marquisate of Villena, which should not be missed. A local road from Belmonte rejoins N301 at El Pedernoso. 28 km to the south-east is the left-hand turning to **San Clemente**. Here, by contrast, the principal buildings belong to the Renaissance period and were put up after the power of the nobles had been broken. In 1487 the inhabitants delivered the place to the Catholic Sovereigns against a written promise that it would never again be granted to a nobleman or any other private person. The Plaza Mayor is entered by an arch matched by a twin on the opposite side, attached to the Ayuntamiento. This has a fine façade over an arcaded pavement with a raised central panel carrying the arms of Philip II. The figures alternating with a wheel and spoke pattern in the frieze under the eaves represent Philip (on the left-hand corner) and other kings and heroes. The belfry appears to be a later addition. Part of the ground floor is occupied by a large old-fashioned bar and next door is the low white façade of the posada, which produces abundant cheap meals.

Almost facing this hostelry is the south entrance of the impressive ex-collegiate church of **Santiago el Mayor**. The three western bays are Gothic giving way in the fourth to the hall-church plan. The transition to the new style is ingeniously effected by the conversion of the fourth pair of piers, rising

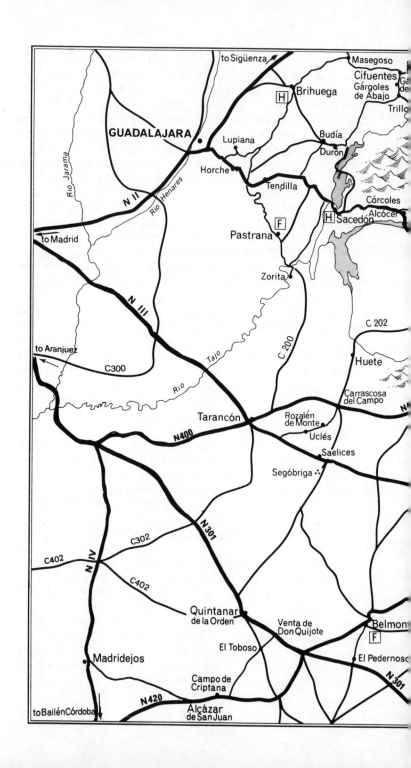

from wicker-work Gothic bases, into rounded columns with Ionic scroll-capitals on the side facing the altar. The elegant sanctuary frames a remarkable alabaster cross, which came from a little chapel at the entrance of the town; it is unusually rich in detail for a simple cross-roads symbol of which there are so many in Spain. Possibly the wealth of the Marquis was so great that he was able to engage such a master as Gil de Siloe even for a minor commission of this nature. The shaft is carved with apostles and angels and yet more angels are perched on the arms with cups to catch the blood. Local legend has it that the cross was carved by Benvenuto Cellini to the order of Philip II and brought from Italy on a cart drawn by oxen who refused to move a pace beyond San Clemente, where it therefore remained. But one can hardly credit that the will of the builder of the Escorial would have been baulked by the whim of a pair of beasts and the work is in any case by an earlier hand. The chapel of the Pallares family houses a pretty Baroque gilt and glass altar front belonging to the Virgen de Rus, who is brought from her country hermitage to spend forty days a year in her best clothes in town. When the Renaissance extension was made, this family sued the chapter on the grounds that they would no longer be able to see the high altar from their private chapel and would thus have to hear mass with the plebs. They lost.

Between the church and an arcaded building facing the Ayuntamiento is a Baroque arch leading to a second plaza. The Civil Guard barracks on the left, once the *pósito* or communal grain and cereal storehouse, has a handsome entrance of 1585. On the far side of the square is the lawcourt with an unusual doorway of 1698, brought from the house of the Inquisition which stood on another site. Also worthy of mention is the Plaza de Carmen Martínez with a firm squat tower with ajimez windows called the Torre Vieja, probably belonging to the twelfth or thirteenth century. The Pensión Florida is extremely clean and the posada also provides beds.

From San Clemente C3214 runs north to join NIII at Honrubia. Proceeding towards Madrid we find on the left, 2 km before La Almarcha, the castle of Garcimuñoz which is stone-built on a square plan with round towers and mullioned windows. The village church has been put up within the walls, using part of the old fabric. A plaque records that the soldier-poet Jorge Manrique died outside the gate, fighting for Isabel the Catholic in the war over her succession. At La Almarcha we rejoin N420, which runs north via Olivares de Júcar towards Cuenca. At El Castelar the road crosses the river Júcar; just before the modern bridge is a hump-backed single-span Roman bridge in good condition. La Mancha is now well behind. The countryside is hilly and wooded and pockets of mist tend to lie in the hollows, giving it a mysterious air, especially under a full moon.

Cuenca, that is to say old Cuenca, is an interesting mediaeval city dramatically situated on a spine between the gorges of the Júcar and the Huécar. Although slightly farther north than Toledo, it was not wrested from the Moors until nearly a century later, when Alfonso VIII in 1177 reduced it after a long siege. Until very recently the place was still considered so remote as to be virtually inaccessible. In the last century Street omitted the cathedral altogether from his *Some Account of Gothic Architecture in Spain* and even Hemingway complained of the bad roads. The one I have indicated is now very adequate, so also is N400 from Madrid via Tarancón. The lower town contains all the modern development, which is much of a muchness with that of any other provincial capital. It is clearly divided from the old city by the narrow channel of the Huécar, which is easily reached from the Parque San Julián, the modern centre with the Gobierno Civil, the Post Office and the Hotel Alfonso VIII. A pleasant old street, the Calle de los Tintes, follows the curve of the stream. The bridge over this launches the pedestrian on the ascent of the old quarter by Calle del Pósito. On the right is the Archaeological Museum (see p. 354), beyond which the street widens into the Plaza del Cardenal Anaya. We continue by Calle San Vicente, always climbing, to the Plaza del Salvador, at the top of which a steep flight of steps passes between the churches of San Andrés on the left and San Felipe Neri on the right to emerge in the Calle de Alfonso VIII. Almost any other permutation of streets and alleys – always provided they lead upwards – will achieve the same result. The motorist must make a longer circuit, following the main shopping street, Avenida de José Antonio, until he comes to the Plaza de la Trinidad where a right turn over a bridge initiates a steep ascent by Calle de Palafox, which turns into Calle Alfonso VIII and brings him to the same point already reached by the pedestrians. A little farther on is the Ayuntamiento built like Admiralty Arch over an arcade. This Baroque building of the early eighteenth century was restored in 1881 and again in 1960. Passing under it we come into the elongated Plaza Mayor overlooked by tall plain houses.

On the right is the west front of the **Cathedral**. The original façade was not completed till the seventeenth century and was then seriously damaged by the fall of the north tower in 1902, after which it was demolished. The present unfinished front follows plans by Vicente Lampérez and was designed to give the old church a face consistent with its interior. Pedantry was even pushed to the point of allowing for the normal mediaeval time-lag between the beginning and completion of a cathedral – this explains the conscientiously fourteenth-century air of Lampérez's work. To date, the result is not disastrous though it will look a great deal better when the stone has weathered in two or three centuries' time and it is much to be hoped that the unpromising towers projected in the model will not be built and the present upper windows on either side (which are higher than the old aisles) will simply be left as screens. The new rose-window does serve a purpose in lighting the nave and a reasonably successful junction is made inside between the first two bays, rebuilt with quadripartite vaults, and the other four, which are covered by the original sexpartite vaulting scheme. Despite his rejection of the sexpartite system Lampérez has preserved the pretty device of the earlier bays whereby a circular clerestory window is set in the outer wall above a triforium gallery. The shape of the window is repeated by a crocketed circlet of tracery forming part of the triforium screen, which also incorporates angels sheltered by canopies in the centre of each section of the balustrade. The old tracery is lacking except in the third bay, which also preserves some remains of original colouring. This part of the church was completed about 1250 and affinities have been suggested with Lincoln and Ely.

The crossing belongs to the earliest part of the structure begun about 1197 and consecrated in 1208. The square tower with lancet windows immediately over the crossing (masked by the vault with only a circular opening for light) and the long presbytery – designed to hold a choir – are other features pointing to a foreign, perhaps Anglo-Norman, origin. The sexpartite vaulting, later continued in the nave, covers both presbytery and transepts. This system, by which each compartment shelters two steeply pitched arches, has always seemed to me one of the happier Gothic inventions, far more striking and aspiring than the later flattened vaults. The four parallel apses – two on each side of the sanctuary – of the early church were pulled down to make way for the present double ambulatory inspired by Toledo's and built between 1448 and 1490. The switch from the rectangular to the semicircular plan has been achieved by means of some very complicated but clumsy vaulting compartments and while the inner ambulatory becomes bulbous rather than strictly semicircular, the outer walk – which begins the wider of the two – is squeezed to much narrower proportions at the east end. Throughout the building the same solecism has been committed as at Avila of colour-washing the walls and picking out the stones with gold paint. But in architectural terms this is one of the most fascinating cathedrals in Spain.

The high altar retablo by the Neo-Classical Ventura Rodríguez, in which porphyry columns are employed to frame low-relief scenes in white stone, is in the anodyne good taste of the late eighteenth century, a far cry in spirit from the daring and often beautiful building. This is enclosed by Baroque grilles on the sides (showing that the tradition of iron craftsmanship survived more healthily than sculpture into a later age) and by a particularly splendid and exceptionally tall Renaissance screen with a great crestwork of angels and putti in beaten tin by Hernando de Arenas, an ironsmith of Cuenca itself. Opposite this is another good grille of more standard composition by the same master, protecting the choir. The ironwork throughout the cathedral is of very high standard, yielding only in excellence to Toledo and Seville.

As we have already seen, the older and more interesting choir stalls were sold by the chapter to Belmonte. The present set are good standard Baroque, though untypically there is only one female figure, which appears to represent Saint Theresa. The matching organs of the same period are reached by a pretty trellised loft. Along with the side and back walls, they form part of a general design that has been attributed to Martín de Aldehuela, architect of the great new bridge of Ronda, who fell to his death while inspecting his work there in 1784.

While in this part of the church one can hardly fail to notice the **Arco de Jamete** in the north transept. This over-adorned archway of 1546–1549, opening into a vaulted recess whose door led to the cloister, was severely damaged by the fall of the great tower in 1902. Next to it is the **Capilla de Múñoz** with a flamboyant Gothic entrance and a window grille called a *comulgatorio*, through which plebeians might receive communion without entering and defiling this family's private chapel. Both these features have later been framed by a refreshingly exuberant Plateresque entablature on engaged columns whose lively fancy almost seems to mock the pomposity of the neighbouring arch. At right angles to this is the more solemn **Capilla de los Albornoz** of double size and containing in the floor the tomb of Doña Teresa de Luna, mother of Cardinal Albornoz – only the head and hands project in carved stone from the flat slate slab. The retablo has a Crucifixion by Hernán Yáñez de Almedina, also an Adoration of the Kings and a Descent by the same painter, who combines Leonardesque or Raphaelesque physiognomy and gesture with Castilian Grand Guignol – he is especially liberal with his skulls. Both these chapels are notable too for their fine ironwork. Together with the egregious Arco de Jamete they form one of the most interesting corners of the church.

Starting the circuit of the ambulatory on this side we come next to the **Capilla de Santiago** with two good Gothic tombs. We then pass two chapels of little interest before reaching the glass doors of the **Capilla Honda**, used as a winter choir. In order to make it snugger, it was decided to raise the floor, which is now so close to the deeply coffered Renaissance ceiling with its fiercely spiked bosses as to make these seem positively menacing. There are five rather hack paintings by Juan de Borgoña. The shallow axial **Capilla de Santa Elena** has a small retablo in natural wood. Facing this and forming the main feature of the trasaltar is a so-called **Transparente** (cf. Toledo cathedral) of the same period as the high altar and also by Ventura Rodríguez, enshrining the remains of the cathedral's patron, Saint Julian, in a silver casket. The high relief stone panels above include on the left a scene showing the saint and his assistant Saint Lesmes making a basket. Apparently he took up this simple craft as a means of relaxation and sold the products to succour the poor. Farther round the trasaltar, now on the gospel side, this theme is repeated over a Rococo

Toledo, Plateresque entrance of the Hospital de Santa Cruz, 'conceived by
Cardinal Mendoza and built between 1494 and 1515 by Enrique de Egas'.

Cuenca. The celebrated Casas Colgadas, which now house the Museo de
Arte Abstracto Español.

Left, Cuenca, the Cathedral tower and chevet. 'The square tower with lancet
windows immediately over the crossing . . . and the long presbytery are . . .
features pointing to a foreign, perhaps Anglo-Norman origin.'
Right, Casas Colgadas of the type not shown on tourist posters but alive
with human interest.

Village street in the Vera (Avila).

Farmhouse near Cuenca.

Sierra de las Mamblas near Covarubias (Burgos).

Hamlet near Soria.

Pastrana. '... impressively situated but like many places of a region that
disdains the cosmetic treatment of whitewash it crouches back into its hillside
and is barely discernible in fading light.'

Priego under its great escarpment.

Co-cathedral of Soria. Capitals 'of obviously Celtic inspiration' in the twelfth-century Augustinian cloister.

San Baudelio de Berlanga (Soria). 'The structurally fascinating San Baudelio is . . . a tragic witness to collectors' greed. In 1922—five years after its official declaration as a National Monument—an international dealer acquired the frescoes for the United States. Six of these have found their way back to the Prado.'

There is something irresistible about a good tower and these abound in Spain;
Spanish skies at once require and inspire them.
Top left, the transitional (pointed Romanesque) tower of Santa Maria del
Azogue, Benavente; *right,* a Plateresque example, rare in church architecture,
at Morón de Almazán; and two Baroque specimens: *below left,* one of a
pair belonging to the Clerecía, Salamanca; *right,* Domingo Ondategui's fine
contribution to the Cathedral of El Burgo de Osma.

altar in a Flamboyant Gothic frame – here he is shown as a mitred bishop with two baskets and, it would seem, a client. This is known as the **Capilla de San Julián**; above it is a compartment with a fancy grille in which his remains lay before their removal to Ventura Rodríguez's Transparente. Backing onto the ambulatory pier nearest Saint Julian's chapel is the handsome Renaissance altar of Saints Fabian and Sebastian.

Reverting to the outer circle, so to speak, we come to the late Gothic **Sacristía** containing part of the 'treasure'. There are some good vestment chests by Ventura Rodríguez, who was also responsible for the display cabinets containing the usual collection of church plate and reliquaries. Among the works of art there is an attractive small Flemish carved group of the Betrothal of the Virgin (59), while in the anteroom leading to the chapter house we find an angular Calvary of the thirteenth century, called Alfonso VIII's (50) and a damaged alabaster Pieta with a homely Virgin of the fifteenth century (54). A very decorated Plateresque doorway with carved wooden doors attributed to Alonso Berruguete opens into the **Sala Capitular** whose cavernously coffered artesonado ceiling was absurdly painted in the eighteenth century with excessively pretty Rococo colours – baby pink, baby blue, white and gold – quite at odds with its ponderous craftsmanship. This grand room houses a rather poor collection of paintings from churches in the diocese. Beyond it steps lead down to a little room containing the rest of the treasure. Over the entrance to this treasure-chamber are two works by el Greco – an Agony in the Garden (303) of about 1605–1610 and a small head of Christ with the Cross of the same period (305). Sharing the passage with these is a Calvary attributed to Gerard David (301).

After the sacristy comes the Baroque **Capilla del Santísimo** with a lantern-cupola, where mass is celebrated daily. Then, passing a pair of tombs of the Montemayor family – the top tenant died in 1465 – we find the altar of Saint Martin, who is shown as usual slicing his cape in two in order to give half to a naked beggar. The south transept has little of interest, nor have the south aisle chapels, unless we except the Capilla de la Virgen del Pilar of double size with a Plateresque entrance and a comulgatorio as in the Múñoz chapel. The cloister is not one of the strengths of this cathedral and is now used as a stonemason's yard for the craftsmen working on the west front. It is not usually shown to the public but on the way into it is the **Capilla del Espíritu Santo** of the sixteenth century containing tombs of the proud family of Hurtado de Mendoza, Marquises of Cañete, each of which is topped by a skull and crossbones.

Three short itineraries from the cathedral can be recommended. First, continuing uphill, we pass between staid old houses until the street opens out by the octagonal church of San Pedro, which has a circular core. On the left steps lead down by an assortment of alleys and arches to a cobbled walk overlooking the gorge of the Júcar. On the right, the church side, similar passages lead to points of vantage over the humbler Huécar. A little higher up the slope beyond the provincial prison stand the remnants of Alfonso VIII's castle. From the parapet just under the prison there is a good view of the cathedral from the north side and whoever cares to continue through the arch will find a number of good standpoints from which to look back on the old city.

The second route, a short one too, takes us under the arcade of the Ayuntamiento as if to return to the lower town. Immediately on the right is a tall square old house, once the property of the Marquises of Cañete, who ceded it to the Mercedarian order. There is a door open to the public but anyone tempted to enter should be warned – to avoid an unpleasant shock – that it leads into a modern convent chapel with some truly appalling stained glass. To the left of the building an alley leads up to the small but rather distinguished Plaza de los Colegios. In front is the large Baroque portico of the seminary and at right angles to this the Neo-Classical façade of the seminary church. The other doorway on this side belongs to the nuns. The alley continues between religious buildings with a doorway of 1746 on the right to the platform once occupied by the Moorish Alcazaba, overlooking the brown waters of the Júcar. From this rises the slender square **Torre de Mangana**, which is thought to have belonged to a mosque, though the machicolations of the parapet were certainly added later. The tower has been stripped recently of its plaster decorations and left proudly naked with a brand-new clock-face at the top. From here we retrace our steps to the cathedral west front.

To the right of Lampérez's façade a slope leads down past the eighteenth-century episcopal palace to the much publicised

Casas Colgadas or hanging houses, three of which have been cunningly knocked together to house the **Museo de Arte Abstracto Español**. This is an amusing visit and one is led by an intricate network of stairs through a series of differently shaped rooms on different levels. Some of the works may arouse indignation, even outrage. They raise a question many would prefer not to have to ask, namely: What is Art? In most cases they deny that it is a perfectly realised, static statement of the artist's intentions. Some of them assert that it is a game, in which the viewer must participate. Torner's stainless steel and scrap works invite one to experiment with one's own dimmed reflection in the steel panel. His Vanishing Point lures one into the picture like a child drawn to the exact point where the rainbow ends. The showmanship is such that one is innocently drawn on (one way only) through the whole collection before emerging in a pleasantly arranged sales department where one is invited to buy prints by the artists represented. In the same building there is a good restaurant, in which food that no one can quarrel with is presented with the same aplomb as the art.

A passage under the Casas Colgadas slopes sharply down to the iron pedestrian bridge with a wooden slatted walk 130 feet above the Huécar, whose narrow stream winds between tiny strips of cultivation called *hocinos*. Perched high on the opposite bank is the late Gothic church of **San Pablo** with a fine spreading vault reminiscent of Juan de Alava. The Valencian Baroque portico featuring the cross of Calatrava has a strikingly elongated decorative panel over the door. The building attached is a seminary and the terrace provides a good view of the Casas Colgadas and the chevet and tower of the cathedral. The road down from the seminary brings the less prettified but more genuine cliff-hanging houses into prominence with their faded colour washes and their domestic washing and TV aerials. At the bottom of the slope we recross the Huécar and continue under the walls to the Puerta de Valencia, where the Calle de los Tintes begins.

Outside the enclave bounded by the twin rivers Cuenca has no buildings of enormous interest, though the steps opposite the motor bridge over the Huécar (on the way up to the cathedral) lead to the decent plain Hospital de Santiago with a portico of 1634 and a Baroque church, while just across the more important bridge over the larger Júcar is the Virgen de la

Luz whose discreet pale ochred outside hides a Rococo lining so extravagant that it swiftly fatigues the eye and encourages retreat. A few hundred yards beyond this on the Madrid road is the workshop of the most esteemed local potter, Pedro Mercedes, whose decorated work weaves an ingenious path between ancient Iberian themes on the one hand and Disneyland on the other; some of his plain pots and pitchers in the reddish clay of the region are excellent.

The **Museo Arqueológico** installed in the old co-operative grain store in the Calle del Pósito should be seen before the sites of Valeria and Segóbriga, from which it draws most of its exhibits. The best pieces are the headless Roman statues with their crisp folds from Segóbriga and the boldly incised Corinthian capitals from the same city. From Roman Valeria and other sites in the province come some beautiful amphorae, several of which have almost pointed bases. Valeria also provides carvings of heads ranging from the solemn and sophisticated to the popular and grotesque. The contents of the cases cannot be described in detail but one may single out the Celtic cinerary urns (the Celts appear to have brought urn burial with them in the eighth century BC), the Roman Terra Sigillata items (this moulded ware had a wide dissemination throughout the Empire in the first to third centuries AD), the collection of coins from the Roman period to the Cordoban Caliphate and the Arab oil lamps and Visigothic ear-rings. The upper walls are hung with modern renderings of the paintings found in two shallow caves between the villages of Villar del Humo and Boniches de la Sierra; the hunters pursuing goats and bulls belong to the transition period from Palaeolithic to Neolithic culture but the scene representing a man leading a horse or ass falls well within the Neolithic period which began about 6000 BC and saw the domestication of animals.

Finally, Cuenca is a good base for the expeditions I am about to recommend. The prices are not high, the people are not spoiled and the Hotel Alfonso VIII, if not exciting, is perfectly comfortable. Whilst in the town I sprained my ankle very painfully and received the most disinterested consideration from everyone I had to rely on. I must plead this mishap in extenuation of any shortcomings in what follows.

Cuenca – Arcas – Valeria – Almodóvar del Pinar – Motilla del Palancar – (Villanueva de la Jara) – Alarcón – Segóbriga – Uclés – Carrascosa del Campo – (Huete) – Cuenca

This interesting circuit can be taken at a leisurely pace if a night is spent at the Parador of Alarcón (it is advisable to telephone for a reservation). Setting out on N320 for Motilla, we shortly turn right on a local road to **Arcas**, which has a church with a single Romanesque apse and a pointed Romanesque doorway. The belfry is attractively placed over an arch. 24 km to the south via Tórtola lies **Valeria**, now a decayed village with a series of terraces on the way in, which are used as threshing floors; these are littered with sections of Roman columns that have been turned to agricultural account as rollers. On the reverse face of the hill there are substantial remains of some important Roman thermae. The first inhabitants of the site were Celtiberians who first fought against Hannibal and then with him against the Romans. The place survived to become the seat of a Visigothic bishopric between 589 and 693. The most important 'finds' are in the Archaeological Museum at Cuenca. On the opposite slope are the ruins of a mediaeval fort. Valeria, sometimes called Valera de Arriba, should not be confused with Valera de Abajo some 5 km farther on, to which the road winds through the grisly gorge of the Río Gritos (river of shrieks). Our route takes us through the upper village to Olmeda del Rey whence we continue to Almodóvar del Pinar. From here N320 leads through pine woods to Motilla del Palancar on NIII and may be followed for another 15 km south between compact clumps of umbrella pines reminding one irresistibly of Botticelli to **Villanueva de la Jara** with an impressive single-span sixteenth-century church and remnants of a castle wall recalling Belmonte. The village also has one of the Carmelite convents founded by Saint Theresa, though there are now insufficient vocations to keep it open and the rump has been posted to other houses of the order. Motilla itself is a market town of no particular interest, though it does boast an ironmonger with the good old Visigothic name of Chindasvinto N. Zornoza.

Sixteen kilometres to the west of Motilla on NIII is the turning to **Alarcón**, which is situated in one of an inverse pair of hairpin bends of the river Júcar. It is accessible only by a narrow neck of land guarded by a tower and a wall on the mainland side, as it were, of the causeway and another gatehouse and wall on the castle side. The Moorish fort here fell temporarily in the tenth century to Muza-ben-Nuseir, the wide-ranging rebel leader and convert who shook the Caliphate to the core from his stronghold in the Serranía de Ronda. It was he who razed the abundant forests for miles around for reasons of defence. Alarcón is said to have been brought to the Castilian Crown as part of the *Dote de Zaida*, Zaida's dowry. She was the daughter of Mutamid, King of Seville, and became the wife (or concubine) of Alfonso VI. Even so, the place had to be recaptured under Alfonso VIII in 1184. The siege lasted nine months and the Christian commander, Martínez de Ceballos, himself scaled the walls using two Basque daggers as pinions to lever himself to the top – he and his family became hereditary governors of the castle, a position they maintained despite the delivery of the villa to the order of Santiago a few years later. In the time of the Infante Juan Manuel, Alarcón became one of the chain of castles, each at a day's ride from the next, belonging to this poet-prince and stretching from Peñafiel to Alicante. The round turreted keep on the adjacent promontory to the north was built by him. The curtain wall across the end of the promontory with its pentagonal tower is of Moorish construction.

The villa was later acquired by who but – one guess should be sufficient! – Juan de Pacheco, Marquis of Villena and Grand Master of Santiago, whose immense possessions stretched from Toledo to Murcia. In the war over the succession of Queen Isabel, Villena's son, the second Marquis, not only fought on the wrong side but had been one of the prime movers of the opposition. All the same, his power was such that he was neither executed nor attainted and the monarchs, still on relatively shaky ground with the nobles whose power they planned to break, preferred to make peace with him. He lost many of his domains and fortresses, it is true, but Alarcón remained in the possession of the Pacheco family until the last century. It is worth remarking here that the sad state of so many 'Castles in Spain' is as much due to the demolition policy of Ferdinand and Isabel as to the ravages of time. In Galicia alone over fifty were demolished after the battle of Toro. Alarcón has luckily survived to become a Parador Nacional.

In the thirteenth century the villa had five parishes and

12,000 inhabitants with its extramural dependants. Now only one church is in use and the population is in the three hundreds. The main church was **Santa Maria la Mayor** near the castle. The Plateresque triumphal portico is by Jamete of Cuenca cathedral fame and the retablo of 1574, damaged during the Civil War, may have been designed by the same master – who was apparently a good drinker and got himself into trouble with the Inquisition. The stucco sacristy ceiling also appears to be by the same hand. At the rear of Santa Maria is the ruined Santo Domingo with a thirteenth-century entrance and Herreran tower. The opposite end of the promontory to the castle is occupied by the Plaza del Ayuntamiento with an arcaded town hall of the time of Charles V and the Herreran church of San Juan. Following the curve of the road back towards the causeway we come upon the only church actually in operation, **La Trinidad**, with a thirteenth-century nave, fourteenth-century aisles and fifteenth-century presbytery arch. There is an ingenious spiral staircase leading to the tower, which straddles an arch over the street.

From Alarcón NIII continues past the castle of Garcimúñoz to the cross-roads at La Almarcha with N420 from Belmonte to Cuenca. 41 km beyond this is the village of Saelices and just before this on the left is the turning to the site of **Segóbriga**, which was inhabited in Iberian, Roman and Visigothic times. The original inhabitants supported Viriathus in his vigorous campaigns against the Romans and the place was probably subjugated by Tiberius Sempronius Gracchus. The excellent sculpted figures we have seen in the Archaeological Museum of Cuenca suggest a city of considerable importance under the Empire. The smallish amphitheatre is being restored and the structure of the theatre, probably of the third century AD, is clearly revealed. Above the amphitheatre are remnants of the Iberian walls and higher up still a large Roman water deposit has been discovered with its attendant thermal baths; there are more thermae on the lower ground to the west. Like Valeria, Segóbriga became the seat of a bishopric between 589 and 693 and a Visigothic necropolis (some objects from which we have seen at Cuenca) existed round the present museum – which is in the process of formation. The mound at the junction of the track to the site with the road was excavated in the last century and found to cover a Visigothic basilica, which remains interred beneath it.

Continuing west for 13 km beyond Saelices on NIII we find the right-hand turning to Uclés, whose monastery is visible from the main road well before arrival. This impressive pile claims to be 'the Escorial of La Mancha'. It is built on the platform of an old castle which was one of the principal seats of the knights of Santiago. The present buildings which date from the mid-sixteenth to early eighteenth centuries graphically illustrate in one complex the development of Spanish architecture over nearly two centuries, preserving at the same time a remarkable homogeneity. Construction began in the Plateresque style on the side overlooking the village. The refectory is in this wing and has a deeply coffered ceiling in natural wood of 1548. The sacristy charmingly combines a low, spreading Gothic vault with Plateresque decoration of the window and cupboard frames. The uncarved bosses were made to receive the heraldic metal plaques called arandelas. The church was largely carried out to Herreran designs by Francisco de Mora – one notes the bold Escorial-type double cornice. The oldest arcade of the great patio is that on the church side but the others were completed with considerable fidelity to it; there is more ornament but the proportions are the same. The grand double staircase is in a very elegant uncluttered Baroque taste; the most decorated feature of all is the great portico of 1735, by which one enters, but this – as usual in Spanish Baroque – is an isolated feature in a plain façade. It is well worth walking round the outside of the building and noticing the strictly Herreran west front and outer flank of the church. The lower part of the apse, however, with figures in niches, was built at the same time as the Renaissance façade, which exhibits a certain disorder in the placement of the windows in their elaborate Plateresque frames encrusted with conches and other devices. One deduces the absence of a firm guiding hand such as produced the orderly north façade of the Alcázar of Toledo at a slightly earlier date. The regular topmost floor is a later addition.

It was to Uclés that Queen Isabel rode post-haste from Valladolid on the death of the first Marquis of Villena, Grand Master of Santiago, in 1476. The motive of her journey is best explained by a brief account of the influential military orders. Some say they were modelled on the monastic orders of the Holy Land, others on similar Arab organisations. The Templars certainly obtained extensive rights in Spain and it was partly on the ruins of their empire that the Spanish orders flourished so exceedingly. The most important, that of Santiago, sprang up when a number of knights came together in the mid-twelfth century to protect the pilgrim route to Compostela from Moorish raids. This order, which required conjugal chastity but not celibacy, received papal approbation in 1175. The order of Calatrava came into being when the Templars abandoned the convent-fortress of Calatrava to the south-east of Ciudad Real as untenable. Sancho the Beloved offered it to whatever knights would undertake its defence. A soldier-monk of Navarre and his friends responded and the order was ιgiven papal sanction in 1164. The strict rule of Saint Benedict applied. The order of Alcántara, founded in 1177, started as a subordinate of Calatrava and later became independent. These orders had almost exclusive rights over the territories they reconquered. They were administered by a council of Grand Master and Commanders (among whom the territories were apportioned). With the advance of the frontiers the increasingly rich offices and benefices of the orders became the objects of the greedy ambitions of the higher and lower nobility alike, while their huge rents and the powerful forces they could put into the field made the parent bodies almost uncontrollable by the Crown. This was the situation Queen Isabel had resolved to end. When she arrived at Uclés, she found the chapter assembled to elect the new Master of Santiago. Arguing the undesirability of any one individual so powerful in the land, she persuaded the knights to put the administration of the grand mastership into the hands of the King, her husband – who waived it in favour of Alonso de Cárdenas. On the latter's death in 1499 the office reverted in administration to the Crown. Calatrava followed suit in 1487 and Alcántara in 1494. In the following reign the masterships were annexed in perpetuity to the Crown and the subordinate offices, in Prescott's words, 'degenerated into the empty decorations, the stars and garters, of an order of nobility.'

From Uclés a local road leads via Rosalén del Monte to **Carrascosa del Campo** on N400. Here there is a handsome church with a Gothic-Plateresque entrance and an interior of six bays, whose stone has recently been cleaned throughout. The Gothic vaults of presbytery and crossing have pleasing curvilinear ribs. Thirteen km to the north of Carrascosa on C202 is the quiet agricultural town of **Huete**, once a stronghold of the Moors and later a possession of Catherine of Lancaster's. Under John II the place was advanced to the rank of city. There are several monastic and religious foundations, all very decayed. The largest of these is the Convento de la Merced, whose seventeenth-century sandstone church with giant pilasters gives on to the square of the same name. Half-way up Calle Mayor on the right is the Convento de Jesús; the church here has a well-proportioned and richly-carved Renaissance portico attributed to Alonso Berruguete. Among the sons of Huete was a certain Alonso Díaz de Montalvo who, on the orders of Ferdinand and Isabel, codified the laws of Castile. He took four years to carry out this work, which was called *Ordenanzas Reales de Castilla* and was printed in 1485 on a press brought to Huete for this purpose alone and carefully dismantled when the job was done. One didn't leave such potent machinery around for anyone to use. When I remarked in the town hall on the fine church at neighbouring Carrascosa, they smiled condescendingly and said, 'Ah, but *they* haven't got anything else!' From here C202 continues, crossing N320 to Priego (see p. 361). Those returning to Cuenca are advised to rejoin N400 at Carrascosa.

Cuenca – Fuentes – Carboneras – Arguisuelas – Yemeda – Villar del Humo (and return)

The main object of this itinerary is to see the cave paintings I mentioned in the Archaeological Museum. Throughout this book I have made it a fundamental rule to speak of nothing I have not seen myself. This is the first exception. Owing to my sprained ankle I couldn't make the trip but I am assured by the director of the museum that it is well worth making. Access is not easy. One starts out on N420 for Teruel. At 18 km is Fuentes, whose church of La Virgen del Rosario has a Romanesque apse similar to that of Arcas. 26 km farther on is Carboneras from where a local road must be taken southwards past Arguisuelas to Yemeda. Here there is a turning to Villar del Humo, where a guide should be obtained, as the rest of the journey to the caves – called Peña del Escrito and Selva Pascuala – can only be made by donkey or on foot. The best person to consult in the village is the municipal judge (*Juez Municipal*), who is also the local schoolmaster (*Maestro Nacional*). Obviously, the attempt is best not made by those who have no Spanish.

Cuenca – Villalba de la Sierra – Las Majadas – Parque Cinegético Experimental Hosquillo – Tejadillos – Río Cuervo – Tragacete – La Toba – Ciudad Encantada – Villalba de la Sierra – Cuenca

I was also unable to undertake this circuit of about 150 km (with an extra 24 km to and from Ciudad Encantada) owing to my wretched ankle. It is the only other exception to my general rule. The strange natural rock formations of Ciudad Encantada, the so-called 'Enchanted City' are already well-known but the wild life park of Hosquillo is not. The entrance is 8 km after the village of Las Majadas and the total extent is about 2500 acres along the upper reaches of the river Escabas. The road through the park leads to viewing platforms over the animal compounds and there is even a footbridge over the bears. The route continues to the source of the river Cuervo, said to be very beautiful, near Tejadillos. The return journey via Tragacete (where one can lunch) leads past the turning to Ciudad Encantada through whose fantastically eroded shapes one can wander in the evening (preferably avoiding a week-end).

Cuenca – Villar de Domingo García – Priego – Valdeolivas – Alcócer – Córcoles – Sacedón – Zorita de los Canes – Pastrana

This drive provides a nice balance between the pleasures of Nature and the works of Man. We set off on the Madrid road. After 6 km N320 branches right to Guadalajara. It is possible to continue on this road all the way, crossing the Embalse de Buendía by ferry but it is more enjoyable on balance to circumvent this great reservoir to the north. Accordingly, immediately past Villar de Domingo García we take the road marked to Albalate, which follows the river of this name fringed with market gardens. In Albalate there is a turning to Villaconejos, where we join C202 to **Priego**, a boldly sited town whose church stands up well under the surrounding escarpments and above the river Escabas. This stream, which is fished for trout, here winds through a serpentine canyon called the Straits of Priego with a flat cultivated floor and almost vertical sides. The presbytery of the church has a sixteenth-century vault rising from round columns; the rest has been given a Classical face-lift. The town hall and some of the houses have welcomed the Renaissance with a fervent rustic embrace. There are remains of the old wall and Priego as a whole is a sturdy, healthy-looking place, living off local industries based on wood. We now return to the junction 3 km before the town and take the road to Albendea and Valdeolivas, which takes its name from the olive cultivation that begins just before we reach the village. These olives are short and stunted, more bushes than trees, and they are not planted in the strict military files of their Toledan and Andalusian brethren. An impression of great distances is given by the successive ridges of flat-topped hills receding to the horizon. The predominantly ochre tones of the fields are freshened by the passage of streams lined with poplars, beech and the odd weeping willow. One can understand why the early tribes followed by the Romans and Visigoths should have favoured this easily defensible and well-watered region – once the bed of some immemorial sea – for their camps and settlements. And, though less dramatic, it runs the province of Avila close in terms of natural beauty.

At the entrance to **Valdeolivas** stand two handsome windmills of dressed stone, not yet tarted up for show. The pleasant village has a single-nave Romanesque church with pointed barrel-vault. Beyond it the road offers sweeping and exhilarating views across the Embalse de Buendía, fed by the river Guadiela, to the serried ranks of table-mountains on the other side. Then we come down to **Alcócer** set a little back from the new system of lakes. Here there is a large ungainly transitional church with heavy vaulting whose ribs do not always end where they should. It is an ambitious church to which an ambulatory has been added in the fifteenth century. The tower has a curious belfry, ungainly like the rest but the awkwardnesses of this venerable and rather touching pile are shrouded by the noble trees that surround it and fill the decaying town with bird-song. Eight km farther on is **Córcoles** an earthy village almost camouflaged by its earth-coloured tiles; just below it are the ruins of a once considerable monastery. Thus we descend to **Sacedón** on the neck of land separating the Buendía and Entrepeñas reservoirs, which are jointly glorified in the tourist hand-out as **El Mar de Castilla**. Sacedón is a plain village with a large plain church and may be left on one side. From here the road swoops down towards the dam and carries us right through the rocky bulkhead between the two reservoirs by means of two tunnels. We then enter a series of curves bringing us to the left-hand turning (C204) marked to Sayatón. This road starts off along the banks of the Tagus, which resumes something like its normal size until it runs into the smaller Embalse or Lago de Bolarque, where it is joined by the Guadiela after the latter's distension by the Buendía reservoir. After Sayatón the road again returns to the river, now quite reduced to its natural proportions after the hydraulic tricks it has been subjected to. On the left we soon come to a nuclear power station vaunting its straight lines and smooth curves in red and gleaming silver against the old earth tones and infinitely various contours of the hills. Right by the power station is a road junction. The left turning is marked to Almonacid de Zorita and the right to Pastrana. If time permits, it is worth following the Almonacid road a short distance to the fork marked **Zorita de los Canes**, where there is a ruined castle wrenched by Alfonso VIII from the Castro family and given to the nascent order of Calatrava along with the town of Pastrana. There is a sympathetic little village church just inside the old gate, which opens onto a bend in the Tagus where the water is a healthy green and moves swiftly and confidently after its release from the great lakes upstream. Backing on our tracks to the nuclear cross-roads, we continue the remaining 9 km to Pastrana.

A large Franciscan monastery, prison-like at dusk, rises up on the left 3 km before the town. The fork leading past it also leads to the town centre but it is less confusing to continue on the road. **Pastrana** is impressively situated but like many places of a region that disdains the cosmetic treatment of whitewash it crouches back into the hillside and is barely discernible in fading light. The main square is open on one side with a pleasant view over the river Arias. Facing this is the **Palacio de los Duques de Pastrana**, built in the time of Charles V for Ana de la Cerda, Countess of Mélito. Her children sold it to Ruy Gómez da Silva, intimate of Philip II, whose widow, the celebrated one-eyed Princess of Eboli, was later to be confined to the building – in which she died – on account of her liaison with the King's secretary, Antonio Pérez. The severely symmetrical façade is flanked by two towers and the whole first floor has carved ceilings, the best preserved of which is the one in the room occupied by 'la Eboli', protected as it is by the upper floor of the tower from the damp that has rotted all the rest. The coffered artesonado of the main saloon is in bad shape but the friezes are delightful, displaying the full Spanish Renaissance repertoire of medallions, warriors, satyrs, shields, urns, swags, fruits etc. in unpainted wood. Restoration is planned by the State.

A narrow street runs straight from the palace square to the **Colegiata**. The old doorway has been almost hacked away and the four-bay fourteenth-century church (which preserves its square tower with a little clock-tower on top) is almost completely encased by the later building of 1637 in a transitional Herreran-Baroque style by Fray Pedro González de Mendoza, son of the Princess of Eboli and Bishop of Sigüenza, for the burial of his parents, himself and the future descendants of his house. The retablo by Matías Jiménez is of the same period. The choir occupies three of the four bays and contains a plain set of seventeenth-century stalls – Pastrana supported 48 canons in that century and the church continued in collegiate use until the eighteen-fifties. The trascoro is encumbered with a plaster and paint mock-up of the grotto of Lourdes. The 'treasure' deserves to be seen. In the long sacristy above the handsome vestment chests hang four tapestries woven in Brussels between 1471 and 1476 celebrating the exploits of Alfonso V of Portugal (supporter of the claim of Joan la Beltraneja against Isabel the Catholic) in North Africa. These have been cut down a bit in size but are still among the finest fifteenth-century tapestries in Spain. Their predominant shapes are helmets, mast-heads, spears and the roofs of besieged cities; the main colours are pink, blue and silver, recalling the Honours and Virtues at La Granja (Segovia) – though there are no written legends here. The Moors leave by the back gate of a typically Flemish Tangiers, looking like prosperous unruffled merchants, while the Portuguese conqueror, making no attempt to stop them, enters by the other gate. There is also an outstanding thirteenth-century Crucifixion in natural wood with a rib cage as rigidly formal as a pair of harps.

A short street leads from the church to the tiny Plaza de los Cuatro Caños, where most of the trading and shopping goes on. The fountain has four water-spouts just out of arm's reach and the technique, as at many Castilian pumps, was to use a hollow bamboo cane to direct the water into pitcher or pail, not wasting a drop. We noted the large Franciscan monastery on the way in. The church is sombre Spanish Baroque and from the terrace there is a good view of the town across the tight-packed patches of cultivation. This was one of two convents – the male branch – founded by Saint Theresa; down below near the river is the grotto occupied by Saint John of the Cross who was master of novices here long before the present building was put up. Energetic Theresa's sister foundation for nuns (1569) lasted only a few years, for on the death of Ruy Gómez da Silva in 1573 the activities of the widowed Princess of Eboli made the place unsuitable for a religious order – in fhe eyes at any rate of the reformer of the Carmelite order. So she removed her nuns to a safer place and the Princess brought in another lot, the Conceptionists.

Pastrana – Brihuega – Cifuentes – Gárgoles de Arriba – Gárgoles de Abajo – (Trillo) – Durón – Budía – Tendilla – Lupiana – Guadalajara

From Pastrana C200 continues north-west to join N320 for Guadalajara. 1 km beyond this junction going west is the right-hand turning to **Brihuega**, which has much to recommend it as a centre for excursions in this region, known as the Alcarria. The road follows the pretty valley of the Tajuña until it reaches this extremely pleasant little town, which preserves long stretches of its outer walls and lesser portions of its castle. The Alcarria belonged to the Moorish kingdom of Toledo and it seems perfectly possible that Alfonso VI of Castile came here on hunting expeditions with his host the Toledan King during his exile by his brother Sancho. The longest remaining strip of city wall is on the west and there is also a fine gate called the Puerta de Cozagón. The castle has become the town cemetery and one treads on tombs ancient and modern to reach its chapel. The main church, **Santa Maria de la Peña**, rises on ground that was once embraced by the castle's outer wall. It is a successful and assured building of the thirteenth century, not one of the fumbling ones. Semi-circular arches are used in the nave and pointed ones in the aisles and over the entrance to the sanctuary. The elegant pentagonal apse contains the Virgin after whom the church is named. She was found in a grotto, they say, in the rock face below the building (*peña* is a crag) where there is still a shrine to her, accessible by a modern functional staircase. She is one of those 'black' Virgins of indeterminate date and mysterious origin, usually supposed to have been hidden during the Moorish occupation and rediscovered by some miracle, to which Spain is so addicted.

At the top of the town is the church of **San Felipe**, recently restored by Bellas Artes. The nave consists of five bays leading to a presbytery with a pointed barrel vault terminating in a semi-cupola. A low vault of later date was demolished to reveal the pointed clerestory windows; nave and aisles were then re-roofed in wood in accordance with the original plan. This is another thirteenth-century church of clean design and fine execution. Taking advantage of the town wall which passes near by, a belfry was erected on one of the tubby round towers and connected with the church by a covered passage. In this district there also stands the Puerta de la Cadena with a plaque commemorating the victory of the forces of Philip V in 1710 over the English and Dutch during the War of the Spanish Succession. The battle, fought outside the walls, is generally known as Villaviciosa and was decisive for the Bourbon cause in the Peninsula.

A road climbs past the belfry of San Felipe to a circular building surrounded by cypresses which has been visible from various points below. This was the **Royal Cloth Factory** erected under Charles III in his attempt to stimulate local industries. The looms were set up in the circular naves and the platform outside was used for drying the cloth. In those days the gardens occupied a terraced slope stretching from below the parapet to the now ruined church of San Miguel. When the cloth industry declined and the buildings passed into private hands, the gardens were happily moved up to their present position, where they have been gently maturing for a century and a half. They belong to that charming, romantic type of Spanish garden which is formal but a little unkempt, well-born but down-at-heel. Cypresses are trained into arches but fallen chestnuts litter the paths in autumn. Long dahlia necks and tangles of other flowers rise above the clipped box-hedges. It is a delightful place to stroll in and from the edge there are entrancing views over the Tajuña valley.

Amongst its various delights Brihuega has a good hostelry

called the Princesa Elima, where the food and beds can be recommended. Immediately opposite this is a pointed arch in a stretch of wall with the legend **Cuevas Arabes**. Application to the owner of the adjacent butcher's shop secures admission to this curious warren of subterranean passages with pointed vaults and arches cut in the soft stone, which served no doubt as an emergency communications system between the castle and other principal houses in the place; the Arabs were given to this tunnelling and a similar network was made at Ronda (Málaga) with passages vaulted in brick. Here, at almost every turning there is a large Ali Baba vat and some of these are used by the butcher who is also a cellarman for the storage of his wine; he tells with glee, as he offers one a glass, how some fifty Italians took refuge down here in the Civil War – presumably at the time of the great battle of Guadalajara – only to be hunted down and killed and dumped three or four to a vat by the victorious Government troops.

It is worth making the circuit from Brihuega on C201 via Masegoso to **Cifuentes**, dominated by the old castle of its counts, whose ancestor played an important part in the final war of Granada. A cobbled ramp leads up from the triangular Plaza Mayor to the Plaza de la Provincia overlooked by the ample five-bay parish church, whose four westernmost piers are raised on crude bases of different shapes, covering outcrops of living rock beneath. The altars are poor but there is a fine Gothic alabaster pulpit on the epistle side. The entrance to the baptistery is by a small cusped Romanesque doorway and the west front of the church has a Romanesque entrance with damaged figures, though the outer archivolt conserves some fearsome devils. Forming a right angle with this church is a ruined Renaissance temple with half a belfry (the rest has fallen) which was devoted to Saint Domingo Guzmán, spiritual father of the Inquisition. At Cifuentes one can get good cheap lamb chops at the Fonda. C204 now runs south to Gárgoles de Arriba with a pointed tower and Gárgoles de Abajo with a square tower, whence a left fork leads to Trillo, once a watering place and now a leper colony. From hereabouts the twin peaks called Las Tetas de Viana are clearly visible. *Tetas* (nipples) do not describe them well, unless they have been amputated; they are in fact rather higher and more sharply defined versions of the table mountains we have seen in the province of Cuenca. C204 continues along the western bank of the Embalse de Entrepeñas to the junction with a local road marked to Guadalajara, which we take. The first village on the left is Durón, which is pleasant enough, and a little beyond this is Budía, whose town hall is carried over the pavement by columns capped with rustic Renaissance capitals. 12 km farther on we rejoin N320, which passes through Tendilla, a long village hugging the road. The Count of Tendilla, like his neighbour of Cifuentes, played a significant part in the last phase of the Reconquest, becoming Governor in 1483 of the newly captured and freshly beleagured Alhama de Granada, where his promissory notes to his soldiers became common currency in the shops and are considered to have been in effect the first bank-notes ever issued in Spain. The road rises to the picturesquely sited village of Horche and then descends towards Guadalajara. Another 3 km brings one to a right-hand fork to **Lupiana**, a village deeply set in its valley, above which is a one-time monastery almost hidden in the woods. This belonged to the Jeronymites and is a good instance of a religious building put on the market by Mendizábal in 1836 and bought up by an ambitious layman, in this case the Marquis of Barzanollana, whose bust is to be found in the garden. He and his descendants turned it into a country pleasure-dome. The walls of the ruined church are clad with creepers and enclose a decorative water tank. The rather gloomy gravel walks with statues also provide welcome glimpses of the village and the open valley. The so-called **Patio Hermoso**, once the cloister of the monks, is a sumptuous Renaissance construction. The lower arcade is semicircular with medallions recalling Juan de Badajoz, while the gallery has shallow mixtilinear arches, possibly of Salmantine inspiration. On one side there is a second or upper gallery with bracket capitals more in the style of the Casa de Miranda (Burgos). The architect in effect anthologises the styles of various regions and the date would appear to be between 1530 and 1550. The house is private but the concierge is happy to oblige for a tip.

Guadalajara, capital of a province, is almost bound to come as a disappointment. It suffered terribly in the great battle that was perhaps the major Republican success of the Civil War. Its main – really its only – show-piece is the **Palacio de los Duques del Infantado**, whose façade and patio survived. The famous ceilings – the one covering the Salón de Linajes was the most outstanding with its cornices of stalactites and frieze of choir-stall intricacy – all perished. The building was carried out by Juan and Enrique Guas for the second Duke of Infantado between 1480 and 1492. The main front is regularly studded with stones faceted like diamonds – which will recall to some the Casa de los Picos (Segovia), also attributed to the Guas team. Over the entrance, whose columns and entablature are entirely covered with ball and basket-work motifs, is the shield of the Mendoza family supported by wild hairy men. The upper part of this façade has an external loggia in which pairs of decorated windows with slate shafts alternate with semicircular miradors. As at Manzanares el Real (Madrid) – also by Juan Guas for the same patron – this seems to me a rather successful development of the loggia, hitherto almost unknown in inward-looking and defence-conscious Spanish building, even of the most luxurious sort. The patio arches inside are forerunners of the Salmantine variety. The lower arcade rests on plain Doric columns but the spandrels both below and above are filled with an orgy of heraldry outstripping even the same master's twelve-fold repetition of the royal arms at San Juan de los Reyes (Toledo).

Apart from this palace Guadalajara has only modest offerings. The seat of the bishop of Guadalajara-Sigüenza is at Sigüenza. The brick church of **Santa Maria de la Fuente** has co-cathedral status. It has a handsome Mudéjar tower and two restored doorways of distinctly Arab stamp. The interior has been completely relined in the most anodyne Baroque imaginable. On the opposite side of the road is the curious chapel of Luis de Lucena, which appears from its Moorish-type eaves and toy-fort corner turrets to be a folly of the nineteenth century – it was built in 1540. In the same street as the post office the tall three-bay Gothic brick church of **Santiago** has a skilful apse vault and some blind arcading that seems to indicate Mudéjar craftsmanship. The Capilla de los Zúñiga, with Plateresque altar and niches and a Gothic vault, is by Alonso de Covarrubias, who was also responsible for the entrance with candelabra-columns to the chapel of the **Instituto** on the other side of the street. The other Renaissance entrance in this precinct with military impedimenta on the pilasters is by Lorenzo Vázquez, at one time architect to the great Cardinal Mendoza. Proceeding up the main street past the nineteenth-century town hall, still clinging nostalgically to

Renaissance medallions and warrjors' heads, we find on the left the Baroque church of San Nicolás, which is well enough in its way with connecting side-chapels on the usual Jesuit pattern. Higher up on the right is San Ginés with the mutilated Plateresque mausoleum of Don Pedro Hurtado de Mendoza. We are right in the heart of Mendoza country.

And that is all that needs to be said of Guadalajara, which lies just off NII from Madrid to Zaragoza. The fascinating and little-known hinterland to the north of the main road – including the cathedral cities of Sigüenza and Burgo de Osma and the provincial capital of Soria – deserves a fresh chapter, which will be the last of this book.

CHAPTER TWELVE

Sigüenza and Soria

✤

Guadalajara – Hita – (Cogolludo) – Jadraque – Atienza – Sigüenza

Leaving Guadalajara on NII towards Zaragoza we find after 4 km the left-hand turn (C101) marked to Atienza. As this road carries us north, the flat-topped ridges of the Alcarria splay out behind us like fingers stretched to their utmost but not quite able to take a grip on the plain. 23 km along C101 is **Hita,** clinging to a hill under the remnants of its castle and preserving some stretches of town wall. The place is now almost uninhabited and semi-ruinous. A restored gateway commemorates with a plaque Juan Ruiz, Archpriest of Hita and author of the *Libro de Buen Amor,* popular rhymed essays of the Middle Ages. The Road continues via Jadraque to Atienza. **Cogolludo,** however, at 20 km by a good local road from Hita, has an interesting palace façade. Built for Luis de la Cerda y Mendoza, 1st Duke of Medinaceli (d. 1501), this is one of the earliest works of the Spanish Renaissance. The whole front is of dressed stone in the Florentine style with no windows on the ground floor and six Gothic windows lighting the piano nobile. There is a strong resemblance between the doorway and that of the Colegio de Santa Cruz, Valladolid, restyled by Lorenzo Vázquez for Cardinal Mendoza. This and the fact that Vázquez also worked at Mondéjar and Guadalajara in this region suggest that he was probably the architect. However that may be, there is no doubt whatsoever of the important role played by the powerful Mendoza clan in introducing the Renaissance to Spain. Iñigo López de Mendoza, Count of Tendilla, Ambassador to the Vatican, was responsible for presenting to the court the great Italian sculptor Domenico Fancelli, who carried out the royal tombs at Granada and Salamanca. It is also likely that he introduced Lorenzo Vázquez to his uncle, the Cardinal, and to his relative the Duke of Medinaceli. The interlocking ramifications of Spanish noble families can be tedious to trace but at this period they produced some positive results in the field of architecture.

From Cogolludo the road may be taken direct to Atienza – 7 km beyond the old mining village of Hiendalaencina is a sign to the Robledo de Corpes, site of the famous Afrenta de Corpes in the *Poema del Cid*, where the Infantes de Carrión stripped and abandoned their wives in an oak wood (cf. p. 158). But this route is mostly unsurfaced after Veguillas and the prudent motorist will return to Hita and continue via **Jadraque**, whose grey stone castle, a long thin one rising on a conical hill, is faintly reminiscent of Peñafiel. C101 leads on to **Atienza**, an ancient feudal stronghold which – unlike Hita – has been taken in hand. The main gate, consisting of a tunnel with four pointed arches, leads from the lower square with the town hall to an upper plaza which has been persuasively rebuilt. On one side of this is the fine big parish church with nave and aisle vaults of the same height containing a pair of small Renaissance retablos with charmingly vivid painted panels. The castle is perched on living rock and within the limits of its outer wall is a church with a decent Romanesque apse. Knightly doorways, overhanging eaves and a rustic bullring of poles and joists complete the picture. We now take C114 from Atienza to Sigüenza. Some 5 km before the cathedral city is the turning to **Palazuelos**, a little fortified villa still surrounded by an almost complete mediaeval wall.

If Guadalajara disappoints, **Sigüenza** exceeds expectation. The castle and cathedral still possess the skyline and everything is subordinate to them. The name of the town is derived from ancient Segontia, which lay a little to the north-east. The Visigoths seem to have preferred the site of the castle, which became in due course the Moorish alcazaba. This was taken from Islam in 1123 and the diocese was founded in the following year. The **Cathedral** can be seen in its entirety from a distance, a well-composed mass with twin fortress-like west towers, low square lantern and thin elegant south-east tower, all rising without any competition above the clustered roofs of the town. The west towers make a particularly strong impact, for they are to all intents and purposes identical (the one with the belfry is in fact a metre or so lower than its fellow), having been faithfully completed at a later date in accordance with the original design. French influence is predominant, though tempered with Spanish gravity. The first Bishop was Bernard de Agen, a nominee of the powerful Bernard de Sédirac, Abbot of Sahagún and later Archbishop of Toledo. He was succeeded by Pierre de Leucate who began the church and died in 1168, leaving funds for the completion of chevet and transepts. When consecration took place in 1169, the work probably consisted of five parallel apses, the crossing and transepts, all rising to a lower level than at present. Sanctuary and transepts were then raised and covered by sexpartite vaults, possibly the earliest in Spain.

The nave, begun in 1192, seems to have been laid out under Bishop Cerebrun of Poitiers and continued as then planned, for the towers standing outside the aisles and forward from the west front are directly based on Poitiers cathedral. The work went on throughout the thirteenth century. Slightly pointed arches are used for the clerestory windows, though the side columns are essentially Romanesque, as are the corbel tables under the eaves. The south-east tower is a happy addition of about 1300. It comes as a surprise to learn that the attractive low lantern, which seems such an essential part of the whole composition, was put up after the destruction of the crossing vault in the Civil War. As the crossing and sanctuary vaults were rebuilt between 1468 and 1495, it is not known whether the original design included a lantern, but the modern architect has certainly recaptured the spirit, if not the form, of the earlier building with notable success. The outside as a whole is remarkably homogeneous, though one regrets the addition of a Neo-Classical porch in 1797 to the south transept and the Baroque panel of the investiture of Saint Ildefonso with the chasuble over the west door – this subject is almost boringly repetitive in Spanish iconography and could have been dispensed with here. The stone, alternating between yellow and red ochre, gives the building a pleasing warmth. The towers, appropriately, are a little greyer and grimmer than the rest.

Entering from the west, we find ourselves in a nave of four massive bays. The trascoro with its twisted columns strikes the first discordant note. Proceeding up the aisle on the epistle side (this has no side-chapels) we reach the south transept, from which we can appreciate the bold sexpartite vaulting of both transepts and sanctuary and the fine consonance with the old design of the new lantern. The rose-windows also glow pleasingly though their glass is not original. Here, at the core of the church, one cannot help remarking that while both the eastern piers and the south-west pier of the crossing are enclosed by clusters of columns, the north-west pier and the next pair of nave piers are simply circular drums; the remainder of the nave reverts to the cluster principle. The first big structural disappointment is that all the parallel apses, apart from the Capilla Mayor, were demolished to make way for a disappointingly dark ambulatory, erected between 1567 and 1606. This is covered by sections of coffered barrel-vaulting and contains five conch-shaped recesses with as many altars.

Following the ambulatory round, we emerge in the north transept whose elaborate decoration must have already caught the eye. This area of the church – which is distinctly reminiscent of the Arco de Jamete, Capilla de Muñoz and Capilla de Albornoz occupying the identical part of Cuenca Cathedral – might well be called Covarrubias Corner. The main feature is this versatile architect's Plateresque monument in painted stone to Santa Librada, patroness of the diocese. The relics of the saint are contained in an urn protected by a grille on the second floor, so to speak, of this fancy construction, whose main recessed arch houses a little retablo with six Mannerist panels of her life and martyrdom. The east wall of the transept is filled by another large monument, also by Covarrubias, to Don Fadrique of Portugal, who became bishop of the diocese. To the left of the saint's mausoleum is a Baroque door in a Plateresque frame leading to the elegant but rather cold cloister built by Alfonso de Vozmediano between 1503 and 1508 and notable for its tall Gothic windows of three lights. The Summer chapter-house opening off the cloister has a flat painted Mudéjar ceiling studded with gold stars. Among its contents are a no-more-than-average collection of Flemish seventeenth-century tapestries, some interesting manuscripts and a plaster reproduction of the beaten silver container of the patron saint's remains, now lost to sight in the depths of Covarrubias's grandiose casket.

If we return to the crossing, we can now visit the **Capilla Mayor** with its seven tall windows separated by web-like vaulting ribs. The retablo was made by Giraldo de Merlo between 1609 and 1611. On the epistle side is the tomb of Cardinal Albornoz with some of his relations below him. The pulpits are worth notice. Both are of alabaster and the one on the gospel side is in the Renaissance taste, while the other is Gothic on a budding Renaissance stem. Turning to the **Coro**, we find a good set of 'geometrical' Gothic stalls not unlike those of Miraflores and Oña. These were ordered by Cardinal Mendoza, who retained the bishopric of Sigüenza even after his elevation to the primacy of Spain. The carving was carried out before 1491 by Rodrigo Duque and Francisco de Coca. The canopy of the episcopal stall may be by Rodrigo Alemán, who was at this time carving his great series of stalls for the Cardinal at Toledo. The painted balustrade appears to date from the Covarrubias régime. Leaving the choir, one notices against the south-west pier a painted alabaster image called the Virgin of the Milk – she too belongs to the period of Renaissance innovation that ran like wildfire through the stern old building.

We have yet to see the show-piece of the Cathedral. This is the famous **Tomb of the Doncel**, Don Martín Vázquez de Arce, in the Capilla de San Juan y Santa Catalina, founded by the Arce family. He died in 1486 under the Duke of Infantado during the final war of Granada. The tomb, commissioned by his parents who lie in the same chapel, shows him reclining at ease on one elbow, unconcernedly leaving the weeping to the page at his feet. The sculptor is unknown and it is also uncertain when or why the term *doncel* – masculine of *doncella*, maiden, and used in the fifteenth century for members of a corps of court-trained pages of tender years, aspirants to knighthood – came to be applied to a young man already knighted, who was 25 when he died and left a daughter behind him. Probably the term was first applied by some nineteenth-century romantic, moved by the plain cap, 'page-boy' haircut and a certain air of youthful melancholy in the features. However the name came about, the figure with its posture of refined lassitude can well be taken as a swan-song in stone of the Middle Ages. In the same chapel lies Martin's brother, who became first Bishop of the Canaries, and in the chapel sacristy are parts of the original retablo mayor by the Master of Sigüenza (the rest is in the Prado).

The north aisle chapels are not of the greatest interest though the **Capilla de la Inmaculada** has an extraordinary entrance arch in which Mudéjar tracery is combined with elements from the Florentine Renaissance and the whole is

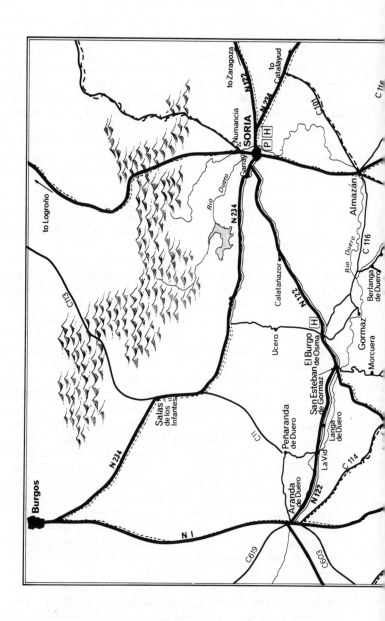

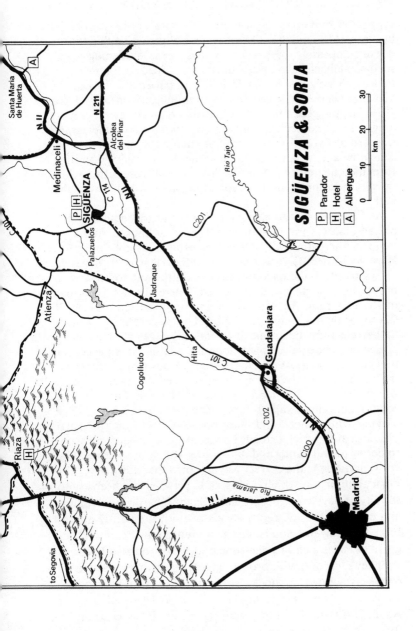

SIGÜENZA & SORIA

P Parador
H Hotel
A Albergue

km
0 10 20 30

Santa Maria de Huerta
N II
A
Medinaceli
N 211
Alcolea del Pinar
C 114
SIGÜENZA
P H
Palazuelos
Atienza
Riaza
H
to Segovia
Cogolludo
Jadraque
Hita
C 201
N II
Rio Tajo
C101
Guadalajara
C102
C100
N II
Rio Jarama
N I
Madrid

topped off by Gothic crest-work. The date would seem to be between 1510 and 1520. The Mudéjar filigree is so fine that it doesn't appear to be plaster. If it is, some hardening agent such as alabaster dust must have been added to the mixture. In this chapel, besides its founder, is buried the Bishop of Sigüenza who was killed by the Republicans on July 27th, 1936. Stepping back from this chapel into the nave, one can no longer avoid confrontation with the massive and unpleasant trascoro of 1676 with its spiral Solomonic columns of marble. This now acts as an unsuitable shrine for the faintly smiling Romanesque image of Nuestra Señora la Mayor, patroness of the city, who previously occupied the place of honour on the high altar.

At Sigüenza we do not have to peer at inadequately displayed objects forming part of a 'tesoro' or 'museo' in one or more of the cathedral's dependencies as is usually the case. Here the **Museo Diocesano de Arte Antiguo** is sensibly installed in a separate building opposite the south-west tower and is properly catalogued and numbered. There are two paintings of the first rank. In room E is an Annunciation (*65*) by El Greco, belonging to his last period. The Virgin almost appears to be rejecting the proposition of the angel apologetically poised on his dense sculpted cloud but as usual it is the colour that counts and most especially the vigorous white strokes on the angel's wing shivering up to join the celestial radiance with which the Holy Spirit breaks out of Heaven. The adjacent room F contains a superb Inmaculada (*86*) by Zurbarán. The Virgin's white smock and blue robe display the artist's usual plastic genius, which extends impartially and in equal measure to her head and hands and in fact over the whole picture. The crescent moon is the correct way up, or rather down, over the Guadalquivir, on which a ship sails between the horns with the city of Seville on the left and a Spanish garden with palms and cypresses on the right. Heads of putti are lightly adumbrated among the clouds. After the repose of this, as full of grave peace as a child's bed-time prayer, the frenzied Baroque Prophet Elias (*89*) with broken fingers – possibly by Salzillo – comes as a bit of a shock. The patio houses archaeological pieces and two strange big-headed, short-legged figures of Adam (*142*) and Eve (*140*) with fig leaves; Eve's head on its funny short pregnant trunk is beautiful. The pair is ascribed to the late fifteenth century. In the patio also is one of those gadgets that delight the Spanish heart. It is an iron chest of the sixteenth or seventeenth century, whose key inserted in a keyhole in the lid (cunningly masked by a sliding stud that looks exactly like all the rest) turns fourteen tongues at once; there is a false keyhole in the normal position on the front.

The rest of Sigüenza lives up to its cathedral, whose south transept gives onto the rebuilt Plaza Mayor with arches of rounded profile in the old Castilian style. From here Calle Mayor climbs past an ex-convent to the castle, first a Moorish fortress, then a residence of battling bishops. Occupying a commanding position above the town, it is now the Parador Nacional Castillo de Sigüenza. It preserves a fine gatehouse whose twin round towers – known as las Torres Gemelas – are connected by a covered passage over the arch. A stroll in the upper town requires no detailed itinerary. It is enjoyable to wander where the spirit takes one. Probably one will come across an old house in the Travesaña Alta known as the Casa del Doncel. Almost opposite this is the church of San Vicente, whose rectangular presbytery appears to be of the same period as the original chevet of the cathedral. Farther west along the same street is a small plaza with the old prison and near this are two of the city gates – the Puerta de Hierro and Arco del Portal Mayor. Lower down the hill on the south side is a long range of buildings, which includes the seminary and the eighteenth-century episcopal palace. The lowest sector of all has a pleasant shady alameda, at whose east end is the genuinely Baroque church of the Ursuline Convent with a curved front and a gracious raised nuns' choir at the rear. At the town end of this promenade is a *humilladero* or shrine and facing it an excellent two-star hostelry called, inevitably, El Doncel. Enquiries for rooms should be made at the restaurant El Motor just beyond the Banco Central on Calle Calvo Sotelo. Round here are grouped the main bars and restaurants, of which El Motor is the best. The station is in a decent nineteenth century style of railway architecture and even the latest building development near the alameda is quite tolerable. I can find virtually no fault with Sigüenza except that its student population is almost too high – nearly 50% owing to a number of residential colleges – with the result that the flood of youth released at week-ends makes the place unexpectedly noisy. Beware week-ends, therefore, in Sigüenza, which is otherwise ideal for artistically inclined honeymoon couples and for romantic lovers of all ages.

Sigüenza – Medinaceli – Santa Maria de Huerta – Almazán – Soria

From Sigüenza C114 continues to meet NII at Alcolea del Pinar. **Medinaceli,** raised high on a breezy platform above the main road is more remarkable for its exhilarating situation and superb configurations of moving clouds than for its buildings. **The Roman Arch** – whose silhouette is reproduced on all the signposts to national monuments throughout the country – is so sited that it frames and thus seems to lay territorial claim to successive ranges of flattish hills to the south and west. But the sky floats free on all sides, unimpressed by a mere human structure, even one that has survived over two millennia of wind, rain, snow and ice. Vestiges of the wall of the mediaeval villa remain and one of the gates has been rebuilt. The fortress of the Moors has become the cemetery of the Christians. The ex-collegiate church of the sixteenth century with three single-span bays and a polygonal Capilla Mayor has a plain set of seventeenth-century stalls at the rear. An old woman talks aloud to her favourite saint and then suffers visible torment in plucking up courage to ask for alms. The parish priest has painstakingly assembled the rudiments of a museum. On the gospel side of the sanctuary is a tribune gallery by which the ducal family had access to the mass and this is matched by an identical mock gallery on the other side. Flanking the high altar are cupboard-like doors surmounted by the armorial bearings of the dukes of Medinaceli with the pendent lamb of the Golden Fleece; these contain the remains of the first ten dukes, moved from the abbey of Santa Maria de Huerta.

In the church square a courageous Anglo-American couple run an art gallery to exhibit their own works and those of their friends. There is a small foreign colony and a population explosion at the week-ends and on public holidays, for Medinaceli is just near enough to Madrid to attract the jaded lungs of the capital, panting for the air that is freely available here in large, almost intoxicating quantities. The Plaza Mayor is filled on one side by the façade of the ducal palace, plain to dullness; a prettier building is the old porticoed and galleried

Alhóndiga, once the communal grain store and now cultural and tourist headquarters. The place is certainly agreeable enough to wander in but it is always the sky and the great distances that steal the show. The highlands surrounding Medinaceli are, incidentally, a triple watershed. At Yelo, a little to the north-west, a stream is born that runs through Berlanga to join the Duero. To the south near Esteras de Medinaceli rises the Jalón, a tributary of the Ebro, while at Horna a little to the south-west is the source of the Henares, which feeds the Tagus.

At 10 km on a local road, just beyond the village of Ambrona, is the unusual **Museo Paleontológico**, in fact a shed covering an excavated site, which reveals *in situ* the remains of giant elephants dead some 300,000 years. Opinion has come down against this being an elephant cemetery where they came to die of their own accord and it is thought more likely that it was a watering place to which they were driven and then slaughtered by men, while unable to charge. The area has always been known as the hill of bones by local farmers. If the guard is not to be found in his little hut, apply in Ambrona or – on Mondays – to the bar of the weird mid-country railway junction of Torralba where he spends his days off.

From Medinaceli we can proceed north on N111 via Almazán to Soria. However, it is well worth continuing a further 27 km along NII to **Santa Maria de Huerta**. This Cistercian abbey founded in 1162 is still occupied by a small community of Benedictine monks. A sixteenth-century arch leads into an outer yard and immediately ahead is the severe pointed door of the twelfth-century church with remnants of the original colouring and above this a restored rose-window with spokes like a great wheel. On the left is the abbey entrance. The first court or Claustro de la Hospederiá was begun in 1582 on the high tide of the Herreran style. From here we pass into the Domus Conversorum, which was probably the lay brothers' refectory. This is a crypt-like chamber on columns of Romanesque stamp with a slightly pointed vault. The capitals are of the severest and most formalised vegetal variety. The darkening of the ceiling is due to prisoners who lit fires to warm their bones during the Civil War. We are now led into the Claustro de Caballeros with a thirteenth-century arcade, partially blocked in, under a sixteenth-century gallery. Round the walls are sepulchres of the Finojosa and other noble families. Opening off the north-west corner is the Gothic kitchen with a huge central rectangular funnel covering not only the fireplace but the whole workspace of the cooks. This was connected by serving hatches both with the Domus Conversorum and with the great **Refectory of the Monks**, into which we are now shown.

Few imaginations will fail to be seized by this superb hall with its rose-window in the south wall, its sixteen pointed windows (those abutting on the kitchen are blind) in the west wall and the elegant little arcaded staircase in the thickness of the east wall leading to the pulpit. The whole is covered by a very fine example of sexpartite vaulting. There is some doubt whether this preceded or followed Sigüenza's. The most recent chronicler of the abbey, Fray Tomás Polvorosa, dates the building of the refectory after the battle of Las Navas de Tolosa in 1212 with the implication that the work was undertaken in celebration of this important victory. If this is so and if, as some sustain, the high vault of Sigüenza was not raised till after 1226, then Huerta can claim the earliest example of this type of vaulting in Castile.

We now continue by the Staircase of Honour, built in 1600 with a cupola added in 1691, to the upper gallery of the cloister, begun in 1531 and completed in 1547, with its flattened arches combining very successfully with the pointed arcade underneath. The south walk provides good views of the rose-window of the refectory and of the belfry-tower. The sixteenth-century chapter house on this level leads to the raised choir at the rear of the **Church**. The walnut stalls, also of the sixteenth century, have back-rests decorated with designs reminiscent of stamped leather; the lower stalls are divided by caryatids on fluted columns whose heads are topped by cushions supporting the continuous lectern above. The organ of the same period was rebuilt in 1760 with horizontal as well as vertical pipes. From the choir we descend into the body of the church, whose first stone was laid by Alfonso VIII in 1179. Despite a complete Baroque face-lift the lines of a noble building are apparent under the stucco mask and there are plans to strip it back to its original form. It still retains a Capilla Mayor flanked on each side by two parallel apses – a design that was to be superseded at Moreruela (Zamora) by a reversion to the ambulatory and of which a notable example was lost by the conversion of Sigüenza to the ambulatory principle in the late sixteenth century. The dukes of Medinaceli were buried in the sanctuary here before the removal of their remains to the town of their own name. On the way out we are shown the sarcophagus of Jiménez de Rada, who became Archbishop of Toledo in the twelfth century. We emerge under the reconstituted rose-window with its cart-wheel spokes. Before leaving it is worth walking round the outside of the main apse with its tall recessed Lombard bands flanked by the humbler side-chapels – this gives a good idea of the east end of Sigüenza when new. And when Huerta's church has had a good scrape inside, the abbey will constitute the best Cistercian complex in Castile.

Near the abbey there is an Albergue or roadside Parador, where the night may be spent comfortably. Another 7 km along NII in the direction of Zaragoza is a left-hand turning (C116) marked to Almazán. This is a good second-class road leading past Monteagudo de las Vicarías, which conserves clearly the rectangular outline of its old walls on which later houses have grown up, to **Morón de Almazán.** The church here has a Plateresque tower, which is unusual as this style, used often enough for the corner towers of palaces, did not usually extend beyond the retablos and doorways of religious buildings. C116 joins N111 from Medinaceli to Soria at **Almazán,** a strong place in a commanding position on the banks of the Duero. Reconquered from the Moors in 1128 by Alfonso I of Aragón, it gained considerable importance in the Middle Ages. It was one of the towns (which also included Monteagudo) given by Henry II of Trastamara to Bertrand du Guesclin in reward for his services in the civil war against Peter the Cruel. In 1464 it was chosen as the site for a treaty between John II of Castile and the Kings of Aragón and Navarre. And Ferdinand and Isabel honoured the villa with their presence during part of the summer of 1496.

The main square is dominated by the plain façade of the Hurtado de Mendoza palace, which has a charming fifteenth-century gallery at the back over the river. Next to this is the unusual Romanesque church of **San Miguel** (declared a national monument by the Republic in 1931), whose eaves and corbels show Muslim influence. The windows of the octagonal Gothic tower have curious cusped intradoses and this is crowned by a brick belfry in which Mudéjar-type brickwork is put to the service of Classical themes. The interior has nave, sanctuary and transepts in the pointed Romanesque style, while the Muslim influence bursts into full flower in the fascinating lantern-cupola with parallel ribs in the manner of the mosque of Córdoba. In the north transept there is an interesting carved scene of the murder of Saint Thomas à Becket by four knights in chain mail. On the evidence of my travels he ranks as the most popular British saint in Spain. This may be because Queen Eleanor of Castile showed her dislike of her father, Henry II of England, by encouraging the cult of the murdered Becket. The other churches are of rather moderate interest but Almazán conserves some fine gates. The mediaeval stone Puerta de la Villa with a brick clock-tower of 1886 is pierced in a stretch of wall so massive that one is led to think of the Roman walls of Astorga and León. The other gatehouses still standing, both impressive, are called Puerta de Herradoreś and Puerta del Mercado. From Almazán to Soria it is only 36 km on N111.

Soria has been badly afflicted by the building blight that affects all provincial capitals to a greater or lesser degree. The modest domestic architecture and unpretentious civil buildings that left the skyline to the tower of San Pedro, the Gomara palace and Nuestra Señora del Espino have given way to tall unsightly blocks. But some buildings of great interest remain, particularly from the Romanesque period, and the town preserves an earnest, vigorous character quite of its own. One senses, correctly, that the region has been inhabited from the earliest times. As far back as the late Palaeolithic and early Neolithic periods shepherds pastured their flocks on these bald grey hills above the Duero. Nearby Numancia was, as we shall see, the scene of one of the bravest local resistance movements in history. The Visigoths followed the Romans and left a necropolis at Deza. The Moors hung on longer here than in the flatter central zone of the country and Christian repopulation of the region did not take place till the early twelfth century. In 1212 Soria, along with Almazán, Medinaceli and San Esteban contributed an important contingent to the battle of Las Navas de Tolosa.

In civil matters the Fuero Extenso of Alfonso VIII, granted in the same year as the battle, furnished an important 'Common Law' antecedent for the Fuero Real of Alfonso X (1256) The mediaeval town council consisted of four theoretically countervailing powers, namely the Crown officers (*regidores*) the local nobility, the representatives of the urban community (*hombres buenos*) and those of the 150 surrounding pueblos (who were called *sexmeros*). In 1273 the Council of the *Mesta* was founded. This extraordinarily powerful sheep-owners' lobby had its senior branch in Soria. Clerical bodies and noblemen who could not sink to agriculture owned migrant flocks. The *Cañadas Reales* or wide drovers' tracks were the high roads of the Spanish Middle Ages and the routes between Castile and Andalusia were thronged. In the thirteenth and fourteenth centuries Soria, with a significant Jewish colony (over a thousand in 1290), reached its zenith. But after the union of the crowns its importance as a communications centre between Castile, Aragón and Navarre declined. By 1602 its population had shrunk to 6500 and by 1710 to 3300. In 1836, along with the monasteries, the Mesta was suppressed – though sheep-dealing is still a real, sometimes passionate factor in local life, as anyone who frequents the Bar Torcuato in Calle Collado on a Thursday will discover. After a recession lasting for centuries Soria's enthusiastic embrace of the high-rise revolution is at least understandable. Although the new buildings may repel us, the city deserves at least one night. There is a modern Parador Nacional on the castle hill. Personally, I prefer to be down in the town, where there is a considerable choice of cheaper lodgings and restaurants. Food – lamb in particular – and wine are excellent in all categories of restaurant and prices very moderate.

As the city has no very clearly defined centre, let us take the pleasant public park called Alameda de Cervantes, which drives a wedge of green into the western sector. On the south side of this are the old walls of a ruined hospital which have been tastefully cleaned up and illuminated by the town council in a rather empty gesture of conservation. In the middle of the park stands the *Arbol de la Música* or Tree of Music, planted in 1611, round whose trunk a mock-Moorish iron bandstand has been very charmingly built. Near by, still in the park, stands the Gothic shrine of Nuestra Señora de la Soledad and across the road from this, next to the Post Office, is the Provincial Museum – to which we will return. The east end of the park opens on to the Plaza Ramón y Cajal surrounded by modern buildings. Proceeding along Calle Collado, the main shopping street, we come to the Plaza de San Esteban, from which the narrow Calle Aduana Vieja climbs north past some noble houses with armorial bearings to the twelfth-century Romanesque church of **Santo Domingo**.

The west front of this, showing Poitevin influence, is very successfully treated as a whole with a rose-window over the porch and two tiers of blind arcading with columnettes stretching from the centre panel to the corners. The carving of the tympanum, in which God the Father presides with Christ on his lap, and of the archivolts is remarkably intact. Working from the outside inwards we are told the stories of the Passion and Resurrection, of the birth and childhood of Christ from the Annunciation to the Shepherds to the Flight into Egypt, of the Massacre of the Innocents whose childish souls are received by archangels in the centre, while the inner-most archivolt of all is devoted to musicians. Inside, the nave and the old presbytery are covered by pointed barrel-vaults and the aisles have narrow semicircular vaults. The church has been widened at the third bay by Gothic side-chapels and the Romanesque presbytery now leads into a late Gothic Capilla Mayor, which acts as choir for the nuns from the adjacent convent. The easternmost pier of the third bay on the gospel side has very vigorous capitals formed by pairs of griffons and other winged beasts.

Returning from Santo Domingo to the Plaza San Esteban and leaving this by the south-west corner, we come to another Romanesque church, **San Juan de Rabanera,** opposite the Diputación Provincial. The west door comes from the ruined church of San Nicolás and was installed here in 1908. In the tympanum this saint presides; his miracles are repre-sented on the epistle side capitals and those on the gospel side show scenes from the life of Christ. Inside, there is some very curious blind arcading on the right-hand presbytery wall. But it is the outside of the main apse that is the most original feature with its three fluted pilasters separating the two windows that light the interior. The capitals of these windows have a Syrian air and on the same level are two pairs of very strangely decorated panels combining oriental and Christian motifs.

If we now take Calle de Caballeros towards the castle hill, we pass on the right the sixteenth-century former church of San Pedro, which has been absorbed into a barracks. A little beyond this we come to **Nuestra Señora del Espino** combining

Gothic and Renaissance features. Outside the church is the *olmo seco*, the withered elm celebrated by the poet Antonio Machado (1875–1939), who came to Soria as teacher of French in the Instituto, married his landlady's daughter, Leonor, in 1909 and left after her early death in 1911. (For his subsequent career see pp. 255–256.) The dead part of the great trunk is held together with rubble, mortar and nails, but the healthier part still puts out *algunas hojas verdes*, the few green shoots of the poem. Continuing uphill we find that almost nothing remains of the castle, though the modern brick Parador, named after Machado, occupies a fine site overlooking the Duero. This river was so important a source of inspiration in Machado's work that I cannot refrain from attempting a translation of some of his finest lines:

> A wide-winged vulture with majestic flight
> crosses, alone, the pale blue of the sky.
> I devised, far off, a tall sharp peak,
> and a rounded hill shaped like a beaten shield,
> and livid heights above the murky earth
> – the scattered rags of an old suit of mail – ,
> the bald flanks there where the Duero curves
> to bend its archer's crossbow
> around Soria – Soria is a barbican
> upon Castilian soil confronting Aragon.
> I saw the horizons closed by dark
> hills, crowned with oaks and holm-oaks;
> naked screes, the odd humble meadow
> where sheep graze and the bull, with knees
> on the grass, chewed its cud; the river banks
> sporting their green poplars in the summer sun.
> And, silently, far-off travellers,
> so small! – carts, riders, muleteers –
> crossing the long bridge, and beneath the stone
> arcades the silvered waters of the Duero
> turn to dark.
> 　　　　　The Duero crosses the oak heart
> of Iberia and of Castile.

At the highest point of the castle hill there is a dull monument erected in the time of Charles IV but no one with sufficient Spanish should omit to bring the original poem – it is called

A Orillas del Duero and is the second in *Campos de Castilla* –
to this spot and read it here before turning downhill towards
the 'long bridge' over the river.

Just above this bridge – which gave Soria its strategic importance, opening the way to Pamplona and Zaragoza –
stands the collegiate church of **San Pedro**. This (like Santa
Maria of Guadalajara with Sigüenza) shares cathedral status
with Burgo de Osma. The co-cathedral here, however, is of
far greater interest than Guadalajara's. The earlier Romanesque
church was destroyed by fire in 1520 and replaced between
1547 and 1551 by the present very handsome hall-church of
five bays modelled – as we shall see in due course – on the
collegiate church of Berlanga de Duero. The seventeenth-
century tower is distinctly Herreran. Inside, the building is
dark and it takes some time for the eye to pick out the various
retablos: the retablo mayor by Francisco del Río belongs to
the late sixteenth century, while the one on the epistle side is
somewhat earlier, recalling Alonso Berruguete. On the gospel
side is an unusual Rococo confection of great intricacy painted
in bluish white but never plastered or gilded – until one
touches it, it might be alabaster. From the north aisle a flight
of steps leads up to a door, which opens into the very different
world of a twelfth-century Augustinian cloister. Sadly, one
wing of this was taken down to make way for the north wall
of the new church but the other three wings remain. Immediately on the right as we enter is a cusped doorway flanked
by two cusped rose-windows (giving light to the present
Capilla de la Santísima). The main arcade round the cloister
garth is supported on well-separated pairs of columns with
twinned capitals. On the east side these feature vegetal
motifs, winged and snarling beasts and a fine Celtic swirl
spread over two capitals (pier number 6). The west wing, which
seems to be the oldest of the three, has heavier capitals more
solidly joined (see piers 2, 3, and 5). On this side there are also
deep wall recesses lined with columnettes and covered by
pointed barrel vaults, which must have been intended for
tombs. If this cloister is not so rich as Santo Domingo de
Silos (Burgos) it is still a pleasure to wander in and one is not
hustled on, as one is by the busy Silos monks. A local historian
has attributed the capitals to Moorish craftsmen. One may
accept this in the case of the formalised vegetal variety, which
show affinities with the Caliphal style, though it is more

difficult to agree in the case of those of obviously Celtic inspiration.

Leaving San Pedro and crossing the river, we find the turning to **San Juan de Duero** only a few yards beyond the bridge on the left. Here there is yet another cloister, now roofless, of the Spanish Romanesque period, though it appears to be somewhat later than San Pedro's and has a strong Mudéjar flavour. There are as many as four main varieties of arcading resting on various types of pillar and column; at three of the four corners is a pointed horseshoe doorway opening on to the enclosed area of grass. This capricious construction is really delightful and I don't think too much punditry is required to explain such a hotch-potch. It is clearly a sort of folly in which Mudéjar craftsmen were given their head, respectfully imitating some traditional Christian designs, inserting some of their own and letting their imagination rip for the rest. It reflects the open-mindedness and disposition to co-existence of the several communities in Spain in the thirteenth century. Part of the original church remains too and the apse is used to display some archaeological pieces. Below the sanctuary steps is a very interesting pair of templetes or baldachinos supported on clusters of four columns (like those in the cloister). The capitals on the gospel side in particular repay study. In the re-roofed nave there is a good non-figurative Roman mosaic floor from Cueva de Soria.

On the same side of the river as San Juan de Duero the gateway of San Polo leads under a building that once formed part of a Templar monastery to the shrine of **San Saturio**, the anchorite, raised over the cave in which he fasted and prayed. The church was built in 1703 on an elongated octagonal plan and is decorated with murals of 1704–1705 by the local Antonio Zapata. Machado wrote also of this distinctly spooky place. The austere Saturio seems to have found favour with the Sorians, for high up on the town side of the river in front of the chapel of Nuestra Señora del Mirón (reached from the Logroño road) is a kind of totem-pole of curiously mediaeval feeling also dedicated to the anchorite. It was in fact put up in the polite eighteenth century, which virtually appears to have passed Soria by, leaving the old border town to slumber amongst its memories and superstitions and allowing it to choose a most unfashionable hero in the shape of a man who turned his back on the world.

The civil buildings of Soria are mostly modern. The Plaza Mayor, however, is mildly distinguished. The House of the Twelve Noble Lineages (who furnished one of the four estates of the mediaeval council), built in 1628, now houses the Ayuntamiento. Forming a right angle with this is the porticoed building that was formerly the Ayuntamiento and is now the Law Court. On the north side is the church of Nuestra Señora la Mayor built on the site of the Romanesque church of San Gil, whose doorway it retains. Next to the church, passing under a building that used to belong to another of the four estates, the Commons, is the Arco del Cuerno – which served as *toril* when bull-fights were held in the square – leading to the Calle Zapatería. A few yards up this on the right Calle del Común continues to the very large palace of the counts of Gomara, whose façade is 109 metres long with a square tower at the east end. This was finished in 1592. In the right-hand wing there is a first-floor gallery of twelve arches on Tuscan columns and above this an upper gallery of 24 arches in the Ionic mode. But the pure size of the building is the most lasting impression that it makes.

The old Museo Numantino next to the post office has changed its name to **Museo Arqueológico Provincial** but is still in the first place a depository of artefacts from the Celt-iberian civilisation that so heroically resisted the Roman steam-roller sent to crush it, with Scipio Africanus at the wheel. Although there are interesting objects from other civilisations, the most exciting exhibits are the really lovely Celtiberian hand-turned pots of a great variety of shapes and sizes and extraordinarily incisive decoration. Fish, birds, horses, warriors and bogeymen execute a sometimes frightening pattern round the subtle curves. Vultures are particularly important, for it was their sacred role to pick the bones of warriors killed in battle (who should on no account be burned). The best pottery is in the case along the end wall nearest the entrance. A pale ochre and a black are used on the reddish clay. Among many fine examples numbers *11873*, *11970* and *2049* may be noted. In one of the central vitrines the ex-voto bull with tail swished over rump (*6132*) should be seen; so should the tiny mummified bronze figurines and the praying male figurine with erect penis in the same cabinet.

All these artefacts show far greater inspiration and variety than the very standard Roman Terra Sigillata ware and ex-votos by which they were superseded.

Numancia itself lies 7 km from Soria on the right of the road to Logroño and just beyond the village of Garray. It is a bleak place on a mound above the confluence of the Tera and the Duero with dark ominous hills filling all the horizons. A vigorous indigenous culture was achieved here by the fusion of iron-age Celtic skills with those of the Iberian tribes from the valley of the Jalón. The city of some 10,000 inhabitants had streets on the plan of a grid inscribed within a circle. Surrounded by outer walls, it was cleverly laid out so that street junctions did not form perfect crosses with the object of denying direct passage to the bitter winds that blew and still blow over such an exposed site as this. A subterranean chamber or cave formed an important part of every house; for several months a year the climate must have driven the inhabitants into these warmer basements and even the Romans did not disdain the system when they occupied Celtiberian cities.

The peace agreed between Gracchus and the Celtiberians lasted from 179 BC to 154 but Roman abuses led to a rising in the latter year. In the campaign of 153–151 the Consul Nobilius completely failed to subdue Numancia. Marcellus then negotiated another peace but in 144 Viriathus the Lusitanian leader applied for assistance to the Celtiberians, which they agreed to give. In the campaign of 141–140 Quintus Pompeius failed twice to take Numancia – and these were by no means the only defeats suffered by Roman generals in the Numantine war. Finally, in 134, the task was confided to Publius Scipio Emilianus, victor of Carthage, who set about reducing the stronghold in the most business-like way. 60,000 Romans in seven camps cut off the 10,000 Numantines (4,000 of military age) from all connection with the world outside their walls. Supplies ran out. Cannibalism was resorted to. Rather than fall into Roman hands the warriors burned their houses and possessions and fell to mortal combat among themselves, preferring to die on each other's swords than those of the enemy. Much has been written of the horrors of the last days of Numancia. When capitulation took place in late July or early August of 133 only a small remnant of the population remained. Scipio reserved 50 Numantines to grace his Triumph, sold the rest and razed the city to the ground.

Soria – Almazán – Berlanga de Duero – San Baudelio de Berlanga – Gormaz – El Burgo de Osma – San Esteban de Gormaz – Tiermes or Termancia – (Ucero) – Calatañazor – Soria

This very interesting circuit could be made in a day but it would be a rush and it is advisable to plan a night at El Burgo de Osma. Returning to Almazán on N111 we rejoin the Duero and then take C116 along this pleasant valley, never far from the river whose course is always marked by its fringe of poplars. After 28 km we reach the left-hand turning to **Berlanga de Duero**, a villa granted by Alfonso VI to the Cid. Much later in 1529 Charles V raised Juan de Tóvar to the rank of Marquis of Berlanga. The major works of the place are due to this family. The magnificent **Colegiata** was built in only four years (1526–1530) by Juan de Racinas for the first Marquis. Consisting of four bays with aisles, nave and transepts all the same height, this is one of the finest, if not the finest, hall-church in Castile with interlocking curvilinear ribs (reminiscent of the great Juan de Alava) rising from huge round columns. No doubt it influenced the lower, wider and later co-cathedral of Soria (1547–1551) – from which, however, it still wins on points. Here, for instance, there is an original treatment of the Capilla Mayor, which has diagonally sited arches opening up a direct view of the high altar from the transepts. The greater height and light are also to Berlanga's advantage. The huge unpainted Churrigueresque retablo mayor is rather impressive.

The outside mass of the church is satisfyingly plain with hardly any relief but that provided by the articulation of the buttresses. The principal door in the north transept is treated something like those of the west front of Segovia Cathedral (designed 1522) but surmounted by a steep Renaissance pediment. There is a general tendency in Spanish church architecture to conservatism of form combined with novelty of ornament. In the same way that Romanesque for a long time resisted Gothic, conceding only some attributes of the new style but not the spirit, so Gothic resisted the Renaissance allowing the innovations free play only in set-pieces such as doorways, tombs and altars. This is what Plateresque is about. There are no Plateresque cathedrals even in the Plateresque period. It is a rarity to find even a Plateresque church tower, as at Morón de Alamazán. However, there is no doubt that a real national style managed to break through in the hall-churches of the sixteenth century, in which the Gothic vault (to which Spain happily clung) was combined with a Renaissance sense of space without the addition of excessive ornament. Berlanga is a very distinguished example of this period.

The castle with its round towers and thick walls looks as if it means business; only the donjon with its round corner turrets and decorative merlons shows any sign of the fantastication that accompanied the decline of the castle as a serious stronghold. The ruined Renaissance palace below the castle hill on the town side shows the decorative restraint that is common to the rest of the place. The walk or drive to the avenue of young poplars along the river (follow the signs to Campo Deportivo Rodrigo Díaz de Vivar) is worth while for the views it affords of the castle with its curtain wall, the palace and the church. The main square and many of the streets of Berlanga are lined with porticoed houses on hefty wooden supports, making an appropriate foil to the grander buildings.

A few kilometres to the south-east of Berlanga is the eleventh-century Mozarabic church of **San Baudelio de Berlanga**. One must continue past the sign to this as far as the village of Caltojar and there seek out Félix el Molinero, who holds the key. He is a cheerful character who will offer or accept a drink with equal pleasure and proudly boasts that he still mills his grain in a thirteenth-century mill powered by water. He will probably insist on showing the church of Caltojar itself which has an unusual double arched entrance unsupported by a central column and a pointed Romanesque nave with very formalised capitals, mainly of the vegetal variety. After a glass or two at the main bar we can proceed with our real object. The structurally fascinating San Baudelio is also a tragic witness to collectors' greed. In 1922 – five years after its official declaration as a National Monument – an international dealer acquired the frescoes for the United States. Six of these have now found their way back to the Prado but in the little church nothing but the faded traces remain and the building seems to have lost heart ever since the rape. Even so, it is of singular interest, if only for the unusual nave construction of eight radial horseshoe arches on a central column; at the west end there is also a gallery raised over nine miniature vaulting compartments on 18 columns. This has been supposed to be for women or for a choir but a more likely explanation seems to be that it served the hermit (whose cave opens off the church) and his disciples, for it is extended by a little barrel-vaulted oratory with one tiny horseshoe window in which only one kneeling person can fit.

We now return through Berlanga to C116 and continue towards El Burgo de Osma. After a few kilometres in this direction we find a left-hand turning via Quintanas de Gormaz to **Gormaz**. The castles or fortified towns along the Duero were of the greatest importance to the Christians once the Reconquest had reached and consolidated itself on this line. Here, on a thin spine above the river, is the ruin of a Moorish fortress taken by Alfonso VI and granted by him, like Berlanga, to the Cid. It is of enormous size and when first seen against the light it is hard to believe it is not a jagged natural formation. It still conserves a double Moorish arch in the south wall and from almost any point on the grass plateau enclosed by the walls there is an immense view – to the north as far as the Sierra de la Demanda and to the south-west as far as the Guadarrama.

From Gormaz a local road leads direct to **El Burgo de Osma**, a town that rivals Sigüenza in charm and interest. The nearby Cerro del Castro was settled by the Celtiberians and later by the Romans. In the Middle Ages the town of Osma moved down on to the river Ucero where there is still a small hamlet with a mediaeval bridge. San Pedro de Osma, who was Bishop from 1101–1109, caused a cathedral to be built on the other side of the river and this was the origin of El Burgo de Osma, now a sober Castilian villa with porticoed houses carried over the pavements on wooden pillars. To an unprepared visitor it might come as a surprise that the many accretions to the **Cathedral** conceal a very pure Gothic church. The large eighteenth-century sacristy with its slate-hung tower conceals most of the chevet. From the Plaza de San Pedro on the south side two of the windows of the sanctuary are visible – they are the only external sign of the Romanesque period. But the hard core soon shows through. The great south door with very beautiful statues speaks of the influence of Burgos, despite its recession under a Renaissance coffered barrel vault and balustrade. The south side of the nave has flying buttresses with figures and finials added in the late fifteenth century; these are cleverly echoed by the pinnacles of the great Baroque tower. Designed and built by Domingo Ondategui between 1739 and 1744, this must be accounted one of the most successful works of its time because its Baroque inspiration is total – it is no mere accumulation of fashionable mannerisms – yet the large plain panels under the cornice do not quarrel with the rest of the building. A walk round the north side is not feasible owing to the houses and gardens, though the tower soars into view again when we reach the canal and a stretch of the old town wall is also visible from here.

The present church was started in 1232 and completed in its essentials about 1300. The plan may derive from Cuenca and some of the details from Burgos, but the first impression inside is of a plainer and purer building than either of these. There are five bays and the absence of a triforium leaves an expanse of plain stone between the tops of the nave arches and the moulding running under the clerestory windows. A rather cold ambulatory was added by Juan de Villanueva between 1772 and 1781, giving access to the same architect's circular Neo-Classical chapel in honour of the Venerable Juan de Palafox – at the time it was hoped that this ex-bishop (who also became Viceroy of Peru) would be canonised but the claim did not prosper and the gilt and porphyry rotunda remains without its saint.

The choir occupies the second and third bays from the west, leaving two clear nave bays to the crossing. The **Capilla Mayor** is, or was, lit by seven tall windows of pronounced Romanesque stamp belonging to the very earliest stage of the building. These are partly obscured by the retablo mayor by Juan de Juni, Juan Picardo and Pedro Andrés. This large construction, devoted to the Virgin, is certainly arresting. Her death is represented in the central scene with Saint Peter holding her hands in Juni's best pathetic manner. On the left of this is the mystical embrace of Saint Joachim and Saint Anne (the Virgin's parents); on the right the Annunciation . . . and so on upwards. There is no doubt that Juni is best seen in a big framework like this, where the rather 'ham' vigour of his expressions and gestures does not immediately capture the attention. Both high altar and choir are enclosed by fine grilles made by Juan Francés from Toledo.

The north transept seems to be the favourite stamping-ground of high fantasy in Spanish cathedrals. One has only to think of the Escalera Dorada at Burgos, the Arco de Jamete at Cuenca and the confections of Covarrubias at Sigüenza. El Burgo de Osma is true to form with the double staircase (1530–1547) in brass, porphyry and painted stone leading to the curious rather than beautiful chapel of San Pedro with a Baroque lantern-cupola over a Rococo baldachino containing the casket with the patron saint's remains. All this is in the wildest imaginable contrast to the chamber immediately underneath housing his earlier tomb – where we begin the visit of the cathedral's treasures conducted by an erudite enthusiast, Don Tomás Leal. The chamber itself is remarkable with nine transitional vaulting compartments resting on four columns whose capitals perform a 45° twist from their bases and two recently uncovered Romanesque double windows on spiral central columns communicating with the cloister.

This is the setting of the **Tomb of San Pedro de Osma**, one of the most moving painted stone productions of the thirteenth century. The saint lies with his head turned slightly to one side. His pillow is held by angels singing from scrolls, while along the edge of his robe on the right crouch the halt, the lame and the blind whom he cured or helped in his lifetime. The right-hand face of the casket shows the upsetting by the devil of an evil knight who sallies out to bar the passage of the saint and a canon. The foot shows the saint administering a fish to a sick man, while the left-hand panel depicts him freeing a priest from prison, casting out a devil, drawing water from an oak and finally dying – in a niche near the corner sits a scribe writing his life. The head of the casket shows the coffin borne by a horse from Palencia, where he died, to El Burgo. Immediately above this are three bishops including himself raising the lids of their coffins in protest at the burial of an unorthodox bishop beside them, while under the pillow is a charming rural drinking scene. This tomb was carved in 1258 and has no rivals of its period, except perhaps those of Villalcázar de Sirga (Palencia).

From the burial chamber we are led to the **Museum** of four rooms. In addition to some interesting fifteenth-century panels by the first and second Masters of Osma, the cathedral has the best collection of Codices in Spain after the Escorial, consisting of 221 items; also 87 early printed books and a goodly number of illuminated *cantorales*. A selection is always on display. One of the show-pieces is a version of 1086 of the Mozarabic commentaries written by el Beato de Liébana in 784; this is usually open at a fascinating double-spread Mapa Mundi of the period. A document of 1211 is said to be extremely similar in calligraphy to the *Poema del Cid* and it is now held in some quarters that the poem was written not about 1150 as was previously accepted but in 1207. The fourth and last room is mainly devoted to vestments and it is interesting to note that San Pedro, the titular saint, wore an Arab robe and that his winding sheet was of Persian material. This is one of the better cathedral museums; with the church itself and other dependencies the visitor should allow two hours, arriving preferably at midday or four in the afternoon.

Leaving the museum we pass through the cloister, begun in 1510, still in the Gothic style with very tall windows of fine perforated tracery on slender shafts enclosing eight narrow lights. Traces of an earlier Romanesque church have been uncovered and can be seen on strolling round the cloister. Among the dependencies, the large eighteenth-century sacristy (where Don Tomás should be sought) is beginning to droop from Baroque into Neo-Classical. The Capilla del Cristo del Milagro between the north transept and the ambulatory has a recumbent alabaster Christ of the School of Gregorio Fernández and a Romanesque Crucifixion of the eleventh century. The trascoro has a Renaissance screen built for Bishop Acosta (who also commissioned the retablo mayor). Berruguete and Juni have been suggested as possible authors of this work, which is dedicated to the Archangel Michael, but it shows neither the vulgarity of Juni nor the mighty wind that blew through Berruguete's best pieces. The episcopal palace just beyond the Cathedral on the left of Calle Mayor is without distinction, though the double cusped entrance arch surrounded by a Gothic label is worthy of notice.

Continuing along Calle Mayor we come to the Plaza Mayor with the **Hospital de San Agustín** facing the town hall. This building makes a significant contrast with the total Baroque of the cathedral tower, for it is essentially a reversion to the plain Herreran style with some Baroque features superimposed – one may mention the Escorial-type slate spires with added

Baroque scrolls, the elaborate episcopal shields and the central panel-and-pediment with Solomonic columns framing Saint Augustine which breaks the roof line. Inside, there is a Baroque dome over the main staircase and a richly decorated lantern raised on a drum over the chapel. The other major building of El Burgo is the **Colegio de Santa Catalina** on the main road, built between 1551 and 1554 for the same Bishop Acosta who patronised Juni in the Cathedral. The patio is harmonious with hardly any decoration except for the Bishop's arms. Having splashed in his church, he tightened his purse-strings and kept his college plain. Nearby, also on N122, are two very adequate road-houses, either of which will serve for a night.

Sixteen kilometres to the north of El Burgo is the village of **Ucero** with the ruins of a castle rising above the confluence of the rivers Ucero and Lobos. Tucked into the gorge of the Lobos in a picturesque setting is a thirteenth-century chapel erected by the Templars and now dedicated to Saint Bartholomew. This road continues north to join N234 for Burgos. If we head west from El Burgo de Osma on N122, we soon reach **San Esteban de Gormaz** with another castle in the Duero chain. In this case the ruins crown a formation reminiscent of the Mappin terraces in the Regent's Park Zoo. There are two interesting Romanesque churches here, both towards the west end of the long thin town. **San Miguel** (take Calle Mayor from the plaza and third turning on the right) dates from 1081 and may thus claim to be the first church in this region to introduce an atrium or porch running all along the south side in the manner of the Segovian churches. (San Salvador, Sepúlveda, with the same arrangement, dates from 1093.) The inside is extremely plain with a wooden tie-beam roof and later choir gallery at the rear. The higher church of **Nuestra Señora del Rivero** is on a more luxurious scale with a barrel-vaulted presbytery ending in a semi-cupola with traces of black, grey and ochre painting. There are weird bird-beast figures on the capital to the left of the sacristy door and the entrance has capitals carved with a serpent, a monkey and a bird of prey pinning down two other birds. But the long southern porch is less complete than San Miguel's.

San Esteban de Gormaz is the best point of departure for an excursion to the Celtiberian Termes, now called **Tiermes** or **Termancia** (probably for no better reason than the consonance with Numancia). The distance from San Esteban is 34 km to the south via Morcuera and Montejo de Tiermes. The road is good and the journey worth while if only for the views, the sensation of vast space and the vicarious escape from the present afforded by the unchanging rhythm of the herdsman's life and the distant unemphatic horizons. The horizons do not limit; they just imply yet more space. At Montejo the road branches left and after another 3 km there is a right fork, which we take. A small Romanesque church with the characteristic southern porch tells us we have arrived at our destination. Tiermes, though occupied and touched up by the Romans, is fundamentally a rupestrian city, most of whose dwellings were underground. But this does not mean it is merely a warren of communicating caves. Far from it. Steps were cut down into chambers and slots made to receive floor or roof timbers. Ramps were carved through the natural walls to permit the passage of wheeled vehicles; there is even a circus shaped largely out of the living rock. Quintus Pompeius failed to take the place in 141 after his earlier failure at Numancia and it did not finally fall to the Romans till 97 BC. After the Roman occupation its very existence was forgotten for centuries. The guardian is extremely proud of the lettuces he grows in a silted-up Celtiberian home – and of the whole half-buried city which is in effect his.

On the return journey from San Esteban de Gormaz to Soria, **Calatañazor** should not be missed. The left-hand turning to this stranded mediaeval village comes up 27 km after El Burgo de Osma going east. The remains of the castle stand proudly above the beautiful valley floor, a secret valley almost, enclosed by a grisly sierra and known to this day as el Campo de Batalla – for here it was, according to local tradition, that the fearsome Almanzor, the scourge of Spanish Christendom, received a mortal wound that brought about his death near Medinaceli in 1002. In the Plaza Alta is a rollo or stone marker indicating the place of Council and Justice. A little lower down is the church of **Santa Maria del Castillo** with a Romanesque doorway inside a curious moulding with Celtic-type decoration; above this is a tiny triple blind arcade with a cusped arch in the centre and set into the wall on the right is a pre-Romanesque stone carved with three low-relief panels of uncertain meaning. These enigmatic pieces all combine to endow Calatañazor with an aura of great antiquity.

The present late-Gothic church has been raised on Romanesque foundations. In the sacristy the parish priest has put on view an interesting series of royal documents confirming the fuero of the town, though the last of these signed by Charles V is no more than a demand for taxes. In that reign community rights perished.

The Roads from Soria

In the Middle Ages, as we have seen, Soria was of considerable strategic importance and it is still the centre of a useful network of roads that allow the traveller a wide choice of routes. Looking eastwards towards Aragón, N122 leads via Tarazona to Zaragoza, while N234 also leads to the Aragonese capital via Calatayud. Northwards from Soria N111 climbs over the Puerto de Piqueras at 1710 m towards Logroño, Pamplona and the Pyrenees. The north-westerly route follows N234, which joins NI only 9 km south of Burgos. This also gives an opportunity for anyone who has not visited Santo Domingo de Silos, Covarrubias or Quintanilla de las Viñas (see Burgos chapter) to take in these interesting places on the way home. Making for the centre, N110 diverges from N122 at San Esteban de Gormaz and leads via Ayllón and Riaza (see Segovia chapter) to Segovia or Madrid. If N122 is followed directly westwards from San Esteban it brings one to Aranda de Duero on NI and this will be the final route described in this book.

Soria – (El Burgo de Osma) – (San Esteban de Gormaz) – Langa de Duero – Peñaranda de Duero – Aranda de Duero

The first town on N122 after San Esteban de Gormaz is **Langa de Duero** with a square keep, Gothic-Renaissance church, wood-framed houses with overhanging eaves and – slightly to the south – a fine mediaeval bridge over the river. But the place is so strung up with wires and cables and transformers and lamp-fittings in the earnest scramble to keep up with the times that it has lost most of its charm. **Peñaranda de Duero** 7 km to the north of the road via La Vid is worth the short detour. On the road from La Vid there is a fine view of the castle and the ex-collegiate church. Entering by the town gate, we find ourselves in the Plaza Mayor, which has been taken in hand by Bellas Artes. As a result it is not enmeshed in hideous light cables like Langa, though the carefully exposed timbers have a slightly mock-Tudor air.

On the left is the grand Renaissance **Palacio de los Condes de Miranda**. This sums up beautifully everything we have seen of civil Renaissance architecture in Spain. The best synthesis, as I have suggested at Berlanga, of native and imported elements was made in the hall-churches. The best secular façade was probably that of the university of Alcalá de Henares. The large town houses are mostly awkward customers with – often charmingly – unassimilated features from the Muslim, Gothic and Italianate worlds. This palace is no exception. A very elaborate doorway is topped off by a statue of Hercules and pretty swags on which putti swing lightheartedly. The piano nobile windows have Plateresque frames. The staircase roof combines the Moorish honeycomb with Renaissance coffering. The heroic heads in medallions so dear to the period decorate the patio. The main floor is characterised by plaster friezes of Mudéjar inspiration and wooden coffered ceilings. The one in the dining hall is supported on honeycomb corner squinches; the window and door surrounds are Plateresque or Mudéjar; the fireplace is Plateresque and the musicians' gallery has a Gothic screen. The third reception room along the front is covered by a small *media naranja* carved wooden dome that might have come from Seville. All this is the product of a culture in a whirl, self-confident and arrogant but needing to impress and grabbing everything stylistically to hand. The disillusionment of the late sixteenth century and the seventeenth was to find expression in a plainer style but to the magnates of the day and their decorators nothing, not even the most bizarre hotchpotch, could have seemed far-fetched in a country that had in sober fact struck gold beyond the seas.

Facing the palace is the sixteenth-century church of generous proportions with an entrance façade of 1722. One has the impression of fine space but poor detail – confirmed by the cheap standard Neo-Classical altars of wood and plaster. The choir stalls are also of poor quality. By the time of their making the glory had departed and the long decline set in. In the plaza outside is a handsome Gothic rollo and the streets have a strong mediaeval flavour still. The only pharmacy conserves the outward aspects of a *botica* of the eighteenth century and there is a small charge for admission to its 'museum'.

From Peñaranda one can return to N122 at Valdecondes or proceed on C111. Both routes lead to **Aranda de Duero** on NI. The filling-station, road-house face that this thriving town presents to the main road conceals an old core, accessible through the arch under the new town hall just north of the bridge. From the Plaza del Caudillo it is only a few steps to the **Plaza de Santa Maria**, whose parish church has a splendid Isabelline-Gothic portico strongly reminiscent of those in Valladolid. This work is usually attributed to Simón de Colonia about 1510. The figure in the travelling habit on the left of the entrance is Saint Jerome. The carved wooden doors are original. The church, which is rather earlier than its great south doorway, is of handsome proportions and contains a carved Renaissance pulpit in natural wood. Just to the west in the same quarter of the old town is **San Juan** with an unusual entrance of eight slender unadorned archivolts. The Baroque retablo incorporates six very good Gothic carvings of the life and death of Saint John, survivors from an earlier altarpiece.

And there we are, dear Companion, back on the main north-south artery, free to turn north to Burgos or south to Madrid, safely back on the highway after our immersion in the older world that most Spaniards would like – if not to forget – at least to set aside as a tourist attraction, a museum without walls, a source of national inspiration and pride if you like, but not, dear God, a way of life! Well, those of us who remember the aching distances of the Tierra de Campos and the dust bowl of La Mancha and the bitter winds of Soria and the shepherds in their blankets and the yawning afternoons in pueblos to the click of dominoes and the rattle of dice will take their point and respect their choice. But our point is not their point. Our slavery to the industrial civilisation we have created compels us to seek space, light, air and architecture that stands up properly against the sky. I will end, therefore, by restating the great experiences that Spain still has to offer. The Church has always been the lodestar of the Spanish imagination, so it is not surprising the greatest buildings are churches and monasteries. Then, there is something peculiarly satisfying about almost all the landscapes – however harsh – from the Old Castilian steppes to the massy

Guadarrama and from the delightful contrasts of the province of Avila to the prehistoric subaqueous contours of much of New Castile. In Spain, building, light and landscape fuse as nowhere else. And in the *interior* of the country people are still themselves. And we are still ourselves. We have not been fed on a conveyor belt into a cynical holiday machine and we have met Spaniards who have not been sucked into the boom. Probably we have found them extraordinarily helpful and touched by our interest in their heritage. Almost certainly very few readers will have had time to follow my whole circuit. But that is to the good, for it means – I hope – that they will come back for more.

Appendices

Chronological Table

DATES	CIVILISATIONS AND RULERS	POLITICAL AND MILITARY EVENTS	ARCHITECTURE AND THE ARTS
	Iberian Civilisation	Ancient Greek historians called the inhabitants of the north-east region of Spain Iberians – probably from the river Iberus (Ebro).	
	Celtiberian Civilisation	Celtic immigrants from Gaul into Iberia mixed with local tribes and spread over the northern and eastern parts of the central plateau.	
239–228 BC	Carthaginian Conquest of Spain		
218–201 BC	Second Punic War	Carthaginians driven out of the Peninsula by 206 BC	
200–27 BC	Spain under The Roman Republic	Resistance of Celtiberian Numancia – destroyed by Scipio the Younger (133 BC)	Ruins of Numancia
27 BC–AD 406	The Roman Empire	Fall of Rome to the Goths (AD 406/407)	Aqueduct, Segovia
AD 412–531	Visigothic Occupation of Spain	Extinction of the Roman Empire of the West (476)	
531–711	Visigoth Kingdom in Spain	Establishment of Catholicism as State religion during reign of Reccared (586–601)	Visigothic church of San Juan de Baños (660)
711–1492	Muslim Occupation of decreasing areas of the Peninsula, lasting nearly eight centuries	Invasion of Spain by Arabs, Syrians and Berbers under Tarik and Musa (711–712)	

DATES	CIVILISATIONS AND RULERS	POLITICAL AND MILITARY EVENTS	ARCHITECTURE AND THE ARTS
718–914	Christian Kingdom of the Asturias (founded by Pelayo)	Battle of Covadonga (718) Muslims cross the Pyrenees, defeated near Poitiers in 732 by Charles Martel	
758–929	Emirate of Córdoba		Mosque of Córdoba (c. 750–c. 950)
914–1037	Christian Kingdom of León	Independent County of Castile (c. 950) Raids of Almanzor Death of Almanzor (1002)	
929–1031 1037–1065	Caliphate of Córdoba Ferdinand I of Castile and León	Establishment of Kingdom of Castile (1037) and first Union of the Kingdoms	
1065–1072 1072–1109	Sancho II of Castile Alfonso VI of Castile and León	Division of the Kingdoms Reunion of the Kingdoms Reconquest of Toledo (1085) Almoravid Invasion (1086) Death of the Cid (1099)	Cluniac influence, brought in by Alfonso's wife Constance, daughter of Robert, Duke of Burgundy
1109–1126 1126–1157	Urraca Alfonso VII, 'Emperor in Spain and King of the men of the two religions'.	Almohad invasion (1147)	Alfonso VII sends for reforming Cistercians, who founded their first monastery in Spain at Moreruela (1151)
1157–1188	Ferdinand II of León	Redivision of the Kingdoms	Zamora Cathedral (1151–1240) Salamanca Old Cathedral (1152–1200)

1157–1158 1158–1214	Sancho III of Castile Alfonso VIII of Castile	Alfonso married Eleanor, daughter of Henry II of England and Eleanor of Aquitaine Reconquest of Cuenca (1177) Foundation of the Military Orders	Sigüenza Cathedral begun (1155) Avila Cathedral begun (1160) Ciudad Rodrigo Cathedral begun (1168) Foundation of Real Monasterio de las Huelgas, Burgos (1187) Cuenca Cathedral begun (c. 1197) First Spanish University founded at Palencia by Alfonso VIII of Castile (1212)
1188–1230	Alfonso IX of León	Battle of Las Navas de Tolosa (1212)	
1214–1217	Henry I of Castile	Berengaria, daughter of Alfonso VIII of Castile had married Alfonso IX of León. She was heiress also to her brother Henry but abdicated the Crown of Castile on his death in 1217 in favour of her son Ferdinand (a great-grandson of Henry II of England)	

DATES	CIVILISATIONS AND RULERS	POLITICAL AND MILITARY EVENTS	ARCHITECTURE AND THE ARTS
1217–1230	Ferdinand III of Castile *becomes*	On his uncle's death in 1217 Ferdinand became King of Castile.	Burgos Cathedral begun (1222)
1230–1252	Ferdinand III of Castile and León (later 'The Saint')	On his father's death in 1230 he also inherited León. Final Union of the two Kingdoms. Reconquest of Córdoba (1236) Reconquest of Seville (1248) [Ferdinand canonised (1671)]	Toledo Cathedral begun (1226) El Burgo de Osma begun (1232) University of Salamanca founded (1230) Plasencia Cathedral Chapter-house (1250)
1253–1284	Alfonso X, the Learned	Fuero Real (1256)	
1284–1295	Sancho IV, the Brave		
1295–1312	Ferdinand IV	First joint Cortes of Castile and León (1301)	
1312–1350	Alfonso XI	Battle of the Rio Salado (1340) defeats last serious Muslim invasion	Palencia Cathedral begun (1321)
1350–1369	Peter I, the Cruel	Peter's eldest daughter, Constance, married John of Gaunt. Civil War. Peter (supported by the Black Prince) murdered by his half-brother, Henry of Trastamara. Change of Dynasty. House of Trastamara	Reconstruction of the Alcázar, Seville, by Peter the Cruel
1369–1379	Henry II	John of Gaunt's claim to the throne of Castile by virtue of his marriage to Constance of Castile surrendered in return for the marriage of their daughter, Catherine of Lancaster, to John I's	Reconstruction of the Alcázar, Segovia, by the early Trastamaras
1379–1390	John I		

Dates	Rulers	Events	Art and Architecture
1390–1406	Henry III, the Ailing		Rogier Van der Weyden (1399–1464)
1406–1454	John II		
1454–1474	Henry IV, the Impotent	Effective rule by the favourite, Alvaro de Luna until his execution in 1453. Marriage of Henry's sister, Isabel, to Ferdinand, son of John II of Aragon (1469). Civil War (1474) between supporters of Henry's putative daughter Joan, 'La Beltraneja' (her father was generally supposed to have been Don Beltrán de la Cueva) and the supporters of Isabel confirmed the latter on the throne of Castile	Hieronymus Bosch (1462 –1516)
1474–1504	Isabel I of Castile and León	Isabel's husband, Ferdinand, inherited the Kingdom of Aragón (1479) but remained only King-Consort in Castile. Establishment of Inquisition in Castile (1480). Reconquest of Granada (1492). Columbus's first voyage (1492). Treaty of Tordesillas (1494) between Spain and Portugal defined spheres of influence in the New World	Isabelline-Gothic style
1479–1516	Ferdinand II of Aragón (los Reyes Católicos)		
1504–1555	Joan the Mad	Marriage (1496) of Ferdinand and Isabel's daughter, Joan the Mad, to Philip of Habsburg the Fair who died in 1506	Plateresque style
1504–1506	Philip the Fair, Regent for his wife		
1506–1518	Ferdinand II of Aragón, Regent for his daughter	Marriage (1509) of their youngest daughter, Catherine of Aragón to Henry VIII of England	Salamanca New Cathedral begun (1512). Plasencia New Cathedral begun (1513)

DATES	CIVILISATIONS AND RULERS	POLITICAL AND MILITARY EVENTS	ARCHITECTURE AND THE ARTS
1516–1558	Charles I of Spain and V of the Holy Roman Empire (abdicated Spanish dominions in favour of his son Philip, 1555/1556)	Ferdinand's grandson, Charles of Habsburg theoretically joint monarch with his mother, Joan the Mad, but in effect sole ruler Beginning of Habsburg Dynasty Revolt of the Commons of Castile (1520–1521)	Juan de Alava active R. Gil de Hontañon active Alonso Berruguete (c. 1480–1561) Juan de Juni (d. 1586) active
1556–1598	Philip II married (1) Mary of Portugal, mother of Don Carlos (2) Mary Tudor (3) Isabel of Valois (4) Anne of Austria, mother of Philip III	Charles's son, Philip, married (1554) to Mary Tudor, who died 1558 Duke of Alba sent to suppress Revolt in the Netherlands (1567) Revolt of the Moriscos (1568–1570) Battle of Lepanto (1571) Portugal annexed (1581) The Great Armada (1588)	The Escorial (1563–1584) El Greco to Spain (1577) Valladolid Cathedral begun (1585) Death of Herrera (1597) Gregorio Fernández (1556–1636)
1598–1621	Philip III	Expulsion of the Moriscos (1610)	Death of Cervantes (1616) Plaza Mayor, Madrid, finished (1619)
1621–1665	Philip IV	Thirty Years War (1618–1648) Rule of the Count-Duke of Olivares Secession of Portugal (1640)	Zurbarán (1598–1661) Velázquez (1599–1660)
1665–1700	Charles II, the Bewitched	Charles died childless, leaving his Kingdom to Philip, Duke of Anjou, son of the Dauphin. This gave rise to the War of the Spanish Succession (1700–1713)	

1700–1724	Philip V	Enter the Bourbon Dynasty	Royal Palace of La Granja (1719–1739)
1724	Louis I	In 1724 Philip abdicated in favour of his son, who died seven months later, on which his father resumed the throne	
1724–1746	Philip V		Reconstruction of Royal Palace of Aranjuez (1727–1752) Plaza Mayor, Salamanca (1728–1755) Royal Palace, Madrid, begun (1737)
1746–1759	Ferdinand VI		
1759–1788	Charles III	Expulsion of the Jesuits (1766)	Charles III able to move into Madrid Palace (1764) Further additions to Aranjuez (1775–1778)
1788–1808	Charles IV	Godoy, the Queen's lover, prime minister (1792). Execution of Louis XVI of France (1793). Godoy, 'Prince of Peace' (1795) Abdication of Charles IV (1808) in favour of Ferdinand, his son, and retirement to Rome. Ferdinand imprisoned in France for six years	Goya (1746–1828)
1808–1814	Joseph Bonaparte	Peninsular War (1808–1814) Constitution of Cádiz (1812) Battle of Talavera (1809); Sieges of Ciudad Rodrigo & Badajoz (1812); Battles of Salamanca (1812) & Vitoria (1813)	
1814–1833	Ferdinand VII	Bourbon Restoration	

DATES	CIVILISATIONS AND RULERS	POLITICAL AND MILITARY EVENTS	ARCHITECTURE AND THE ARTS
1833–1841 1841–1843	Maria Christina, Regent Espartero, Regent	First Carlist War (1833–1840) between supporters of the late King's daughter, Isabel, and her uncle, Don Carlos	The 'Romantic' Movement (c. 1820–1860)
1843–1868	Isabel II	Isabel expelled by General Prim (1868) to the slogan 'No more Bourbons!'	The 'Isabelline' style
1868–1870 1870–1873 1873–1874 1874–1885 1885–1902	Republic Amadeus of Savoy Republic Alfonso XII Christina, Regent	Second Bourbon Restoration Second Carlist War (1874–1876) Alfonso XIII born six months after his father's death	Statue of Alfonso XII as 'The Pacifier' in the Retiro Park.
1902–1931 1931–1936 1936–1939 1939–1975	Alfonso XIII Republic Civil War General Franco Caudillo and Regent	Abdication of Alfonso XIII (1931)	Valle de los Caidos (1940–1959)
1975–	Juan Carlos I	Third Bourbon Restoration; the monarch becomes the guarantor of the Constitution of 1978	

Glossary of Architectural, Art and Allied Terms

✦

AEDICULE literally a little house; applied to shrines and tabernacles, also the smallest unit of Classical and Gothic design.

AMORINI cherubs or juvenile angels used in Renaissance decoration.

ANNULET band of moulding encircling a column, usually at half height.

ARCADE range of arches supported on piers or columns; a blind arcade is a pattern of arches applied as a decorative motif to a wall.

ARCADED I have used the adjective to describe squares and streets whose sidewalks are overhung by the projecting first storeys of the houses supported on pillars or columns.

ARCHITRAVE beam or lowest division of an entablature (q.v.), extending from column to column.

ARCHIVOLT moulding framing and following the contour of an arched doorway, which often had several of them, richly carved.

ATRIUM forecourt or arcaded porch.

BALDACHINO canopy supported by columns over an altar, shrine or tomb (cf. ciborium).

BAROQUE term applied to architecture and design during the late Renaissance period, roughly 1600–1760.

BOMBÉ describes columns wider at the centre than at the neck or base.

CALIPHAL term applied to architecture and design during the period of the Caliphate of Cordoba.

CELTIBERIAN loosely describes a mixed race resulting from the intermarriage of immigrant Celtic tribes from Gaul with native Iberians; the Celtiberians inhabited the north-east and part of the centre of Spain in Carthaginian and Roman times.

CHEVET apse surrounded by an ambulatory with radial chapels; in effect the whole east end of a major church beyond the transepts.

CHINOISERIE affectation of the Chinese style, extremely popular in eighteenth-century furniture.

CHURRIGUERESQUE term applied to the work of the followers and copiers of the Churrigueras, a family of Baroque altarpiece-makers turned architects, who flourished in the first half of the eighteenth century; they were not themselves the perpetrators of the worst excesses of their style.

CIBORIUM shaped usually like a small baldachino, this occupies the centre of a large altarpiece and shelters the vessel containing the host; also by extension this vessel itself. Not to be confused with Spanish *cimborio*, a lantern-dome.

CLERESTORY range of windows sited above the nave arcade of a church and looking out over the aisle roofs.

CORBEL projecting bracket, often carved, supporting eaves.

CUSPED said of an arch whose intrados (q.v.) is decorated with a tracery of semicircles joining to form points or with a series of miniature horseshoe arches projecting like teeth; also called multifoil.

DOMICAL adjective of dome, dome-shaped.

DONJON the great tower or keep of a castle; though of the same etymological origin, it does not now mean the same as dungeon but will probably contain one.

ENCEINTE fortified wall or girdle surrounding a mediaeval town.

ENTABLATURE combination of architrave (q.v.), frieze and cornice, supported on columns.

EPISTLE-SIDE term applied to the right-hand side of a church facing the altar (from whose left side facing the congregation the epistle is read); useful when it is confusing to refer to 'north' and 'south' or 'left' and 'right'.

EXEDRA semicircular or rectangular recess with stone benches in which the disputations of the learned took place in Greek and Roman times.

EX-VOTO offering to a god or goddess for a favour sought or received, usually in the form of a model of the human figure or the part of it affected by an illness.

FIBULA clasp, buckle or brooch, used particularly for objects of this kind found in antique tombs.

FLAMBOYANT applied to Gothic stone tracery forming wavy flame-like shapes; equivalent to English 'Decorated'.

GOSPEL-SIDE term applied to the left-hand side of a church facing the altar (from whose right side facing the congregation the gospel is read), cf. epistle-side.

GOTHIC pointed style of mediaeval architecture, adopted in Spain from the thirteenth to mid-sixteenth centuries.

HALL-CHURCH one in which nave and aisles are of the same or almost the same height, developed in Spain from the secular commodity exchanges of the Levant.

HELIX from the Greek for spiral or tendril; in fact a rather wavy cross somewhat resembling a propeller and a very common decorative motif in Visigothic decoration.

Visigothic decoration

Helix

HELLENISTIC imitating the Greek style.

HERRERAN the plain post-Plateresque and pre-Baroque style developed by J. B. de Toledo (d. 1567) and carried on by his assistant at the Escorial, Juan de Herrera; somewhat unfairly Herrera gets all the kudos.

HISPANO-FLEMISH applied to early Spanish painting, strongly influenced by the Flemish School.

HISPANO-MOORISH applied usually to ceramics, particularly the lustre-ware manufactured by Moriscos (q.v.) at Manises.

HORSESHOE ARCH

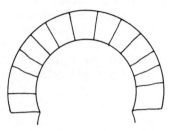

(1) unexaggerated: the Visigothic type, which has a squarer look than the Moorish.

(2) three-centred: same as above, which is theoretically based on the intersection of three arcs.

(3) ultra-semicircular or rounded: this is the Moorish type, in which a semicircle is slightly prolonged on either side, so that it curves inwards before coming to rest on its capitals or impost.

(4) pointed: more like a Gothic arch but also curving inwards at the base.

IBERIAN term applied by early Greek navigators to the inhabitants of the east coast of Spain, possibly deriving from those who dwelt by the river Iberus (Ebro); Iberia is also applied to the whole peninsula. The mingling of the Iberians with the immigrant Celts gave rise to the Celtiberians (q.v.).

ILLUSIONISM term invented by myself to describe the development of Spanish religious imagery in the sixteenth and seventeenth centuries; hence Illusionist, a practitioner of it.

IMPOST moulding supporting the springing of an arch.

INTRADOS the inner curve of an arch.

ISABELLINE applied to furniture and decoration of the reign of Isabel II (1843–1868), roughly equivalent to English mid-Victorian.

ISABELLINE-GOTHIC applied to architecture and decoration of the reign of Isabel I (1474–1504).

LONGITUDINAL applied to arches of exceptionally long span in a church; a whole nave arcade might be composed of one, two or maximum three on each side, running east-west. Space was saved by the fewer and slimmer columns required but such a structure could not resist the outward thrusts of a vault and had to be covered by a wooden ceiling.

MANNERISM term applied to work of the Italian Renaissance architects and artists of the period 1530–1600, mainly characterised by the preferment of personal virtuosity to the strict rules of the Roman canon; hence Mannerist.

MERLON the upstanding part of a fortified parapet between two embrasure openings.

MIHRAB niche inside a mosque indicating the direction of Mecca, to which Muslims turn while praying.

MIXTILINEAR used of a type of shouldered arch developed during the early Spanish Renaissance at Salamanca.

MORISCO Muslim living under Christian rule and nominally converted to Christianity.

MOZARABIC term applied to the art and architecture of the Mozarabs, Christians living under Muslim rule.

MUDÉJAR Muslim practising his own religion under Christian rule; term applied especially to the building and carpentry carried out by this sector of the community for its Christian masters.

NARTHEX vestibule or portico stretching across the west front of some early churches between the towers, separated from the nave by a wall or screen and set apart for converts under instruction before baptism, women and others who might not enter the main body of the church.

OCTOPARTITE describes a vault divided into eight compartments.

OCULUS circular or elliptical window.

PALAEOPUNIC early Punic or Carthaginian.

PATEN shallow dish on which the host is laid during the celebration of the Eucharist.

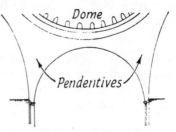

PENDENTIVE triangular curved overhanging surface by
which a dome is supported
over a square or polygonal
chambèr.

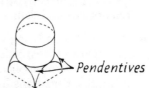

PERPENDICULAR English Gothic style that evolved from the Decorated and produced the fan vault.

PLATERESQUE early period of Spanish Renaissance architecture, so called from the likeness of its intricate decoration to the work of a silversmith (*platero*).

POLYCHROMED (WOOD) usual material of Spanish religious
imagery, which is treated with gesso and then painted and
picked out with gold leaf.

PREDELLA lowest stage of an elaborate *retablo* (q.v.), usually
decorated with painted or sculpted panels.

RENAISSANCE term applied to the reintroduction of Classic
architecture, which began in Italy in the fourteenth century
and spread all over Europe, reaching Spain at the end of the
fifteenth century.

ROCOCO a later development of Baroque with decoration based on rock-like forms, sea-shells, fantastic scrolls etc.

ROMANESQUE style founded on Roman architecture, prevalent in Western Europe from the ninth to twelfth centuries and surviving in Spain almost to the end of the thirteenth century. I have used the term 'Pointed Romanesque' to describe the next phase, which remains essentially Romanesque in layout and feeling with the exception of the introduction of the pointed arch; this is more commonly called Transitional (q.v.).

RUPESTRIAN applied to dwellings or cities hollowed out of rock.

SALMANTINE adjective of Salamanca.

SEMI-CUPOLA type of roof often used over a semicircular apse; in effect half a cupola.

SEXPARTITE type of Gothic vault of six compartments covering two nave bays in contrast with a quadripartite vault, which covers only one.

SOLOMONIC describes a type of spiral column, like a barley sugar stick, very popular in Spanish Baroque buildings and altarpieces.

SPANDREL the triangular surface on either side of the curve of an arch.

SQUINCH diagonal arch across the inner corner of a tower or square chamber; four of these – one at each corner – convert the square into an octagon and serve as supports for an octagonal lantern.

TERRA SIGILLATA type of Roman pottery of red clay, cast in a mould, often with decoration in low relief.

THERMAE public baths of the Greeks and Romans.

TRANSITIONAL term applied to Spanish thirteenth-century architecture in which the Gothic arch first makes its appearance; in some churches I have used the term 'Pointed Romanesque', as this seems to me a more graphic description of a style that retained all the massive weightiness of Romanesque (q.v.).

TREFOIL from the French *trois feuilles*, three leaves, applied to this pattern in Gothic tracery.

TRIBUNE raised dais, rostrum or gallery; in church architecture usually designed to accommodate some important person such as the king and accessible by a private door or staircase.

TRIFORIUM gallery or passage in the wall of a large church running above the nave arcade and under the clerestory (q.v.); as its windows open only inwards on to the nave and not outwards to the sky (from which it is shut off by the aisle roof), it is sometimes called a 'blind storey'.

ULTRA-SEMICIRCULAR see Horseshoe arch.

VISIGOTHIC applied to the architectural and art forms of the Gothic race that invaded the Roman Empire towards the end of the fourth century AD, made its capital at Toulouse and moved into Spain in the mid-fifth century, where it established a kingdom not overthrown until the Moorish invasion of 711–712.

VORTICIST painter practising Vorticism, a development of Cubism concerned with dynamism and movement.

Glossary of Spanish Words

❧

Abolengo ancestry, lineage

Abulense inhabitant of Avila

Adobe unfired, sun-dried brick

Aficionado follower or fan, usually of bull-fighting

Ajimez (*ajimeces*) twin-arched window with central column

Alameda poplar grove, public walk

Albergue inn; applied in particular to the road-houses run by the Government

Alcabala sales tax instituted by the Reyes Católicos

Alcaide governor of a castle

Alcalde mayor

Alcázar fortress, usually belonging to the Crown

Alcoba bedroom or closet

Alfiz (*alfices*) rectangular moulding or 'label' round door or window

Anis strong liqueur with an aniseed flavour

Antecoro antechamber to choir

Antesala anteroom

Aposentador officer charged with lodging arrangements

Apostolado set of carvings or paintings of the Saviour and the twelve apostles

Arandela metal plaque, usually painted with crest or coat of arms, attached to the intersection of vaulting ribs instead of a stone boss

Artesa trough in which bread dough is kneaded

Artesonado wooden ceiling shaped like an inverted artesa, carved with Moorish geometrical tracery

Aula lecture hall

Ayuntado person co-opted to a meeting of the city or town council

Ayuntamiento city or town hall

Bargueño type of chest with many drawers, first made at Bargas (Toledo)

Barrio district, quarter

Bellas Artes Beaux Arts; used in text as an abbreviation of Dirección General de Bellas Artes, a department of the Ministry of Education in charge of ancient monuments and museums

Calesa two-wheeled carriage or trap

Calle street

Calle Mayor main street

Camarín closet behind altar where images are dressed and their ornaments kept

Cantoral large book of choir chant

Cañada Real drovers' path wide enough for large migrant flocks, walled where it passed through agricultural land

Capilla chapel

Capilla Mayor sanctuary

Carta de arras marriage contract

Casa house

Casita cottage

Castillo castle

Castro hill-top with ruined castle

Cátedra university chair

Catedrático university professor

Cerca fence or low wall

Cervatana water duct (Segovia)

Chanquete whitebait

Charlotada burlesque bull-fight with dwarfs and young bulls

Charro was used, well before its adoption in Mexico, to describe villagers of the province of Salamanca, who loved to dress up; the beaded and sequinned costumes remind one of the uniforms of pearly kings and queens.

Cisne swan

Clavero keeper of the keys, treasurer

Cobertizo covered alley running under buildings

Colegiata church with collegiate status, i.e. a number of priests forming small chapter

Comulgatorio communion hatch from which the host was passed to plebeians from a noble or private chapel

Comunero Commoner; leader or member of the party that rose in support of Spanish democratic liberty against Charles V in 1520–1521

Consejo council
Consejal councillor
Convento convent
Coro choir
Corregidor royal magistrate
Corrida bull-fight
Costa coast
Costumbrista genre painter or writer of the nineteenth century
Cuadrilla matador's team; a patrol of four police
Cubo tower protruding from a fortified wall, usually semi-circular or rounded on the outer face and rectangular at the rear
Cuerda seca tile-making technique in which the different coloured glazes of the design are poured into slightly ridged channels to prevent them running together
Custodia monstrance in which the host is carried through the streets on Corpus Christi day

Desamortización disentailing of the monastic lands in 1835–1836, followed by their sale to restore the government's finances; this was in effect the death-knell of the monasteries
Desnudo, a naked
Despacho study or private office
Diputación provincial body bearing some resemblance to a county council
Dolorosa Mater Dolorosa, the Virgin sorrowing over the dead Christ
Donativo gift, offering
Doncel member of a mediaeval corps of royal pages
Doncella maiden, lass
Duende fairy, sprite, goblin; also an intuitive or imaginative quality said to be possessed by some writers and musicians
Dulce sweet

Embalse dam, reservoir
Envolvedora padded dressing platform of a child of royal or exalted birth, something like a small billiards table
Esgrafiado decorative plasterwork or 'pargeting' on the façades of houses, particularly in Segovia
Espino hawthorn
Estación station

Estofado raised ridge of gesso treated with gold-leaf to emphasise haloes, crowns, borders, etc. in mediaeval painting; also a stew

Evacuatorio lavatory

Feria fair, in the past always accompanied by an animal market, though these are becoming rarer.

Fiesta festival, public holiday

Fonda inn without stabling; guest-house, the cheapest form of lodging

Fraile mendicant monk, friar

Fuero a compilation of laws or – and in this sense a very important and emotive word – the particular law or statute conceded by the Crown in the Middle Ages to each reconquered city or district, allowing considerable fiscal and legal autonomy; more recently the rallying-cry of separatist movements hankering for lost privileges

Fuero Extenso fuero granted by Alfonso VIII in 1212

Fuero Real fuero granted by Alfonso X in 1256 to all towns that were still without a charter at that date

Gallo cock

Garganta throat; stream or snow-duct (province of Avila)

Guirnalda painted garland of flowers, usually surrounding an oval picture of the Virgin

Hidalgo (*hijosdalgo*) minor noble or country gentleman, usually untitled but banned from trade and exempted from certain taxes

Hocino narrow cultivated strip by a mountain stream, region of Cuenca

Hombre Bueno good man; in the plural an estate, equivalent to the Commons, of the old Aragonese and Castilian parliaments

Horno de asar brick roasting oven

Huelga modern industrial strike; in the past (usually plural) it meant repose, leisure, recreation, e.g. *Las Huelgas Reales*, the royal pleasure grounds

Humilladero roadside shrine

Iglesia church

Infante any legitimate male child of a Spanish king other

than the heir apparent

Infanta any legitimate daughter of a Spanish king or wife of an Infante

Infantado territory set apart for the maintenance of an Infante or Infanta

Inmaculada term applied to any of the thousands of paintings celebrating the Immaculate Conception of the Virgin (e.g. *La Inmaculada de Soult* in the Prado)

Lector university reader
Licenciado university graduate

Macero mace-bearer; savage figure supporting a coat of arms
Madera en blanco natural unpainted wood
Madera policromada see Polychromed (wood) in glossary of Architecture etc.
Madrileño inhabitant of Madrid
Maestro Mayor master of works of a cathedral
Majo plebeian dandy or swell; some star matadors were majos
Maja moll, mistress, concubine or wife of the above; also there were some majas – flower-sellers, prostitutes – in their own right
Matadero slaughterhouse
Matador torero who kills the bull, head of his cuadrilla (q.v.)
Merindad ancient name for a rural district in Old Castile
Mesta powerful union of owners of migrant flocks, founded in 1273 and dissolved in 1836
Monasterio monastery
Morisco see glossary of Architecture etc.
Mosto must, unfermented wine from the last harvest
Mozárabe Mozarab; Christian living under Muslim rule
Mudéjar see glossary of Architecture etc.

Noria well with a wheel turned by a donkey or mule to bring the water to the surface in little containers; from these it is tipped into the irrigation channels

Obispo bishop
Obras works, repairs
Osa she-bear

Palacio palace

Pantano reservoir

Parador originally a coaching inn; now used particularly for the hostelries of the M.I.T.

Paraninfo university senate house

Parteluz central pillar or column of a double doorway, often carrying a statue

Paseo de Ronda guard walk round the top of a fortification, protected by the merlons (q.v.)

Patio de Armas (see Plaza de Armas)

Pícaro rogue or knave; hero of a picaresque novel

Pico point

Pintor painter

Pintor de cámara painter to the royal family

Pintor del rey painter to the king

Platero silversmith

Plaza de Armas parade ground and rallying point inside a fortress or palace (also Patio de Armas)

Plaza Mayor main square

Posada inn with stabling for pack-animals; these are dying out

Pósito communal grain store

Postigo postern gate; window shutter

Pueblo town or village; also the people as a whole as in *el Pueblo Español*, the Spanish people

Puerto de mar seaport

Puerto de montaña mountain pass

Putti naked children used in Renaissance decoration

Regidor the term has varied a lot in meaning with the changes in constitution of city and town councils over the centuries; recently it meant simply a councillor though in some regions in mediaeval times the regidores were Crown representatives

Reja wrought-iron grille or screen

Retablo reredos, retable, altarpiece

Rey king

Reyes Católicos (*los*) The Catholic Sovereigns; title conferred on Isabel I of Castile and her husband Ferdinand by the Pope

Rollo column marking the spot from which justice was administered and edicts were read.

Sacristía sacristy

Sala hall, parlour
Sala Capitular chapter house
Saledizo projecting upper storey of a house
Santa Forma (*la*) the host
Seco, a dry
Sesmero (*sexmero*) mayor of a rural district
Simpatía charm, congeniality; hence the adjective *Simpático*
Sortija ring

Tanto Monta tantamount; the joint motto of the Catholic
  Sovereigns designed to emphasise their equal status, though
  Ferdinand, King of Aragón in his own right, was never
  more than King-Consort in Castile
Tapa titbit, snack; see appendix on Eating and Drinking
Templete pavilion or shrine sometimes found in the centre of
  a cloister; also a baldachino (q.v.)
Tesoro treasure; cathedral's collection of plate etc.
Tocador dressing room, dressing table
Torero bull-fighter (*toreador* is not used in Castilian Spanish)
Toril passage and door from which bull is released into the
  ring
Transparente altarpiece or chamber behind the high altar, lit
  by a lantern or skylight
Trasaltar wall screening the sanctuary of a major church from
  its ambulatory
Trascoro rear or west wall of an enclosed choir situated in the
  nave of a church
Trastamara(*s*) name of the dynasty that came to the Castilian
  throne in 1369 and was extinguished by the advent of
  Charles I of Spain and V of the Holy Roman Empire

Urbanización urbanisation; suburban development or estate
  in the countryside or on the coast

Válido favourite and effective ruler in the king's name, usually
  remarkable for personal ambition and unscrupulousness
Villa town, usually fortified and of mediaeval origin, with
  jurisdiction over a number of surrounding villages; in some
  places the town hall is called Casa de la Villa; the usage for
  a country or suburban house is quite recent in Spain
Villa ducal ducal town

Vítor (*vítores*) inscription on a wall commemorating a triumph, particularly a doctorate obtained at the university of Salamanca

Volapié method of killing a stationary bull

Yo I – the most important word in the Spanish language

Zaguán porch of a large house, often with mounting block and entrance to stable

Hotels and Tourist Offices

❧

Such has been the spate of hotel building in the past two decades that a complete list for the area under review would be impossibly lengthy. I therefore give below only hotels I have stayed in myself or have some knowledge or report of. All the Paradors in the area are included (though I have not stayed in those very recently opened) because the Government's network (now over fifty years old) maintains a universally respected standard of accommodation and service, often in buildings of great antiquity and charm. But I have some reservations about their food – see appendix on Eating and Drinking. For a wider choice consult the Michelin Guide to Spain and for active assistance in finding rooms the tourist offices listed at the end of this appendix are to be recommended. Obviously, one's freedom of movement is greatly increased if one does not have to book in advance and my experience is that this is not normally necessary except in the case of the Paradors, some of which have only a few rooms (numbers shown in hotel listing), and in Madrid and Valladolid. The great majority of Spanish hotel rooms are doubles with only a small discount for single occupation. If the worst comes to the worst, the inns are full and the tourist office closed, one need never leave a Spanish town without a bed in a private lodging house; a question to a municipal policeman or in a bar will always elicit the name of someone who lets rooms and probably assistance in finding one.

Apart from their commercial signs, all licensed hotels carry a pale blue plaque indicating their type and rating on a scale approved by the Secretary of State for Tourism. In this system of classification **H** stands for a fully fledged hotel, running from one to five stars. **Hs** stands for Hostal which may not occupy the whole of its building and only runs from one to three stars; otherwise it provides the same facilities as the equivalent category of hotel. **HR** stands for a hotel without restaurant and **HsR** for a hostal which only provides bed and breakfast. **P** is for Pension with less than 12 rooms and the right to oblige clients to take full pension terms. The cheapest lodging of all is indicated by **F** for Fonda; these often have only a jug of cold water and a basin in the room but can be very clean.

Stars are to be evaluated as follows. Five indicate *grande luxe* and four as much *luxe* as the average person can absorb. Three stars always guarantee a good standard of comfort with private bath in 50% of the rooms, private showers with lavatories attached to the rest. Two and one stars are a bit of a lottery. I have stayed at good one star hotels which have not been upgraded because they have not put in a lift. My main criticism of recent hotel construction is that too much attention has been paid to individual baths (some of which attention has been paid to individual baths (some of which do not have efficient hot water) at the expense of good building standards; some of the very latest hotels have wafer-thin walls and are extremely noisy. Often the older establishments are to be preferred to the more modern, especially in the cheaper range, though the same criticism sometimes applies also to hotels at the top end of the scale.

With these warnings and reservations I offer the following suggestions. My list is compiled alphabetically by and within provinces. First comes the provincial capital followed by smaller towns in the province.

AVILA	H****	Palacio de Valderrábano
	H***	Parador Nacional Raimundo de Borgoña. Former town house of local nobility, 62 rooms.
Arévalo	Hs*	Comercio
Gredos (Navarredonda de la Sierra)	H***	Parador Nacional. First of the chain, opened 1928, 77 rooms.
Madrigal de las Altas Torres	Hs**	Madrigal
BURGOS	HsR***	Asubio
Covarrubias	H***	Arlanza
Medina del Pomar	H***	Las Merindades

CACERES

Guadalupe	H***	Parador Nacional Zurbarán, 25 rooms.
	H**	Hospedería del Real Monasterio
Jarandilla	H***	Parador Nacional Carlos V, 43 rooms.
Plasencia	Hs**	Iberia

CIUDAD REAL

Almagro	H****	Parador Nacional de Almagro. Former convent of San Francisco, 56 rooms.

CUENCA

CUENCA	H****	Torremangana
	H***	Alfonso VIII
Alarcón	H***	Parador Nacional Marqués de Villena. Converted castle, 11 rooms.
San Clemente	Hs**	Milán
	P*	Florida
	F*	La Fonda

GUADALAJARA

Brihuega	Hs*	Princesa Elima
Cifuentes	Hs**	San Roque
Sacedón	Hs**	Mari Blanca
Sigüenza	H****	Parador Nacional Castillo de Sigüenza. Converted castle, 82 rooms.
	HsR**	El Doncel

MADRID

Over 700 establishments are listed in the Ministry's official hotel guide. Anyone arriving without a booking should, if motor-borne, deposit the car in a multi-storey or underground car park (there is one of the latter in front of the Hotel Palace) and get a taxi; the Madrid taxi-drivers can be almost guaranteed to find something, somewhere, even if it takes a couple of hours. I have only three positive recommendations, all of which fulfil my requirements of easy access on foot to the Prado, the Plaza Mayor and to cheap restaurants. They are:

	H*****	Ritz, Plaza de la Lealtad. Smallish for a grand hotel with 156 rooms.
	H*****	Palace, Plaza de las Cortes. Much larger than the Ritz (518 rooms) and much less character but very handy.
	H***	Victoria, Plaza del Angel. Very conveniently placed half way between the Plaza Mayor and the Prado, surrounded by reasonably priced bars and restaurants, 110 rooms. Try and get one looking onto the Plaza de Santa Ana.
Chinchón	H****	Parador Nacional de Chinchón, 38 rooms.
San Lorenzo de El Escorial	H****	Victoria Palace
	H**	Miranda-Suizo
PALENCIA	HR***	Castilla La Vieja
	HR***	Rey Don Sancho de Castilla
SALAMANCA	HR****	Gran Hotel, just off Plaza Mayor
	H****	Parador Nacional, 108 rooms.
Béjar	H***	Colón
Ciudad Rodrigo	H***	Parador Nacional Enrique II. Converted castle, 29 rooms.
	H***	Conde Rodrigo
SEGOVIA	H****	Parador Nacional, modern building outside walls with views of old city, 80 rooms.

	H***	Acueducto
Riaza	H**	La Trucha
Villacastín	H***	Albergue Nacional

SORIA	H***	Parador Nacional Antonio Machado. Modern building on castle hill, 14 rooms.
El Burgo de Osma	HsR**	La Perdiz
Santa Maria de Huerta	H***	Albergue Nacional, 40 rooms.

TOLEDO	H****	Parador Nacional Conde de Orgaz. Modern building outside walls with views of old city, 57 rooms.
Oropesa	H***	Parador Nacional Virrey Toledo, 44 rooms.

VALLADOLID		
Medina de Rioseco	H***	Hostal de los Almirantes
Peñafiel	H**	Infante Don Juan Manuel
Simancas	H***	Gran Parque
	Hs**	La Barca
Tordesillas	H***	Parador Nacional. Modern building, 73 rooms.

ZAMORA	H****	Parador Nacional Condes de Alba y Aliste. Old town house, 19 rooms.
	HR***	Dos Infantas
Benavente	H****	Parador Nacional del Rey Fernando II de Leon. Converted castle, 30 rooms.
Toro	H***	Don Juan II

TOURIST OFFICES

AVILA   Oficina de Informacion de Turismo, Plaza de la Catedral 4

BURGOS   Jefatura Provincial de Turismo, Plaza de Alonso Martinez 7

C.l.T., Paseo del Espolón (under Theatre)
Medina del Pomar, C.I.T., Martinez Pacheco 6
(CACERES)
Plasencia, Consejeria de Turismo de Extremadura, Pedro de
Lorenzo 2
C.I.T., José Antonio 20
Trujillo, Oficina Municipal de Turismo, Plaza Mayor
CUENCA Jefatura Provincial de Turismo, Dalamacio
García Izara 8
C.I.T., Colón 34
GUADALAJARA Jefatura Provincial de Turismo, Travesía
de Beladiez 1
Sigüenza, C.I.T., Plaza Obispo Don Bernardo 13
MADRID Oficina Municipal de Turismo, Plaza Mayor 3
Patronato Municipal de Turismo, Calle Mayor 83
Alcalá de Henares, Oficina Municipal de Turismo, Callejón
de Santa Maria
Aranjuez, C.I.T., Moreras (Hogar de la Juventud)
PALENCIA Oficina Información de Turismo, Calle Mayor
105
C.I.T., Conde Vallelano 1
Frómista, C.I.T., Oficina de Turismo
SALAMANCA Oficina de Información de Turismo, Gran
Via 41
Oficina Municipal de Turismo, Plaza Mayor
C.I.T., Plaza Sexmeros 1
Bejar, C.I.T., Puerta de Avila 4
Ciudad Rodrigo, C.I.T., Plaza Mayor 1
SEGOVIA Oficina de Información de Turismo, Plaza Mayor
10
C.I.T., Domingo de Soto 3
Soria, Oficina de Información de Turismo, Plaza Ramon y
Cajal
Agreda, C.I.T., Plaza Mayor 1
Almazan, C.I.T., Caballeros 6
Burgo de Osma, C.I.T., Obispo Rubio Montiel 1
Medinaceli, C.I.T., Plaza Gerneralisimo 1
TOLEDO Jefatura Provincial de Turismo, Plaza Zocodover
11
Oficina de Turismo, Puerta de Bisagra
VALLADOLID Jefatura Provincial de Turismo, Paseo de
Zorrilla 48
C.I.T., Paseo de Zorilla 64

Medina del Campo, Oficina Municipal de Turismo, Plaza
   Mayor 27
Tordesillas, Oficina Municipal de Turismo, Ayuntamiento
Medina de Rioseco, C.I.T., Arco de Ajújar
ZAMORA   Jefatura Provincial de Turismo, Prado Tuerto,
   Edificios Multiples
C.I.T., Pelayo 4
Toro, C.I.T., Plaza de España 1

Note on Maps and Symbols:

   The symbols $\boxed{P}$ $\boxed{H}$ and $\boxed{A}$ on the maps in the text denote
respectively Parador, Hotel and Albergue. The latter is a
Government roadhouse, of which only a few remain. The
symbols appear only against place-names possessing one or
more establishments recommended in the above list. The
symbol $\boxed{F}$ for Fonda, which appears in one or two of the
remoter regions indicates clean beds without private toilet
facilities. Accommodation is available in many places not
included in my selection; the complete list of all recognised
hotels in Spain is published annually by the Dirección General
de Empresas y Actividades Turísticas under the title **Guía de
Hoteles.**
   For local information on accommodation, festivities, opening hours etc and for regional maps and town plans the
following addresses may prove useful. The initials C.I.T. stand
for Centro de Iniciativas Turisticas.

Tipping

❧

HOTELS S/T compris

LUGGAGE roughly 50 ptas per large suitcase and 25 ptas for a small one in the middle-rank hotels. In four-star and luxury hotels they may look a bit askance.

RESTAURANTS (other than the hotel where one is staying) 10%.

BARS nothing across the counter except small, loose change, 10% at the tables.

TAXIS in urban areas roughly 10% of the fare. Long-distance journeys are usually done by an owner-driver for a contract price. One might buy him a meal or a drink.

LAVATORIES usually 25 ptas where there is a lady attendant who supplies towel, paper etc.

BOOTBLACKS 50-75 ptas for a shoe-shine, more for boots.

BEGGARS officially these no longer exist but some elderly people *do* beg. Give something, if possible. There may be a gap between the intensions and performance of the Social Security system. If one is accosted by a healthy gypsy with a baby, one must follow one's feelings about gypsies. On no account should one give to children who beg 'peseta, peseta' or 'money, money, money' – this is a patter they have picked up and is only for sweets.

MUSEUMS there is a fixed charge. Solicitous attendants will sometimes hang around for tips but they are adequately paid and should be discouraged, particularly those of the Patrimonio Nacional.

CATHEDRALS entry usually free, though in some disgraceful cases (Seville) not. There is more often than not a ticket for the 'treasure' or 'museum', which will include the more interesting dependencies. If special services are required of the sacristan – i.e. chapels not normally shown etc. – he should be tipped 25 ptas per head of the party. But beware of paying to see inferior stuff. As a general rule, anything I have not mentioned is not worth seeing.

MONASTERIES usually a straight charge and no complications. Don't tip monks.

PARISH CHURCHES these often have to be opened up by the priest or a choir-boy. 50 ptas usually appropriate for the latter. If it is the priest himself or his housekeeper more is expected; it should be accompanied by the words *un donativo para la iglesia*. Obviously they spend it as they like and I have met needy priests who probably put it towards housekeeping.

GUIDES here there is a monstrous abuse. In towns like Toledo or museums like the Prado the reader is likely to be accosted by a 'cultured' individual with or without a number or badge whose aim is to charge a *lot* to show a cathedral, a city or a collection. The tone of the guide is often strident and declamatory and the pace rapid, so that much if not all of the pleasure of looking at things at one's leisure is lost. I humbly suggest that no reader of *this* guide book who has spent a few minutes reading about the places on his following day's programme need *ever* avail himself of the services of such an individual. I don't say there are *no* good local guides, but they are in a vast minority. If a couple or family hire one for an hour or two, they must be prepared for a bill of at least £10, probably a good deal more.

Eating and Drinking

✦

Spaniards have always eaten to live rather than lived to eat. The classic peasant dish of the Castiles was and is *cocido*, a stew of potatoes and chickpeas or beans with pork trimmings and by-products. The liquid and vegetables are drained off first and eaten as *sopa de cocido*, followed by the titbits such as blood sausage, trotters and fat as second course. *Potaje* is similar without any meat ingredient. As a result, Spanish food has not had a good reputation among foreigners, better than Greek perhaps but that's about all. I'll try and disentangle the good – and there is much of it – from the bad. In the first place anyone who owns or leases a house or even buys for a picnic has an opportunity of catering with some excellent materials. Bread is very good, crusty and satisfying, a real food, not a limp accessory as it is in England. Staple vegetables like potatoes, cabbage, broad beans, onions and most especially tomatoes are marvellous. Some vegetables that are almost a luxury in England are common fare; these include artichokes, peppers, young spinach, courgettes, aubergines and olives. Fruit in season is good and the oranges are outstanding, the most delicious varieties being the mandarins of Winter and the *guachis* (Washington navels) in the Spring. Delicious too are the pears, grapes, melons, water melons, figs, custard apples and herbs. The food markets (*mercados* or *plazas de abastos*) are a 'must' for housewives and picnickers alike. Olive oil has got an undeserved bad name, probably from its use two or three times over in cheap pensions. But it is to the Spanish kitchen what mortar is to brick and is most unlikely to be the cause of 'Spanish tummy' – the water is a much more likely culprit, It is also far better for the health than animal fats and more interesting than margarine or soya.

Of the meats, Spanish beef is stringy, partly because of the pasturage and partly because Spaniards like a good chew – they don't want the precious stuff to melt away in their mouths.

Lamb is a strong line in Central Spain. The tenderest and most prized meat is pork. Chicken is universally good. Rabbit is preferred to hare. The red-legged partridge is shot all over the country and usually cooked in a casserole, not roasted. Liver, kidneys, brains etc. are excellent. Fish used to be the poor man's diet and the fish distribution service is the best in the world; it arrives by motor-bike at the remotest pueblos. Shellfish (except clams and mussels), sole, mullet, fresh tuna and the excellent swordfish are now more expensive but fresh sardines and anchovies are still very reasonable and quite delicious, also a variety of whitebait called *chanquetes*. Cheeses lack variety. *Manchego* is a sheep cheese often matured to excessive hardness. The light soft goats' cheeses are pleasant.

How does all this affect eating out in hotels and restaurants? According to category, a meal is usually offered of two, three or even four courses plus *postre* (cheese, fruit, tinned fruit, cream caramel known as *flan*, or ice-cream). I think the general rule in the provinces is to prefer the thick soups, fish soups, hors d'oeuvres (*entremeses*), salads (avoiding the heavy one with tinned tuna), chicken and main fish dishes (avoiding the *rebozado* treatment of heavy batter) to steak (*biftec*) and beef in general (*ternera*). *Huevos a la flamenca* is a good egg dish. Lamb chops (*chuletas de cordero*) are usually a bit meagre though of good flavour. Roast lamb (*cordero asado*) and roast pork (*lomo de cerdo*) can be very good especially in the regions of Soria, Segovia and Avila, though the roast sucking pig (*cochinillo asado*) of Segovia is too rich for my taste. Partridges (*perdices*) are the big thing in and around Toledo. *Paella*, though not a Castilian dish, is found everywhere and is an obvious attraction to rice-lovers; it is usually served in the meat or fish juices and is not fluffy and dry as in England. The Government Paradors have a good reputation for comfort and service but one should beware of getting a dull meal in their restaurants, where a standard four-course, 'International' vaguely French-type meal is offered. It is better to eat fewer courses and ask for the speciality of the region. For those with a sweet tooth the *pastelerías* and *confiterías* make very good pastry and creamy things.

In the TAPAS served in bars the Spanish cuisine reaches its highest peak. These are literally stop-gaps (from *tapar* – to cover or fill in) designed to take the edge off hunger (and incidentally drunkenness) before the late meals. They are not just skimmings of main dishes and their confection is an art in itself. Usually they are served on miniature round or oval dishes. They used to be costed into the price of a drink but in most parts of Spain they are now charged separately and always so in Madrid. The prices are often chalked up on a board. They can be cold or hot. The main cold *tapas* are: olives, almonds, slices of salami-type sausage (*chorizo, salchichón*) and other cold meats, enticing little green salads, very good potato and Russian salads and seafood salads, marinated anchovies, egg mayonnaise, etc. Of the hot variety, *tapas de cocina*, the favourites are: *callos madrileños* (tripes à la mode de Madrid) in a delicious piquant sauce, *pinchitos* (liver, kidneys or minuscule steaks of meat skewered on to a sliver of bread with a toothpick), *calamares* (squid either fried in rings or served in its ink), fried anchovies (*boquerones*) and other fried fish, little baby stews or ragouts . . . but the invention of the individual bar-owner is endless. These appetisers are presented with great artistry in contrast with the often sloppy and heavy handed presentation of regular meals. A variant of the tapa is the media ración, a larger helping served in an earthenware bowl (if hot) and probably costing up to 300 ptas. Some bars specialise in medias raciones, which can be shared between two or three people or combined by the connoisseur to form a whole meal – very often cheaper and more satisfying than one served on a table-cloth. But be careful not to be given a filling media ración if you only want a tapa. Any of these items eaten sitting down and brought by the waiter will cost about 10% more than at the bar and the waiter should be tipped (see Appendix 5).

Madrid is strong on bars serving good tapas and especially on seafood. If it seems rather far from the sea for this, it must be remembered that the fish is brought in from all the ports of Spain by great refrigerated lorries thundering through the night. But I must warn that oysters, lobsters, langoustines and the large prawns called *cigalas* are expensive. They are usually sold by weight, even over the counter with a drink. Clams (*almejas*) and mussels (*mejillones*) are cheaper alternatives.

The capital also offers a very wide choice of restaurants. These are classified from one to five forks, which reflect the comfort rather than the cuisine. Top of the list must come the Ritz with its Edwardian décor, properly spaced tables and charming terrace in good weather. Among other five-fork restaurants, the nearby Las Lanzas in Calle Espalter has good, expensive classic food of the smoked salmon and roast beef variety, while the slightly seedy Lhardy above a confectioner of the same name in the Carrera de San Jeronimo is faintly reminiscent of the Cavendish Hotel in the old days. It is relatively cheap for its class and has one or two private rooms for intimate dinners. For shellfish the Hogar Gallego is good; it has a jolly breezy atmosphere and is not expensive. In the region of the Plaza Mayor in the old town there are a number of restaurants clustered round the Arco de Cuchilleros. These are of the *típico* or deliberately quaint variety and rather expensive. El Púlpito in the corner of the plaza is very popular with tourists and Sobrino de Botín (through the arch and down the steps on the left), one of Hemingway's haunts, is now in the same category with a speciality in sucking pig. Continuing down the street and turning right one comes almost immediately on Casa Paco, a *tasca* or tavern come up in the world. The meat is very good but the place is crowded and it is advisable to book. The barman is a great adept at serving red wine with tapas of cured ham (*Jamón Serrano*) or (Spanish) Roquefort cheese extremely fast. Lower down the scale, there is a multitude of two- and one-fork restaurants with no pretensions to décor where one can get very adequate meals with wine in the 1500-2500 ptas range. Meals in hotels vary from 1200-3000 ptas according to category. A 3-star hotel will normally provide a set meal in the region of 2000 ptas. Half-pension terms, which are more favourable, are a sensible arrangement.

WINE

In the field of drink Spain provides undoubted pleasures at prices ranging from the reasonable to the very cheap. At places like Cogolludo (Guadalajara) you can still get a glass of wine in a bar for twenty-five pesetas. The awful problem of what to drink *before* a meal, which bedevils ones life in France, is solved by the very wide choice of sherries – the finos like La Ina and San Patricio and the dry Olorosos like Rio Viejo head the league. The finos from Montilla near Córdoba are almost as good and nearly every bar serves a house fino. Red and white vin ordinaire – *tinto* and *blanco corriente* – are served over the counter of all but the most expensive bars. Spain has far less of a name than France for table wines and certainly there is nothing in the country to touch the classified Clarets and Burgundies. But almost all the Rioja reds from reputable houses – Paternina, Bodegas

Franco Españolas etc. – are very palatable, if a bit heavy, Marqués de Murrieta has a sound red and fruity white. The Marqués de Riscal light Claret type has decreased in quality because the makers sell too much of it. The Valdepeñas wines from the south of New Castile are much lighter than the Riojas and of lesser quality. The sparkling wines made in Catalonia – no longer allowed to be called *champaña* or *champán,* as a result of a successful lawsuit by the French – are cheap and enjoyable, especially if used in Champagne cocktails. The fantastic cheapness of the *corrientes,* usually sold in litre bottles with capsules, not corks, is due to Spain's over-production of wine – which not long ago gave rise to an officially approved campaign to get people to drink more wine. This was a refreshing change from the usual warnings that line major roads. In quality and alcoholic content these wines vary a lot according to region, though I would say they are better than the French equivalents bottled in the same way. The rosé or *rosado,* incidentally, is sometimes called *clarete* from its colour and has nothing to do with Claret. Burgos has a red wine that is almost black and turns one's teeth the same colour. Those from Aragón and Murcia are rough, strong – as much as 15 or 16 percent alcohol – and heady; they are best avoided if one is driving. In the centre of the country, available in almost every grocer's and at road houses and cheap restaurants, there are some very adequate *tintos* ranging from 12 to 13.5 percent. Spaniards often add colourless fizzy pop called Casera in the summer. Posher restaurants nearly always have a perfectly drinkable house wine in bottle or carafe. *Sangría* is a sort of summer cup jazzed up with fruit and brandy or gin. It can be delicious if properly made but don't pay too much for it, as, apart from the fruit perhaps, the ingredients are very cheap. Spanish brandy – which still gets away with the name *coñac* – is much sweeter than the French but also much cheaper. And, finally, no one should leave Spain without experiencing the spine-tingling, shuddering shock of a neat dry *anis* – preferably from Chinchón near Madrid – about mid-morning. This is guaranteed to set anyone up for the day. The sweet variety doesn't do the trick.

Feast Days and Fairs

❧

No Spanish guide-book can be complete without reference to the many local *fiestas* and *ferias* which still continue despite the introduction of the industrial three-week holiday among large sectors of the population – with the result that most Spaniards get the best of both worlds. The *fiestas*, of essentially religious inspiration, take place either on the day of the local saint or patron or on a great day in the Church calendar such as Easter, Corpus Christi or the Assumption. They are often celebrated by processions bearing images through the streets – the ones in *Semana Santa* (Holy Week) are the most famous of these. Then there are the more rural and festive *romerías*, a rather jolly cross between a picnic and a pilgrimage, to the shrine of some local saint, usually a little way outside the village or town. On the evenings of feast days there are often *verbenas*, which are public dances generally held in the open air.

The *ferias*, of secular origin, started life as animal or produce markets – sometimes lasting as long as a month, cf. p. 206 – round which various attractions inevitably grew up. Some have now lost their original purpose and degenerated into mere amusement parks but others still take place in conjunction with a cattle or other market and these are the best, as it is much more fun to observe the gypsies and dealers and other traditional picaresque types of the Spanish fairgrounds than crowds of respectable bourgeois parents pushing or leading their children between miles of shooting galleries, tombolas and the like.

The feasts and fairs of the small pueblos, sometimes preserving mediaeval rituals of even older origin, are perhaps the most agreeable of all. Sometimes the religious and secular motivations merge and both types of festivity—whether separately or together—are more often than not accompanied by bull-fights. And there is a far better chance of seeing a good one before a critical Madrid public or even in a makeshift ring in a small Castilian village than in any of the showbiz stadiums built for tourists on the coast. Here I think I should briefly sketch the main types of 'taurine spectacle'.

A *corrida* is a proper bull-fight between bulls of four years and over and fully-fledged matadors and their assistants. A *novillada* is exactly the same except that the bull is not more than three and the matador or *novillero* as he is called – who looks and dresses the same but is often much keener than the old hands in the big money – has not yet taken his *alternativa* or doctorate in tauromachy. A *corrida de rejones* is one in which the bull is fought throughout from horseback, as was common till the mid-eighteenth century in Spain, after which it lapsed but was continued in Portugal. It owes its Spanish revival to amateur *rejoneadores* but has since become commercialised. Often one or two bulls are fought in this way as an appetiser to the main business. Unlike those of *picadores* in the normal corrida, the horses are almost never hurt. The words *capea* and *becerrada* describe the playing of young bulls or cows, possibly in a makeshift ring or farmyard, by all and sundry including children using old *capas* (capes), *muletas* (the matador's red flannel cloth) or even shirts and hats. An *encierro* is the rounding up of bulls in the open country by men on horseback and the driving of them through the streets to the ring; in some places it is traditional for the young bloods to run before them, as in Pamplona. A *charlotada* is a burlesque bull-fight with dwarf toreros and tiny bulls, which the squeamish will do well to avoid. Finally, there is the *festival,* in which prominent matadors in country dress (*traje corto*) and Cordoban hats instead of the formal suit of lights (*traje de luces*) fight young bulls, usually in aid of some worthy cause and partly (when the festival takes place in the off-season) for the practice. This is a good type of 'first' fight for those who are not sure if they are going to enjoy bull-fighting or not. It will be seen that taurine events are of different kinds and I shall simply indicate them below by the word 'bulls'. The traveller will do well to enquire in advance what is on offer.

Even if space allowed, it would be impossible to give a reliable list of all the feast-days and fairs in the area covered by this book. Most religious feasts are pegged to dates in the church calendar such as Saint John's day, June 24th, which coincides with the summer solstice, and the Assumption of the Virgin on August 15th, which some scholars link with pre-Christian rites for Astarte. But Easter, as we all know, is a moveable feast and many secular events vary slightly from year to year. The following is a small selection of some of the principal festivities in our area:

Alba de Tormes	Oct 14	Saint Theresa. Dancing in *charro* costume, bulls.
Alcalá de Henares	Aug 24-27	Saint Bartholomew. Classical theatre, processions, bulls.
Almagro	Aug 24-28	Saint Bartholomew. Cattle market, bulls.
Avila	July 18-21	Summer Fair. Open air theatre, dancing, bulls.
	July	*Semana polifónica,* concerts of early music.
	Oct 9-16	Saint Theresa. Concerts, bulls.
Burgos	June 20	Corpus Christi procession to Las Huelgas.
	June 27	Saint Peter. Processions, dancing, romerías, bulls.
Carrión de los Condes	June 24-29	Saint Zoilo. Bulls.
Chinchón	Sept 2-16	*Festivales* for charity; leading matadors, young bulls.
Cuenca	Aug 20-28	Saint Julian. Carnival, horse-show, bulls.
El Escorial	Aug 10	Saint Lawrence.
Guadalajara	Sept 25-27	Autumn Fair. Bulls, discerning audience.
Guadalupe	Oct 12	*Dia de la Hispanidad.* Pilgrimage, dancing, popular festivities.
La Granja	Aug 25	Saint Louis, King of France. All palace fountains play free.
Madrid	May 10-26	Saint Isidro. Bulls nearly every day for three weeks. A 'must' for serious *aficionados.*
Medina del Campo	Sept 1-8	Saint Antolín. Sheep market, *encierros,* bulls.

Medina de Rioseco	June 23-29	Agricultural Fair and Saint John. Bulls.
	Sept 8	Romería with decorated carts.
Palencia	Aug 1-9	Saint Antolín. Regional dancing competitions, bulls.
Pastrana	July 13-18	Patron Saint. Bulls.
Peñafiel	Aug 14-17	Assumption. Bulls, *encierros,* theatre.
Plasencia	Aug 25	Main Fair. Bulls.
Riaza	Oct 25-30	Big Cattle Fair. Bulls.
San Esteban de Gormaz	Sept 8-10	Patron Saint. Popular dancing, bulls.
Segovia	June 24-29	Saints John and Peter. Bulls.
Sigüenza	Aug 14-18	Assumption. Bulls, *encierros.*
Soria	June 28- July 2	Saint John. Bulls, *encierros,* fireworks, regional dancing.
Talavera de la Reina	Sept 21	Saint Matthew. Bulls, discerning audience.
Toledo	June 20-21	Corpus Christi. Bulls, theatre, music and dance.
Toro	June 11	Romería to Romanesque church of Christ of the Battles.
	Aug 28- Sept 3	Saint Augustine. Main Fair. Bulls, *encierros,* processions, regional dress.
Valladolid	Sept 15-23	Patron Saint. Main Fair. Bulls.
Zamarramala	Feb 4	Saint Agatha. Women's day presided over by two elected mayoresses who invite all their sisters but no men to bread and wine. Regional dress.
Zamora	June 11	Romería to La Hiniesta.
	Sept 8-14	Main Fair and Cattle Market. Processions, bulls.

The main months, it will be clear, for fairs, romerías and bullfights are June to September but there are 'rogue' events

as early as February and as late as November. I have not
included Easter above, as it is celebrated in some form or
other almost everywhere. For fuller information on small
town and village festivities it is wise to consult the local tourist
office or Centro de Inicitativas Turisticas (C.I.T.), whose
addresses are to be found at the end of the appendix on
Hotels and Tourist Offices on p.435-437. These offices will also
help with accommodation, suggest routes and provide free
regional maps and town plans. Some are a bit sleepy but on
the whole they give a very good service. Remember that they
are likely to be closed between 1.30 and 4.30 pm in Summer
but will probably reopen till 8.00 pm.

Some Suggestions for Further Reading

❦

ART AND ARCHITECTURE

Bevan, B.	History of Spanish Architecture (1938)
Brown, J. & Elliott, J. H.	A Palace for a King, Yale University Press
Harvey, J. H.	The Cathedrals of Spain, Batsford
Milne, J. Lees	Baroque in Spain and Portugal
Palol, P. de & M. Hirmer	Early Mediaeval Art in Spain
Prentice, A. N.	Spanish Renaissance Architecture and Ornament, 1500-1560 (revised ed. 1970)
Sitwell, S.	Southern Baroque Art
Street, G. E.	Some Account of Gothic Architecture in Spain (1865, revised ed. 1914, since reprinted)
Thomas, Hugh	Goya: The Third of May, 1808
Whitehill, W. M.	Spanish Romanesque Architecture of the 11th Century

BULLS

Blasco Ibáñez, V.	Blood and Sand
Hemingway, E.	Death in the Afternoon, Jonathan Cape
Lafront, A.	Encyclopédie de la Corrida
McCormick, J. & Mario Sevilla Mascarenas	The Complete Aficionado, World Publishing Company
Marks, J.	To the Bullfight Again
Tynan, K.	Bull Fever

HISTORY

Atkinson, W. C.	A History of Spain and Portugal, Penguin
Brenan, G.	The Spanish Labyrinth
Carr, R.	Spain, 1808-1939
Davies, R. Trevor	The Golden Century of Spain
Defourneaux, M.	Daily Life in Spain in the Golden Age

Elliott, J. H.	Imperial Spain, 1469-1716
Herr, R.	The 18th Century Revolution in Spain
Jackson, G.	The Making of Mediaeval Spain
	The Spanish Republic and the Civil War
Kamen, H.	The Spanish Inquisition
Lévi-Provençal, E.	Histoire de L'Espagne Musulmane (30 vols, Paris 1944-53)
Livermore, H. V.	The Origins of Spain and Portugal
Longford, E.	Wellington, the Years of the Sword
Lynch, J.	Spain under the Habsburgs, 1516-1700, Blackwell (2 vols)
Madariaga, S. de	Spain
Menéndez Pidal, R.	The Cid and his Spain
Thomas, Hugh	The Spanish Civil War
Trend, J. B.	The Civilization of Spain
Weller, J.	Wellington in the Peninsula
Vives, V.	Economic History of Spain

LITERATURE AND CRITICISM

Barea, A.	The Forge
	The Track
	The Clash
Bell, A. F. G.	Luis de León
Brenan, G.	The Literature of the Spanish People
	Saint John of the Cross, His Life and Poetry C.U.P. 1973
Entwhistle, W. J.	The Spanish Language
Jones, R. O. (Ed.)	A Literary History of Spain (8 vols)
Orwell, G.	Homage to Catalonia
Peers, E. Allison (Ed.)	The Complete Works of Saint Teresa of Avila
Trend, J. B.	Alfonso the Sage and Other Spanish Essays (1926)

TRAVELS

Baretti, J.	A Journey from London to Genoa (1770, reprinted 1970)
Borrow, G.	The Bible in Spain (1842, often reprinted)
Dumas, A.	From Paris to Cadiz, Peter Owen
	A Handbook for Travellers in Spain, J. Murray 1845 and later editions
Ford, R.	Gatherings from Spain (1846, reprinted 1970)
Lee, Laurie	As I Walked Out One Midsummer Morning

Pritchett, V. S.	The Spanish Temper
Robertson, I.	English Travellers in Spain 1760-1855
Starkie, W.	Spanish Raggle-Taggle
	The Road to Santiago
Tracey, Honor	Silk Hats and No Breakfast
Workman, F. B.	
& W. H.	Sketches Awheel in Fin de Siècle Iberia

MISCELLANEOUS

Braudel, F.	The Mediterranean
Livermore, A.	Short History of Spanish Music
Polunin, O. &	
Smythies, B. E.	Flowers of South-West Europe
Robertson, I. (Ed.)	Blue Guide to Spain

SPANISH LITERATURE

Anon.	Poema del Cid, modern version by Francisco López Estrada, Editorial Castalia
Anon.	Lazarillo de Tormes, Editorial Juventud, Barcelona
Cela, C. J.	Viaje a la Alcarria, Harrap
Cervantes, M. de	Paginas del *Quijote,* U.L.P., Lester H. & Terrádez V. (Ed.)
Lester H. &	
Terrádez V. (Ed.)	Paginas del *Quijote,* U.L.P.
Machado, A.	Campos de Castilla, Editorial Anaya
Ortega y Gasset, J.	Papeles sobre Velázquez y Goya
Perez Galdos, B.	Episodios Nacionales, Aguilar
	(The first series of these throws a fascinating light on the Spanish view of the Napoleonic Wars and the Peninsular War in particular. The best are: Trafalgar, La Corte de Carlos IV, El 19 de Marzo y el 2 de Mayo, Bailén, Zaragoza, Cádiz and Juan Martín 'El Empecinado')
Vega Carpio,	
Lope de	El Caballero de Olmedo
	Fuenteovejuna

Index

❧